*Pitt Series in Russian and
East European Studies*

THE DISABLED
IN THE
SOVIET UNION

Past and Present,
Theory and Practice

*William O. McCagg and
Lewis Siegelbaum*

EDITORS

University of Pittsburgh Press

Series in Russian and East European Studies No. 12

Published by the University of Pittsburgh Press, Pittsburgh Pa. 15260
Copyright © 1989, University of Pittsburgh Press
All rights reserved
Baker & Taylor International, London
Manufactured in the United States of America

Library of Congress Cataloging-in-Publication Data

The Disabled in the Soviet Union : past and present, theory and
   practice / William O. McCagg and Lewis Siegelbaum, editors.
      p.   cm.—(Series in Russian and East European studies ; no. 12)
      "Conference from which this book emerges was held at Michigan
   State University on 11–13 April 1985"—P. 5.
   Includes bibliographies.
   ISBN 0-8229-3622-4
      1. Handicapped—Soviet Union—Congresses.   2. Invalids—Soviet
   Union—Congresses.   I. McCagg, William O.   II. Siegelbaum, Lewis H.
   III. Series.
   HV1559.S65D57   1989
   362.4'0947—dc20   89-40206
                                                                 CIP

Contents

Acknowledgments

MANY PEOPLE and organizations have helped in the production of this book. First, the editors wish to acknowledge their debt to the Michigan Council of the Humanities, which made a grant to the conference on "The Handicapped in the Soviet Union and Eastern Europe," held at Michigan State University on 11–13 April 1985; and to the deans of International Programs, Arts and Letters, Social Science, Human Medicine and the Honors College at Michigan State, without whose support the conference could not have been held. The History Department at Michigan State most generously gave Professor McCagg leave time, during which he could organize this project, and the Russian and East European Program at Michigan State served as project headquarters.

We were greatly helped in shaping this book not only by the individual writers of the papers here published, but by several scholars who participated in the conference or in its planning: especially Barbara Anderson, John Eulenberg, Jonathan Harris, William Frey, Anna Green, Barbara Jancar-Webster, Aliki Coudroglou, Adele Lindenmeyr, Alfred Meyer, Walter Parchomenko, Vladimir Shlapentokh, and Brian Silver. Our thanks are also due to Professors William Chase of the University of Pittsburgh, and Roberta Manning of Boston College, who served as academic readers.

John Micgiel of the Institute on East Central Europe at Columbia University typed the final manuscript. He, as well as Victor Lancina of the Russian and East European Program, and Virginia Vande Voord of the University Center for International Rehabilitation at Michigan State University, contributed a great deal also to the complicated business of coverting the conference papers into a publishable book.

Last, but hardly least, we are most indebted to Louise McCagg and Leena Siegelbaum, who have supported us unfailingly during yet another "scientific" exploration far from the family hearths.

William O. McCagg
Lewis Siegelbaum

THE DISABLED IN THE
SOVIET UNION

Introduction

William O. McCagg and
Lewis Siegelbaum

I

M O D E R N civilization has enormously increased the
ability of people to survive. Because of it, a large portion of our
species has become taller, fatter, healthier, and more independent
of nature's restrictions than ever before. Yet even in the most
developed parts of the world, certain sections of the population
have lagged behind: those who were born, or who have become,
crippled, insane, blind, or deaf—the disabled. Through all the
political and social revolutions of the past two centuries, the problems of such people have proved in no way so malleable as other
social problems. Only the technological revolution of recent decades has suggested some ways out.

The fate of the disabled invites social scientific study because
to an extraordinary extent it provides clues to the inner directions
of modern society. Historically, for example, the modern education of the deaf in Europe dates from the late Renaissance: its
history both coincides with and illustrates the birth of a modern
European social conscience. Likewise, as Michel Foucault has
shown, the treatment of the declared insane is a supremely delicate
index to the shifts in that conscience during the seventeenth- and
eighteenth-century Enlightenment.[1] It may be significant of developments in our own century that the Nazi assault on European
Jewry began with the application of euthanasia to retarded and
crippled Germans.[2]

Why might the fate of the disabled have this weathervane character? A primary explanation is surely that societies always reveal
themselves through their treatment of the helpless among their
own populations. The Poor Laws of nineteenth-century England

3

and France suggest rather better the inner dynamic of the industrial revolution than do the new comforts of middle-class life. The shunning of cancer victims and, more recently, those who have contracted the AIDS virus, betray psychological and moral predispositions that otherwise remain below the surface. And in the case of the disabled, there is another factor at work. Physical deformity, retardation, the loss of hearing or of sight, and insanity, afflict all classes of society indiscriminately. The disabled far more than the poor tend to be the brothers and sisters, the parents and the children, of the elite, who in all societies make social policy. Unlike the poor, therefore, their presence cannot be expunged from the elite mind by means of a new type of poorhouse, by emigration, or by injections of funds. The disabled are a more personal problem, and they stay around.

This book deals with the position and the treatment of the disabled in the Soviet Union. Why this country? Above all, because it is important, constituting one of the larger blocs of population in the world; and the disabled within it are numerous enough to merit study in their own right. Second, the Soviet Union is different. Although it is in the northern tier of the world's population, it does not share the great wealth of Western Europe and North America and therefore is in many ways excluded from adopting the recently developed simple—i.e., technological and financial—solutions to the problems of the disabled that have been applied elsewhere in the northern tier.

Then, third, it is "socialist," which historically has meant that its government justifies itself in terms of providing a more humane alternative to that provided by societies dominated by market forces. But, fourth, it is different from the social-democratic Scandinavian countries, which essentially participate in the wealth of Western Europe. The Soviet Union has built its socialist institutions independently of—and in many ways systematically against—the models of Western Europe and the United States.

There is one last reason for studying the disabled population in this part of the world: very little is known about this subject. In Soviet studies, one expects to encounter different sorts and qualities of data from that available for study of Western societies. But seldom is data so hard to come by as in the present respect. As the reader will find in the following essays, a great deal is done for the disabled. Our subject in fact is enormous. But even within the USSR, the dimension of the disabled population and the extent and effectiveness of its treatment is little publicized,

and for decades virtually nothing on the subject reached the foreigner's eye. It was to fill this lacuna that the conference from
which this book emerges was held at Michigan State University
on 11–13 April 1985.

II

For a long time while modern social science developed, the disabled
as a social group were ignored. This was because, under prevailing
notions, one considered a subaltern group worthy of study only if
one could perceive that eventually it would adopt or catch up to the
values and behavioral patterns of the "normal" middle classes of
industrial society. Obviously, the disabled did not fit this frame. All
the other classes of society could be asked through social science to
abandon their backward-looking mores—"amoral familialism" in
the case of peasants, "tribalism" in the case of various colonial
peoples, and innocence and plainspokenness in the case of urban
workers—for the ideologies, organizations, and modes of expression of the "intelligent" sectors of society. But how could the disabled be persuaded to give up their infirmity? One could (and did)
suggest educational devices for pretending that some disabilities
(notably deafness) might through special effort be cancelled out.
But generally, one premised that there were medical, not social-
scientific, problems here.

Over the decades, then, this positivistic orientation in the social sciences was confronted by a number of new perspectives.
Both social unrest at home and wars of national liberation abroad
left an impact, and attitudes changed. Gradually, one came to view
peasants not as atavistic holdovers from precapitalist times but
rather as part societies interacting with a variety of modes of production in complex ways. One discovered that workers were not
merely potential recruits for intelligent organizers, or a social base
for ideologically oriented political movements, but agents of their
own making. The study of groups previously hidden from
history—not just blacks and ethnic minorities, but women and
homosexuals—now flourished. It was in this context that the disabled also came under study—the last element in society to receive
social-scientific consideration on its own terms.

Two qualities of the disabled population distinguish it fundamentally from the other groups mentioned above, however, and
determine how it should be studied. All those others—workers,
peasants, various ethnic groups, women, and the sexually defined

groups—can be said to share histories of socioeconomic, political, and cultural oppression, and this is why they are studied. In the case of the disabled, contrastingly, such oppression is secondary at best, often incidental. The oppression from which they suffer derives above all from the conditions nature has imposed upon them. This is not to posit an absolute antinomy between social and biological forces. As army recruiters in nineteenth- and early twentieth-century Europe well know, chronic malnutrition among workers and peasants produced a relatively high proportion of "rejects"— individuals whose biological condition made their social condition worse and vice versa. Still, blindness, deafness, the loss of the use of one or more limbs, mental retardation, or insanity can occur among any and every sector of society. Natural facts, rather than any social distinction, define the uniqueness of the disabled as a societal group, and those who study them must observe restraint, accordingly. No revolution will solve this social problem, nor will the disabled ever be a ruling class.[3]

This is a first rule of the game here. A second derives from the fact that, apart from their disabled condition, there is no unifying element holding the diverse categories of disabled people together. There can be, and alas often are, individual overlaps between handicaps—for example, some blind people are also deaf, some physically crippled people are also mentally retarded. Because of these overlaps, a holistic, rehabilitationist tradition exists in the medical history of the disabled, and as we will discover below, this is a major reason for studying them where this tradition has been perpetuated. Indeed, in the USSR, this tradition, under the label *defectology,* thrives.

In most countries such holism is avoided, however. The blind as a social group are treated as absolutely different from the deaf or the insane, and all these are referred to as different social groups from the physically crippled. Attitudes follow the words we use, and the disabled are perceived everywhere as not constituting a single group. Worse, within most of the categories we call disabled there are two by no means homogeneous elements: those who were born disabled and those who acquired their disability. Sometimes, as among the blind and the physically crippled, these sub-groups can develop certain common interests. But among the deaf there exists a fearful chasm between those who were born without hearing and those who lose it later in life. The born deaf used to be called dumb. They are still pariahs, for their education is inevitably sharply curtailed, and they need manual signs to talk. They look the same as other people, but in a real sense they have never been and never will be participants in the normal world. For the postlingually deaf (the deafened hearers), on the other hand, participation has been the dominant life experience. The longer they enjoyed it, the more defensive they tend to be about their exclusion, and the more they look down on, even hate, the dumb, with whom they are now grouped. And among the insane, individual isolation is acute. This absence of group coherence makes the social-scientific study of the disabled objectively much more difficult than comparable study of other social groups.

Such factors directly affect the shape and content of this book. First and above all, we have eschewed in this volume any attempt at overall coverage. None of the chapters here are comprehensive surveys; all of them are informed probes into one aspect or another of the situation of the disabled in the Soviet Union. Because of the disunity of the disabled as group, it has seemed flatly unuseful to attempt any sort of synthesis such as one might attempt if probing the condition of Soviet women, Soviet workers, or other classes. Second, we have considered it as important to get close to the technicians who work with the disabled as it is to view the disabled in their relations with society at large. To the ordinary Western reader, technology—the availability and quality of eyeglasses, hearing aids, wheelchairs, various new medicines and medical therapies—may seem to be dull stuff; but for the disabled themselves, successful technical work is the essence of a freer life. Third, we have left space for the disabled themselves to speak, where possible in person, otherwise through the mouths of creative writers, the traditional voices of the society under consideration. This has been a most difficult task. One of the editors and two of the contributors are disabled, but in general the Soviet disabled have not spoken much for themselves. Still, we have sought to emphasize them wherever possible. The bitterness of disabled humanity must out, or our effort will be wasted.

III

The Michigan State conference addressed itself to a series of concrete questions, the first of which were historical. We asked, Was there a recognition of the disabled as a social problem in Russia before the 1917 Revolution? And what kind of support policies existed then? To what extent did these policies change after the Revolution, and what was the impact of the Second World War?

Six essays in this book respond above all to these questions and bring to light how the treatment of the disabled mirrors in general the wider context in which they lived, and in particular the relationship between state and society.

A second group of questions raised at the conference regarded the actual experience of the disabled. These questions were: What are the dimensions of the handicap problem in the USSR today? What are the present economic, legal, and institutional bases for the treatment of the disabled? How do the treatment methods for the disabled relate to the methods of infant care, primary and secondary schooling, medical service programs, industrial health and safety programs, labor laws and pension programs, and old age treatment? To what extent has the Soviet Union responded to the technological revolution in the treatment of the disabled that has taken place since about 1950 in the West? Does it import technology and new techniques of treatment from the West or does it seek to develop the domestic production of appropriate support for the disabled? It goes with mere mention that few initiatives emerge from the circles of the disabled. But it seems important to inquire whether there is any knowledge in the USSR of Western movements organized by the disabled. Five essays in the second part of the book respond to these questions in particular.

The third group of questions raised at the conference regarded attitudes toward the disabled. They were: In the absence of public opinion surveys about attitudes toward the disabled, how may we gain access to the popular image of them? To what extent can literature, aphorisms, and jokes provide clues to social values? In Eastern Europe, where defectology originated, albeit under another name, there is a "painted bird" literature—a literature focusing on grotesque, often specifically disabled, figures (the reference is to the novel *The Painted Bird* by the Polish writer, Jerzy Kosinski). To what extent does this literature indicate tendencies of normal society to think of itself as disabled—of a psychology of the disabled in society as a whole? These questions provoked the penultimate chapter in our book.

NOTES

1. Michel Foucault, *Madness and Civilization: A History of Insanity in the Age of Reason* (New York: Vintage, 1973).
2. See Gerald Fleming, *Hitler and the Final Solution* (Berkeley and

Los Angeles: University of California Press, 1984), chs. 1, 2; and Robert Lifton, *The Nazi Doctors* (New York: Basic Books, 1986), chs. 2, 4. We have investigated a widely circulated report that the Soviet state persecuted the disabled in similar fashion "during the mid-1930s" by assembling the "blind lyricists" of the Ukraine at a First All-Ukrainian Congress of Bards and Bandulists and then arresting them en masse. The situation of the disabled in Stalin's Russia was clearly less than enviable, but we have been unable to find concrete evidence of generic persecution. For the original report, see Solomon Volkov, ed., *Testimony: The Memoirs of Dmitri Shostakovich* (New York: Harpers, 1979), pp. 214–15.

3. It is exemplary of today's new views that the physically disabled in America tend now to normalize their position by referring to the TABs (temporarily able-bodied) in the larger society. In this connection, one may note also the tendency in the American sign language community to view the deaf as a group characterized by their language (sign) rather than by a defect (deafness). For an extreme expression of this analysis, see Harlan Lane, *When the Mind Hears* (New York: Random House, 1984), Forword. But compare Oliver Sacks' informed remarks on recent research about the neurological basis of sign language in "The Revolution of the Deaf," *New York Review of Books,* 2 June 1988, pp. 23, 26.

SOME BIBLIOGRAPHY IN ENGLISH

Barbara A. Anderson, Brian D. Silver, and Victoria A. Velkoff. "Education of the Handicapped in the USSR: Exploration of the Statistical Picture." *Soviet Studies* 39 (1987): 470 ff.

Walter D. Connor. *Deviance in Soviet Society: Crime, Delinquency and Alcoholism.* New York: Columbia University Press, 1972.

H. P. David. *Family Planning and Abortion in the Socialist Countries of Central and Eastern Europe.* New York: Population Council, 1970.

Mark Field. *Soviet Socialized Medicine.* New York: Free Press, 1967.

Michel Foucault. *Madness and Civilization.* New York: Vintage, 1973.

G. Hyde. *The Soviet Health Service: A Historical and Comparative Study.* London: Lawrence & Wishart, 1974.

Michael Kaser. *Health Care in the Soviet Union and Eastern Europe.* London: Croom Helm, 1976.

Alex Kozulin. *Psychology in Utopia: Towards a History of Soviet Psychology.* Cambridge: MIT Press, 1984.

Bernice Madison. "The Organization of Welfare Services." In Cyril E. Black, ed., *The Transformation of Russian Society.* Cambridge: Harvard University Press, 1960.

———. *Social Welfare in the Soviet Union.* Stanford: Stanford University Press, 1968.

————. *The Meaning of Social Policy: The Comparative Dimension in Social Welfare*. London: Croom Helm, 1980.

Andrew Sutton. "Backward Children in the USSR: An Unfamiliar Approach to a Familiar Problem." In Jenny Brine, Maureen Perrie, and Andrew Sutton, eds., *Home, School, and Leisure in the Soviet Union*. London: Allen & Unwin, 1980.

Vladimir G. Treml. *Alcohol in the USSR: A Statistical Study*. Durham: Duke University Press, 1982.

Joan Valsiner. *Developmental Psychology in the Soviet Union*. Bloomington: Indiana University Press, 1988.

E. R. Weinerman. *Social Medicine in Eastern Europe*. Cambridge: Harvard University Press, 1969.

David Wright. *Deafness*. New York: Stein and Day, 1975.

Part ONE

Historical Essays

Societal Responses to Mental Disorders in Prerevolutionary Russia

Julie V. Brown

Paupers on the face of Holy Russia, wandering psalm singers, Christ's cripples, fools in Christ of Holy Russia—these sugar cakes have adorned everyday life from Russia's very beginnings. . . . These madmen or frauds—beggars, bogus saints, prophets—were held to be the Church's brightest jewel, Christ's own, intercessors for the world.

—*Boris Pilnyak*

> But here's the rub. If you go mad,
> They'll fear you worse than any plague
> And lock you up at once
> Putting you on a chain—an idiot
> Whom they'll come to mock
> As they would a captured beast
> Through its prison bars.

—*Alexander Pushkin*

I

IN SOME ways, old Russia faced the often disturbing dilemmas posed by the mentally disabled just as other societies did. But in other respects, Russian modes of dealing with the problem were idiosyncratic. This duality is not surprising. The aberrant behavior through which madness manifests itself creates many practical difficulties, which are similar for all societies. Yet the disorders most often surface in the form of deviations from socially acceptable modes of thought and action. They are thus especially evocative of culturally specific understandings. The intent of this chapter is to examine changing responses to insanity in

13

prerevolutionary Russia, which added up to a transformation both
of societal perceptions and institutional methods quite as great as
the ones that followed the Bolshevik Revolution.

II

In old Russia, as in most traditional societies, primary responsibility for both the mentally and the physically handicapped rested
with the family and the local community. The only organized care
for the insane was provided by the Russian Orthodox Church. For
the most part, arrangements were informal and their character was
a function of both the specific nature of the problem and the availability of resources. As early as the eleventh century, certain monasteries began to provide shelter for some of the insane as well as
other "unfortunates." The characteristics of those individuals have
not been thoroughly researched, but evidence suggests that many
of them came from privileged families. The monasteries provided,
in addition to physical shelter, spiritual treatment. This was considered to be the only possible remedy for the suffering of those
regarded as victims of malevolent forces.[1]

From an early date, Russian culture fostered a perceptibly benign attitude toward unfortunates of all types and especially toward the insane—an attitude exemplified by Pilnyak's description
of them as the sugar cakes of Holy Russia. This was due primarily
to a religious tradition that regarded some of the insane as particularly close to God and hence deserving of great respect.

The earliest holy fools (*iurodivye*) were, of course, not insane
but were ascetic monks who feigned madness in their efforts to
achieve greater piety. This particular form of asceticism has its roots
in Greek orthodoxy; however, later scholars have concluded that
some of those popularly regarded as holy fools in Russia were not
feigning madness but instead actually were mentally handicapped.
Others are presumed to have assumed the status for the benefits it
conferred. Regardless, in Russia *iurodstvo* caught hold of the popular imagination, becoming in the words of an eminent historian of
Russian religion, "the most popular, a truly national form of ascetic life."[2] Only a few holy fools were ever canonized by the
Russian Orthodox Church, but many were cast in that role by the
people. Popular respect for *iurodivye* was such that they were
sought after for advice, and increasing numbers managed to survive thanks to the faith and generosity of the masses.

Though the *iurodivye* were unquestionably revered by ordinary folk, it would be a mistake to conclude that this was old Russia's only response to insanity, for in Russia, as elsewhere, the uncontrolled behavior of individuals described as insane (*dushevno-bol'nye*) posed a potentially serious threat to both the physical well-being and the property of those around them. So far as we can tell, such persons were feared and could be treated quite harshly. It is recorded, for example, that families of the insane sought help from a variety of religious and lay experts, who attempted to exorcise the bewitching demons assumed to be the cause of the problem. Anecdotal evidence suggests that relatives and neighbors did not hesitate to resort to extreme physical restraint when it was deemed necessary. As late as the early twentieth century, observers reported stumbling into villages in which mad men and women were kept shackled hand and foot. Upon inquiring, they would often be informed matter of factly that the individuals had been confined in that fashion for years, without any accommodation for their creature comforts.[3]

Prior to the sixteenth century, traditional Russian efforts in this area were largely confined to the *dushevno-bol'nye*. However, during the sixteenth and seventeenth centuries the state grew more sensitive to deviant behavior, perhaps because the number of self-proclaimed fools in Christ increased during this era, prompting a heightened concern with accurate diagnosis. Furthermore, some of the holy fools had assumed a political role, chastising rulers for alleged misconduct with relative impunity. Regardless, from about 1550 both religious and secular officials sought to distinguish between fakers and those who were truly insane, taking on themselves the task of making sure that the piety of the masses did not benefit undeserving individuals.

Not only did secular officials begin with much greater frequency to deal with the occasional excesses of the *iurodivye:* they also expressed concern about malingering and fakery in another then proliferating form of aberrant behavior which affected primarily women. Victims of this new disorder, referred to as *klikushestvo* (from the Russian verb *klikat* meaning to shriek or cry out), would suddenly become hysterical, scream out obscenities, and crawl about on the floor like animals. While neither *klikushi* nor those charged with practicing the evil arts were regarded as insane by most of their contemporaries, a twentieth-century perspective would suggest that some of them did suffer from that problem. *Klikushi* often accused others of having bewitched them, charges which more than occasionally resulted in prosecutions of the ac-

cused for witchcraft. This was, of course, an era of witch burning
in many societies. Although there were witchcraft trials in Russia,
by comparison with the West the number was relatively small.
Still, some of Russia's mentally unbalanced population doubtless
fell victim to the epidemics of fear that followed such charges.

One of Russia's earliest historians of insanity attributed the
lower level of witchcraft hysteria in Russian society to the unwillingness of the Russian church to assume a major role in the prosecution of witches. The church was regarded as the principal reposi-
tory of expert knowledge concerning most of the diverse behaviors
we would today lump together as mental disorders, and clerics
were often called upon to render judgments on the nature of the
problematic mental state. It may thus be significant that when Ivan
IV, the Terrible (1533–84), requested the church's assistance in
prosecuting witches, the church declined, responding that the tsar
should handle the problem himself.[4]

The church's reluctance to take on this new assignment may
well be one of the earliest manifestations of what became an escalating disagreement between the church and the state over the appropriate locus of responsibility for society's misfits. Prior to the
middle of the sixteenth century, the church's involvement in caring for the insane had been largely voluntary and self-regulating.
The monastery system of care in particular remained an informal
one. But in 1551, Tsar Ivan convened a major church council (the
Stoglavyi Sobor) to consider a new code regulating the relations
between church and state. One of the provisions made monastery
care for the insane compulsory, and the wording suggests that the
concerns of the state with maintaining social order now superseded any humanitarian, religious, or even mercenary urges which
might have motivated the church.[5] The law stipulated that individuals who were possessed by demons or had lost their reason
(*oderzhimy besom i lisheny razuma*) should be sent to monasteries
"so as not to be a hinderance to the healthy."[6]

In sum, through much of early Russian history the problem
now defined as mental illness was not regarded as a single phenomenon but was understood as several discrete states, each of
which possessed its own particular etiology and cultural meaning.
Most of these conditions were associated with the supernatural.
While some of them were feared, others were highly valued. By
the seventeenth century, these matters were no longer restricted to
the private spheres of family and community. The involvement of
the state made them a public issue. Significantly, public concern, at

least as manifested in government policies, was less for the welfare of the insane than for protecting against the possible danger they might pose to the rest of society. This set of priorities was perhaps a logical consequence of the prevailing assumption that insanity was incurable. Despite subsequent radical changes in that assumption, the emphasis upon social defense would prove a remarkably enduring feature of the Russian state's approach to insanity.

III

Tsar Peter I, the Great (1682–1725), established the first formal procedures for determining mental competency in Russia. They proved to be long-lived, enduring without fundamental alteration until the revolutions of 1917. Given his general record, it is not surprising that the tsar's interest in the insane sprang less from concern for their welfare than from his conception of the needs and welfare of the state. The new procedures were a by-product of Peter's efforts to regularize the service obligations of the Russian gentry. Compulsory state service was not new to Russia; however, under Peter it was much more stringently enforced in accordance with the tsar's mercantilist approach to governance. A growing number of gentry families resisted the requirement that they enter their sons into state service by seeking individual exemptions on the grounds that their offspring were "in no way suited for service, and it is impossible to teach them anything, as they have been *duraki* [fools] since birth."[7] Peter's response was to order, in 1712, that all alleged *duraki* be brought to the capital city to be examined by the Senate, the highest administrative and judicial institution in the country. Certification exempted one from the service obligation. It also limited the property rights of *duraki* and denied them the right to marry, provisions that were designed to negate any potential advantages which might accrue to successful malingerers.[8]

The examiners designated by Peter were secular rather than religious officials. While their charge did not extend to all forms of mental abnormality, the delegation of authority to the Senate was a major step in the shift away from reliance upon religious authority in such matters. Peter apparently wished to remove the church from any responsibility for the mentally handicapped, an attitude consistent with his other efforts to limit its role in society. In 1723 he ordered that the mad no longer be sent to monasteries. A brief effort to provide for the insane in a few secular institutions in St.

Petersburg apparently ensued, but it was abandoned upon Peter's death.

Peter's immediate successors did not share his zeal for secularization. Ironically, it was the church that became the most enthusiastic advocate of secular care for the insane in the half-century following Peter's death. There was indeed a protracted struggle between church and state over this issue. Examination of the various arguments made by the combatants in this dispute reveals a continuing concern on the part of the state with controlling what it regarded as dangerous forms of madness. Over the course of the eighteenth century, the government persistently demanded that monasteries accept "dangerously insane" individuals brought to them by secular officials, including the political police (*tainaia kantseliariia*). The church with equal determination protested that it should not be required to do so. Whether the church's resistance to the state over this issue was a result of its reduced assets (due largely to the confiscatory policies of Peter I) or whether it was merely an expression of opposition to state interference remains uncertain. Quite probably both factors were relevant. In any event, the church increasingly sought to extricate itself from responsibility for providing shelter to the insane. Indeed, it was the Russian church that first argued that the insane were ill and should be treated by physicians, an argument underlying the claim that monasteries were inappropriate settings for treating the insane.

The final transfer of responsibility for institutional care for the insane to the state was made during the reign of Catherine II, the Great (1762–96). From early in her reign, members of her court evidently suspected that there were dangerous numbers of madmen wandering unsupervised and uncontrolled through the streets of the empire's growing cities. Catherine's chief of police, N. N. Chicherin, was particularly troubled by the presence of such individuals in St. Petersburg and repeatedly sought the advice of the empress as to how to deal with the problem.[9] In 1775 Catherine, in her great reform of Russia's local government, established Departments of Public Welfare (*Prikazy obshchestvennogo prizreniia*) in each region and made them inter alia responsible for constructing madhouses.

This was an era in which madhouses began to proliferate in many societies and for reasons not dissimilar to those which account for their appearance in Russia. The first Russian madhouses were in fact modeled after their counterparts in the West. The nature and functioning of the madhouses were clearly spelled out in the statute calling them into existence. The mad were to be "segregated according to their condition," cared for by a "good hearted but firm" watchman (*nadziratel'*), and most importantly "locked up so that it will be impossible for them to cause any harm."[10]

The establishment of the Departments of Public Welfare, or *prikaz* madhouses, finally put responsibility for the care of the insane firmly in the hands of secular authorities. The number of madhouses grew steadily throughout the late eighteenth and early nineteenth centuries. By the middle of the nineteenth century there were over forty of them. Despite the fears prompting their construction, most of these institutions remained small and even then were not always filled to capacity. Public attitudes toward these madhouses are illustrated by the words of Pushkin cited at the beginning of this chapter. Commonly referred to as yellow houses, after the inexpensive paint with which they were covered, *prikaz* madhouses were regarded as places of horror to be avoided at all cost. Nobles were rumored to have sent their unruly serfs to work in the institutions as punishment for misbehavior.[11]

Thus, by the early nineteenth century the Russian government had equipped itself with physical structures within which it could confine and isolate the insane. Most of the population, however, equated the institutions with prisons and continued to deal with the insane in accordance with time-honored traditions. Mild-mannered unfortunates were supported and cared for by their families, while raving lunatics were restrained to protect those around them. Any desire on the part of families to relegate responsibility for the latter to the yellow houses was probably mitigated by the substantial fees charged for the dubious privilege of confinement.

IV

The late eighteenth and early nineteenth centuries are extolled by historians of Western psychiatry as the era of the first revolution in the care of the insane. It was in 1793 that Philippe Pinel ordered the removal of the chains from the mad at the Bicêtre in Paris, and most countries boast of Pinels of their own during this period. What followed is described as a great humanitarian transformation in the response of Western European societies to their insane. Madness became mental illness, the cure for which rested in the reformed asylum.

The ideals of the first psychiatric revolution penetrated Russia during the second quarter of the nineteenth century. Responsibility for initiating asylum reform belongs primarily to Nicholas I, who ruled the country between 1825 and 1855. Nicholas is more frequently remembered as the ruler who had the philosopher Peter Chaadaev declared mad and placed under house arrest.[12] Yet, while it would be an overstatement to assert that this tsar of "orthodoxy, autocracy, and nationality" was obsessed with asylum reform, that was clearly an interest which persisted throughout his life.

Nicholas visited England as a young man before he assumed the throne. While there he was taken to visit William Tuke's York Retreat, an asylum established in 1792 to care for the Quaker insane. Tuke's revolutionary approach was based upon the principle of humane care in a natural yet ordered environment. Like other psychiatric reformers, Tuke insisted that the insane should be treated humanely both because they were ill human beings and because the use of coercion and restraint had been proven by long experience to be ineffective. Given the proper conditions, such early psychiatric revolutionaries maintained, most cases of madness could be cured.

Tuke achieved such success with his first patients that the York Retreat drew international praise as a model institution. Nicholas, like many other visitors, was sufficiently impressed to aspire to replicate Tuke's achievement in his own country.[13] Within a decade after he ascended the throne, Nicholas had built a model asylum. The All Mourners (*Vsekh Skorbiashchikh*) Hospital in St. Petersburg, opened in 1832, was comparable to the best institutions of Western Europe.

Shortly thereafter, the Russian government initiated a plan to replace the (by now appalling) yellow houses with a network of modern asylums. Nicholas kept the matter in the public eye by making repeated visits to provincial madhouses. Many excursions resulted in imperial ukases intended to improve the care of the insane.[14] In the late 1830s the government engaged the physician I. F. Riul' to conduct a census of the insane population in the empire. Carried out with the cooperation of provincial governors, the census suggested great discrepancies between the size of the insane population at large and the capacity of existing madhouses. These findings appeared to provide substance to the continuing complaints of provincial officials that their cities were being overrun by deranged and troublesome individuals. Later, in 1842, following the lead of Nicholas, the director of the central government's

Medical Department personally examined each madhouse. His report characterized them as seriously deficient. The yellow houses were adequate only as places of detention, he declared, arguing strongly for reform on the grounds that better institutions could also provide treatment for the insane.

In the 1840s the government finally established a committee to plan for asylum reform. The committee quickly decided to recommend construction of a network of regional (*okruzhnye*) asylums throughout the empire. However, progress was extremely slow. The cost of the endeavor greatly exceeded anticipated levels, and for a while the project was tabled. It was later resurrected because of continuing pressure from provincial officials. The first regional asylum opened in Kazan in 1869. It was based upon the latest Western architectural designs, but it incorporated much touted variations more appropriate to the demands of the harsh Russian climate. It was supposed to serve four or five provinces. The reformers acknowledged this to be an extremely large area, but they had concluded that the cost of building more asylums was prohibitive.

The changes in the response to insanity in Russia during this era were predicated upon the notion that insanity was a disease that, like any other, could be treated and even cured. According to its charter, the Kazan Regional Asylum was to admit only those patients who could benefit from the specialized treatment it offered, that is, those deemed curable. In reality, the treatment accorded to the patients was as much a consequence of their social status as their condition. For example, Nicholas I's showcase institution, All Mourners, had as its primary beneficiaries members of the empire's wealthiest and most privileged stratum. All Mourners was a luxurious facility, a reflection more of its clientele than of the scientific principles upon which it was supposedly based. As the willingness of monasteries to provide care for the insane had declined over the course of the eighteenth century, wealthy families had come to rely more heavily upon foreign physicians and institutions to help alleviate their burden. All Mourners provided them with a domestic alternative but had virtually no impact upon the conditions faced by the overwhelming majority of Russia's mentally ill population.[15] This was true irrespective of the fact that the reformers continued to insist that the disorder was an illness with a physiological base.

Asylum reform in Russia thus occurred within the framework of the existing social structure. Furthermore, as the protracted process culminating in the construction of the Kazan Regional Asylum illustrates, reform was propelled by aims that were, at their core, incompatible. Sincere humanitarian concern for the welfare of suffering human beings certainly provided one motivation. However, those government officials who spearheaded the reforms never lost sight of the need to maintain order and to protect society from the dangerously insane. Early in the planning, the conflict between these two goals was not readily apparent. The most progressive treatment of mental illness was dependent upon institutionalization. Indeed, the institution itself was regarded as the principal therapeutic weapon. Similarly, the social defense concerns of officials were well addressed by plans to confine more of the insane. Only later, as the unanticipated costs of the bold new endeavor became clear, did the incompatability of the two goals become apparent. The fact that it continued only because of the repeated complaints from government's provincial representatives suggests that humanitarianism alone was not deemed sufficient justification for such enormous expenditures.[16]

V

The opening of the Kazan Regional Asylum was accompanied by much fanfare. However, in the long run it proved of little practical consequence. In the interval between the conception and execution of the project, the Great Reforms of Alexander II (1855–81) had fundamentally altered the institutional structure within which social and medical services were provided to provincial Russia. The Great Reforms of the 1860s abolished serfdom and brought significant changes to educational, judicial, military, and administrative institutions throughout the country. Among the reforms was the creation of the zemstvo system of local self-government in 1864. The zemstvos were given responsibility for the provision of a variety of services to the population in their geographic areas. These included education, public health, and famine relief.

Although the government had spent the preceding two decades planning a network of regional asylums, its Ministry of Internal Affairs, which had overseen the project, now decided instead to transfer responsibility for institutional care for the insane to the zemstvos. The cost of the Kazan Asylum had continued to escalate, and the territory it was designed to serve was far too large to be satisfactory to provincial officials. Furthermore, it was underutilized. Not only was it located at some distance from much of its potential constituency, but fees charged for care placed it beyond the means of most of the population. While the institution provided special accommodations for the elite, that group apparently remained reluctant to utilize it.

The zemstvos proved far from enthusiastic about their new assignment. Faced with limited sources of income, they were not eager to take on any unnecessary obligations. Zemstvo representatives argued to officials in the capital that institutions for the insane fell outside of their charge to protect the public health.[17] Pointing to the presence of insane individuals in prisons and workhouses, they noted that the government seemed to regard the insane more as a public safety problem than as a medical one. Given that definition of the situation, the zemstvos would have no responsibility.

The central government, however, insisted that the zemstvos must provide institutional space for the mentally disturbed. Indeed, the order went even further. In 1875 the zemstvos were told that they must continue to expand their facilities as much as necessary to accommodate all individuals who required either care or confinement.[18]

The foundations upon which the zemstvos were to build systems of rural medical care were the existing Department of Public Welfare institutions, including the *prikaz* yellow houses, the condition of which had continued to deteriorate. In the years after the Great Reforms, most of them were filled to overflowing. An observer described the one in the provincial city of Poltava in the following vivid fashion: "The facility is indescribably dismal. The sight of the high fences, the iron bars on the windows, the heavy bolts on the doors, and the stern figures of the guards leads one to the conclusion that prisoners are held here. But the unprecedented crowding and the chaotic noises persuade one that this is none other than a lunatic asylum. . . . The laughing, crying, singing, swearing, and brawling result in an unbearable racket, which continues without pause both night and day."[19]

Many of the zemstvos sought to restrict admissions to the institutions. The establishment of these quotas prompted the government decree that "the number of patients supported in madhouses is not to be limited to any specific number."[20] As had been the case on earlier occasions, the government acted because of complaints by provincial governors. In this instance, tsarist officials protested that they could not maintain order because they were being denied use of the institutions to confine the dangerously insane. The government did attempt to lessen the burden it laid at the door of the zemstvos. At the insistence of local self-government officials, the Ministry of Internal Affairs earmarked some of the funds that had been set aside for the regional asylum project to support new asylum construction by the zemstvos. Moreover, the Ministry of Internal Affairs' decree of 1879 formalizing this arrangement stressed the government's humanitarian motivations and argued for the importance of a scientific approach to the treatment of the insane. Nonetheless, the zemstvos had to accept primary responsibility for caring for the insane. There is a measure of irony in the fact that its call for radical improvements in asylum conditions throughout the empire came as the government was transferring the primary responsibility for carrying them out to another party. As had been true in the debate between church and state a century earlier, the argument in favor of a medical approach to insanity was made by the authority seeking to extricate itself from the responsibility.

The decade that followed the ministry's promise of assistance brought much asylum construction to provincial Russia. Local governments in many areas began to renovate and expand existing structures and to build new ones where necessary. That they took their obligation seriously is suggested by their increasing tendency to bring in experts to help with the construction and to work in the institutions. Many zemstvo representatives not only traveled to St. Petersburg and other university cities to recruit psychiatric physicians, but in a number of instances they paid to send their new employees abroad where they could examine model Western asylums first hand. Each new asylum was carefully planned both to meet Ministry of Internal Affairs specifications (without which subsidies could be denied) and to ensure that local needs would be met. The opening of every institution was accompanied by confident declarations that it would easily and comfortably accommodate all of the region's insane for many years to come.

In almost every case, however, the demand for institutional space rapidly outstripped the supply. No sooner would a new mental institution open than it would be filled to capacity, and calls would go out for still more beds and more buildings. The seemingly endless demand for psychiatric care quickly shattered the confidence and optimism of the 1880s. Those sentiments were replaced by rising frustration, as the cost of asylum construction and maintenance escalated to the point where other zemstvo projects were threatened. Exasperated local officials charged psychiatrists with both underestimating the problem in the planning stages and exaggerating it later by admitting patients indiscriminately. As one psychiatrist lamented, "Dishonorable individuals are beginning to assert that [we] are inventing the insane in order to enhance our reputations."[21] Both zemstvo representatives and their psychiatric employees continued to blame the tsarist government for their predicament. Fiscal realities were such, they complained, that the zemstvos could not possibly continue to meet the government's requirement of unlimited access.

Bowing to increased pressure, the government gradually clarified its intent. In the 1890s it acknowledged that to provide institutional care to those who could reasonably remain in the community was for Russia "an unattainable luxury." Therefore, the requirement that the zemstvos provide asylum space as needed, government officials declared, should be interpreted as applying only to the dangerous, that is, "to those whose admission is ordered by the administration and the courts."[22] By the turn of the century, these priorities had been clearly stated. Local self-governments were relieved that their obligation had been lessened. However, neither they nor their asylum psychiatrists were especially pleased with the direction of government policy. Both worried that unwanted police interference in the internal operation of the institutions would likely follow in its wake. Liberal zemstvo officials and psychiatrists considered the asylums to be institutions of healing and resented demands that they fulfill police functions as well.

In addition, the tsarist government had by its own efforts brought into being a group of indigenous medical experts who opposed its policy on madhouses. These were the psychiatrists, graduates of the university psychiatry departments set up in the 1860s to produce staff for the planned state institutions. The government had doubtless anticipated that these specialists would serve as technicians and would loyally carry out policies stipulated from above. The new professional group perceived its role quite differently. Psychiatrists quickly declared themselves advocates for Russia's insane population against the social defense priorities of the state. In their view, they alone possessed the knowledge that was essential to the proper diagnosis and treatment of mental disturbances. With increasing vehemence they demanded a deciding voice in asylum affairs. By the end of the nineteenth century, Russia's psychiatric profession had emerged as a particularly aggressive defender of what it perceived to be the interests of the mentally disturbed.

VI

The tsarist government had long reserved to itself ultimate authority to determine who would be confined in the asylums of the
empire. In the decade or so before the Bolshevik Revolution it
availed itself of that privilege somewhat more than it had in previous years. Nonetheless, rising government concern with social control is not alone sufficient to explain the dramatic growth in asylum
populations that occurred during the decades after the Great Reforms. Government commitments accounted for only a portion of
the increase. To understand the increasing utilization of institutions
for the insane, other factors must be taken into account.

The expansion of institutions for the insane over that half century was quite remarkable. In 1860 on the eve of emancipation
there were 43 madhouses in Russia with a combined inmate population of 2,038.[23] By 1912 the number of institutions had nearly
quadrupled to 160, while the number of individuals within them
had reached 42,489.[24] This was a period of rapid population
growth in Russia, as elsewhere; however, the growth in the number of institutionalized insane far exceeded the rate of increase in
the overall population. Furthermore, according to the calculations
of psychiatrists, most of Russia's insane population (both institutionalized and uninstitutionalized) was of peasant origin. A census
of the insane in Moscow Province conducted in the 1890s, for
example, revealed that over 90 percent of the province's mad were
peasants.[25] Other statistical reports reached similar conclusions.

Some observers interpreted the increase as indicating a rise in
the number of individuals suffering from mental disorders. The
stresses associated with modernization were most often blamed for
the problem. Emancipation as well as accelerating urbanization
and industrialization were regarded by these theorists as having
increased the intellectual and physical demands on a peasant population poorly equipped to cope with them. Social and economic
change had come to Russia far more rapidly than to most other
societies, they contended. In consequence, many more individuals
experienced mental and physical exhaustion, succumbing thereafter to depravity or mental illness.

Many psychiatrists disagreed with that argument, proposing
instead that the rise in asylum admissions merely reflected a growing faith among the masses in the efficacy of psychiatric care. The
profession devoted considerable effort to the task of public education. Psychiatrists wrote and distributed numerous brochures in

which they sought to convince the reading public that insanity was a treatable disorder of the brain and that the *iurodivye* and *klikushi* who still resided throughout the countryside were ill and could be cured of their disorders. To reach the illiterate masses, they gave numerous public lectures in both urban and remote rural areas. Recognizing the enormity of the task, the St. Petersburg Society of Psychiatrists even sponsored contests to encourage innovative strategies by which to enlighten the public.

The numerous and varied attempts to bring modern ideas to the dark masses of rural Russia clearly had some impact upon peasant thought and behavior. Yet evidence for the persistence of traditional attitudes toward insanity is remarkably strong, casting doubt on any explanation of the increased number of institutionalized peasants in terms of the new ideas alone. Despite the many efforts of psychiatrists to eliminate what they regarded as potentially dangerous superstitions, the population continued to adhere to ancient beliefs and to resort to time-honored remedies for madness. Indeed, it was reported that there were clergymen who specialized in exorcism. According to one account, these were generally the single individuals. Others avoided the assignment because of fears that the expelled demons would wreak their vengeance on the exorcist's near and dear ones.[26]

In the event that priestly ministrations failed, there were also numerous lay healers who could be called upon to employ their own personal remedies for madness. Some of these idiosyncratic methods were relatively benign. Others were probably life threatening. Among the approaches described by contemporary observers were imbibing of complicated herbal concoctions, forcing disturbed individuals to jump over bonfires, burying them underground, and inducing terror by the most fearsome means that could be devised. To be effective, it was said, the terrorizing event had to be so horrible that it would drive the demon away. One can only imagine what the effect must have been upon the mentally disturbed individual in whose interest it was supposedly carried out.

While psychiatrists may have exaggerated the strength of their opposition, they claimed that even wealthy and educated people utilized these unscientific methods. They also asserted that lay healers and priests actually sought to dissuade the masses from using mental institutions. The Moscow psychiatrist V. I. Iakovenko, for example, reported at the turn of the century that peasants from the districts bordering the province of Tver (to the north of Moscow) most often turned to a monk in the town of Staritsa, who advised them, "under no circumstances should the patient be sent to a hospital."[27]

Psychiatric physicians who conducted a census of the insane of St. Petersburg province in 1908 reported 233 cases in which individuals, whom they judged to be mentally disturbed, had been taken by their families to exorcists. While commenting sympathetically on the "loving attention and patience" with which families showered their disabled members, the census takers went on to report hundreds of instances in which the mad had been physically restrained, mocked, and abused.[28]

The St. Petersburg census also uncovered eighteen holy fools scattered throughout the province, evidence that popular veneration of them remained very much a feature of Russian life. Even though the church had ceased to canonize *iurodivye* several centuries earlier, the population at large continued to invest certain individuals with those qualities, nurturing them and looking to them for advice. Even the institutionalization of a famous holy fool was generally insufficient to tarnish his reputation. Perhaps the best known example was that of I. I. Koreisha, a holy fool who lived for almost a half-century in Moscow's Preobrazhenskaia Hospital. People from all walks of life came to the hospital to pay their respects to this holy madman and to seek his advice. The psychiatrist N. N. Bazhenov, who was for a time director of the hospital and later wrote a history of the institution, reported that many merchant families in Moscow would not embark on any new endeavor without first consulting Koreisha. He was often discussed in the press, and even Nikolai Gogol reportedly traveled to the Preobrazhenskaia to meet him.[29]

The noted historian of Russian religion G. P. Fedotov once observed that, "sincere or feigned, a madman with religious charisma (prophecy, clear-sightedness, and so forth) is always a saint, perhaps the most beloved saint in Russia."[30] The social response to Koreisha indicates that those sentiments were not restricted to the peasantry but were found even among Russia's most educated members, the intelligentsia. While the Preobrazhenskaia's famous resident died in the late 1860s, the intelligentsia continued to write about him and to idealize similar figures well into the twentieth century.

The fascination of the Russian intelligentsia with insanity was multifaceted. Many writers populated their fictional worlds with mentally abnormal individuals, most of whom conformed to traditional images of madness and were portrayed with great sympathy. Fictional and journalistic portrayals of the institutions within which Russian society confined madness were much less flattering. The stigma associated with the yellow houses remained, despite the best efforts of psychiatric reformers to expunge it. Instead, the reformers themselves increasingly came under attack by virtue of their association with suspect ideas and institutions.[31] While most members of the intelligentsia had come to accept the basic premise that mental disorders were a type of illness, many were skeptical of both the motives and the methods of psychiatry. By implication if not by direct declaration, they equated existing psychiatric approaches with coercion and oppression and contrasted them with traditional ones based upon sympathetic understanding and respect.

The Russian people clearly clung to traditional approaches to insanity in the late nineteenth and early twentieth centuries. Indeed, efforts to eliminate these old ideas have persisted well into the Soviet period. Those who knew the peasantry well in the late imperial era also described them as having an intense dislike for institutional methods of caring for any of their dependents, including the insane.[32] Psychiatrists continually complained that families waited far too long before bringing their disturbed members to the asylum and that they came to reclaim them before their treatment could be completed. In short, much of the available evidence seems to suggest that the population regarded mental institutions as last resorts, to be utilized only after they had exhausted all other options.

How then to account for the fact that the peasants' resorted to this widely abhorred solution in ever increasing numbers toward the end of the imperial era? In order to answer this question one must consider the changing economic and social circumstances of the Russian peasantry. Most historians have argued that emancipation did not bring a marked improvement in the economic condition of the peasants. The requirement that they reimburse the gentry for the land transferred to them saddled the peasants with a debt far beyond their means and which continued to mount over the remaining years of the nineteenth century. As is well known, rising numbers of peasants sought to better their lot by migrating to urban areas to seek work.

To some degree, the rise in asylum populations was a reflection of changes in family support structures brought about by increasing geographic mobility. Although migration to the cities did not terminate an individual's legal ties to the countryside, it could alter the emotional ties, especially for those peasants who lived in the city on a more or less permanent basis. Thanks to the laws, all peasants remained legal residents of their native region even though they might not have set foot in it for decades. By the late nineteenth century, it was a rather common practice for overburdened city officials to transport those who became disabled or insane to the area from which they had come, even if that legal residence was long abandoned and quite some distance away. Not surprisingly, villagers resented the troublesome human parcels returned with such formality to their doorsteps. Their willingness—already undermined by economic hardship—to care for "their own" insane often did not extend to individuals whose involvement in the community amounted to little more than a line in a passport. As a result, some such persons were abandoned; others were taken to the police, who could insist upon their admission to the nearest asylum.

Evidence from asylum annual reports of that era leads to the further conclusion that peasant families increasingly used the mental institutions to ease the burden of caring for some of their troublesome members. A sizable contingent of asylum patients consisted of individuals whose confinement corresponded to periods of relatively greater economic hardship for their families. Approximately half of all patients were released within a year after they had been admitted. Most of those lived within close proximity to the institution. Seasonal variations in both admissions and discharges from these mental hospitals suggest quite strongly that an ever rising number of peasant families elected to send some of their disabled members away to winter in the asylum, reclaiming in midsummer those who could assist with the harvest.[33] These tendencies were most pronounced in those zemstvo asylums that had eliminated fees for care, an escalating trend by the late nineteenth century. In short, one need not conclude that attitudes toward the institutions had changed in order to account for rising asylum populations. Rather, the combination of economic privation and the new availability of an inexpensive institutional alternative to caring for dependents at home appear the more important factors. The fact that families withdrew their members from the institution when their labor was needed (and often against medical advice) indicates that the populace used the institutions less because of faith in medical ministrations than because to do so could bring a marginal improvement to what was for many an increasingly precarious existence.

VII

The nineteenth century brought to Russia both new institutions for the insane and new ideas regarding the etiology and treatment of their condition. Nonetheless, despite elite support for the asylum and growing utilization of it by the population, there is little evidence to suggest widespread acceptance of the notion that insanity could actually be cured by institutionalization—or any psychiatric intervention, for that matter. Even psychiatrists grew increasingly pessimistic about the curability of mental illness during the latter part of the nineteenth century. An ardent supporter of the curative system at midcentury, the psychiatric profession later focused much of its energy upon the complex and costly problem of chronic incurable insanity.

From its beginnings, the Russian psychiatric profession had taken sociocultural factors into account in the planning of institutional regimens for treatment. The Kazan Regional Asylum, for example, was designed to treat patients from every walk of life, yet virtually all aspects of the treatment varied according to the social origin of the patient.[34] As its chief architect, the psychiatric physician A. Iu. Freze, commented, "insanity, even the same nosological form, takes on a totally different character among the common people than it does among the educated classes."[35] Because insanity manifested itself differently in these different social groups, treatment, in his view, was of necessity class specific.

These supposed differences between the educated insane and their uneducated counterparts provided a scientific rationale for far greater expenditures on the care of the former. These distinctions were quite apparent when the goal for both categories of patients was complete recovery. By the early twentieth century, the accumulation of chronic, seemingly incurable, patients had shown that to be a futile expectation. Although expenditures had always been highest for the most privileged patients, substantial outlays for the treatment of common folk had also seemed justified so long as they were accompanied by the expectation that many would eventually resume productive roles in society. As it became apparent that large numbers of the insane would not recover but instead would be permanently disabled, the willingness of the zemstvos to fund expensive asylums declined accordingly.

Russian psychiatrists grappled at length with the problem of what constituted appropriate care for incurably insane peasants. While the educated classes also produced their share of chronic patients, those individuals were of less concern to both psychiatrists and the zemstvos. Their numbers were relatively small, and their personal resources proportionally greater. Care for peasants, on the other hand, was provided at public expense.

No one was willing simply to fling open the doors of the institutions and release those who could not be helped to fend for themselves. The very presence of asylums and experts had conditioned all those involved in decision making to the necessity of some type of organized care, or at the very least supervision, of the insane. Nonetheless, the approach increasingly adopted throughout the empire did represent a retreat from the asylum, a path that distinguishes Russia from most Western societies.

This new approach, usually referred to by the French term *patronage familial,* involved returning incurable patients to the peasant milieu from which they had come. As the name suggests, this idea was not unique to Russia, although it was more widely implemented there than in many other settings. For the most part, patients were not returned to their own families but were placed in foster care with carefully selected peasant families. There were many local variants on this theme. In some instances, entire villages were chosen as centers for extramural care; in others, individual families near an asylum were selected to serve as hosts for deinstitutionalized patients. In either case, the family was paid a stipend for its efforts (generally between eight and twelve rubles a month), and the expectation was that the patients would contribute to the extent possible to the family economy. "Women patients were expected to help with the housework and child care and the insane men took their place in the fields along with their hosts. If the patients were too feeble or incapacitated to work, the families usually received a higher stipend."[36]

In important respects, *patronage familial* encapsulates the distinctive features of the Russian response to the insane. Its proponents advocated it on the grounds that it was especially suited to Russian culture and to the economic conditions of the empire. The sympathy and compassion of the Russian peasants toward those less fortunate than themselves (and especially toward the mad) provided the assurance that the patients would be well treated, while pervasive poverty provided motivation for peasant participation. From the standpoint of the zemstvos, the most important advantage of the *patronage familial* was that it eliminated the need for further asylum construction and significantly lowered the per capita cost of psychiatric care.

Psychiatrists were ambivalent about the concept. Most continued to regard institutional care as the treatment of choice. However, they were well aware of the fiscal realities. Furthermore, *patronage familial* provided them with a setting within which they could function with a minimum of outside interference. That was becoming less and less true of the asylum. Mounting pressures on the autocracy in the early twentieth century had further stimulated its already significant concern with social and political control. In the aftermath of the Revolution of 1905 in particular, increasing numbers of "dangerous" individuals were confined in both the prisons and the mental institutions of the empire. The government insisted upon using shackles and its own policemen to guard those inmates, intrusions that provoked open conflict between the government and the psychiatric profession. *Patronage familial* may not have been ideal in the view of psychiatrists, but at least it was their domain and relatively free from police interference.

Finally, the movement toward extramural psychiatric care in Russia was itself a response on the part of officials to the escalating concern with social and political stability. For complex reasons, many psychiatric hospitals and asylums had been centers of unrest during 1905 and 1906. Their role in the strikes and demonstrations of that era made them suspect in the minds of increasingly conservative zemstvo and tsarist officials. Consequently, both were eager to tighten their control over the institutions, and neither was disappointed to see a diminution in the asylum's role in the countryside.

VIII

Many of the changes in pre-1917 Russia's care of the mentally handicapped were similar to changes in the West. These include the increased involvement of the state, the expansion of a network of institutions to confine and treat the problem, the acceptance by elites of a medical definition of mental disturbance, and the associated delegation of limited authority for it to psychiatric experts. Similarly, the tension between concern for the personal suffering of unfortunate individuals and the desire to maintain social and political order is a dynamic underlying developments in many lands. Still, this ambivalence was somewhat more acute in imperial Russia, on the one hand, because of the adoration and respect that continued to characterize the popular response to certain types of madness and, on the other hand, because of the extraordinary defensiveness of the autocracy.

The expansion of the asylum in other societies has been correlated with urbanization, industrialization, and the growth of a capitalist economy. As Russia had not progressed as far as most Western societies along those paths, it is perhaps not surprising that the asylum system was less well developed there. As indicated earlier, the number of asylums increased several times over during the final decades of the tsarist era. Even so, the proportion of the population institutionalized in many Western countries was much greater. Late twentieth century critics of the total institution might well argue that this was for Russia but another manifestation of the advantages of backwardness, although contemporaries clearly did not perceive it in that way. Similarly, from the perspective of present-day policies of deinstitutionalization, Russia's rejection of the asylum in favor of foster care, with its emphasis on treatment in natural settings, appears particularly enlightened and worthy of more extensive examination.

The ravages of war and revolution brought much destruction to Russian mental hospitals and an end to the *patronage familial* system. Still, the system of psychiatric care as reconstructed in Soviet Russia was similar in form to that which existed prior to World War I. *Patronage familial* was not reinstituted, although there was some debate in the 1920s and the 1930s about the wisdom of doing so.[37] Nonetheless, it has its present-day counterpart in the neuropsychiatric dispensary, through which outpatient care is provided to both acute and chronic mental patients.

Finally, it would appear that ambivalence and contradiction remain aspects of the contemporary response to mental disorders. Concern with maintaining social and political order is still evident, as later chapters in this volume will attest. Nor have traditional attitudes of sympathy and respect disappeared over the course of the twentieth century. On the one hand, this suggests the historical importance of those values. On the other hand, it may also reflect the fact that madness was never segregated in Russia to the extent that it was elsewhere. Hence, it was not transformed into a strange and fearsome state, associated primarily with thick walls and barred windows, but remained a relatively ordinary feature of everyday life.

NOTES

1. A. Shul'ts, "Prizrenie pomeshannykh v Rossii," *Arkhiv sudebnoi meditsiny i obshchestvennoi gigieny* 1 (1865): 1–47.

2. George P. Fedotov, *The Russian Religious Mind,* vol. 2 (New York: Harper and Row, 1946), p. 317.

3. There were many such reports by psychiatrists, who recounted them in the effort to persuade the population of the importance of institutional care for the insane. An interesting journalistic account is to be found in V. G. Korolenko, "Smirennye," *Sobranie sochinenii* (Moscow: Gos. izd. khudozh. lit-ry, 1953), pp. 282–98.

4. I. V. Konstantinovskii, *Russkoe zakonodatel'stvo ob umalishennykh. Ego istoriia i sravnenie s inostrannymi zakonodatel'stvami* (St. Petersburg, 1887), pp. 17–18.

5. Some Soviet historians have argued that caring for the insane was a money-making proposition for the church and that its interest in doing so declined when secular officials began to demand the incarceration of the "dangerous" irrespective of their financial condition. See, for example, A. M. Shereshevskii, "Sozdanie v Rossii pervykh spetsial'nykh uchrezhdenii dlia dushevno-bol'nykh," *Zhurnal nevropatologii i psikhiatrii im. S. S. Korsakova* 78 (1978): 132–34.

6. Ia. G. Il'on. "Materialy k istorii organizatsionnykh form otechestvennoi psikho-pomoshchi i razvitiia aktivnoi terapii psikhozov," Diss. dok. med., Gor'kii, 1940, p. 42. See also Shul'ts, "Prizrenie pomeshannykh," p. 2.

7. L. Z. Slonimskii, "Zakonodatel'stvo o dushevno-bol'nykh," *Vestnik klinicheskoi i sudebnoi psikhiatrii i nevropatologii* 1 (1883): 132.

8. G. V. Morozov, D. R. Lunts, and N. I. Felinskaia, *Osnovnye etapy razvitiia otechestvennoi sudebnoi psikhiatrii* (Moscow: Meditsina, 1976), p. 15.

9. Konstantinovskii, *Russkoe zakonodatel'stvo,* p. 51.

10. Quoted in Shul'ts, "Prizrenie pomeshannykh," pp. 10–11.

11. Ibid. The epithet yellow house has survived in popular usage down to the present day.

12. Zhores and Roy Medvedev, *A Question of Madness* (London: Macmillan, 1971), pp. 198–200.

13. N. N. Bazhenov, *Psikhiatricheskaia besedy na literaturnyia i obshchestvennyia temy* (Moscow, 1903), p. 83.

14. On one occasion, an ukase forbade the use of military sentinels in mental institutions. On another, officials were forbidden to use physical restraints on the insane. See J. V. Brown, "The Professionalization of Russian Psychiatry, 1857–1911," Ph.D. diss., University of Pennsylvania, 1981, pp. 65–66.

15. Several other private madhouses were opened during this era in St. Petersburg and Moscow. Each was quite small and catered to the wealthy. For a discussion of their role, see Brown, "Professionalization," pp. 64–65.

16. P. Ostankov, "Vinnitskaia Okruzhnaia Lechebnitsa," *Obozrenie psikhiatrii, nevrologii i eksperimental'noi psikhologii* 1 (1896): 440.

17. During their early years, the zemstvos attempted to minimize

and in some instances even to avoid their public health responsibilities. See N. M. Frieden, *Russian Physicians in an Era of Reform and Revolution* (Princeton: Princeton University Press, 1981), p. 89.

18. Cited in N. N. Bazhenov, "Proekt zakonodatel'stva o dushevno-bol'nykh i ob'iasnitel'naia zapiska k nemu," in *Trudy pervago s'ezda soiuza psikhiatrov i nevropatologov sozvannago v Moskve v pamiat' S. S. Korsakova* (Moscow, 1914), pp. 201–202.

19. Cited in T. I. Iudin, *Ocherki istorii otechestvennoi psikhiatrii* (Moscow, 1951), pp. 213–14.

20. Bazhenov, "Proekt zakonodatel'stva," pp. 201–02.

21. P. I. Kovalevskii, "Polozhenie nashikh dushevnykh bol'nykh," *Arkhiv psikhiatrii, nevrologii i sudebnoi psikhopatologii* 5 (1890): 83–84.

22. J. V. Brown, "Psychiatrists and the State in Tsarist Russia," in S. Cohen and A. Scull, eds., *Social Control and the State* (New York: St. Martin's Press, 1983), p. 275.

23. Shul'ts, "Prizrenie pomeshannykh," p. 12.

24. *Sovremennaia psikhiatriia* 6 (1912): 848–49.

25. V. Iakovenko, *Dushevno-bol'nye moskovskoi gubernii* (Moscow, 1900), p. 150.

26. K. P. Sulim, "Koe-to o polozhenii dushevno-bol'nykh v iugo-zapadnom krae," *Arkhiv psikhiatrii, nevrologii i sudebnoi psikhopatologii* 6 (1885): 51.

27. Iakovenko, *Dushevno-bol'nye,* pp. 54–55.

28. P. P. Kashchenko, *Kratkii otchet po perepisi dushevno-bol'nykh v S-Petersburgskoi gubernii* (St. Petersburg, 1910), p. 15.

29. The story of Koreisha is discussed in K. S. Dix, "Madness in Russia 1775–1864: Official Attitudes and Institutions for its Care," Ph.D. diss., University of California at Los Angeles, 1977, pp. 231–33.

30. Fedotov, *The Russian Religious Mind,* p. 324.

31. See, for example, A. P. Chekhov, "Ward No. 6," and "The Black Monk,"; N. Gogol, "Diary of a Madman"; V. M. Garshin, "The Scarlet Flower"; L. N. Andreev, "A Dilemma"; and G. Korolenko, "The Meek." Many of Fyodor Dostoevsky's novels contain characters who are mentally handicapped. Leo Tolstoy was one of the most vocal literary critics of psychiatry; and newspapers reported scandals involving psychiatrists and psychiatric hospitals with some frequency. For a discussion of several of these scandals, see Brown, "Professionalization," ch. 5.

32. See Adele Lindenmeyr, "Work, Charity and the Elderly in Late Nineteenth Century Russia," in Peter Stearns, ed., *Old Age in Preindustrial Society* (New York: Holmes and Meier, 1982), pp. 232–47.

33. See J. V. Brown, "Peasant Survival Strategies in Late Imperial Russia: The Social Uses of the Mental Hospital," *Social Problems* 34 (1987): 311–29.

34. See J. V. Brown, "Mental Illness as a Social Disease: Elements of Psychiatric Thought in Late Imperial Russia," paper delivered at the

Conference on the History of Russian and Soviet Public Health, Toronto, 1986.

35. A. Iu. Freze, *Ob ustroistve domov umalishennykh* (Moscow, 1862), p. 38.

36. See J. V. Brown, "A Sociohistorical Perspective on Deinstitutionalization: The Case of Late Imperial Russia" *Research in Law, Deviance and Social Control* 7 (1985): 167–88.

37. Z. N. Serebriakova, *Organizatsiia psikhiatricheskogo patronazha i perspektivy ego razvitiia v SSSR* (Moscow: Meditsina, 1965).

The Origins of Defectology

William O. McCagg

I

THE WORD *defectology* (*defektologiia*) is the official term in the Soviet Union for the academic discipline (*sistema nauchnopedagogicheskikh znanii*) in which those who teach handicapped children receive their training. The word is attached to teacher training faculties at the most important institutes of higher learning. It is also present in the name of the Scientific Research Institute for Defectology at the Academy of Pedagogical Sciences of the Russian Republic (*Nauchnoissledovatelskii Institut Defektologii Akademii Pedagogicheskikh Nauk RSFSR*).[1] Because the Institute of Defectology has direct input through the Ministry of Education into the administration of, and teaching at, schools for the handicapped, it dominates the world of Soviet handicapped children.

Subsumed to the defectological faculties are various teacher training departments covering the education of the deaf and hard of hearing, the blind and weak sighted, the weak of mind, and children with speech difficulties (*surdopedagogika, tyflopedagogika, oligofrenopedagogika, and logopediia*). These departments are today described as autonomous, which suggests that in practice they are as separate as the corresponding areas of child rehabilitation are in the West. In the special school system, there are likewise areas of autonomy. The schools for the deaf and blind, for the retarded, and for speech improvement are under the Ministry of Education. Those for children with clearly psychological disturbances are under the Ministry of Health, however, even if these are logopedic in character; and so are the schools for crippled children and many asylums.[2] Still, the blanket term *defectology* remains important. The objective in the present chapter is to give the reader some idea

39

of the origins and character of the educational discipline that it denotes.

II

We had best begin by dispelling the mystery of the term, for it is puzzling. In Russian, a great many scientific terms and the names of many scientific specializations are Western in origin, so it is perhaps not surprising to find one here too. Yet *defektologiia* is not just Western. It incorporates negative attitudes toward the disabled that would not survive for three minutes in a discussion of the handicapped in the Western world today. Defectology is boasted as being a new and special discipline within Soviet academe, one that attempts to overcome the heritage of the past. How can it be that the very title of this new discipline seems so redolent of prejudice? And then, second, there is a practical matter that makes the Soviet use of this collective term seem puzzling: in the West one tends to believe that deafness, blindness, and weak-mindness are entirely different afflictions, requiring entirely different treatments. How can it be that among handicapped children in the Soviet Union, all the defects seem lumped together?

Some of the puzzle disappears when one probes for first usage.[3] It turns out that the term *defectology* was introduced in Russia in 1912 by a psychiatrist, Professor V. P. Kashchenko (1870–1943), who in 1908 at Moscow had organized a private "sanatorium-school" for retarded "abnormal" children.[4] Kashchenko was among the first in the country to pioneer into an area that was then and still is in the West called special education. But there are many other scholars who were pioneering at the same time into other special fields: as is well known, that was a time of considerable experimentation by intellectuals in Russia. The education of advanced as well as retarded children was being investigated, and the Russian words for special (*spetsial'nii, iskliuchitel'nii*) were in current use to cover both. Consequently, when in 1912 Kashchenko and his colleagues published a collection of papers recounting in international perspective the experience of his institution, they needed some other terms to denote the retarded groups with whom they dealt. At the time, the word *defective* did not conjure up, even in the West, the connotations of prejudice it does today. One may find it as a classifier term in the New York Public Library catalogue, for example, which was composed in that day. It was perfectly respectable.[5] Consequently, Kashchenko used the term *defektivnii* to serve his ends.[6] It was soon taken up by a prominent neurologist, Professor G. I. Rossolimo (1860–1926), who headed a clinic at the University Hospital.[7]

The puzzle of the Soviet use of the word defectology seems even less when one recalls the early development of this discipline. In the heady atmosphere of the Revolution of 1917, Dr. Kashchenko, like many other Russian intellectuals, leapt into the future. In 1918 he transformed his school into a public and revolutionary Child Teaching House (*Dom Izucheniia Rebenka*), and shortly thereafter guided it into a further incarnation as the Medical-Pedagogical Experiment Station (*Mediko-Pedagogicheskaia Opytnaia Stanitsa*) of the new People's Commissariat of Education, a clinic for retarded children, of which he himself became the director.[8]

As head of this clinic, and as an Education Commissariat official all through the early Soviet period, Kashchenko was an important figure in the development of a centralized all-national Soviet system of special education for handicapped children. It was quite natural, therefore, that his vocabulary should have been applied to the new revolutionary institutes that sprang up in 1918–20 in Moscow, Petrograd, Kiev, and other cities for training teachers of abnormal children. He himself actually headed the one in Moscow; the one in Petrograd was founded by his collaborators, professors A. S. Griboedov and A. N. Graborov. From early on, they were called pedagogical institutes for child defectiveness, and their graduates were labeled defectologists.[9] It was equally natural that Kashchenko's terminology should appear also in the title of the First All-Russian Congress for Struggle against Child Defectiveness, Delinquency and Homelessness (*Detskaia Defektivnost', Prestupnost' i Besprizornost'*), which met from 24 June to 2 July 1920, under the leadership of A. B. Lunacharsky and Maxim Gorky, and founded a new centralized Soviet system for educating physically abnormal and mentally retarded children.[10]

One may still ask, why has the term defectology not only caught on, but survived? It was all very well for old Russia's child rehabilitationists to solve a temporary terminological problem through the use of this word in 1912. But why sanctify it down to the present day? Professor Kashchenko was no Bolshevik, after all. He was an old-regime doctor who collaborated of necessity with the new revolutionary regime after 1917, but who was deposed from positions of influence once the Stalin revolution began, about 1930. Why has his terminology lasted?

The answer may be that after the 1920 congress, it was boasted

that "except in America [and Soviet Russia], nowhere else in the
world could one find institutions of *higher* education devoting attention to the problem of teaching retarded children."[11] Between the
wars, and especially in the period 1917–22, Russian intellectuals
were doing things vigorously their own way, and Dr. Kashchenko's
work was seen as a Soviet humanitarian breakthrough. By the late
1920s and into the 1930s, therefore, when in the West doubts may
have begun to surface about the expression *defectiveness,* perhaps
there was no going back for Soviet *defectology.* Perhaps its label was
by then too well established, too revolutionary-national, to be cast
aside.

III

Let us turn now to the other question we have asked about defectology. Does not everyone know that the principal child afflictions that Dr. Kashchenko treated and that present-day Soviet
defectologists treat—blindness, deafness, mental retardation, and
physical disability—are entirely different from one another? Does
not everyone know that these disabilities require very different
treatments? Should not enduring etiological factors therefore mili-
tate against the word *defectiveness,* making it seem unuseful in the
Soviet context?

To answer such questions, it is useful to refer back to the
beginnings of the modern history of the disabled in Europe, and to
recall some principal features of their early rehabilitation.[12] It
comes immediately to light that, though our languages of course
had different words from very far back for blindness, deafness,
feeblemindedness, and physical disability, the diagnosis of their
presence in children was for many centuries difficult, and certainly
not among society's primary concerns. One may add, indeed, that
children with such afflictions most frequently did not long survive
in order to have their problems diagnosed. It follows in all probability that our special words for deafness, blindness, and even
insanity are derived not from the diagnosis of childhood afflictions
but rather from those of adults—people articulate about their afflictions and who from long observation had a clear idea of what was
wrong. By implication, our languages may lend an unreal clarity
of the differences between the afflictions.

To go a step further, let us note that for a long time the diagnosis of disability even among adults was notably difficult, as we can
tell from the horrifying imprecision that throve in the old days.

From the beginnings of Western civilization, for example, the born deaf were believed to be uneducable, as well as the non-hearing, because they were unable to speak. Because of this assumed quality, the deaf were by law excluded from civic rights, and the word "dumb" came to mean "stupid."[13] Correspondingly, the born incompetent were grouped in the Middle Ages together with the insane and the deformed as fools. With the beginnings of modern social legislation in the seventeenth century, moreover, these born idiots, the deformed and the insane alike, were often incarcerated indiscriminately together with the poor and the criminal, because all were vaguely seen as noxious and nonuseful members of society.[14] The reason for such vagueness is clear enough: even today one hears of cases where a born deaf child is mistakenly diagnosed as retarded. Who could then tell the difference? As is today widely known, there is frequently in individual cases an overlap between blindness, deafness, deformity, and mental retardation, albeit it is always in different forms; and there are all sorts of different degrees of retardation among children and adults alike. If the etiology of disability is acknowledged today in specialized circles as so exceedingly difficult, should one not ask again, who in the old days was in a position to tell the difference? And does it not follow that vagueness about defects was nigh excusable in an earlier age because our words blind, deaf, and weak-minded deceive—because the differences between the defects are in nature hard to tell?

It is well known that toward the end of the eighteenth century an epochal change abated some of the worst of Western society's diagnostic confusions about the disabled. In the 1780s the revolutionary emperor Joseph II in Austria ordered the establishment of special asylums for weak-minded children, as well as separate school institutions for the blind and the deaf. Just after he died, the French Revolution opened the gates of Bicêtre, striking off the chains that bound the insane in the same prison with the criminal and poor. Hereupon, the medicalization of disability began to advance in most European countries. Soon there were schools for the deaf and institutes for the blind even in distant Russia.

But did emancipation mean that immediately the problems of treating the handicapped, and particularly handicapped children, were solved? And with medicalization, did it quickly become easy to distinguish between the various handicaps? The sad fact is that despite the emancipation of the handicapped from the prisons, for a long time, even in the West, the institutional network fell far short of an ability to care for the actual numbers of the disabled. In

countries such as Russia an almost insuperable gap remained between the number of institutions available and the demand. Furthermore, one should have no illusions about medicalization. In
most places the problems of diagnosing disability were hardly
touched, if only because there were too few doctors, because too
much misinformation was left over from the past, and because in
any case scientific research takes a long time.[15] And to this one
must add, that almost coincidentally with emancipation an entirely
new set of problems arose to plague those who cared for the
handicapped.

Enlightened Europe was aspiring not just to the establishment
of science and reason as the fundament of civilized life, but to
universal literacy. In all countries, the Enlightenment produced a
vision whereby education was a prerequisite for social and economic success, and it led to a proliferation of schools. The result
was that the handicapped began to stand out from the norm much
more than before. Because of the new schooling of all children, in
city and village alike "abnormal people" began to experience an
exclusion from society even in their childhood, and of course this
increased later on with the ever greater differentiation between the
educated and uneducated classes.

For such reasons, one began early in the nineteenth century to
ask a host of new questions. Should all the different kinds of
mental abnormality, for example, be considered equally uneducable? Should no effort be made to improve the children (or the
adults, for that matter) who fall short of some, often non-
specifiable, standard of normal behavior? If society is to attempt
the education of some categories of disability, why not all? After
one has set up special schools for the deaf and special homes for the
blind of all ages, can it be considered that the insane asylum is the
right place for the simpleminded child?

All told, coincident with the medicalization movement, the
question of schooling retarded and disabled children came onto the
European agenda, with all that implied in terms of pressure to
diagnose disability in childhood, when, as we have seen, it is much
more difficult. And this development had significantly different
consequences in different places. In England and its erstwhile
American colonies, where a primary school network was already
well laid out before 1800, it was relatively easy to respond to the
new questions. It seemed feasible to establish separate schools for
separate categories of disabled children, or at least to set up separate classes in the grade schools. Though practice remained far

behind theory, especially in the public sector, there was relatively little pressure to follow the expedient path of challenging the linguistic categories by lumping all the disabled together. But on the Continent, and especially in the German and Eastern European lands, where a broad primary elementary school network was either less advanced or nonexistent, there was a temptation to take shortcuts, if such came to light. This brings us toward our point, which is that on the Continent the old etiological confusion of the handicapped groups, which had been based on sheer ignorance, gave way to a new lumping together of these people based on expediency, as well. Given the pattern of overlaps mentioned above, this was in no way a bad thing, a step backward. It was simply different.

Other factors hereupon also tipped the Germanic and Eastern European lands further in the same direction. One may dramatize one of these by contrasting the classic problem educational researchers investigated in France, with its parallel in Germany. In France in the early decades of the nineteenth century Dr. Jean Itard of the Paris Institute for the Deaf undertook the education of a wild boy and then widely published his findings. Though Itard was a medical man working in the heartland of the Enlightenment, he made the problem of special education seem above all a problem of getting through somehow to a natural mind—a pedagogical, not a medical, issue. Further east, however, the classic problem facing such researchers was cretinism—an environmentally caused idiocy that was widespread in the valleys between the Alps.[16] One could not help but guess, even in the days of primitive diagnostics, that the solution here would have to be medical, not just pedagogical. The cretins were clearly not just uneducated: they were physically defective. Their treatment could not be handed over just to educators, but clearly had to be retained in the hands of the medical profession.

There were of course in the German lands, as in France, wild men enough to stimulate pedagogically inclined minds. But disability here seemed in general more a social question than in France, and the result was a holistic tradition of disability rehabilitation, which increasingly contrasted with the individualistic pedagogical tradition of the Atlantic countries. Some well-known historical factors reinforced this tradition, which—to repeat—was in no small degree appropriate, given the extreme difficulty of disability diagnosis. In general, scholars in Germany tended for nationalistic reasons to scorn theories of natural education derived in France from Rousseau, and to prefer the high philosophical approaches of Kant and Herbart. Perhaps one may say that the Germans out of nationalism came to crave a comprehensive, all-explaining theory of rehabilitation first, before they turned to practical experimentation. In any case, even before the introduction of state systems of primary education, German experts were insisting that all varieties of human deficiency be studied together, rather than separately; that medical doctors as well as pedagogues be deeply involved in the care of the handicapped; and that science, not accident, dominate such serious matters. In Germany, one began before the middle of the nineteenth century to refer to the schooling of the handicapped not just as a new branch of education, but as a specifically medical curative pedagogy—*Heilpädagogik*. As early as 1861, two Austrian doctors, J. G. Georgens and his partner, H. Deinhardt, who had in 1856 established a medical and educational establishment, named Levana (Heilpflege- und Erziehungsanstalt, Levana) near Vienna, used this term in a book title, as if it were a separate, integrated science.[17] The term gained broad use when in 1865 two other medical men, Dr. Kern and Dr. Stötzner, established a *Heilpädagogische* section at the All-German Congress of Teachers.[18]

Scientific rigor and holism led German disability scholarship to outrageous abuses, there can be no doubt. Notoriously, it was Germans who in midnineteenth century developed the theory of deaf education, whereby one must not only insist on training deaf children to learn a spoken language by reading lips, but also rigorously and rigidly exclude from their lives sign language, which they use naturally to express themselves (and which, incidentally, Frenchmen had until then used for teaching the deaf). Why so? This theory held that a mode of thinking dominated by images, and allegedly encouraged by sign language, was inhibitory to the abstract mode of thinking that was considered necessary to produce a cultured person. This was science and holism carried to unintelligent excess.[19]

Nonetheless, science and holism also brought the Germans great success and world renown. In the 1880s, the German oralist method of educating the deaf conquered the whole world, including pragmatic America, so great was its scientific credibility. All the more did German solutions to disability problems enjoy great prestige in Eastern Europe. In tsarist Russia, characteristically, the treatment of the deaf was frequently in the hands of the practitioners of the Germanic exclusively oralist method.

So it was that in Germany in the last decades of the nineteenth century, a new approach to the education of the retarded took root, one that had a particular appeal to Eastern Europeans. At this time when the cities of Germany, like those all over Europe, were swelling enormously with immigrant populations, it became clear that there were many parents who knew their children were having trouble keeping up in the now obligatory state-run *Volkschulen,* but who were unwilling to send them to the various extant institutions for the feebleminded. First in Saxony and Prussia, therefore, then in other German states, the government-run *Volkschule* authorities began to organize special classes—*Nebenklassen*—and later on, entire remedial schools—*Hilfsschulen*—for the slower students. In 1893, 110 such classes existed in 32 German cities with 2,290 children in them. By 1902/03 there were some 575 classes in 138 cities, and they serviced some 12,000 children. In 1913/14, some 1,850 classes in 320 cities serviced some 43,000 children.[20]

In a population of 65 million, these were by no means earthshaking figures. But they reflected a strong market for the advocates of *Heilpädagogik,* whose audience had hitherto been more or less confined to teachers in old-fashioned and usually ill-financed private institutions. Now suddenly lots of teachers and school administrators had to find out rapidly about how to educate retarded and otherwise abnormal children. There resulted a positive blossoming of relevant literature and a good deal of imaginative innovation in *Heilpädagogisch* teaching theory and method (though one must stress that there was absolutely no unity of content here, to supplement the unity of basic approach). By 1904 Theodor Heller, the director of a school for retarded children in Vienna-Grinzing, felt free to publish a volume entitled *Grundriss der Heilpädagogik,* implying that this was already an independent science. Contrary to what some of his colleagues (and many earlier advocates of *Heilpädagogik*) believed, Heller asserted that feeblemindedness was not akin to deafness and blindness, the result of a medically treatable defect in the human constitution.[21] But when in 1911 Dr. Dannemann, Dr. Schober, and Dr. Schulz at Halle undertook to publish an *Enziklopädisches Handbuch der Heilpädagogok,* they made no such genteel distinctions. They included essays on the treatment and history of all aspects of abnormality, most specifically including blindness and deafness. Already they were pointing to a sort of quasi-political teacher activism, which between the wars would thrive in the *Verband der Hilfsschulen Deutschlands,* which would regard the *Hilfsschulen* as a useful way to educate the masses, and which would insist that *Heilpädagogik* had unitary scientific foundations.[22]

Just as earlier German theorists had acquired with their science a broad foreign audience, so now did the advocate of curative education. Their first victory was in Hungary. By 1898 Alexander Naray-Szabó, a prominent official in the Hungarian Ministry of Education, was so impressed with the literature and achievements of the German *Hilfsschulen* that he instituted a special section for *Heilpädagogik* (or *Gyógypedagógia,* as it is known in Magyar) under his own leadership in the Budapest ministry. He and his colleagues then undertook to provide guidance and training to all teachers of the blind, the deaf, the feebleminded, and the speech impeded in Hungary. They soon organized a special two-year teacher training institute, and made it the first such obligatory state defectological school in all Europe. In 1906 their department absorbed a *Heilpädagogisch-psychologisch* laboratory organized a few years earlier by a well-known psychiatrist, Dr. P. Rauschburg.[23] The attraction of *Heilpädagogik* to the Magyars was no doubt in part nationalistic. When they instituted it, they were consciously grabbing at a new idea before even the Germans, the great "culture bearers" of Europe, had done so. In addition, they were being different from and more progressive than their Austrian rulers. But one may recognize also that *Heilpädagogik* and the *Hilfsschulen* may have seemed extremely interesting to an Eastern European government faced with the problem of spreading education among a large population that the ruling classes had traditionally regarded as stupid peasants. In the socioeconomic backwardness of Hungary, defectiveness may have seemed a far broader phenomenon than the officially recorded statistics regarding the deaf, blind, and weak-minded might imply.

In the years just before the First World War, *Heilpädagogik* found a following also in Russia, and it will not surprise the reader that Professor Kashchenko's school faculty were among the converts. We do not know much about them, but significantly Kashchenko labeled the school he founded in 1908 a sanatorium school, implying a joint medical and pedagogical approach to retardation. In 1912 one of his colleagues at the sanatorium school, Maria P. Postovskaia, together with her husband, Dr. N. I. Postovskii, published a book reporting on the "development, present situation and organization" of comparable schools in Germany.[24] In 1915, a member of Kashchenko's staff, S. Kriukov, who had been responsible for the international chapter in Kashchenko's earlier defectological book, published a report: "The *Hilfsschulen* in Germany from Personal Observation." In 1919 as noted earlier, Kashchenko named his clinic in Moscow a medical pedagogical station, literally translating the term *Heilpädagogik*. In 1929 he and his close collaborator, G. V. Murashev, had a book in press entitled *Korrektivnaia (Lechebnaia) Pedagogika,* an even more literal translation of *Heilpädagogik*. In a Soviet defectological encyclopedia published in the 1960s, the leading advocates of *Heilpädagogik* in Russia are listed as Dr. Kashchenko, Dr. Rossolimo, and Dr. Griboedov, who of course were precisely the founders of defectology itself.[25]

It is not known when exactly or how this group of Russian special educationists acquired their knowledge of the German curative-educational approach to treating disabled and retarded children. But the transfusion of ideas is not surprising, given the universal prestige of German science at the time, its dominance in Russian universities, and the frequency with which Russian intellectuals visited the German lands. It thus seems most probable that what these Russians came to call defectology derived from this transfusion, more or less in the same fashion as did the *Gyógypedagógia* just previously established in Hungary. The diagnostic and rehabilitative tasks they faced in Russia were enormous. The ideas of *Heilpädagogik* were fresh, appropriate, and seemed progressive. Especially when the Revolution of 1917 provided both an opportunity and a demand for quick solutions to enormous social problems, the hardly tried German model for remedial education must have seemed the answer to a prayer.

IV

There remains an important question: has the early Soviet, holistic, *Heilpädagogist* education of the handicapped remained unchanged in all the years since 1920? Is the defectology of today the same as that of Dr. V. P. Kashchenko? Of the several possible approaches to an answer to this question, one, the statistical approach, leads to certainly negative results.

Let us first assess the statistical picture in Kashchenko's day. On the eve of the First World War, tsarist Russian authorities were aware of some 45,000 deaf-dumb children and some 28,600 blind children. Of these about 3,000 deaf and 460 blind children were attending special schools. In addition, by 1916, 796 retarded children were attending recently organized special institutions.[26] Comparable Soviet statistics on this subject are rare—no questions were asked about the disabled in the 1939, 1959, 1970, and 1979 censuses; we have census data only for 1926, and even that is rather too general.[27] But there is extant a report based on data from 1930 that Dr. A. S. Griboedov, the director of the Defectological Research Institute in Leningrad, submitted to a German encyclopedia in that year.[28] Griboedov reported that in the special schools for the deaf there were now in all 6,700 pupils, as opposed to the 3,000 in 1911; 5,400 of these were in the Russian Republic (RSFSR), 800 in the Ukraine, 150 in Belorussia, and 300 in the other republics. In the thirty-seven special schools for the blind, there were about 2,000 children, as opposed to the 460 of 1911. Of these, 1,500 were in the Russian Republic and 500 in Moscow and Leningrad alone. From another source we know that much of these increases occurred only in the late 1920s. In 1925 there had been less than 1,200 children in the deaf schools; in 1926 there had been only twenty-six schools for the blind.[29] And meanwhile, there had been even greater growth in the education of the retarded.

Griboedov reported that in the whole USSR some 20,000 such children were actually enrolled in special courses, as opposed to the 769 in 1916. Of these, about 7,000 were in the Moscow region, 4,500 in Leningrad, 3,000 in thirty other cities of the Russian Republic, 2,700 in the Ukraine, 640 in Belorussia, 300 in Uzbekistan, 140 in Turkmenistan, 240 in Transcaucasia, and 1,000 in institutions controlled by the state railroads. There were no such courses in the countryside. This was certainly a remarkable change from 1916. Griboedov further provided statistics about 200 special homes for difficult children, which had been set up since the Revolution. They contained about 11,000 pupils, of whom some 800 were in the RSFSR, the rest in the national republics. All told, thus, according to Griboedov, defectology was in 1930 reaching some 40,000 Soviet children, though most of them were concentrated in the Moscow and Leningrad regions; and he indicated that the trained teachers and staff overseeing all these children numbered 3,530 persons. Since 1917 some 500 teachers of defective children had completed the four-year course at the two principal teacher training faculties of the USSR, those at Leningrad and Moscow. All this was the accomplishment of Kashchenko's defectology.

Striking as these figures are compared to the prerevolutionary situation in Russia, they have been wholly eclipsed in recent decades. In the last prewar year, 1940–41, according to a Soviet handbook, there were some 1,095 schools for handicapped children with an enrollment of 274,000.[30] The war then caused a sharp drop: in 1945/46 there were only 705 schools with 85,000 children.

But by 1959/60 there were 966 such schools, with 122,000 children enrolled. As will be seen below, these last figures may represent a plateau of sorts, resulting from a deliberately egalitarian school policy that discriminated not just against the handicapped but also against all categories of special education—against special classes for advanced, as well as for retarded, children.[31] If so, the plateau was rapidly left behind in the 1960s. As a result of the great Soviet education reform of 1958/59, the number of special schools increased to 2,026 by 1970, and the number of pupils to 362,000. By 1980 the total number of pupils was in the range of 500,000.[32]

A recent study has shown that the increase in the number of special schools was most pronounced in the more advanced, wealthier areas of the Soviet Union, the RSFSR, and the Baltic republics.[33] This was as it was back in Kashchenko's day. Still, defectology has not only changed absolutely in its dimensions since then but shows strong signs of becoming an all-nation discipline. In 1950, 76.7 percent of special school children were still in the Russian Republic, 17.5 percent in the Ukraine and Belorussia, and only 2 percent in Central Asia. By 1980, despite the vast increase in the sheer numbers of enrolled children, only 58.9 percent were in the Russian Republic, 12.0 percent of them were now in Central Asia.

V

Defectology has also undergone tremendous ideological changes since the mid-1920s, and this perhaps most of all because of the work of L. S. Vygotsky, the revolutionary of early Soviet psychology.

Vygotsky, born in 1896, was the scion of a Jewish family in a small city in Belorussia. He graduated in law from Moscow University in 1917. But he had a mind that transcended academic disciplines. His interests were in history, psychology, philosophy, and literature. His eventual (postwar) dissertation was on the psychology of art, and involved not only a study of *Hamlet,* but also of Ivan Bunin's "Gentle Breath," various fables, and contemporary psychoanalysis. And by the end of the revolutionary period, early in the 1920s, he was displaying his talents by teaching both literature and the history of art at schools in Gomel.

Vygotsky broke onto the academic scene of the Soviet Union very suddenly in January 1924, when he delivered a seemingly extemporaneous presentation on consciousness at the Second All-

Russian Psycho-Neurological Congress at Leningrad. Until then, Soviet psychology and Soviet defectology as well had been dominated by men who had thrived even under the old regime: by Chelpanov, Bekhterev, Kornilov, Pavlov, Blonsky in the first discipline; by Kashchenko, Rossolimo, and Griboedov in the second. There had been revolution, of course, and a purge of bourgeois intellectuals in both disciplines. This had happened especially in psychology, which had been much more developed before the war than defectology, and where old-fashioned, antirevolutionary intellectuals had been more common. But in both disciplines, revolution had taken the form of prewar specialists more or less opportunistically jumping on the Bolshevik bandwagon. Pressure to go further—to base the discipline on Marxism—existed. In psychology, it led in 1924 to the establishment of K. N. Kornilov as head of the Moscow Psychology Institute on the grounds that he was more materialist than his colleagues. And there was plenty of young blood in both disciplines. But before the arrival of Vygotsky, neither new blood nor Marxism were particularly visible in the leadership.[34]

Vygotsky's presentation at the 1924 congress was so brilliant that it earned its author an invitation to become a member of Kornilov's just-then-reorganized Institute of Psychology in Moscow. Although only twenty-eight years old at the time and not yet qualified either as a Ph.D. or as a psychologist, Vygotsky was an ardent, believing Marxist, and was possessed by a nigh messianic energy. He had a dynamic effect on the younger members of the institute. He soon seemed to incarnate the revolution there. And he soon had a comparable effect in defectology. In Gomel, Vygotsky had developed his interest in psychology by organizing a laboratory for the study of defective children at the teacher's college that employed him. Even then, he apparently admired the clinical method of studying child cognitive processes that Jean Piaget was developing abroad.[35] Arriving in Moscow, he decided to pursue his study of consciousness on an experimental basis. Outside of old Professor Rossolimo's neurological laboratory at the First Moscow University, little was being done in this area of research. Vygotsky chose to organize, not at the universities, but under the Education Commissariat, a Laboratory for Study of the Psychology of Abnormal Childhood. It was modeled, one may presume, on the one he had set up earlier at Gomel, and brought him into close contact with the Moscow defectologists, who were also under the ministry.

This injection of brilliant researchers—for Vygotsky brought with him the cream of the Psychology Institute—transformed defectology. Hitherto, it consisted of teacher-training by Old World professors and had involved the organization of remedial classes and schools. Its doctrine had insisted on medical involvement in the education of abnormal children, on a vague linkage between various social and physical abnormalities, and on an activist approach to all of them.[36] Now, Vygotsky made it over into a specifically Marxist, high philosophical science. As will be detailed in a subsequent chapter of this volume, he made no pretense that all physical and mental defects were in any way similar. To the contrary! But he worked out in detail a theory whereby all of them caused distortions in a child's psychological development; and whereby, as a result, the task of the psychologist and the educator of the handicapped becomes encouragement of a psychological compensation for the distortions. Herein lay a justification of a unified defectology that was vastly superior to Kashchenko's.

In the short decade of Vygotsky's eminence (he died in 1934), he spread himself over the whole landscape of Soviet psychology and education.[37] By 1929 he had expanded his laboratory, renaming it the Experimental Defectological Institute; and he was publishing a professional journal entitled *Voprosy Defektologii*. But his ascendency did not last long. As early as 1930, for reasons to be discussed below, one of his colleagues, I. I. Daniushevskii, took over the leadership of the institute, which was renamed the Scientific-Practical Institute of Special Schools and Child Homes. In 1931, the *Voprosy Defektologii* ceased publication, not to be replaced until 1958.[38] After 1936, Vygotsky's name came under a shadow, his works were banned, and much of his intellectual accomplishment was reattributed to Pavlov.[39]

Still, Vygotsky had infused an intellectual backbone into Soviet defectology, which made it a far more respected, and objectively a far more respectable, discipline than Kashchenko's had been. During the Stalin years, Soviet defectology was underfunded, understaffed, terrorized like the rest of the academic world, and certainly no great thing. (Indeed, may the education of handicapped children ever, in any country, under any regime, be considered a great thing?) Yet characteristically, in those years because of its intellectual heritage, it served as a refuge of sorts for Soviet psychologists.[40] They felt they could work here, while their own disciplines were paralyzed. And after Stalin, a less dogmatic spirit fairly rapidly manifested itself.[41] First in 1956, then in the later 1960s,

Vygotsky was rehabilitated, his works were published, and his memory lent to his whole discipline a national and international prestige, which it never would have had without him.[42]

VI

The third major area in which Soviet defectology has changed since Kashchenko's time is curriculum. As observed earlier, the German *Hilfsschule* tradition and early Soviet defectology alike had a strong activist aspect: they minimized the difference between social and biological handicaps and maximized the social value of helping all children through school. Toward the end of the 1920s, various factors lent special emphasis to this aspect; then in the 1930s it was cut off, never really to be restored.

One of the circumstances that led to an activist defectology during the later 1920s was an ambition, embedded in the socialist ethos, to make education universal. In 1926 the Soviet government promised state funding for an increase in the number of special schools. This precipitated the fairly rapid expansion of the special schools network that we observed earlier, and encouraged the defectologists to race ahead. Then in 1931 the Sovnarkom specifically legislated that education must be available to all defective children.[43] Decrees do not reality make! But from that moment on, the pressure on defectology to become yet more activist was very great indeed. In all probability, it was this pressure that led to the coincident eclipse of Vygotsky's scientific defectology by I. I. Daniushevskii's practical defectology.

Meanwhile—in the later 1920s—the continued presence in Soviet society of the victims of the civil war—the delinquents and orphans—sustained pressure for remedial education. These people were now rapidly passing through young adulthood. Soon the time for providing them with a regular education would be gone for good. When after 1926 state funds became available, the defectologists were tempted to include such people among the anomalous beneficiaries of the new schools. And this pressure increased with the start of the Stalin revolution, which on the one hand brought out of the depths of civil society a vast number of uneducated proletarians and peasants, who needed quick training; and on the other hand released the radical intellectuals in the Soviet pedagogical establishment—the red professors and their like, many of whom were intrigued with the then-new Western science of pedology.

What exactly happened within Soviet defectology in these years we cannot tell: we have only snippets of information—signs and symptoms. There seems no doubt that some esoteric activist theories did gain currency. Increasingly during the 1920s, for example, the defectologists had struggled against what they considered the patronizing and philanthropical views of bourgeois special educators, whereby defectives were considered irreparable. In 1930, thereupon, Soviet special school curriculum writers decreed that, since deaf children were by nature identical with other children, therefore the tasks of deaf education must be identical with those of a normal school—the learning of language and speech must not interfere with the acquisition of a normal accumulation of data.[44] Nice as this decree sounded, there was a considerable contradiction within it between ideal and reality. And in the following years, a similar leftist theory emerged according to which retarded children could, through correct application of pedagogical principles, be brought up to norms—as it were, cured.[45] But the essence of defectology in these years seems to have been what later on was called differentiation within special education. Distinctions were made between the deaf and the hard of hearing (*tugoukost'*) and between the blind and the shortsighted (*slabovidenie*), with special courses designed for each. Logopedia was developed as a separate branch of defectology from surdopedia. Schools and classes also were developed for many different gradations of retardation and abnormality. IQ testing was used extensively to determine not only these different gradations, but also to winnow out of the normal schools candidates for special (defectological) training. It was this differentiation that really opened up the special schools to those sectors of the population who were in need of remedial education.[46] The result was a staggering rise in the number of schools to over 2,000 in 1932/33 and in the number of children attending to 140,000, over half of them in rural areas.[47] "Remedial schools, multiplying rapidly, filled up not with retarded children, but with pedagogically neglected, undisciplined students and children who for one reason or another couldn't pass tests."[48]

Hereupon a cloud broke. On 4 July 1936, the Central Committee of the Soviet Communist Party issued a resolve entitled: "On Pedological Perversions in the Commissariat of Education."[49] With the slashing sarcasm characteristic of Stalin's time, party authorities now labeled all variety of testing as bourgeois perversions. They lavished special scorn on the defectologist testers and opened the way for a net ban on further defectological differentialization, a ban that would last for twenty years. Oddly enough, it was not Daniushevskii, the living defectological activist, but Vygotsky, the deceased theorist, who incurred the party's displeasure. Daniushevskii remained in charge of the defectological establishment until 1944, and seems to have possessed enough political prestige to protect his colleagues, and even refugee psychologists, all through the worst years of the great purge. But for the time being, the erstwhile main activist theme of Soviet defectology was dead. In 1937/38 the number of children in the special schools was down to 116,000, a 25,000 cut since 1932, taken overwhelmingly from the rural area contingent.

It will be impossible here to review all the matters that occupied the minds of the Soviet defectologists during the Stalin decades. Suffice it to mention that they, like other academics, had to wrestle with the problem of the class struggle, with the tasks of integrating physical labor into their curricula, and with the need for patriotism.[50] And this is not to speak of the war, which destroyed many of the leading schools and dispersed a good many of the provincial staffs.

For present purposes the main thing that needs to be said is that gradually things got better. In 1943 younger men, A. I. D'iachkov in the lead, undertook to reorganize Vygotsky's old laboratory under the title, Defectological Scientific Research Institute, which it retains today.[51] This had the effect of aligning defectology with other disciplines of Soviet academia that possess separate research and teaching branches. The following year, in connection with the formation of the RSFSR Academy of Pedagogical Sciences, Daniushevskii's School Institute was dissolved. After the war, a gradual rebuilding of the school system took place. And then new opportunities opened for defectology on the occasion of Khrushchev's great educational reform of 1958.

Again, the exact course of events is unclear. We know that the great reform had as its stated objective the countering of the Stalinist trend toward educational elitism. Channels were supposed to be reopened whereby proletarian and peasant children could rise socially; and the children of the elite were supposed to be subjected to a work ethic through the introduction of manual labor at all educational levels. Egalitarianism was supposed to be reinforced, special schooling for the gifted and privileged were supposed to be cut back. All in all, however, the reforms not only ran counter to the interests of the elite but tended to exacerbate some of the major extant difficulties of the educational system—in particular a very high dropout rate due to lack of family encouragement in rural areas; and low quality graduates due to lack of special training. At a very early date, resistance to the reform was widespread, and immediately after Khrushchev's fall in 1964, many of its provisions were withdrawn.[52] Meanwhile, however, defectology, with its past record of social activism, may have seemed a useful remedy to the system's failings.

In 1956 and 1957, while the reformers were at the height of their power, there was a sharp drop both in the number of special schools for the handicapped and in the number of attendant children. This seemed to reflect the reformers egalitarian urge. But then suddenly in 1958, the year of the reform, not only did the long precipitous rise in the number of special schools begin, which we have mentioned earlier, but the Defectological Scientific Research Institute acquired for the first time since 1931 a professional journal of its own, the *Spetsial'naia Shkola* (later, in 1969, renamed *Defektologiia*). Virtually on the masthead of the new journal—in other words, figuring as a major theme in its lead articles during the following years—was the notion of differentiation: differentiation by degree of physical disability, and, according to social environment, differentiation by degree of mental retardation.[53] Pedological testing was not rehabilitated, but an elaborate system of qualitative analysis emerged, whereby defectologists could assess why children do badly in school, and very great attention was paid to remedial work. All told, the Soviet authorities seem to have given back to defectology some of its old social mission, in a brand new, much more scientific form.[54]

VII

Defectology, to recapitulate, is a very special Soviet invention. It is an academic discipline for teaching people how to tend the handicapped. Despite the broad development of rehabilitative science outside the Soviet Union, defectology has no real parallel in the Western world. The name of this discipline, it must be admitted, is unprepossessing. It is a terminological relic from prerevolutionary Russia. Yet the term does recall a heroic aspect of the impact of the Bolshevik Revolution on the field of medicine. Though the disabled elements of society could not help make that upheaval, the new regime to which it gave birth in Russia very visibly took them into consideration.

Today's defectology recalls a major tradition in the history of the handicapped worldwide that is often ignored in Western histories; the German *Heilpädagogik* tradition, that responded in the nineteenth century to the age-old diagnostical difficulty of childhood disability. But defectology is very different from the curative education that Dr. Kashchenko and his colleagues brought to Russia in the early years of the country's revolution. Not only is it dimensionally completely transformed, it has intellectual backbone based on the inspired work of L. S. Vygotsky; and the social mission of the early *Heilpädagogists* has been transformed into a unique emphasis on differentiation in the curricula of remedial work.

NOTES

1. "Defektologiia," and "Nauchno-isledovatel'skii Institut Defektologii," in A. I. D'iachkov, ed., *Defektologicheskii slovar'*, 2d ed. (Moscow: Pedagogika, 1970). This work is cited henceforth as *DS*. It was originally published as *Kratkii defektologicheskii slovar'* (Moscow: Prosveshchenie, 1964). This work is cited henceforth as *KDS*.

2. "Spetsial'nye uchebno-vospital'nye uchrezhdeniia v SSSR," in *DS*, p. 427.

3. The following explanation follows V. P. Kashchenko and G. V. Murashev, *Iskliuchitel'nye deti. Ikh izuchenie i vospitanie* (Moscow: Rabotnik Prosveshcheniia, 1929), p. 22.

4. Biographical data in Kh. S. Zamskii, *Istoriia vospitaniia i obucheniie umstvenno otstalykh detei* (Moscow: Prosveshchenia, 1966), pp. 111–12; and in *DS*, p. 141. This Kashchenko was the brother of the psychologist P. P. Kashchenko (1858–1920), after whom a well-known Moscow hospital is named. For Kashchenko's school, see Zamskii, pp. 112–15.

5. See for example T. N. Kelynack, ed., *Defective Children* (New York: W. Wood, 1915). In England, a National Association for the Support of Defective Children was organized in 1903.

6. *Defektivnye deti i shkola* (Moscow: Tikhomirov, 1912).

7. *DS*, p. 339. According to this entry, Rossolimo published in 1914 a book entitled *Psikhologicheskie profily defektivnykh uchashchikhsia v otnoshenii vozrasta, pola, stepeni otstalosti i dr.*

8. In the first year of the Revolution, Kashchenko's projects were subordinate to the School Sanatorium Department in the Education Commissariat. In 1918 this department was bodily transferred to the Health Commissariat. The Social Services Commissariat also claimed a share. In December 1919 the Sovnarkom finally assigned responsibility for defective children to the Education Commisariat. See Zamskii, *Istoriia vospitaniia*, pp. 129–37; and *DS*, p. 56; A. I. D'iachkov, "Razvitie sovetskoi defektologii za 40 Let," *Spetsial'naia shkola* 2 (1958): 4–6.

9. Kashchenko and Murashev, *Iskliuchitel'nye deti,* p. 14.

10. Ibid., "S'ezdy," in *DS,* p. 395; and *Detskaia defektivnost', prestupnost', i bezprizornost'. Po materialam 1-go vserossiiskogo s'ezda 1920 g.* (Moscow: Gosizdat, 1922).

11. Kashchenko and Murashev, *Iskliuchitel'nye deti,* p. 14.

12. The following relies extensively on the long essay, "Schwachsinnigenbildungs-und-fürsorgewesens nebst Sonderschulwesen, Geschichte d.," in Adolf Dannemann et al., eds., *Enzyklopädisches Handbuch der Heilpädagogik* (Halle: Marhold, 1934), colls. 2331–448 (this work is cited henceforth as *EHHP*); and Theodor Heller, *Grundriss der Heilpädagogik* (Leipzig: Wilhelm Engelmann, 1904).

13. See David Wright, *Deafness* (New York: Stein and Day, 1969), ch. 2.

14. Compare George Rosen, *Madness in Society: Chapters in the Historical Sociology of Mental Illness* (Chicago: University of Chicago Press, 1968), ch. 1; and Michel Foucault, *Madness and Civilization* (New York: Random House, 1965), ch. 1.

15. Compare Morris J. Vogel and Charles E. Rosenberg, eds., *The Therapeutic Revolution* (Philadelphia: University of Pennsylvania Press, 1979).

16. *EHHP,* coll. 2335–36.

17. *Die Heilpädagogik,* 2 vols. (Leipzig: F. Fleischer, 1861); reissued in 1 vol. (Giessen, 1979).

18. *EHHP,* coll. 2343–44.

19. This is well expressed in A. I. D'iachkov, *Sistemy obucheniia glukhikh detei* (Moscow: Akadpednauk, 1961), ch. 3.

20. *EHHP,* coll. 2356.

21. Heller, *Grundriss,* pp. 2–3.

22. *EHHP,* coll. 2367. Compare "Heilpädagogik, Begriff und Umfang der," in ibid., coll. 1083–84.

23. See the short history of *Gyógypedagógia* by Janos Berkes in *Magyar Siketnema Oktatás* 25 (1923): 12–15.

24. *DS,* p. 459. The Postovskiis' publications, and the others mentioned below, are cited in Kashchenko and Murashev, *Iskliuchitel'nye deti,* pp. 21–22. Zamskii makes no bones about the foreign origin of defectology, perceiving Belgian, Swiss, and Italian, as well as German, ideas behind Kashchenko's work. See *Istoriia vospitaniia,* pp. 112ff.

25. *DS,* p. 267.

26. D'iachkov, "Razvitie sovetskoi defektologii," p. 4. Compare Mary S. Conroy, "Education of the Blind, Deaf and Mentally Retarded in late Tsarist Russia," in *Slavic and European Educational Review* 1–2 (1985): 29–49.

27. See Barbara A. Anderson, Brian D. Silver, and Victoria A. Velkoff, "Education of the Handicapped in the USSR: Exploration of the Statistical Picture," *Soviet Studies* 39 (1987): 470.

28. The following is from *EHHP,* colls. 2433–40.

29. D'iachkov, "Razvitie sovetskoi defektologii," p. 8. Both D'iachkov and Zamskii, the outstanding Soviet authorities on this subject, are oddly evasive about numbers here. D'iachkov says, for example, that the growth in the number of schools was especially rapid for deaf children but, as evidence, states: "in 1928 1,077 new children were taken into the deaf schools, representing a 45% overall increase in the number of students relative to 1925." No figure is given for 1925. In *Sistemy obucheniia,* he mentions no statistics at all, despite his much more detailed treatment of the subject of deaf education (cf. pp. 168–69ff). In his overall essays in *DS,* pp. 454ff, likewise, there are no numbers, nor are there any in Zamskii's *Istoriia vospitaniia,* despite a wealth of other information.

30. These and the following figures are from M. A. Korolev and G. A. Obcharenko, eds., *Narodnoe obrazovanie, nauka i kul'tura v SSSR* (Moscow: Statistika, 1977), p. 27.

31. Andrew Sutton, and after him Anderson, Silver, and Velkoff, comment thus on a net fallback in the number of special schoolchildren during the later 1950s: Andrew Sutton, "Backward Children in the USSR: An Unfamiliar Approach to a Familiar Problem," in Jenny Brine, Maureen Perrie, and Andrew Sutton, eds., *Home, School, and Leisure in the Soviet Union* (London: Allen & Unwin, 1980), p. 174; Anderson-Silver, and Velkoff, "Education of the Handicapped," p. 472.

32. Compare Anderson, Silver, and Velkoff, "Education of the Handicapped," p. 474.

33. See ibid., pp. 477ff.

34. Compare the remarks in Michael Cole and Sheila Cole, eds., *A. R. Luria, The Making of Mind: A Personal Account of Soviet Psychology* (Cambridge: Harvard University Press, 1979), chs. 1–3; and Alex Kozulin, *Psychology in Utopia* (Cambridge: MIT Press, 1984), ch. 1.

35. Cole and Cole, *Luria, The Making of Mind,* p. 42.

36. Kashchenko and Murashev, *Iskliuchitel'nye deti,* seems a good example of the intellectual level of the original defectological movement in the Soviet Union. Listing chapter by chapter the different "causes of defectiveness" in children, the authors skip blithely from genetic factors to medical problems—pregnancy and birth difficulties and infant undernourishment, for example—to social factors—alcoholism in the family—to the impact of the war and revolutionary social upheaval on family life, etc. They not only lump deafness and blindness together with feeblemindedness, as had the *Heilpädagogists* in Germany, but feed in also any sort of socially caused weakness in school, including the then widespread phenomenon of orphanism *(bezprizornost').* Physical defectiveness and social delinquency are here, as in the title of the 1921 congress, one and the same.

37. Compare James V. Wertsch, *Vygotsky and the Social Formation of Mind* (Cambridge: Harvard University Press, 1985), pp. 11–12.

38. *DS,* pp. 49–50, 80.

39. For the extent of the de-Vygotskianization of defectology, see

A. I. D'iachkov and A. D. Dobrova, *Khrestomatiia po istorii vospitaniia i obucheniia glukhonemikh v Rossii* (Moscow: Uchpedgiz, 1949); and D'iach-kov, "Kritika reaktsionykh burzhuaznykh teorii vospitaniia i obucheniia glukhonemykh detei," in *Uchebno-Vospitatel'naia rabota v spetsial'nykh shkolakh* (Moscow: Uchpedgiz, 1950).

40. James J. Gallagher, ed., *Windows on Russia: United States–USSR Seminar on Instruction of Handicapped Children* (Washington, D.C.: HEW, 1972), p. 108.

41. For example, the head of the Defectological Scientific Research Institute, the historian of deafness, A. I. D'iachkov, as early as 1961 entirely revised the book cited in note 39 and republished it in more flexible form as *Sistemy obucheniia glukhikh detei* (previously cited).

42. Compare T. A. Vlasova and M. S. Pevsner, *O detiakh s otklo-neniiami v razvitii* (Moscow: Prosveshchenie, 1973), pp. 6ff.

43. *DS*, p. 57; Zamskii *Istoriia vospitaniia*, pp. 145ff.

44. D'iachkov, *Sistemy obuchenia*, p. 169.

45. *DS*, p. 245; Zamskii, *Istoriia vospitaniia*, pp. 146–48.

46. *DS*, p. 400.

47. Korolev and Obcharenko, *Narodnoe obrazovanie*, p. 27.

48. *DS*, p. 269. Zamskii says that by 1936 the pedologists had shifted 7–8 percent of all Soviet school children into the special schools, remov-ing virtually everyone who in any way made difficult the work of the regular schools: *Istoriia vospitaniia*, p. 147.

49. *Pravda*, 5 July 1936. Compare the commentary in Sutton, "Back-ward Children," pp. 164ff.

50. Compare Beatrice Beach Szekely, "The Establishment of the Academy of Pedagogical Science of the USSR," Ph.D. diss., Columbia University, 1976, ch. 2.

51. The first head of the new institute (1943–50) was evidently D. I. Azbukin (1883–1953), an older oligofrenist, who was dean of de-fectology at the Lenin Pedagogical institute in Moscow. But D'iachkov (1900–68), by profession a surdopedagogue, seems to have been the leading ideologist of the new institute from the start, and from 1951 until his death in 1968 he was its director. See *DS*, pp. 11, 105; Szekely, "Establishment of the Academy," pp. 9ff.

52. For the reform, see Nicholas De Witt, *Education and Professional Employment in the USSR* (Washington, D.C.: National Science Founda-tion, 1961); Jeremy Azrael, "The Soviet Union," in James S. Coleman ed., *Education and Political Development* (Princeton: Princeton University Press, 1965); and Mervyn Matthews, *Education in the Soviet Union: Politics and Institutions since Stalin* (London: Allen & Unwin, 1982), ch. 1.

53. See especially D'iachkov, "Razvitie sovetskoi defektologii"; D'iachkov, "Puti perestroiki spetsial'nykh shkol," in *Spetsial'naia shkola* 3 (1959): 3–14; and D'iachkov, "O perestroika spetsial'nykh shkol'," in *Spetsial'naia shkola* 1 (1959): 3–6.

54. For evaluation, see Sutton, "Backward Children," pp. 185–88.

The Vygotskian Tradition in Soviet Psychological Study of Deaf Children

Jane E. Knox and
Alex Kozulin

The history of cultural development in an abnormal child constitutes the most profound and critical problem in modern defectology. It opens up a completely *new line of development* in scientific research. . . . There are three fundamental points, which
define the problem of cultural development for an abnormal child:
*the degree of primitivism in the child's mind, the nature of his adoption of
culture and psychological tools and the means by which he makes use of
his psychological functions.*

—*L. S. Vygotsky*

I

LEV VYGOTSKY (1896–1934), who is primarily
known in this country as a pioneer psycholinguist, has a much
broader recognition in the USSR.[1] He is an undisputable founder
of the Soviet school of cognitive developmental psychology, still
one of its most controversial theorists, and in addition to this,
often perceived as the founding father of modern Soviet defectology, a discipline concerned with the study of physically and
mentally handicapped children.

James Wertsch, a contemporary follower of Vygotsky, recently
described him "as a polyphonic thinker," indicating the full scope
of this man's work. According to Wertsch, Vygotsky's "life goal
was to create *a psychology* that would be theoretically and method-
ologically adequate for the investigation of all aspects of human
consciousness."[2] In assessing Vygotsky's specific contribution to
defectology, two questions arise. How does Vygotsky's advocacy
of a special pedagogy for the learning disabled, the use of many
significant sign factors, and the modulation of the social conse-

quences of a physical or mental handicap relate to his primary concepts? Second, to what extent do Vygotsky's theory of psychological development in general and his defectological ideas in particular affect contemporary Soviet study of handicapped children?

These are the central questions of the present chapter, and we will discuss them fairly narrowly, mainly in the context of defectology and the education of deaf children. We will point first to various fundamentals in his theoretical writings, showing how closely Soviet defectology has stuck to them. We will then discuss some present problems of Soviet defectology, indicating why Vygotskian principles remain a guide to practice.

II

Vygotsky's psychology—and more distinctly, his defectological program—began to take shape in a paper he published in 1925 at a critical moment in his career.[3] In the mid-1920s he had combined his scientific research at the Institute of Psychology with work at Narkompros (the People's Commissariat of Education) in the subdivision for education of defective (handicapped) children. In 1925/26 he organized a laboratory for the psychology of abnormal childhood in the medical-pedagogical sector of Narkompros, housed at 8 Pogodinskaia Street in Moscow. As noted in the preceding chapter, this laboratory later became known as the Experimental Defectological Institute of Narkompros and today is formally called the Scientific Research Institute of Defectology of the Academy of Pedagogical Sciences of the USSR. The major goal of Vygotsky's 1925 article was to restore the legitimacy of the concept of consciousness, but not at the expense of a return to introspective mentalistic psychology. Vygotsky had a major objection against the mentalistic tradition; he felt it confined itself to a vicious circle in which states of consciousness are explained through the concept of consciousness. Vygotsky argued that if one is to take consciousness as a subject of study, then the explanatory principle must be sought in some other layer of reality. Vygotsky suggested that socially meaningful activity (in German, *Tätigkeit*) may play this role and serve as a generator of consciousness.

Vygotsky's first step toward establishing this suggestion was to premise that individual consciousness is formed from outside through relations with others. He explained: "The mechanism for knowing oneself and the mechanism for knowing others are one and the same. . . . We are aware of ourselves in that we are aware of others; and in analogous manner, we are aware of others because in our relationship to ourselves we are the same as others in their relationship to us. I am aware òf myself only to the extent that I am another for myself."[4] One cannot but find a startling similarity between this premise and the concept of significant symbols developed by G. H. Mead. In Mead's view, "The same procedure which is responsible for the genesis and existence of mind or consciousness—namely, the taking of the attitude of the other toward one's self, or toward one's own behavior—also necessarily involves the genesis and existence at the same time of significant symbols, or significant gestures."[5] It seems that Mead's revision of behaviorism and Vygotsky's struggle to define consciousness had much in common; both authors pointed to the same phenomena and followed similar methodological paths.

But Vygotsky went beyond Mead. He now made a principal distinction between "lower," natural mental functions, such as elementary perception, memory, attention, and will, and the "higher," or cultural functions, which are specifically human and which appear gradually in a course of radical transformation of the lower functions. The lower functions do not disappear in a mature mind, he said, but they are structured and organized according to specifically human social goals and means of conduct. Vygotsky used the Hegelian term superseded (*aufgehoben*) to designate their transformation from natural functions into cultural ones. His assumption does not imply that the higher functions can be reduced to lower ones. Decomposition shows only the material with which the higher functions are built, but says nothing about their construction. The constituent parts of the higher functions are nothing but the natural, lower skills. This fact, argued Vygotsky, secures the scientific status of his method, which needs no speculative metaphysical categories to approach the higher forms of behavior. All the building blocks of higher behavior seem absolutely materialistic and can be apprehended by ordinary empirical methods.

Hereupon he came to the vital point in his program. He proposed that the constructive principle of the higher functions is "mediated activity" which lies outside the individual—in interpersonal functions and "psychological tools." Vygotsky wrote: "In the instrumental act, humans master themselves from the outside through psychological tools."[6] In what concerns the structural role of the first external mediator—interpersonal relations—Vygotsky followed Pierre Janet, who claimed that intrapersonal processes are just transformed interpersonal relations. "Each function in the child's cultural development appears twice: first, on the social level, and later, on the individual level; first, between people (interpsychological), and then inside a child's (intrapsychological)."[7]

Vygotsky presented the concept of psychological tools—his other external mediator—in loose analogy with the material tools that serve as mediator between the human hand and an object of action. And in developing this concept he obviously took over the Hegelian notion of the "cunning of Reason"—the notion that reason causes objects to act and react on each other in accordance with their own nature, and in this way, without any direct interference in the process, to carry out reason's intentions.[8] Vygotsky felt that, like material tools, psychological tools are artificial formations. Both are social in nature. But while material tools are aimed at the control over processes in nature, psychological tools master natural forms of behavior and cognition in the individual. For Vygotsky, the principal psychological tools were gestures, language and sign systems, mnemonic techniques, and decision making systems based on casting lots; he considered that sensory-motor schemas connected with practical actions might become psychological tools, but in general he felt that these tools usually have a semiotic nature. And he considered them to be internally oriented; they transform natural human abilities and skills into higher mental functions. He would give the example: if a simple and elementary act of memorizing connects event A with event B through the natural ability of the human brain, then in mnemonics this relation is replaced by two others: A to X, and X to B, where X is an artificial psychological tool like a knot in a handkerchief, a written note, or a mnemonic scheme.

From 1926 through 1930 the focus of Vygotsky's research program was the experimental study of the mechanisms that transform natural psychological functions into higher functions such as logical memory, selective attention, decision making, and comprehension of language—in other words, internalization. Besides Aleksandr Luria and Alexei Leontiev, who had joined him as early as 1924, his group of collaborators included Lidiia Bozhovich, Aleksandr Zaporozhets, Natali'ia Morozova, Roza Levina, Liia Slavina, Lev Sakharov, and Zhozefina Shif.

In concrete experimental practice, the idea of internalization of psychological tools acquired two different, and ultimately even conflicting, forms. One was internalization of functions seen as the process of transformation of external actions into internal psychological processes. This was thoroughly studied by such followers of Vygotsky as Petr Zinchenko, Aleksandr Zaporozhets, and Petr Galperin.[9] Their studies undoubtedly had much in common with Piaget's concept of the development of intelligence through the internalization of sensory-motor schemes.

Vygotsky himself, however, was much more interested in internalization as a process of transforming *symbolic* psychological tools and social relations. He was greatly impressed by the works of the French sociological school of Emil Durkheim and by related ideas of Maurice Halbwachs, Charles Blondel, and Pierre Janet, who studied the internalization of so-called collective representations.

To understand this aspect of Vygotsky's thought, consider how the indicatory gesture appears in a child's behavioral repertoire: at first it is simply an unsuccessful grasping movement directed at an object. Vygotsky used the term gesture-in-itself to designate this stage of the development of the gesture. Later on, when a mother comes to the aid of her child, the movement acquires a different character. A gesture-in-itself becomes a gesture-for-others. Others, a mother in our case, interpret a child's grasping movement as an indicatory gesture, thus turning it into a socially meaningful communicative act. And then there is a third stage, when the child becomes aware of the communicative power of his or her movement. The child then starts addressing his or her gesture to adults, rather than the object that was the focus of interest in the first place. It is essential to recognize that the child is the last person who consciously apprehends the meaning of his or her own gesture. Only at this later stage does a gesture become a gesture-for-oneself.

Using a method of double stimulation, that is, marking each object in the sorting test by a coded triplet of letters, Vygotsky succeeded in setting up an experimental situation in which one could follow the instrumental process of sorting and classification and identify corresponding stages in the development of a child's concepts. Vygotsky discovered a number of such stages, from that of unorganized congeries through that of complexes and pseudoconcepts to that of scientific, logical concepts.[10] Vygotsky's student Zhozefina Shif later extended the study of concept formation to an educational setting.[11] She put different forms of child experience into correspondence with appropriate stages in the development of concept formation. Her work closely resembled that of

Heinz Werner. It is not surprising that Werner's disciples enthusias-
tically used Vygotsky's sorting test in their study of the pre-
conceptual thinking of schizophrenics.[12]

The instrumental aspect of Vygotsky-inspired research in the
1920s focused on the use of external means, psychological tools
that facilitate the development of higher forms of memory, attention, and decision making. Here Alexei Leontiev's study of natural
and instrumentally mediated memory and attention remains a classic.[13] In his experiment, children were asked to memorize several
colors that would be forbidden according to the rules of the play
and should not be named while answering the experimenter's questions. Colored cards were offered to the children as possible aids.
The results showed that children of preschool age failed to make
use of the colored cards. They made as many mistakes, naming
forbidden colors, with cards as without them. Adolescents, on the
contrary, used cards extensively, separating out forbidden ones and
consulting them before answering. Their percentage of mistakes
was much higher when the experiment was conducted without
cards. It is interesting that for adults the performance with cards
was not significantly better than without them, although in both
cases the results were better than for adolescents. Vygotsky explained this as a result of internalization. Adults do not cease to use
psychological tools to structure their memory, but their tools are
emancipated from the material form of the color card. The external sign that schoolchildren need is transformed by adults into an
inner sign.

This does not exhaust Vygotsky's study of concept formation.
He also distinguished two forms of experience, which gave rise to
two different, albeit interrelated, groups of concepts. The first
group, which Vygotsky designated as scientific, has its roots in the
specialized and operational activity of educational instruction,
which imposes scientifically defined concepts upon a child. The
second group, which comprises concepts emerging from the reflection upon everyday experience of a child, was labeled spontaneous
concepts. Vygotsky made it a point to argue that scientific concepts, far from being units assimilated by a child in a ready-made
form, in reality undergo substantial development. This development essentially depends on the existing level of the child's ability
to comprehend concepts. The level of comprehension, in its turn,
is connected with the development of spontaneous concepts: "In
working its way slowly upward, an everyday concept clears a path
for the scientific concept in its downward development. It creates a

series of structures necessary for evolution of a concept's more primitive, elementary aspects, which give it body and vitality. Scientific concepts in turn supply structures for the upward development of the child's spontaneous concepts toward consciousness and deliberate use."[14]

Two forms of learning were thus distinguished. One of them, highly structured learning in an educational setting, later attracted the total attention of Soviet psychologists and has been thoroughly investigated in the works of Vasilii Davydov and Petr Galperin.[15] The much less articulated spontaneous learning of a child was perceived rather as an obstacle on the road of concept formation, and its characteristic features were mostly neglected.

Finally, the study of concept formation in an educational setting helped Vygotsky develop the idea of the dialogical character of learning. In his analysis, Vygotsky took as a point of departure what he perceived as the inability of Piaget's theory to reconcile the spontaneous character of a child's reasoning with the scientific— and thus adult—nature of concepts learned at school. Where Piaget saw confrontation, Vygotsky found dialogue. Vygotsky was also critical of those methods of mental testing that routinely took into account the progress made only by the child who is left alone to perform a task. Vygotsky argued that progress in concept formation achieved in cooperation with an adult would be a much more sensitive gauge for a child's intellectual abilities. The area that lies just ahead of a child's independent achievements was named zone of proximal development (zo-ped). Zo-ped is a meeting place, that is, the place where a child's empirically rich but disorganized spontaneous concepts meet the systematicity and logic of adult reasoning. As a result of such a meeting, the weak points of spontaneous concepts are compensated by the strong aspects of scientific ones. The depth of zo-ped varies, reflecting a child's relative abilities to appropriate structures introduced by adults. The final product of this child-adult cooperation is the solution of a problem that, once internalized, becomes an integral part of the child's own reasoning.

Before turning now to the contributions of the Vygotsky school to present studies of postnatal development of children with physical and mental handicaps, it is necessary to emphasize that Vygotsky approached the personality of each child as a unique organic and psychological structure. This is the fundamental psychological principle underlying all Vygotsky's work in the area of handicapped children. In *The Fundamentals of Defectology,* published long after his death, Vygotsky stated, "A child whose development is impeded by a handicap is not simply a child less developed than his peers; rather he has developed differently."[16] In each stage of his growth, a handicapped child represents "a qualitatively different, unique type of development." In this work on the development of handicapped children, Vygotsky leaned strongly on Alfred Adler's study of abnormal psychology, which postulates that any limitation or abnormality continually stimulates and intensifies higher development. "If any organ, due to morphological or functional abnormality, does not fully cope with its tasks, then the central human nervous system and mental apparatus compensate for the organ's deficient operation by creating a psychological superstructure which shores up the abnormal organism at its weakened, threatened point."[17] For example, if a hearing loss occurs, then the other sensory systems (sense of taste, touch, sight, etc.) take over in processing external signs and stimuli,

Thus, for Vygotsky, it was a fundamental law that the educational content be the same for both handicapped and normal children; the entire difference lies in the fact that one organ of perception takes over for another, while "the qualitative content of the reaction remains the same." Central to this position is the view that the deaf child is entirely capable of full psychological and intellectual development, and therefore an active, useful life. In Vygotsky's words, "the uniqueness of this type of education simply boils down to the substitution of one path of training for another."[18]

The primary problem of a handicapped condition is, generally speaking, not the handicap itself but its social consequences. This secondary effect becomes the major difficulty because, while handicapped children do not consider themselves handicapped, they are seen from the point of view of others (the nonhandicapped) as a social abnormality. Addressing this concern, Vygotsky wrote:

> Any physical handicap—be it blindness or deafness—not only alters the child's relationship with the world, but above all affects his or her interaction with people. Any organic defect is realized as a social abnormality in behavior. It is understandable, of course, that blindness and deafness in and of themselves are biological factors and to no degree social factors. However, the educator must deal not so much with these factors by themselves, as much as with their social consequences. When we have before us a blind boy as the object of education, then it is necessary to deal not so much with blindness by itself, as with those conflicts which arise for a blind child upon entering life.[19]

As is argued elsewhere in this volume, Vygotsky's theses fitted neatly with the holistic tradition of European disability treatment, out of which Soviet defectology had been born. Even in Europe there had been a tendency to premise that the groundwork for a deaf child's development must begin in early childhood so that his adult educators and intercessors could begin immediately to manipulate the environment of all his sensory systems. Vygotsky's fundamental principles emphasized that the educational process should implement all possible tools in real situations that foster normal social activity and, most importantly, work. The environment of the *internat,* the Soviet special school for the deaf, was from the start, therefore, one of rehabilitation, training the child to become a useful and active participant in society.

III

Ivan Sokolianskii (1889–1960) was one of the first to apply in practice what Vygotsky sketched as a theory. As the founder of the Khar'kov School for the Deaf-Blind, Sokolianskii introduced what he called the principle of shared activity, which is closely related to Vygotsky's notion of dialogical learning. First the adult was to carry out the entire action himself, then at the final stage the teacher merely provided the signal for action. In this way, Sokolianskii introduced the zone of proximal development in almost pure form. He also employed the concept of internalization of social relations. The school became well known for its many successful students, some of whom matched Helen Keller with their remarkable achievements in language acquisition and knowledge. During World War II, the Khar'kov School was bombed, and Sokolianskii was forced to set up his school again, this time at the Institute of Defectology in Moscow.

Aleksandr Meshcheriakov (1923–74), one of Sokolianskii's graduate students at the institute, carried on the Vygotsky tradition by setting up a celebrated special school for the blind-deaf-mute children in Zagorsk. Here the role of humanized environment and tools became the guiding principle. In his published study about the Zagorsk program, Meshcheriakov wrote: "These first elements of human mental processes take shape because the child's needs are satisfied with human objects (clothing, household articles and implements, the paraphernalia of child care) and through human methods (feeding, dressing, using the pot). . . . Child's physical needs become human needs since they are satisfied with the help

of human objects through human methods."[20] Meshcheriakov
speaks not only of a humanized environment but also humanized
time, stressing the importance of having a well-organized time
table. All actions of the child should become elements of the integrated system of behavior; normally, this integration is lacking in
cases of blind–deaf–mute children. In these children especially,
everyday concepts appear as scientific. They must be learned systematically with the help of instructors, because these children lack
experience and the knowledge of the simple things in the world
about them.

From this point of view, the role of tools is most crucial for the
deaf–blind child. He or she must develop in an environment of
work, learning to manipulate objects in a socially useful way.
Meshcheriakov stressed the role of tools in a meaningful interaction with a child's environment: "The thing does not present itself
directly to the subject as the object of his need, but as a tool with
its various objective properties . . . the socially evolved mode of
action constitutes the social significance inherent in the tool or
thing. In this way, between the subject (child) and object of his
need there comes a thing (tool) complete with its intrinsic social
significance."[21] In summation, Meshcheriakov wrote: "Only the
sum of the above-listed conditions, i.e. the need for practical action, the utilization of social modes of action, and the orientation
of action to the satisfaction of needs, makes possible the appropria-
tion by the individual of socially evolved knowledge."[22]

These were two model programs, but their point was not lost.
Today, the special school plays an extremely crucial role in the
Soviet system for educating the handicapped. A 1978 survey by
the Ministry of Education and Academy of Pedagogical Sciences,
Hearing Impaired Children and the System of their Education, sets forth
as the basis of the deaf educational system the development of
special corrective methods that allow the remaining healthy sensory systems to compensate for the initial handicap. The survey
cites the research of R. M. Boskis, who reiterated Vygotsky's basic
position, namely that a differentiated special education must be
created for a child with a handicap or else "the loss of normal
function in childhood will impede the normal course of psychological development and lead to abnormality, that is, the emergence of
delays and deficiencies, resulting in abnormal development."[23] In
order to prevent secondary handicaps in the deaf, such as retarded
intellectual development, abnormal behavior, and lack of speech,

"a most important role is played by the pedagogical conditions in which the child is placed from the moment of the sensory loss."[24]

We learn from the 1978 Ministry of Education report also that "for children born with hearing loss (the deaf), or those who lost their hearing due to illness in early childhood (the hard of hearing), the USSR has a wide network of special pre-school institutions adjusted to demand. Here children are educated between the ages of three and seven, and sometimes from an even earlier age."[25] Depending upon regional demands, the following types of pre-school setups for young deaf children allegedly exist: special kindergartens, preschool boarding homes where children live year-round, preschool divisions of the regular boarding schools for the deaf, and special groups for the deaf at regular kindergartens. In these special boarding schools (from which children go home only for vacations unless the distance to the home permits otherwise), deaf children receive in twelve years the equivalent of eight years of general educational preparation, the exception being the special emphasis placed on industrial-vocational training for the deaf. Today in the Soviet Union, this system is openly attributed to the theoretical and clinical research carried on by Vygotsky and his collaborators.[26]

IV

Although the concept of higher mental functions embraced such functions as memory, attention, and will, Vygotsky himself was primarily interested in the development of language in connection with concept formation. He started with an instrumental model but later went beyond the original schema. Vygotsky argued that it is not the development of a single function that should be made a center of study, but rather the development of an interfunctional system, like that of verbal intelligence. Neither language nor thought can be adequately described unless the history of the changing relationships between these two functions is revealed. Later, this idea of functional systems became the theoretical basis of Luria's neuropsychological works.[27]

This was the point from which Vygotsky took off in his work on the methods of deaf education. He saw language as the child's primary tool for manipulating and interacting with the environment. It followed that paramount importance must be placed on the teaching of language to the deaf and on surmounting the main obstacle that stands in the way of every deaf child, namely, the impairment of that very sensory system thought to predominate in the intake of information about the environment—the hearing system. In Vygotsky's view, however, two specific fundamentals must be kept in mind in the setting up of a system of special education for the deaf: (1) meaning is never listed to the spoken word alone but is also conveyed by many other significant sign factors, such as facial expressions, intonation, gestures, and pantomime, which taken all together determine the sense or ultimate motivation behind communication; (2) language acquisition is a living process and as such is the result only of meaningful interaction with others and the environment and not the product of rote memory of dead language, that it, phonetics and articulation reproduced artificially without meaningful context.

In *The Fundamentals of Defectology,* Vygotsky wrote that basically "the states and phases of speech development should be the same for a deaf child as for a normal child: the difference lies only in the means, the methods and time."[28] A deaf child, as is the case of the normal child, should be introduced to live speech, or integral forms of speech, phrases, and words, which carry meaning for the child in his or her specific environment. In play, work, and in the daily life of the boarding school, functional and communicative speech should be used. According to Vygotsky, active interest in speech will be killed if it is introduced by the old traditional methods of teaching the deaf speech—those artificial measures of repeating isolated elements or sounds. Articulation in and of itself is not meaningful—live speech but dead language. Vygotsky claimed that,

> if we were to wait until a child has learned to correctly utter each
> sound and only after this teach him to put sounds together into
> syllables, and syllables into words, if we were to proceed from the
> elements of speech to its synthesis, we would never hear from a
> child live, authentic speech. The reverse path seems more natural—
> mastering integral forms of speech before the individual elements
> and their combination. Both in phylogenetic and ontogenetic devel-
> opment, a phrase precedes a word, a word a syllable, a syllable, a
> sound. Even a separate phrase is almost an abstraction; speech arises
> rather in greater wholes than the sentence. Therefore, speech comes
> to children as something intelligible, necessary, and vitally
> essential.[29]

In examining the nature of thought and its relationship to language, Vygotsky asserted also that a thought is a complex whole, "engendered by motivation, that is, by our desires and needs, our interests and emotions."[30]

Such views about the method of teaching the deaf fitted well with the holistic tradition behind early Soviet defectology. Once again, therefore, we may underline here the degree to which Vygotsky confirmed and reinforced the tendencies in that tradition to see speech as the most crucial sign system in human semiotic activity. In its 1978 report, the Ministry of Education even states that, since the 1930s, "the principle of communication has become the guiding principle for teaching language to the deaf." The report adopts S. A. Zykov's statement of 1961 that "the realization of this goal presumes not only teaching deaf children language for everyday application, but also the internalization of language as a basis of verbal thought" (*rechevoe myshlenie*).[31] Such statements advance the very essence of Vygotsky's fundamental position on the semiotic dimension of human nature.

In addition, it is clear that Vygotsky made several indirect inputs into Soviet defectology's methods of language teaching. Vygotsky collaborated very closely, for example, with Luria, who after the official rejection of his mentor's work in 1936, continued to investigate the systemic organization of sensory inputs in acquiring language. Luria studied the relationship of tongue movement to the "kinesthetic analysis of sounds." According to Luria, in the absence of such kinesthetic contributions the act of writing becomes much more difficult. Concerned with the integrated operations of all the brain's areas, Luria devised an experiment to illustrate the integrative role that "kinesthetic analysis of sounds" played:

> When a child is learning to speak or an adult is learning a foreign language, both of them must "feel" all the speech sounds with their tongue, lips, teeth and palate. If you visit a first grade class where the pupils are learning to write, you will hear a constant buzz as the children say what they are writing, sound after sound. Some teachers are irritated by the noise in the class. But the wiser ones say that if the children are doing so, they must have a need to do it, and let them go on whispering. We divided the class into two groups, in one of which the children were allowed to whisper while they wrote, and in the other, they were told to hold the top of the tongue between their teeth. *The "mutes" made six times more mistakes. The elimination of sound impeded writing.*[32]

Luria's experiment had far-reaching implications for the advisability of teaching deaf children spoken language.

Natal'ia A. Rau, organizer of the first Soviet kindergarten for deaf children, also worked very closely with Vygotsky and wholeheartedly propagated his ideas. The author of many books and articles, she developed a synthetic (*sinteticheskii*) method of lipreading, which followed her master in his call for the development of "live, logical speech, of verbal thought, and for the reinforcement of bonds between deaf-mute pre-school children and the hearing world. On the basis of this method a link is formed between concepts and 'the picture of the movement of the mouth' . . . and tongue, so that pronunciation becomes internalized."[33]

Soviet educators of the deaf still place primary emphasis on the teaching of spoken and written Russian. Like Vygotsky and his collaborators, they insist that language must be taught in a meaningful fashion—that speech must be as meaningful for the deaf as it is for the hearing. They reject, as did Vygotsky, the tedious drilling of sound without regard to sense, that in the distant past stifled all natural desire of deaf children to learn speech. The Soviet Ministry of Education report on the situation in deaf education even states that three forms of verbal language are to be used in deaf schools as a basic means for communication and instruction, all reinforcing the acquisition of speech: (1) spoken language, with strong emphasis on the development of residual hearing, coupled with lipreading and other special methods; (2) finger spelling; and (3) written language.

Two well-known Soviet defectologists, F. F. Rau and N. F. Slezina, developed, moreover, an integrated method for teaching the deaf speech, or a spoken language. They introduced an abbreviated system of phonemes, consisting of eighteen sounds. Their system "allows, first of all, for the introduction of speech formation in stages (speech that approximates the pronunciation of these sounds); second, it advances a solution to the problem of communication for deaf children."[34] While the Rau-Slezina method develops spoken language, finger spelling (*daktil'naia rech'*) reinforces the internalization of speech by facilitating the learning of its written manifestation. As handwriting in the air, finger spelling represents item for item what appears on the printed page and should accompany the oral articulation of words, integrating sight, sound, and touch.[35]

Perhaps Vygotsky was not the actual inventor of the present-day Soviet defectological methods for teaching language to deaf children, but he certainly exercised a considerable influence, and he certainly would have approved the current direction of research. Soviet defectology carries out his principal goal: the full development of children's personalities and consciousness through meaningful interaction with the world in which they must operate with the help of the specific tools readily available to each child.

V

In *Fundamentals of Defectology,* Vygotsky did not pay overwhelming attention to the role of mimed gesticulated language among the deaf. Nor does the present-day Soviet defectological system make much room for it. "Fingerspelling must not," according to the ministry report, "be mixed with the mimed-gesticulated language, the sign language used as the natural form of communication among deaf adults outside of school."[36]

According to the definition given in the Defectological Dictionary compiled by members of the Institute of Defectology, sign language or mimed-gesticulated language is a rather primitive form of communication among the deaf. Its limitations, according to this dated definition, are elaborated as follows: (1) meanings of signs do not always correspond with word meanings—the verb *to fly* is given as an example of this, because the sign will differ depending upon the context; (2) the overall number of signs is considerably less than the number of words in the spoken language—there are very few or no signs, for example, for certain generic categories, such as clothes or transportation; (3) at the same time, certain concrete or specific labels cannot be differentiated—bonfire, fire, dream, day dreaming, or fantasy. In general, the structure and syntax of sign language is characterized as an approximation of simplified or spoken dialogue, which develops only primitive forms of cognition.[37] Implicit here is the recognition that such a system of communication has not yet achieved the higher level of historical-cultural development characteristic of the dominant spoken and written language, and therefore its use will not allow a child to develop fully the inner semantics of verbal thought and written sign.

But before surrendering to such negativism, let us reexamine Vygotsky's basic position. In the earlier stages of his activity (1924/25), he appeared to reject outright mimicry (the Russian term popularly used to signify the mimed gesticulated language of the deaf) as a viable means of communication with and instruction for deaf children in the classroom. While he viewed this means of communication as "the natural language of the deaf," not to be

discouraged outside the classroom, he stated that the very natural-
ness of gestures prevented development of higher mental functions, and in particular linguistic competence.[38] In "The Principles
of Social Education of Deaf-Mute Children" (1925), Vygotsky
devoted a section to this question and concluded that mimicry
cannot serve as an instrument of abstract-logical thinking.

In principle, however, Vygotsky supported any means of semiotic mediation of practical activity. As previously stated, he saw
the development of higher mental processes occurring whenever a
sign is united with an object of action in a meaningful way. Does it
not follow that, for Vygotsky, the semantics of the underlying
object-sign or act-sign relationship was more significant than the
sign in itself? In his analysis of the multifaceted nature of human
semiotic activity, Vygotsky did not concern himself with the study
of the spoken word alone. For example, when he examined the
dialogue between characters in Lev Tolstoy's *Anna Karenina,* he
noticed the mutual perception between intimate partners who understand each other so well that their inner speech is made intelli-
gible to one another by a mere glance, a gesture, and so forth.
Vygotsky observed from his experiments that, when inner speech
seemed to be at the forefront, vocalization decreased: "When we
converse with ourselves, we need even fewer words than Kitty
and Levin did. Inner speech is speech almost without words. . . .
Inner speech works with semantics, not phonetics."[39]

In the same light, Vygotsky took great interest in the dramatur-
gical method of K. Stanislavskii (1863–1938), because the famous
theater director insisted that his actors master the underlying psychology of a role before learning the words, gestures, and actions.
Here, meaning precedes words. Vygotsky wrote: "The theater
faced the problem of thought behind the words before psychology
did. In teaching his system of acting, Stanislavskii required the
actors to uncover the 'subtext' of their lines in a play."[40]

Vygotsky attempted to establish the very essence of inner
speech, which, he believed, "is to a large extent thinking in pure
meaning." In his early studies of semiotic activity, together with
Luria, Leontiev, and others (Zaporozhets, Slavina, Levina, Bozhovich, and Morozova), Vygotsky even set up an experimental lab at
the Krupsakaia Academy to deal with pictography. This was a
method of studying what Vygotsky called indicative activity, or
the mental process whereby signs are invented. In these experiments, children who had already grasped concepts such as happi-

ness or fidelity from their own practical experience were asked to depict these difficult concepts in signs. According to Luria, in spite of the difficulty some adults would have describing these concepts in words (usually many words), these children "almost invariably came up with some signs."[41] In such cases, thought was adequately expressed in means other than words. In the same light, as noted earlier Vygotsky was fond of citing the example of a knot tied in a handkerchief as a mnemonic device. This example, however primitive, serves to illustrate how an external, nonverbal sign (here, the knot) can be united with a simple mediated act in order to "control one's own behavior and organize mental operations."[42]

Finally, in the 1930 essay, "The Questions of Speech Development and the Education of the Deaf-Mute Child," Vygotsky reversed his position on sign language, and emphasized that the full development of deaf children dictates an expansion of the system of verbal means used in the educational process: "One must reevaluate the traditional, theoretical and practical attitude toward the various individual forms of speech used by the deaf-nute, and *above all toward mimicry*."[43] One must bear in mind that speech, for Vygotsky, meant any verbal means used to communicate and does not imply the narrower meaning of only oral speech. Furthermore, he now stated that sign language of the deaf "is an authentic language with an entire wealth of functional significance."[44] This later recognition of sign language (mimicry) allowed Vygotsky to determine the uniqueness of a deaf child's development under conditions of polyglossia—the acquisition of speech by various verbal means. Here he advanced polyglossia as the most productive path of development and growth for a deaf child: "the maximal use of all forms of speech" is the necessary condition for the radical improvement of a deaf child's education.[45] In Luria's words, "Vygotsky was engaged in the study of the semantic and systems structures of human consciousness until his last days."[46]

Luria continued Vygotsky's study of semiotic activity by observing the communication between young children and their mothers. In an interview granted to the American psycholinguist Michael Cole in the 1970s, Luria pointed out the importance of sense-conveying gestures in the initial stages of ontogenesis of speech. He gave an example where language influence would seem to be minimal while the gesture directed at a tool takes on a maximum significance. A mother helps direct her child's attention to a specific object (tool), which will have a significant function for the child. "She changes the child's perception by pointing and naming the object. The pointing and naming isolate the cup from the rest of the environment and make it a figure set against a background."[47]

Luria concluded that such gestures accompany words only in the first stage of language development and are often totally absent once a child has internalized the concept. Yet, in spite of the primitiveness of such single gestures or operations, the semantics of inner speech remain the same even when the child later learns to replace the external sign with many words in order to describe the function of the isolated object. In this sense, the experiments carried on by Vygotsky and Luria on alternative nonverbal sign factors demonstrate that the gesticulated language of children and adults is a very natural and significant means of communication. Such experimental work paves the way for a serious, scientific examination of the mimed-gesticulated sign language systems of the deaf.

Building on this foundation in the past few years, researchers at the Institute of Defectology have begun to carefully analyze the structure and complexity of sign language. In particular, Galina Zaitseva has advanced the position that the sign language of the deaf does not limit mental thought to concrete ideas and, more importantly, that, as the language most natural for the deaf, it is rich in meaning, inflection, and linguistic structure. If this assessment is true, then mimed-gesticulated language is a significant alternative sign system for the deaf. Zaitseva's laudable efforts to advance a new understanding of "conversational gesticulated language" are most clearly illustrated in her book *Use of Sign Language at Lessons of Literature in the Evening Schools for the Deaf and the Hearing Impaired.*[48] Here she pointed out that the process of language acquisition for a deaf child (with deaf parents) by means of sign language is much the same as it is for the hearing child, involving as it does "the process of communication with others." Referring repeatedly to research by American linguists (in particular, W. C. Stokoe), Zaitseva described the specific, grammatical structure of mimed-gesticulated language. She also outlined the three structural elements of signs that correspond to the phonemes of words: (1) the configuration of the hand; (2) the spatial position of the hand; and (3) the type of movement.[49]

To support her study of Russian Conversational Sign Language, Zaitseva also cited the research of A. P. Gozova, T. B. Rozanova, N. V. Chulkov, and N. V. Iaskova, who observed "the high effectiveness and conceptuality [*osmyslennost' zapominaniia*] of signs in the deaf."[50] Further, Zaitseva based her deductions on her own observations of deaf students from the evening division of classes at the institute. Her experimental subjects from various age groups all recalled signs better than words. In the study of literature, they demonstrated a better understanding when signs were used to accompany words. For example, literary concepts of general and analytical categories, such as artistic image, plot, character, romanticism, and critical realism, were better comprehended and retained longer in the memory when they were introduced with the help of sign language.[51]

When called upon to provide a basic linguistic definition of Russian Conversational Sign Language, Zaitseva called it a variety of syncretism, invoking Luria's notion that words are a semantic heap. She suggested that, in the same fashion, signed gestures potentially have multiple meanings (polysemy), of which one is selected and all others excluded in a specific communicative act. Such application of Vygotskian and Lurian semantics evidently helped Zaitseva in her Soviet environment support her view that the mimed-gesticulated language of the deaf is not a primitive but a complex alternative sign system. Syncretism or complexity of word meanings reflects an advanced stage of language acquisition—as language develops so does meaning.[52]

VI

The intent of this study has been determination of whether the principles proposed by Vygotsky form the basis for modern Soviet defectology and, in particular, whether they determined the development of Soviet special education for the deaf.

We hope we have shown that current Soviet defectologists have inherited from Vygotsky and his research collaborators firm principles on which to build, namely the principles of shared activity or dialogical learning, the uniqueness of every child, the internalization of sign factors and tools, the priority of semantics, and last, the principles of rehabilitation. Vygotsky is to be commended for rejecting philanthropic welfare and the notion of being handicapped. He rightly called attention to the fact that these children are handicapped only in the eyes of others and do not perceive themselves as defective. We conclude our assessment by quoting a statement that well illustrates Vygotsky's belief in the miraculous, inexhaustible potential of higher mental functions inherent in all humans:

The world pours, through a large funnel, as it were, in thousands of stimuli, drives and callings; inside the funnel are constant struggles and clashes, all the excitations issue from the narrow end as response reactions of the organism in greatly reduced quantity. The actualised behavior is but an infinitesimal part of the possible behaviour. Man is full of unrealized opportunities at any given moment. These unrealized opportunities for behaviour, the disparity between the broad and narrow ends of the funnel, is an indisputable reality, just as real as the reactions which have prevailed.[53]

The real advantages of the Vygotskian tradition and its practical application within Soviet defectology go well beyond the scope of our work. This presents a challenge for subsequent research in the USSR in collaboration with Soviet defectologists and educators. Needless to say, questions do arise from his approach to the disabled. Researchers at the prestigious Moscow Institute of Defectology assert that only a truly differentiated learning environment can fully develop a deaf child's cognitive skills and overall personality, because only in the specially manipulated setting proposed by Vygotsky and his followers will the entire staff be able to exclusively serve the individual needs of a handicapped child, building on strengths and uniqueness, not on handicaps. By contrast, American educators, now generally committed to the mainstreaming of all handicapped children, will respond to this by asking: How can a deaf child, or any other handicapped child, grow into a normal, well-adjusted, and useful member of society if, from an early age, he is severed from society at its roots, from his family, and placed in an isolated hothouse environment?

Each pedagogical system would seem to have its own advantages, and critical assessment of this controversy is the topic for another study. Here let us state that the enriched, holistic psychology of human nature, bequeathed to us by Vygotsky, demands great respect and further attention in the West by psychologists, linguists, and pedagogues.

NOTES

1. Vygotsky left behind a huge collection of unpublished papers, the majority of which appeared in book form only after Zh. Shif, T. A. Vlasova, and other members of the Institute of Defectology worked many years to compile and edit them for final publication. L. S. Vygotsky, *Osnovy defektologii*, in L. S. Vygotsky, *Sobranie Sochenenii,* vol. 5 (Moscow: Pedagogika, 1983). An English translation of this collection

(translated and edited by Jane Knox and Kira Stevens) will soon be published as R. W. Rieber, ed., *L. S. Vygotsky: Problems of Abnormal Psychology and Learning Disabilities* (New York: Plenum Press, forthcoming).

2. James Wertsch, *Culture, Communication, and Cognition: Vygotskian Perspectives* (Cambridge: Cambridge University Press, 1985), p. 66.

3. L. S. Vygotsky, "Consciousness as a Problem of the Psychology of Behavior," in K. Kornilov, ed., *Psikhologiia i Marksizm* (Moscow: Gosizdat, 1925); translated in *Soviet Psychology* 17 (1979): 29.

4. Ibid.

5. G. H. Mead, *Mind, Self and Society from the Standpoint of Social Behaviorist* (Chicago: University of Chicago Press, 1974), pp. 47–48; originally published in 1934.

6. L. S. Vygotsky, "The Instrumental Method in Psychology," in J. Wertsch, ed., *The Concept of Activity in Soviet Psychology* (New York: Sharpe, 1981), p. 141.

7. L. S. Vygotsky, *Mind in Society* (Cambridge: Harvard University Press, 1978), p. 57.

8. Ibid., p. 54.

9. A. Kozulin, "Vygotsky in Context," in L. S. Vygotsky, *Thought and Language,* rev. ed. (Cambridge: MIT Press, 1986), originally published in 1934.

10. Vygotsky, *Thought and Language,* pp. 96–145.

11. Zs. Shif, *Razvitie zhiteiskikh i nauchnykh poniatii* (Moscow: Uchpedgiz, 1935).

12. H. Werner, *The Comparative Psychology of Mental Development* (New York: International Universities Press, 1948); E. Hanfmann and J. Kasanin, *Conceptual Thinking in Schizophrenia* (New York: NMDM, 1942).

13. A. Leontiev, *Razvitie pamiati* (Moscow: Uchpedgiz, 1931); also A. N. Leontiev, "The Development of Voluntary Attention in the Child," *Journal of Genetic Psychology* 40 (1932): 52–81.

14. Vygotsky, *Thought and Language,* p. 194.

15. V. V. Davydov, *Vidy obobshcheniia v obuchenii* (Moscow: Pedagogika, 1972); V. V. Davydov and A. Markova, "A Concept of Educational Activity in School-children," *Soviet Psychology* 21 (Winter 1982–83): 50–76; P. Galperin, "Stages in the Development of Mental Acts," in M. Cole and I. Malzmann, eds., *A Handbook of Contemporary Soviet Psychology* (New York: Basic Books, 1969) p. 69.

16. L. S. Vygotsky, *Osnovy defektologii* (Moscow: Pedagogika, 1983), p. 7.

17. Ibid., p. 10.

18. Ibid., p. 14.

19. Ibid., p. 102.

20. A. Meshcheriakov, *Awakening to Life: Forming Behaviour and Mind in Deaf-Blind Children* (Moscow: Progress Publishers, 1979).

21. Ibid., p. 292.

22. Ibid., p. 293.
23. V. I. Foman, *Deti s narusheniem slukha i sistema ikh obucheniia* (Moscow: Min. Prosv., 1978), p. 4.
24. Ibid., p. 5.
25. Ibid., p. 6.
26. J. T. Gibson, "A Comparison of Soviet and American Approaches to Special Education," *Phi Delta Kappa*, Dec. (1980): 264–67.
27. A. R. Luria, *Language and Cognition* (New York: Wiley, 1981).
28. Vygotsky, *Osnovy defektologii*, p. 106.
29. Ibid., p. 105.
30. Vygotsky, *Thought and Language*, p. 252.
31. Foman, *Deti*, p. 12.
32. Luria, as cited by K. Levitin, *One Is Not Born a Personality* (Moscow: Progress Publishers, 1982), p. 11, emphasis added. For a similar discussion of the kinesthetic inputs, see Vygotsky's *Osnovy defektologii*, p. 77. Here Vygotsky discusses the important role of kinesthetic sensations (during articulation) in the process of language internalization in deaf children.
33. Vygotsky, *Osnovy defektologii*, p. 351.
34. Foman, *Deti*, p. 14.
35. Ibid., p. 10.
36. Ibid., p. 10.
37. A. I. D'iachkov, *Defektologicheskii slovar'* (Moscow: Pedagogika, 1971), p. 198.
38. Vygotsky, *Osnovy defektologii*, pp. 77–78.
39. Vygotsky, *Thought and Language*, p. 244.
40. Ibid., p. 149.
41. Luria's description of this collaborative work, cited by Levitin, *One Is Not Born*, p. 162.
42. Ibid., p. 172.
43. Vygotsky, *Osnovy defektologii*, p. 217, emphasis added.
44. Ibid., p. 215.
45. Ibid., pp. 218–19.
46. Levitin, *One Is Not Born*, p. 172.
47. Ibid., p. 166.
48. G. L. Zaitseva, *Ispol'zovanie zhestovoi rechi na urokakh literatury v vechernikh skolakh dlia slaboslyshashchikh* (Leningrad: Leningradskii vostanovitel'nyi tsentr VOG, 1981).
49. Ibid., p. 29.
50. Ibid., p. 9.
51. Ibid., pp. 12–13.
52. Ibid., p. 25. Compare Luria, *Language and Cognition*, pp. 52–53; and Vygotsky, *Thought and Language*, p. 217.
53. Vygotsky as quoted in Levitin, *One Is Not Born*, p. 130.

Industrial Accidents and Their Prevention in the Interwar Period

Lewis Siegelbaum

Capitalist production . . . is very economical with the materialized labor incorporated in commodities. Yet, more than any other mode of production, it squanders human lives, or living labor, and not only blood and flesh, but also nerve and brain. Indeed, it is only by dint of the most extravagant waste of individual development that the development of the human race is at all safeguarded and maintained in the epoch of history immediately preceding the conscious reorganization of society.

—Karl Marx

I

KARL MARX was not wrong. Although work-related disability, injury, and death certainly predate industrial capitalism, two features of the capitalist epoch vastly increased the danger to the lives and limbs of those engaged in material production. One concerns the inherent properties of the new materials and means of production—whether toxic chemicals or electric sparks, razor-sharp cutting blades operated at high speeds, or, to take a more modern example, nuclear radiation. The other has to do with what Marx called the social relations of production, that is, the ever increasing specialization of labor that induces monotony and fatigue; piece rates and other material incentives used by managers to urge on workers a fiercer pace of production; and the efforts of owners of capital to minimize production costs by ignoring occupational safety.

It should logically follow that a radical revision of relations of production, or better still the "conscious reorganization of society" along socialist lines, would dramatically reduce the squandering of blood, flesh, nerve, and brain. The question this chapter addresses is whether history has followed that logic. To be more precise, it considers whether what Marx regarded a consequence of "the natural tendency of capitalist exploitation" persisted in the first society to be consciously reorganized along principles radically different from capitalism—that is, the Soviet Union. In recounting how this putative workers' state handled the problem of industrial accidents, we shall be concerned with whether there was a distinctly Soviet approach to preventing accidents, and what features of that society as it emerged in the 1920s and was then transformed by the Stalin revolution impinged on the problem and the ways it was understood.

The chapter thus has a dual focus. It deals not only with the incidence of industrial accidents and disability, but with the evolution of the professions most closely associated with the study of these phenomena before and during Russia's rapid industrialization. Assessing the impact that those claiming expertise had on state policy, it also considers the degree to which both the persistence of high rates of accidents and the political leadership's changing priorities determined the fate of those experts.

II

The half century that separated the writing of *Capital* from the Russian Revolution saw concerted efforts both in Europe and the Americas to reduce the incidence of industrial accidents. As in the case of the Factory Acts and the inspection system in Britain (which Marx acknowledged as having "markedly" reduced accidents), state intervention was to play a major role.[1] Standardized building codes, workers' compensation and social insurance laws, the systematization of accident data collection, and the promotion of safety consciousness were among the most important measures. Not surprisingly in view of its adherence to the *Rechtsstaat* principle and its attempts to weaken the appeal of the Social Democratic Party, the German state was in the forefront of such intervention. Its compulsory accident law, passed in 1884, served as a model for other European countries (Austria in 1887, Norway in 1894, Britain in 1897, France and Italy in 1898, Russia in 1903), though notably not the United States.[2]

Nevertheless, by the turn of the century, progress in reducing industrial accidents was slow. On the one hand, many employers continued to circumvent safety regulations (where any existed), with such catastrophic results as the New York Triangle Shirtwaist Company fire, which killed 146 women in March 1911.[3] On the other hand, increased mechanization, the introduction of assembly line production, and the rapid growth of clerical and office staff occupations exacerbated problems of monotony and mental fatigue, which soon became recognized as major causes of accidents and disabilities.[4]

It was at this juncture that "science" intervened in the form of applied chemistry, physics, physiology, and above all, psychology. The first two decades of the twentieth century saw a veritable explosion of research in Europe and North America into the causes of work-related disabilities and accidents, and the corresponding emergence of two new professions—industrial hygiene and industrial psychology, or psychotechnics.[5]

Physicians, many of whom served as factory and mining medical inspectors, were especially prominent among hygienists, though toxicologists and safety engineers were also represented. Some hygienists, most notably in Germany and Britain, worked in conjunction with trade union committees; others carried out research in universities and state-financed institutes; still others were employed by major insurance companies that held the policies of industrial corporations. Irrespective of their institutional affiliation, industrial hygienists were active in national and international associations and published in professional journals, most of which were founded in the period just before and just after the First World War.[6]

If industrial hygienists were primarily concerned with the effect on workers of environmental conditions—temperature, ventilation, lighting, and the condition of equipment and the plant in general—then the central thrust of psychotechnics was to measure the effects of various kinds and intensities of work on individual workers' attentiveness, muscular reflexes, pulse rates, and other psychophysiological functions. Put another way, whereas industrial hygiene sought to modify working conditions as a means of reducing accidents and disabilities, psychotechnical research took the environment as a given and aimed to develop methods by which appropriate individuals could be selected for specific jobs.

Psychotechnics had diverse roots. It clearly was derived from the work of Francis Galton and J. McKeen Cattell, the pioneers of differential psychology. It also drew upon advances in intelligence, motor coordination, and alertness testing. Finally, it shared much in common with (and was no doubt influenced by) Frederick Winslow Taylor's scientific management, particularly its emphases on the analysis of work into its constituent elements and mathematical precision in evaluating output.

Although the term psychotechnics was coined as early as 1903, it was not until the publication of Hugo Münsterberg's *Psychology and Industrial Efficiency* ten years later that a comprehensive program of research was developed.[7] Münsterberg's program included tests in the selection of workers, in training techniques, in the assessment of motivation, and in factors producing fatigue. Characteristic of the appeal that technocracy had in war-weary and strife-torn Europe, industrial psychotechnics flourished in the 1920s, particularly in Germany. With its several psychotechnical institutes, numerous laboratories attached to major industrial firms, and at least three professional journals, that country was the envy of industrial psychologists everywhere, including Soviet Russia.[8]

Tsarist Russia had not been immune from these developments, but it had exhibited certain peculiarities. A factory inspectorate was established in 1882, originally to enforce laws protecting juveniles and women. Following the first serious outbreak of strikes in 1884/85, the brief of the inspectorate was expanded to include peaceful mediation of labor disputes, supervision of labor contracts, ensuring workers adequate medical assistance and protecting their lives, health, and morals. Indeed, such was the breadth of the inspectorate's responsibilities and the shortage of staff that, in the words of one historian, "the factory inspector's work, like a housewife's, was never done."[9]

There were other problems as well. Like their contemporaries in the *zemstvo* administrations, many inspectors were highly educated and intrepid social reformers who sought to expose and thereby alleviate the abuses they witnessed.[10] However, their exposures, contained in the annual reports of the inspectorate, were so embarrassing to the tsarist government that no reports were permitted to be published until 1900. Even more tellingly, most inspectors eventually succumbed to pressure from the Ministry of Finance and individual industrialists and refrained from filing grievances on behalf of workers in the provincial governors' factory councils. In 1901, of 2,712 reported violations of rules on the safety, health, and morals of workers, inspectors forwarded for the councils' deliberation only 213.[11]

All the while, the number of industrial workers was growing as a consequence of industrial expansion, and desperate conditions on the land. Precisely because of its relative lateness and intensity, industrialization in Russia generated almost ideal conditions for industrial accidents and disabilities. The combination of large-scale factories employing advanced technology and a working class that was scarcely removed from the countryside was sufficient in itself to cause extensive carnage.[12] Added to this, working hours for adult males were not regulated until 1897, and workers were deprived of any legal opportunities—at least until 1906—to collectively remonstrate to improve working conditions.

The tsarist government was only slightly less hostile to the growth of autonomous professional groups, as witnessed by its repression of student organizations, liberal-oriented academics, and zemstvo personnel. The contribution of civil society to the development of occupational hygiene and accident prevention was thus limited. A case in point was the fate of F. F. Erisman, Russia's most outstanding hygienist. Having been appointed professor of hygiene at Moscow University in 1882, Erisman was dismissed from his position in 1896 in connection with student disturbances. Until his death in 1915, he continued his work in occupational hygiene, not in Russia, but in his native Switzerland.[13]

The creation of the State Duma and other concessions wrested from the authorities during the 1905 Revolution did not significantly alter the situation. The only piece of legislation concerning industrial accidents—the Workers' Insurance Laws of 1912—took nearly five years of deliberation and debate. Providing for elected representatives of workers to administer funds jointly with employers, it singularly failed to address the matter of accident and disability prevention or to extend the provisions to state-owned and nonindustrial enterprises.[14]

Whatever progress had been made in these respects by 1914 was undone by the First World War. The recruitment of many skilled workers into the army, the running down of capital stock, and the resort to intensification and overtime by employers eager to fulfill war orders took their toll on workers. At the Putilov Works, Petrograd's (and the empire's) largest heavy industrial plant, there were 211 cases of mutilation in 1914, but 305 in 1915. For every thousand workers in Ekaterinoslav's factories in 1915, 322 sustained injuries; in Perm's armaments factories, the rate was nearly 300 per 1,000 workers in 1916.[15] Undoubtedly, the actual rates were even higher, for monetary inflation convinced many workers that they could not afford to seek compensation or disability pensions.

III

Industry-related accidents and disabilities were merely one of the multitude of social problems inherited by the Soviet government from its tsarist predecessor. In comparison to most others, it was not a pressing issue. Even among the disabled, those who had become so in the course of industrial work constituted a small minority. In addition to the victims of nonindustrial accidents, there were the maimed, crippled, and blinded of the First World War and the ensuing Russian Civil War. Still, a government characterizing itself as a dictatorship of the proletariat had, perforce, an obligation to safeguard the members of the class in whose name it ruled.

Early Soviet legislation on industrial safety reflected the impact of workers control as it had evolved in the course of 1917/18. On 18 May 1918, the prerevolutionary system of factory inspection was abolished and replaced by one that called for the nomination of inspectors by the factory committee of each industrial establishment and their appointment by respective trade unions and social insurance organizations. In addition, the new law enjoined each factory committee to form a special subcommittee on labor protection, which was to contain from three to seven members, depending on the size of the work force. The administration of this and other laws pertaining to safety was placed in the hands of the Commissariat of Labor (*Narkomtrud*), which created a Bureau for the Protection of Labor especially for that purpose.[16] By 1920, similar provisions had been made for the appointment of technical and health inspectors.[17]

As promising as these initiatives may appear, their immediate impact was severely limited by circumstances prevalent during the civil war years. With industrial production at a fraction of its pre–World War I level and the industrial proletariat dispersed throughout the countryside, mobilized for the Red Army, or barely surviving in the cities on whatever could be pilfered from the idle plants and bartered on the black markets, the regulations governing industrial safety had little more than a paper reality.[18] Even after the introduction of the New Economic Policy (NEP) in 1921, the system of labor inspection remained rudimentary, the collection of statistics on occupational diseases and industrial accidents was haphazard at best, and analysis of the causes of accidents was speculative.[19]

This situation began to change in 1923. That year saw the

founding of both a Central Museum for the Protection of Labor and Social Insurance and the Obukh Institute of Occupational Diseases. The former was devoted to the display of protective devices and methods of accident prevention; the latter employed both a research and clinical staff and issued periodic bulletins on dangerous substances used in industry and instances of occupational disability.[20] Two years later, in 1925, the State Institute for the Protection of Labor was established in Moscow under the auspices of *Narkomtrud,* the Commissariat of Health of the RSFSR, and the USSR Supreme Council of the National Economy. Its director was S. I. Kaplun, a twenty-eight-year-old professor at the Moscow Medical Institute and a Communist Party member since 1917.[21]

In the meantime, the first monographs, collections of articles, conference proceedings, and journals dealing with industrial hygiene in the USSR were beginning to appear. Clearly, the most important among the latter was *Gigiena truda* (Labor Hygiene), a monthly journal published by the Central Council of Trade Unions under the editorship of Kaplun. *Gigiena truda* reported on the work of labor, technical, and health inspectors, provided space for the discussion of appropriate terminology, reprinted decrees of Narkomtrud and other Soviet organs on labor protection, and summarized international developments in its and related fields. So impressive was the scope of activity in the USSR that Alice Hamilton, the pioneering American industrial toxicologist, could write of her visit to that country in 1924 that "indeed, it seemed to me that there was more industrial hygiene in Russia than industry."[22]

Hamilton's assessment would no doubt have pleased Soviet hygienists, but the lack of industry was, to say the least, disturbing to higher authorities. Industry's slow pace of recovery after the civil war was reflected in the high costs of production, which in turn created the "scissors crisis" of 1923. If the NEP was to succeed, the goods offered to the peasantry in return for grain had to be produced in greater quantities and at less cost.

It was in this context that various schemes for rationalization were advanced. Among them was the Soviet version of Taylorism, embodied in the Central Institute of Labor and articulated by the institute's visionary director, A. K. Gastev. The institute, from its founding in 1921, had absorbed a number of specialists who were interested in labor psychology, fatigue, and the selection of workers for different tasks. But the research program mandated by Gastev was not to everyone's taste. Far from seeking to mitigate the dangers of the factory regime, Gastev asserted that "History urgently demands of us to pose, not these small problems of the protection of personality by society, but rather a bold design of human psychology in reliance upon such an historical factor as machine production."[23] As suggested by his aphorism that "machines, from being managed, will become managers," Gastev's notion of relying on machine production was rather extreme.[24]

So, at least, it appears in contrast to the more classically humanist perspective offered by the dean of Russian psychophysiologists (or reflexologists), V. M. Bekhterev. "In a socialist society," Bekhterev asserted, "the rationalization and scientific organization of labor must be based on the fundamental principle that the maximum of productive work can only be procured by fully protecting the health of workers and by guaranteeing the complete development of their personalities."[25] Although Gastev and his institute would develop a number of simple and successful techniques for training machine and metal workers, they did so without the services of Bekhterev and others who shared his antipathy to Gastev's vision. Among them was I. N. Shpilrein, the father of Soviet psychotechnics. Initially associated with Gastev's institute, Shpilrein defected to the Institute for the Protection of Labor shortly after its creation. Between 1923 and 1928, he was a member of the editorial board of *Gigiena truda,* to which he frequently contributed articles.

It is testimony to the relatively pluralistic character of the period that competing approaches to the protection of workers from the hazards of industrial work and corresponding institutional rivalries could be sustained. Common to both Gastev's scientific organization of labor and its alternatives was the assumption that it was possible to serve both scientific rationality and the building of socialism. Only in the early 1930s, when hygienists and industrial psychologists were under assault for their own and their professions' bourgeois origins, did they have to choose between the two.

IV

Having thus laid out the socioeconomic and institutional settings within which Soviet research on industrial safety was undertaken in the 1920s, we can now turn to what such research revealed. Not surprisingly, investigators found that, as industry revived, so did the rate of reported accidents. Mining, which had all but ceased during the civil war, graphically exhibited this trend (see table 1).

But to what extent the reported increases reflected the real situation or an improvement in data collection is not clear. Comprehensive data covering the major branches of Soviet industry only began to be compiled in 1926 (see table 2). They suggest a leveling off of accident rates beginning in 1927, but there remain problems of interpretation. The fact that the overall accident rate for industry in the RSFSR was less than half that of Ukrainian industry surely requires an explanation. Did it have something to do with working conditions and labor forces, or was it a function of the concentration of light industry in the RSFSR and heavy industry in the Ukraine? Other questions arise. How useful is it to divide industry into its constituent branches when within each branch there were some occupations that were far more dangerous than others and several occupations that were common to more than one branch? Finally, these figures tell us nothing about the severity of accidents, nor do they indicate disabilities that did not result from accidents.

Statistics are available for 1927 and 1928 indicating the periods of recuperation from industrial accidents. They show that, whereas in 1927 8.5 per 1,000 insured workers in the USSR required more than thirty-five days to recover, in 1928 the figure had risen to 9.6 per 1,000. There appears to have been a strong correlation between the severity and frequency of accidents. Thus, whereas for every 1,000 coal miners, 23.5 in 1927 and 25.5 in 1928 required more than thirty-five days to recuperate, for machine building workers the corresponding figures were 11.0 and 13.2; and for textile workers, only 2.6 for each year.[26] It should be pointed out, however, that these computations exclude fatalities and permanent disability.

Taking these limitations into account, can we at least use the national (or republic) figures to make international comparisons,

TABLE 1
Mining Accidents, Deaths, and Serious Injuries, 1923–1927

	1923/24	1924/25	1925/26	1926/27
Accidents per 1,000 workers				
All mining	115.2	131.4	179.8	221.8
Coal mining	146.3	169.7	213.3	253.9
Deaths[a]	214	248	411	452
Serious injuries[a]	853	896	1,628	1,812

Source: *Trud,* 5 Feb. 1928, p. 3.
    a. Represents total recorded for all mining.

say, with Germany, where the same statistical criterion—per 1,000 fully insured workers—was used? If there is such a basis, then the comparison would appear to have been very much in Germany's favor. There, the rate of accidents was as follows: 77.37 (1927); 82.23 (1928); and 80.73 (1929).[27] As two Soviet statisticians were quick to point out, however, accidents resulting in the loss of even one day's work were included in the USSR, whereas in Germany the minimum for reportable accidents was three days.[28] Yet this alone would not entirely explain the difference, for in 1927 and 1928 only some 16 percent of all reported accidents in the USSR involved the loss of less than three day's work.[29] There are, in fact, grounds to suspect that the actual difference was even greater than a comparison of the two sets of figures would suggest. Under-reporting of accidents in the Soviet Union due to incomplete information provided by the social insurance offices was estimated at between 10 and 15 percent during these years.[30] This does not include cases where workers, fearful of losing their jobs, failed to report to the enterprise's medical station. Second, it should be noted that the category *workers* includes managerial-technical personnel, whose chances of incurring accidents were considerably less than manual workers.[31] Still, in order to make a more precise

TABLE 2

INDUSTRIAL ACCIDENTS IN THE RSFSR AND UKRAINE, 1926–1928, RATES PER 1,000 INSURED WORKERS

	1926 RSFSR	1927		1928		% Change In RSFSR, 1926–1928
		RSFSR	Ukraine	RSFSR	Ukraine	
Coal mining	283.3	471.3	479.5	469.8	457.9	+39.7
Oil extraction	251.2	338.8		298.3		+15.8
Ore mining		215.7	422.6	197.7	429.1	
Metallurgy	259.5	269.4	355.4	256.4	391.1	− 1.2
Machine building	281.8	276.6	350.8	286.1	398.4	+ 1.6
Other metalworks	169.2	175.7	354.1	175.6	362.0	+ 3.7
Woodworking	318.2	333.6	317.8	384.2	330.9	+17.2
Chemicals	221.9	164.3	227.2	157.8	210.7	−28.9
Textiles	72.2	76.1	149.4	72.8	175.1	+ 0.9
All industry	169.2	175.7	354.1	175.6	362.0	+ 3.7

SOURCES: For 1926, N. I. Sinev and I. F. Engel', "Promyshlennyi travmatizm v SSSR," *Gigiena, Bezopasnost' i Patologiia truda* (Hereafter *GBPT*) 3 (1929): 69–70; for 1927 and 1928, I. Engel', "Metody ucheta neschastnykh sluchaev i promyshlennyi travmatizm v SSSR," *GBPT* 11 (1929): 71.

comparison, we would need to know more about the reporting of accidents in Germany, what proportion of the work force was fully insured, and a number of other factors.

For the purposes of this chapter, however, it would be better to take a closer look at how the situation in the Soviet Union was analyzed by Soviet specialists. Among the vast number of studies produced in the latter half of the 1920s, three research strategies can be discerned: locating as precisely as possible which workers suffered accidents and when they had occurred; studying the impact of changes in the labor process on fatigue and accidents; and investigating the nature and degree of severity of occupational diseases and disabilities.

V

Let us look at the first of these strategies. As might be expected, Soviet investigators found that accident rates differed markedly from one occupation and age group to another, and that they also depended on a number of other variables, some more tractable than others. The two studies by Shkliar, Trakhtenberg, and Krol' of accidents at the Petrovskii metallurgical factory in Dnepropetrovsk may be taken as representative of such studies. They found that accidents occurred most frequently during the second of three shifts and in the "hot" shops, especially the foundry section; that the rate was three times as high among nineteen- to twenty-three-year-olds as among those who were eighteen and under; and that those with one or two year's production experience (*stazh*) had a considerably higher rate than those with less than one year or those with more than two years. Finally, the accident rate among the enterprise's female workers was negligible, a fact that was explained in terms of the relatively safe if menial tasks performed by women.[32]

In the follow-up study, the researchers noted the continuing rise in the number of accidents per worker—0.96 in 1926, 1.08 in 1927, and 1.18 in 1928—but also the decline in the proportion of accidents resulting in either temporary or permanent disability. Two other trends, related to the work regimen, were discussed. The rise in the rate of accidents toward the end of each shift was related to the early meal break followed by as much as six hours of continuous work. And, whereas in 1926 and 1927 the frequency of accidents was greatest on Fridays and Saturdays, the introduction in 1928 of a system of staggered days appeared to have eliminated end-of-week fatigue.[33] Other studies of individual metallurgical enterprises, shipyards, machine tool factories, and coal mines tended to replicate the methodology and findings of Shkliar et al. In some cases, though, a downward trend in the frequency of accidents per worker was recorded.[34]

Industrial hygienists were not content, however, merely to record differential rates of accidents. They sought both to refine their analysis and to generalize about the causes of accidents. Both strategies had important policy implications. Refinement of analysis consisted, in the main, of going beyond the specification of the most dangerous occupations to breaking them down into constituent tasks and body movements. Here, hygienists depended on industrial psychologists' reconstructions of the workday via time and motion studies and minutely detailed occupational schemas, known as *professiogrammy*.[35]

When it came to explaining the causes of accidents in more general terms, hygienists pointed to several factors that were unrelated to work. Poor living conditions, alcoholism, and family problems—the latter often being a consequence of the first two—were frequently cited. But overwhelmingly, it was conditions in the factories that bore the brunt of criticism. Inadequate lighting; excessive temperature, humidity, and dust; antiquated equipment; crowding of machinery and workers; insufficient rest periods; and other violations of safety codes and factory rules figured prominently in reports of technical and health inspectors.[36] Criticism was also expressed of the tendency of management to staff their safety bureaus with poorly educated and lowranking technical personnel and to burden them with other duties.[37]

Occasionally, responsibility was placed directly with the economic system itself. For example, two of Kaplun's assistants at the State Institute for the Protection of Labor went so far as to assert: "Under the influence of the sharp demand for its products, our industry has had to raise its productivity without at the same time being able to renew or improve its equipment. This circumstance in connection with the application of unlimited piece rates could not but have negative repercussions on the dynamics of accidents."[38] This assertion, or at least part of it, was supported by another article, which demonstrated a positive correlation between increased labor productivity and the rate of accidents at the Petrovskii metallurgical factory.[39]

VI

Now for the second strategy: scrutiny of changes in the labor process. The question of how to raise labor productivity without doing damage to the health of workers was a highly controversial issue in the late 1920s. One of the earliest and most exhaustive studies devoted to this question was conducted in 1925 by V. V. Isakov and Iu. N. Khalturina.[40] The study investigated the effects of increasing the number of weaving machines from two to three, which were operated by female weavers at two textile mills. Isakov and Khalturina neither condemned nor unequivocally endorsed the change. Rather, they pointed to the importance of ancillary factors in determining different rates of productivity and fatigue. Among these, hygienic conditions and the socioeconomic condition of those who had volunteered to work on three machines were given special emphasis.

Although the study was carried out before the state had launched its economy and rationalization drives, by the time the study was published, those campaigns were in full swing. Their most concrete manifestation was the seven-hour workday and three-shift systems, which were first introduced in the textile industry in January 1928.[41] Hailed by party leaders as a great innovation of the socialist state, these changes presupposed a more intense pace of production and raised the question of fatigue to a matter of urgency. In this context, the cautionary notes sounded by Isakov and Khalturina take on added significance. It was asserted, for example, that "to raise productivity by means of increasing the weaver's intensity of effort is only possible if, in addition to commercial considerations, the . . . physical expenditure of the vital energy of the worker is taken into account."[42]

Other researchers noted that the shift to three machines could only be considered rational if proper atmospheric and other environmental conditions prevailed and if rest periods were properly observed. Yet the reported rise in 1928 of absenteeism and illnesses among Moscow textile workers was attributed precisely to "unsatisfactory sanitary-hygienic conditions and increase in fatigue as a result of the lack of normal breaks for food and rest, and the greater intensification of work consequent upon the consolidation (*uplotnenie*) of the workday."[43]

On a broader, theoretical level, O. A. Ermanskii, an ex-Menshevik whose oeuvre defies categorization as either industrial psychology or hygiene, questioned the identity between the intensity and productivity of labor. In his view, human progress could be measured not by a secular increase in the quantity of human energy expended in the transformation of nature (intensity of labor) but rather the reverse, that is, by its reduction per unit output. Mechanized, and in particular assembly line, production could thus vastly contribute to human progress, but only if certain physiologically based norms or optima of energy expenditure were maintained.[44] It was in this respect that Ermanskii considered early Soviet experience with conveyor production as dangerous. Writing in March 1927, he noted "the excessive intensification of labor as the first consequence of introducing the conveyor."[45]

But this begged the question of what was the optimum of energy expenditure, or to put it another way, at what speed should conveyors be operated and how long should workers be on the line without a break. A detailed comparative analysis of manual and assembly line production of harrows at the Hammer and Sickle factory in Khar'kov found that there was a "significant economization of energy expenditure" among workers on the assembly line, but that this did not necessarily mean a reduction of fatigue. On the contrary, the investigators concluded that "workers on the conveyor, although conscious of expending less energy and approving of the collective nature of the work, nonetheless raise an arsenal of complaints ranging from leg and back aches to emotional disorders and protests against the compulsory, elementary and fatiguing monotony (odnoobraziia) of work."[46]

In short, mental fatigue—the subjective element—would have to be taken into account in assessing fatigue and regulating assembly line production. So too, come to think of it, would differential tolerances among individuals. Soviet industrial psychologists did think about these questions, but could not reach any consensus about how to integrate them with physiological considerations. The First All-Union Conference on the Psychophysiology of Labor and Occupational Selection, which met in May-June 1927, merely concluded that there were "certain theoretical problems" that still needed to be worked out and that no one approach to the study of fatigue could be unequivocably endorsed.[47] This remained the situation for several years.

Meanwhile, on the practical level, industrial psychologists sought to determine proper rest intervals for a number of occupational groups through a variety of measures. These included the Bourdon cancellation and other attention tests, tremometer readings of hand and arm steadiness, metabolic rates, and the so-called work method, whereby investigators performed all the tasks associated with a given occupation.[48] The advantages of physical exercise during rest periods was also emphasized, and it is partly thanks to their emphasis that organized calisthenics was introduced into the workplace.

VII

Aside from the specification of high-risk occupations and working conditions and the study of work fatigue, Soviet investigators of the late 1920s also studied occupational disabilities and diseases. Much of their research dealt with analyzing the toxicity of chemical substances used in industrial production and the incidence and nature of diseases such as silicosis, lung cancer, and other respiratory and pulmonary disorders. Cases of mass poisoning documented by technical inspectors also received close attention. Perhaps the most interesting research, however, had to do with eye and ear disorders. Analyzing statistics on eye injuries incurred by workers at the Red Sormovo Metalworks Factory, S. Ia. Glezerov noted the inverse relationship between age and accident rates and attributed this in part to the fact that older workers tended to wear spectacles. "Out of the enormous and ever-growing number of varieties of protective glasses," he remarked, "not one can be worn by metalworkers. . . . Either they are too heavy, too large, or restrict the range of vision."[49]

The extent of eye injuries, particularly in the metalworks industry, was consequently staggering. At the Khar'kov Electromechanical Factory, 22 percent of all workers in 1925 were victims, mostly of flying splinters, but also of burns. At the Stalingrad Metallurgical Works, the figure was 30 percent. Over the course of two and a half years, there were 1,512 cases at the factory, including 20 that resulted in complete blindness. Not all occupational groups were at equal risk. Among three Leningrad factories, eye injuries affected 18, 20.6, and 55 percent of all workers in 1928. But for polishers, the range was 263–700 percent and for turret lathe operators, the average was 350 percent, or 3.5 eye injuries per worker.[50]

The problem with respect to hearing defects was not so much accidents as the cumulatively debilitating effects of noise. Among workers employed for ten or more years in the flyer-frame division of several large textile mills, 24.8 to 42 percent were found to have had partially or completely damaged cochleae. Studies of railway workers and telephonists revealed that "reduced hearing ability" was widespread.[51]

VIII

By the end of the NEP period, Soviet psychotechnics and labor hygiene could boast of an impressive record of scientific investigation and a sound institutional basis for future research. In addition to those already mentioned, institutes for the study of occupational diseases and labor hygiene existed in Leningrad, Kazan', Kiev, Khar'kov, Stalino, and Tbilisi. In 1927, the All-Russian (later, All-Union) Psychotechnical Society was established, with Shpilrein as its chairman. The society's journal began to appear the following year. By 1930, according to one estimate, there were some 500 psychotechnologists in the Soviet Union, and in just three years, the total number of books and articles in the field had reached over 400.[52]

If despite this overall impressive growth the rate of accidents and injuries remained intolerably high, the extent of the problem was far better known and analysis of its causes was far more advanced than in the early or even mid-1920s. While the introduction of new technology and revisions to the organization of labor had exacerbated the problem of fatigue, the absence of any artificially imposed consensus about how to deal with it meant that lively and fruitful debate could prevail. Moreover, there were grounds for optimism in the draft figures for expenditure on technical safety during the First Five-Year Plan. The amount to be allocated in 1932/33 was to be nearly two-thirds more than what was spent in 1927/28.[53]

But in this respect as in so many others, the correspondence between plan and reality proved to be illusory. It was one thing to apportion funds among industrial enterprises, but quite another for them to be applied toward the intended purpose. On more than one occasion in 1929, Narkomtrud called attention to the failure of enterprise management to utilize funds for occupational safety, characterizing such inaction as negligent.[54] By 1932, N. Shvernik, chairman of the Central Council of Trade Unions, used stronger language, referring to the "criminally slipshod relation on the part of management to technical safety and the protection of labor."[55]

This problem, however, paled in comparison with that of absorbing and safeguarding the new labor recruits who poured into the cities and industrial construction sites from the surrounding countryside during the First Five-Year Plan. Ill nourished and clothed, crowded into barracks and dormitories, frequently working overtime and even two successive shifts, these largely unskilled peasant workers injured themselves and their work mates in unprecedented numbers.

Exactly what those numbers were is impossible to determine. The statistics presented in table 3 are even less meaningful than those in table 2, if for no other reason than the two Soviet sources for 1931 and 1932 show such marked variation. But there are additional reasons. In order to properly assess their verisimilitude, we would need to know whether the reporting of accidents during the chaotic years of the First Five-Year Plan was of the same standard as prior to 1929, whether the proportion of insured workers remained constant—which in view of the huge influx of seasonal workers and the phenomenal turnover rates in many industries, is doubtful—and what the impact of frequent changes in wage policy was on social insurance.

Unfortunately, there was no discussion of these factors in the main journal devoted to labor hygiene and safety. Nor was there any comment on or reference to the increasing rate of accidents in 1927–30. Observing that no two factories or shops maintained identical conditions, one statistician concluded that "the summarization of accidents for all branches of industry in the existing system of statistics represents a typical example of the divorce of

TABLE 3
INDUSTRIAL ACCIDENTS IN THE USSR, 1929–1933, RATES PER 1,000 INSURED WORKERS

	1929	1930	1931	1932	1933
Coal mining	509.3	477.0	341.1 (359.0)	282.3 (269.6)	291.6
Ore mining	314.4	327.8	330.3 (379.2)	223.7 (239.5)	192.1
Metalworking	337.6	315.6	256.3 (267.7)	209.4 (211.0)	198.1
Machine building	298.6	307.6	268.1 (297.6)	180.1 (192.1)	168.5
Chemicals	230.1	215.4	235.0 (227.9)	157.9 (170.5)	
Rubber	94.9	110.9	98.3	78.6	
Woodworking	281.5	268.1	252.7	186.3	173.9
Textiles	67.8	76.9	72.6 (72.6)	55.4 (76.7)	48.0
Hides and leather	239.9	219.8	204.6 (204.6)	146.7 (137.2)	111.3
Footwear	184.5	183.9	158.1	111.1	91.2
Construction RSFSR	157.1	166.0	136.1	93.0	95.3

SOURCES: For 1929–32, *Sotsialisticheskoe stroitel'stvo SSSR Statisticheskii ezhegodnik* (Moscow: TsUNKhU 1934), p. 424; for 1933, ILO, *Industrial Safety Survey* 12 (1936): 52–53. Figures in parentheses from *Gigiena i bezopasnost' truda* 1 (1933): 4.

statistics as a method from the material reality towards which it is applied."[56] Presumably because material reality was ever changing even within a single factory, such an argument could be used to justify the suppression of statistical series over time. In any case, after 1933, no aggregate figures for industrial accidents or occupational disabilities are available.

It was as if a fog had descended over these questions, a fog that became thicker still by the mid-1930s.[57] When in 1936 an elaborate statistical compendium appeared on the health of Soviet citizens and the state of health services, there was but one table on temporary disabilities as a result of industrial accidents. The table compared 1930 with 1934/35 for four branches of industry, but expressed the comparison in terms of the almost meaningless percentage decline.[58] Statements in the periodical and monographic literature to the effect that there were "13.3 per cent fewer accidents among Union of Machine Tool Workers in 1937 than in 1936" and that industrial accidents declined in 1938 compared to 1937 by 10 to 20 percent in the major branches of industry need to be regarded with a large dose of skepticism if only because of the political context within which the statistics were reported.[59]

None of this is to deny that the rate of industrial accidents may have declined during the 1930s as the growth in the industrial work force tapered off, the proportion of skilled workers increased, and industrial equipment was modernized. Yet in the absence of any concrete data, it is impossible to be precise about the extent of the decline or any other aspect of occupational disability and accidents. On the other hand, the fate of the two professions that were devoted to the investigation of these phenomena is at least partially documented and can be discerned in its broad outlines.

IX

Like other professions, industrial hygiene and psychotechnics experienced profound upheaval during the period that has been characterized as the Cultural Revolution. As summarized in a volume devoted to the subject, the Cultural Revolution in the professions arose out of, and interacted with, already existing disputes among different schools of thought—sometimes, though not always, reflecting different political orientations and philosophies. Its prime agents were usually young communist intellectuals, who "were often extremely aggressive, but at the same time unsure of their credentials. They tended to question their own value to society, suggest that factory workers could do their jobs better, and [engage in] what one observer called the disease of self-flagellation in a collective of intellectuals."[60] The human behavioral sciences were not immune to this disease, though in their case, there was the added factor that "political leaders and scholarly professionals claim[ed] privileged understanding of the same subject matter: people."[61]

Psychotechnics and industrial hygiene illustrate the combination of these two factors perhaps more clearly than any other professions. First, they dealt not only with people but people in the process of production, a subject that was particularly dear to the hearts of party leaders.[62] Second, being of recent provenance and having lower status than the "pure" sciences from which they were derived, they did not generate a very intense degree of either professional autonomy or confidence. These two factors alone, not to speak of the traumatic impact of the First Five-Year Plan on Soviet workers, ensured that the Cultural Revolution would reverberate among industrial hygienists and psychologists with particular force.

The opening blast was a shrill polemic against Shpilrein's approach to psychotechnics that was published in the journal *Psikhologiia*. The polemic was written by N. F. Kurmanov, a former student of Shpilrein, who had died before the article was published.[63] The essence of the attack was that Shpilrein had never really lost his earlier admiration for the idealism of William Stern and had failed to learn anything from Feuerbach, Marx, Engels, Plekhanov, and Lenin. At best, he had adopted a "neutralist empiricist position," but this was only a cover for retaining his idealist perspective. In his reply, printed in the same issue, Shpilrein was indulgent toward Kurmanov, but insisted that he had misinterpreted his former teacher's approach.[64]

However, no doubt aware of similar attacks against the philosopher A. M. Deborin, Shpilrein tried to distance himself from his past and the objectivist and biological orientation of the field over which he had presided. In September 1930, he delivered a report on "What Is Fatigue" to a joint session of the Psychotechnical Society and the newly formed Society of Materialist Psychoneurologists.[65] The report repudiated the decision taken by the Psychophysiological Congress in 1927 to accommodate different approaches to this complex subject. Shpilrein explicitly denounced the "purely biological method of studying social processes, whereby the human organism was treated in mechanistic terms." He also condemned the concept of the optimum because of its marginalization of "the social factor." "In reality" he remarked, "the optimum moves (*sdvigaetsia*). The optimum for a worker engaged in socialist construction will be different from the worker of a capitalist factory and significantly higher than for the worker under serfdom. But however great is this optimum (defined as the socially acceptable coefficient of the expenditure of an organism's resources), its biological limit is the energetic maximum."[66]

Still, Shpilrein refrained from characterizing these approaches as anti-Marxist or associating them with any individual except Ermanskii, who had been something of a maverick in the profession for a number of years in any case. He may have gone a long way toward applying the lessons of struggles in related fields, but at least for some of his listeners, he had not gone far enough. Why, it was asked, had he avoided any mention of what workers were doing now, of socialist competition and shock work, "since sometimes one hears . . . discussion about the overwork of workers and a whole series of other purely technical objections leveled against shock work?"[67] Since precisely at this time, the Council on Technical Norms was redefining the basis for output to be the performance of "workers demonstrating an intense tempo, that is, shock workers," this was a pertinent question.[68]

Kaplun too was subjected to the same sort of criticism. His definition of the burning questions of labor hygiene was found to be inadequate by several practitioners. In the era of socialist construction, it was now argued, industrial hygiene had to abandon its passive, defensive nature and instead assist in speeding up the tempo of construction—"of course not at the expense of the physical and spiritual powers of the proletariat, but on the contrary, by developing them."[69] Another critic said, "From the point of view of improving the health of the proletariat, it is much more important to study and establish the most advanced regimen of labor and forms of labor cooperation, than to take multitudinous measurements of energy expenditure."[70]

By 1931, these forays had become more generalized and, one cannot help thinking by their sheer repetitiveness, ritualized as well. Under attack from the advocates of "the Marxist-Leninist revolutionary theory of knowledge and practice," were Menshevik idealism and rotten liberalism (read, the notion of protecting labor), neutralism (read, objectivity), eclecticism (read, employing methods devised by Western researchers), empiricism (read, paying attention to data), and so forth and so on. Virtually none of the leading lights in psychotechnics and labor hygiene emerged unscathed, although some were attacked more vigorously than others. Two examples will suffice. One was Professor N. A. Vigdorchik of the Leningrad Institute of Occupational Diseases. He had the courage, or stupidity, to suggest in December 1930 (!) "The Role of Socialist Competition and Shockwork in Increasing Morbidity" as a subject for investigation, and was rewarded by being denounced in the resolutions of several conferences and journal articles. The other was K. Kh. Kekcheev, whose *Labor Physiology* appeared in a second edition in 1930. Aside from retaining enough of a biomechanical approach to be accused of several of the above-mentioned heresies, the book also contained the statement that "from the productive point of view, man must be exploited as judiciously as the machine."[71]

Kaplun had devoted eight pages of his journal to withering criticism of Kekcheev's book, but what Vigdorchik and Kekcheev had asserted, he only doubted. He, therefore, also came under fire, finding himself the target of a *Pravda* article by six militants. Kaplun responded by confessing his mechanistic and Menshevik idealist views and admitting that among his friends were several Deborinites, that is, disciples of the recently discredited philosopher of science, A. M. Deborin. Further bouts of self-criticism followed.[72]

In the meantime, industrial psychologists were undergoing their own process of socialist reconstruction. The All-Union Psychotechnical Congress, meeting in Leningrad in May 1931, was the occasion for much self- and mutual recrimination. As if to underscore the necessity for the radical reorientation of the profession, the opening speech was delivered by M. B. Mitin, who was then leading the assault against the Deborinites and who would soon assume the mantle of authority within the field of philosophy.[73] The conference was noteworthy in another respect. For the first time, "conciliarism, the establishment of a philosophical line by resolutions of conferences," was employed, and again a first, *partiinost'* (party-mindedness) was formally invoked.[74]

Thus armed with the insights of Marxist-Leninist teaching, Soviet psychotechnologists were ready to confront their Western counterparts at the Seventh International Psychotechnical Conference, which was held in Moscow in September 1931. "The position of the Soviet delegation," we are told, "can be characterized as the active, militant contraposition of Soviet psychotechnics and psychophysiology of labor to bourgeois psychotechnical science."

This strategy, according to the same account, was a great success. "Soviet psychologists emerged as passionate propagandists of Marxist ideology," contributing to the growing division among the representatives of science in capitalist countries between idealists and mechanists on the one hand and Marxists on the other.[75]

But the unity within the Soviet camp was superficial.[76] As soon as the conference was over, the denunciations were renewed. Now it was the turn of specialists in occupational selection and industrial accidents to be pilloried. It was discovered that, here too, biologism had crept into Soviet research in the form of the concept of accident proneness, which was associated with the German psychotechnologist Karl Marbe. The concept had never been well received in the USSR, but its fatalistic implications were even more anathema once the Cultural Revolution's transformatory zeal took hold of the profession. One zealot went so far as to assert that not only *proneness* but *accident* (*neschastnyi sluchai*) ought to be purged from the vocabulary of Soviet psychotechnics, since each mishap could be explained by the sociomaterial conditions where it occurred.[77] The notion, put forward by Iu.O. Shpigel', that psychophysiological conditions should also be taken into account, was regarded by Gellershtein as "very closely connected to the views of Marbe."[78]

In this manner, the fundamental premises on which industrial hygienists and psychologists had operated—that workers needed protection from harmful substances, dangerous conditions, and overwork, and that statistical analysis and psychological testing could lead to a better understanding of what changes were necessary and which workers were suited to which jobs—were challenged as ideologically incompatible with the tasks of socialist reconstruction. It would thus appear that both labor hygiene and psychotechnics were casualties of that process. But if only to avoid sanctimoniousness with respect to fields that in the West saw their fair share of distortions and charlatanism, several points need to be made.

First, although the struggles within these professions owed a great deal to the initiative and encouragement of the political authorities, their outcome cannot be considered to have been predetermined by them. As David Joravsky has pointed out, the insistence by Stalin (among others) that theory be subordinated to practice still left open the question of exactly what practice meant and how it was to inform theory.[79] That this dogma was interpreted in the way it was must be attributed to the apocalyptic nature of the times as well as to the intelligentsia's instincts for survival. The predictions by Communist intellectuals that the contradictions between town and countryside were about to be resolved, that the distinction between mental and manual labor was withering away, and other equally utopian notions, were not just flights of fancy but can be seen as "a kind of running commentary on contemporary processes of institutional disintegration and social flux" under the impact of vast and largely uncontrolled socioeconomic changes.[80]

Second, as simplistic and overschematized as the denunciations of "bourgeois psychotechnics and labor physiology" were, subsequent developments within these fields have demonstrated the justice of some of the accusations. The culture-bound nature of many psychological tests, class-based assumptions implicit in the search for psychically maladjusted workers and psychopathic personality types among those who do not stand up to stress, and the lack of corroborating evidence that accident proneness is a fixed personality trait have been widely if not universally recognized by industrial psychologists.[81] Put another way, on present evidence, the reconstructionists were right to stress the social factor and the malleability of individual personalities. Nor should their antipathy to laboratory methods be dismissed as mere abolitionism or antiintellectualism. For they were only repeating the criticism leveled by worker delegates against the Moscow Institute of Labor Protection for its failure to study fatigue as experienced in everyday assembly line work.[82]

The problem was that the reconstructionists' impulses were taken to their extreme and absurd limits and transformed into axioms. Emphasizing the social factor did not have to mean eliminating the personal or physiological; invoking practice should not have restricted investigators to the study of the performance of shock workers or precluded laboratory experimentation. Yet, those who reminded their colleagues of these points earned rebukes to the effect that their positions were objectively consistent with bourgeois pseudoscience.

Nevertheless, neither labor hygiene nor psychotechnics entirely disappeared. Indeed, by 1932, as the storm whipped up by the Cultural Revolution began to subside, many of those who had been its chief victims resumed their scientific work, occasionally finding that their earlier positions had been vindicated. The case of D. I. Reitynbarg, who wrote extensively on safety propaganda, well illustrates this ironic, if temporary, turnabout. An advocate of socialist competition to reduce accidents in production, Reitynbarg had also urged the adoption of techniques pioneered in the United States. These included brief orations during the intermissions of theatrical performances, the inclusion of a lucky number among tickets distributed to workers before meetings, and street theater performances.[83] In his writings regarding safety posters, he pointed out that, in contrast to the positive and often humorous content of their Western counterparts, Soviet posters tended to depict blood, severed limbs, and other negatively emotive themes.[84]

At the height of the upheavals within the profession, Reitynbarg came under attack and duly engaged in self-criticism. Indiscriminately borrowing from American experience, he had failed to relate his work to Soviet circumstances. This was largely because he had not worked out any theoretical approach, but rather had unconsciously relied upon utilitarian and empiricist instincts.[85] Yet within a year, the effectiveness of signs hung in the lavatories of workers' clubs and the buffet of a workers' theater in Moscow could be measured in precise percentage terms of before and after, naturalistic posters in factories were being condemned for frightening newly recruited workers, and the theory that was being advanced seemed decidedly utilitarian.[86]

This is not to suggest that the professions had returned to the status quo ante. The scope of what could be published and, presumably, researched had been considerably narrowed, and public debate about the merits or weaknesses of different approaches had ceased. Nonetheless, something of a modus vivendi had been achieved. So long as they invoked (if only in preamble form) the classics of Marxism-Leninism—appropriately digested by the now-chastened authorities within the field—the specialists were able to pursue their specialized work. Psychological testing and vocational training methods and the rationalization of technical processes now came back into vogue.

But this arrangement did not last. As in the past, official faith in technics eventually gave way to a violent swing in the direction of voluntarism and an intolerance of technical experts. The termination of the journal *Sovetskaia psikhotekhnika* in 1934 and the closure of the psychotechnical Society the following year marked the beginning of a new onslaught on the professions that was more devastating and long lasting than the Cultural Revolution. This time, the challenge came not from zealots within the professions but from outstanding workers, known as Stakhanovites, whose production feats appeared to confirm political authorities' suspicions of the experts.

Stakhanovism, which emerged in the autumn of 1935, was to have immense significance for industrial hygienists and psychologists. It served to discredit all the old calculations about the productive capacity of workers and their machines (dubbed the theory of limits) and hence all those associated with their formulation. Not only did Stakhanovites smash the old technical and output norms but, after doing so, they testified to being less tired than previously.[87]

Separating fact from fiction in the accounts of Stakhanovites' records is not easy. It would appear that in many cases their achievements were not the result of the speedup of production processes, or sweating, but rather an increased division of labor or a more rational use of their tools. However, to replicate the rather special circumstances in which they set their records was beyond the capacity of management, notwithstanding pressure from above to do just that. The resultant gross disparities in output and wages between Stakhanovite and non-Stakhanovite workers and the herky-jerky pace of production exacerbated tensions throughout the industrial system, which fed into the Great Terror of 1936–38.

Some industrial hygienists and psychologists salvaged their careers (if not their self-esteem) by attesting that Stakhanovites had fewer accidents, produced a smaller proportion of defective goods, and suffered less fatigue than other workers.[88] Given that Stakhanovites generally were better equipped and serviced and had a higher standard of living, these claims could well have been true. But the empirical evidence provided was so slim as to preclude a definitive judgment.

We know from various sources that accidents involving Stakhanovites or occurring in the midst of so-called Stakhanovite days, and five- and ten-day periods were frequent. Both Kravchenko and Scott attributed accidents in their plants to overstrain of machines and workers.[89] Soviet officials had another explanation, namely sabotage. With rare exception, the only industrial accidents reported in the Soviet press from 1936 to 1938 were in connection with accusations against hapless engineers and managers, many of whom received the ultimate sentence or long prison terms.

The politicization of industrial accidents, coinciding with the virtual cessation of research into this and related phenomena and the closure of the institutes that had sustained such research, constitutes a terminal landmark for this chapter. In 1940, the Commissariat of Health published a large and well-illustrated textbook by Kaplun, which it recommended for use in the medical institutes of the USSR. The book was remarkable in a number of respects, not the least of which was its failure to even mention psychotechnics. Typical of its approach to topics that had been burning questions a decade earlier was the following statement: "In rare cases, fatigue among individual workers is still possible, but as a whole, the problem of fatigue as a mass, typical phenomenon in the contemporary stage of the construction of communism has already unquestionably been removed, since all possibilities for the maximal prevention of reduced work capacity and the breach of both urban and rural workers' health have been created.[90] Public acknowledgment that fatigue and other phenomena associated with accidents and disabilities had not disappeared would have to await the post-Stalin era.

The fates of those who had been active in the fields of industrial hygiene and psychology were varied. Shpilrein was arrested some time in the late 1930s and died not long thereafter; but his close associates, Gellershtein and Shpigel', were able to preside over a revival in the late 1950s and early 1960s of the field they had helped to pioneer. Kaplun continued to write propagandistic literature on Soviet achievements in occupational safety until his death in 1943. Meanwhile, Ermanskii, the ostracized ex-Menshevik, continued to lead a charmed existence. In 1940, not without difficulty, he managed to publish a study of Stakhanovism that was critical of the many distortions and excesses inspired by that movement. The book remains to this date the most interesting on the subject to have been published in the USSR.[91]

X

The foregoing suggests that during the formative decades of Soviet power, industrial accidents and disabilities became sufficiently sensitive matters that their investigation and prevention ultimately depended less on expertise than political savvy. While the most creative theoretical and empirical investigations into the causes of accidents and prophylactic measures against them were done during the NEP years, their immediate practical benefit was marginal, and no less importantly, their usefulness as a basis for mobilizing and training the masses was dubious. This apparent paradox was sufficient to heighten impatience among the younger, more party-minded members of the institutes. Whether inspired by the new tasks of socialist construction or eager to make a name for themselves, they went on the attack against the relatively narrow professionalism of their elders. At the same time, as industrial hygienists and psychologists immersed themselves in criticism and self-criticism, the rate of accidents soared and the incidence of fatigue among workers increased. By the end of the First Five-Year Plan, the worst appeared to be over. But what had happened was only a prelude to the traumatic events of 1936–38.

Viewed in comparative terms, the USSR appears to have avoided the pressures of market competitiveness and corporate profitability, which have been and remain major underlying causes of industrial accidents in both underdeveloped and advanced capitalist societies. Yet, it must be acknowledged that the forced pace of industrialization itself and the suppression of experimentation and statistical enquiry into the effects of that process meant that Soviet workers were no less at risk of becoming maimed, blinded, deafened, or otherwise disabled than their Western counterparts—and perhaps even more so.

NOTES

1. Karl Marx, *Kapital,* vol. 3 (Moscow: Progress Publ., 1959), p. 88.

2. See Bernhard J. Stern, *Medicine in Industry* (New York: Commonwealth Fund, 1946), pp. 17–32; Ludwig Teleky, *History of Factory and Mine Hygiene* (New York: Columbia University Press, 1948), pp. 48–74; Irma Ritternhouse, "Industrial Hygiene: Legislation and Reform," in *Encyclopaedia of the Social Sciences,* vol. 7 (New York: Macmillan, 1937), pp. 702–04.

3. Many of the deaths occurred because some of the doors of the burning building were locked. Speaking at a memorial service, an organizer active in the Women's Trade Union League noted: "This is not the first time girls have been burned alive in the city. Every week I must learn of the untimely death of one of my sister workers. Every year thousands are maimed. The life of men and women is so cheap and property is so sacred." Quoted in James R. Green, *The World of the Worker, Labor in Twentieth Century America* (New York: Hill and Wang, 1980), p. 75.

4. For discussions of these processes and their relationship to fatigue, see A. Mosso, *Fatigue* (New York: Putnam, 1904); F. B. Gilbreth and L. M. Gilbreth, *Fatigue Study* (New York: Sturgis and Walton, 1916); and Morris S. Viteles, *Industrial Psychology* (New York: Norton, 1932), pp. 438ff.

5. Psychotechnics may be taken as synonymous with applied psychology. Industrial work is thus only one of many spheres in which psychotechnical investigation has been conducted.

6. For example, the Berlin-based Institute of Industrial Hygiene and its journals, *Zentralblatt für Gewerbehygiene und Unfallverhutung* and *Schriften aus dem Gesamtegebiet der Gewerbehygiene,* both of which were founded in 1913; the U.S. National Safety Council (1913); the American Foundation of Occupational Health (1915); and the *Journal of Industrial Hygiene* (1919). International congresses on occupational diseases and the study of the medicine of accidents were held before the First World War in Milan (1905) and Brussels (1910). Teleky, *Factory and Mine Hygiene,* pp. 90–92, 176–77.

7. William Stern, coeditor of the *Zeitschrift für Angewandte Psychologie,* is credited with coining the term. Münsterberg, who served as director of Harvard's Psychological Laboratory, originally published his seminal work in German in 1912.

8. For a brief summary, see Viteles, *Industrial Psychology,* pp. 49–51.

9. Theodore von Laue, "Factory Inspection under the 'Witte System,' 1892–1903," *American Slavonic and East European Review* 19 (1960): 356. In 1894, there were a mere 143 inspectors. See also Frederick C. Griffin, "The 'First Russian Labor Code': The Law of June 3, 1886," *Russian History* 2 (1975): 83–100. The classic Russian study is A. A. Mikulin, *Fabrichnaia inspektsiia v Rossii, 1882–1906* (Kiev: Tip. S.V. Kul'zhenko, 1906). For a revealing personal account by the first chief inspector in Moscow, see I. Ianzhul, *Iz vospominanii i perepiski fabrichnogo inspektora* (St. Petersburg 1907).

10. In addition to Ianzhul, this would include E. M. Dement'ev, A. V. Pogozhev, V. V. Sviatoslavskii, and undoubtedly many others.

11. Von Laue, "Factory Inspection under the 'Witte System,' " pp. 359–60.

12. Indeed, many workers were seasonal, and therefore sought overtime as a means of supporting their families back in the village, to which they periodically returned. See Robert Eugene Johnson, *Peasant and Proletarian: The Working Class of Moscow in the Late Nineteenth Century* (New Brunswick: Princeton University Press, 1979), pp. 29–30, 35–40, 43–50.

13. See entry in *Bol'shaia sovetskaia entsiklopediia,* vol 64 (Moscow: Sovetskaia Entsiklopediia, 1933), p. 594.

14. For two different assessments of the debates, see V. Ia. Laverychev, *Tsarizm i rabochii vopros (1861–1917gg.)* (Moscow: Mysl', 1972), pp. 236–43; and Ruth Amende Roosa, "Workers' Insurance Legislation and the Role of Industrialists in the Period of the Third Duma," *Russian Review,* 34 (1975): 410–52.

15. L. S. Gaponenko, *Rabochii klass Rossii v 1917 godu* (Moscow: Nauka, 1970), p. 202.

16. *Vestnik narodnogo kommissariata truda* 2–3 (1918): 335–40; *Sobranie*

uzakoneniia i rasporiadeniia rabochikh i krestianskikh pravitel'stva (1918), cols. 36–47.

17. Margaret Dewar, *Labour Policy in the USSR* (London: RIIA, 1956), pp. 180, 187, 188; George M. Price, *Labor Protection in Soviet Russia* (New York: International Pub., 1928), pp. 86–93.

18. By 1920, there were an estimated 1.2 million industrial workers as compared with 2.6 million in 1917. Large-scale industrial production in 1921 was one-fifth of what it had been in 1913. See Alec Nove, *An Economic History of the USSR* (London: Allen Lane, 1969), pp. 66–68.

19. As late as 1924, the Ukraine had only forty-one health inspectors. *Gigiena truda* 1 (1924): 86.

20. The latter was named after B. A. Obukh, who had been a Bolshevik since 1902, served as one of Lenin's physicians after the Revolution, and was the founder and director of the institute that bore his name. See *Bol'shaia sovetskaia entsiklopediia*, 3d ed., vol. 18 (Moscow: Sov. Ents., 1970–78), pp. 233–34. This work is cited hereafter as *BSE*.

21. *BSE*, vol 11, p. 361.

22. Alice Hamilton, *Exploring the Dangerous Trades: The Autobiography of Alice Hamilton, M.D.* (Boston: Little, Brown, 1943), p. 332.

23. Quoted in K. E. Bailes, "Alexei Gastev and the Soviet Controversy over Taylorism, 1918–24," *Soviet Studies* 29 (1977): 384.

24. Ibid., p. 378. For these early controversies, see especially S. Leiberstein, "Technology, Work, and Sociology in the USSR: The NOT Movement," *Technology and Culture* 16 (1975): 48–55; Zenovia A. Sochor, "Soviet Taylorism Revisited," *Soviet Studies* 33 (1981): 246–64; Steven Smith, "Taylorism Rules OK? Bolshevism, Taylorism and the Technical Intelligentsia in the Soviet Union, 1917–41," *Radical Science Journal* 13 (1983): 3–27. For the now classical discussion of the many guises that Taylorism assumed in interwar Europe, see Charles S. Maier, "Between Taylorism and Technocracy: European Ideologies and the Vision of Industrial Productivity in the 1920s," *Journal of Contemporary History* 5 (1970): 27–61.

25. Quoted in Richard Schultz and Ross A. McFarland, "Industrial Psychology in the Soviet Union," *Journal of Applied Psychology,* 19 (1935): 266.

26. I. F. Engel', "Metody ucheta neschastnykh sluchaev i promyshlennyi travmatizm v SSSR," *Gigiena, bezopasnost' i patologiia truda* 11 (1929): 72. This work is referred to hereafter as GBPT.

27. F. Ritzmann, "German Accident Statistics, 1928–1930," *Industrial Safety Survey* (ILO) 8 (1932): 151.

28. N. I. Sinev and I. F. Engel', "Promyshlennyi travmatizm v SSSR," *GBPT* 3 (1929): 70.

29. Engel', "Metody ucheta," p. 72.

30. Ibid., p. 69.

31. See V. A. Beleliubskii, "Znachenie orientirovochnoi statistiki pri

izuchenii professional'nogo travmatizma," *GBPT* 10 (1929): 90, where mention is made of this fact with respect to statistics derived from social insurance offices.

32. B. M. Shkliar, M. S. Trakhtenberg, and N. D. Krol', "Dinamika razvitiia na metallurgicheskom zavode im. Petrovskogo v Dnepropetrovske za 1927, *Gigiena truda* 8 (1928): 68–79. The same reason might apply to workers with less than one year's *stazh*.

33. B. M. Shkliar, M. S. Trakhtenberg, and N. D. Krol', "Dinamika travmatizma na metallurgicheskom zavode im. Petrovskogo za 1926–1928," *GBPT* 12 (1929): 96–107.

34. V. N. Popovitskii, "Dinamika travmatizma na metallurgicheskom zavode 'Krasnyi Oktiabr,' " *GBPT* 9 (1929): 83–90; V. S. Ikriannikov, "Travmatizm na pogruzochno-razgruzochnykh rabotakh vo Vladivostoke," *Gigiena truda* 12 (1928): 79–87; A. V. Bronevskii, "Dinamika travmatizma na taganrogskom instrumental'no-mekhanicheskom zavode IuMTa i metody bor'by s nim," *GBPT* 4 (1929): 87–96; A. Plotnikov, "K voprosu ob izuchenii travmatizma v kamennougol'noi promyshlennosti," *Gigiena truda* 8 (1928): 87–90.

35. See extracts from S. G. Gellershtein's 1926 article "Psikhotekhnika" in *Informatsionnyi biulleten'*, 2 (17) seriia: *Iz istorii sovetskoi sotsiologii, psikhologiia truda* (Moscow: n.p., 1969), pp. 45–62; S. G. Gellershtein, "K voprosu o professional'noi tipologii," in *Istoriia sovetskoi psikhologii truda, teksti (20–30 gody XX veka)* (Moscow: MGU, 1983), pp. 118–27; I. N. Shpilrein, "Osnovye teoreticheskie problemy psikhotekhnicheskoi kharakteristiki professiia," in *Vsesoiuznaia konferentsiia po psikhofiziologii truda i professional'nomu podboru. Tezisy dokladov* (Moscow: Orgbiuro, 1927), pp. 64–74.

36. See, for example, S. Ia. Glezerov, "Professional'nyi travmatizm glaz na zavode 'Krasnoe Sormovo,' " *Gigiena truda* 2 (1928): 47–49; D. R. Balianskii, "K voprosu o bezopasnosti raboty na pressakh," *Gigiena truda* 2 (1928): 70–75; S. M. Stakhorskii, "Travmatizm v metallopromyshlennosti Ukrainy," *Gigiena truda* 6 (1928): 82.

37. V. A. Krukovskii, "Ob organizatsii tekhniki bezopasnosti v promyshlennosti predpriiatiiakh," *Gigiena truda* 9 (1928): 78–82.

38. Sinev and Engel', "Promyshlennyi travmatizm," p. 65.

39. B. M. Shkliar, "Promyshlennyi travmatizm i ego sviaz' s proizvoditel'nostiu truda i sverkhorochnymi rabotami," *GBPT* 8 (1929): 58–61. Kaplun dissociated the journal from the article's findings by claiming in an editorial note that "the author's data do not provide a basis for serious methodological or practical conclusions."

40. V. V. Isakov and Iu. N. Khalturina, *Izuchenie proizvoditel'nosti i utomliaemosti pri perekhode na tkatskikh fabrikakh s 2-kh na 3 stanka* (Ivanovo-Voznesensk: Osnova, 1928).

41. See E. H. Carr and R. W. Davies, *Foundations of a Planned Economy*, 3 vols. (Harmondsworth: Penguin, 1974–77), vol. 1, pp. 516–53; and for a Soviet view, A. P. Finarov, "Perevod promyshlennykh pred-

priiatii na 7-chasovoi rabochii den' v 1928–1932 gg.," *Istoriia SSSR* 6 (1959): 107–14.

42. Isakov and Khalturina, *Izuchenie proizvoditel'nosti*, p. 29. The statement appears in the section by Isakov.

43. N. Rozenbaum, Kh. Rivlina, E. Belorets, and L. Seletskaia, "Vliianiia intensifikatsii truda na utomliaemost' tkachei," *Gigiena truda* 8 (1928): 15; N. E. Akim, "Okhrana truda na tekstil'nykh fabrikakh moskovskoi gubernii s semichasovym rabochim dnem," *GBPT* 5 (1929): 98; and the circular dated 9, May 1929 reprinted in *GBPT* 9 (1929): 117.

44. O. A. Ermanskii, *Teoriia i praktika ratsionalizatsii*, 5th rev. ed. (Moscow-Leningrad: NKTP, 1933), pp. 117–18. Earlier editions were not available to me, but see the review of the first edition in *GBPT* 1 (1929): 141–43.

45. O. A. Ermanskii, "Opasnost'," *Komsomol'skaia pravda*, 17 Mar. 1927.

46. E. M. Kogan et al., "Opyt sravnitel'nogo izucheniia ruchnoi i konveirernoi raboty," *Gigiena truda* 8 (1928): 17, 22.

47. *Psikhofiziologiia truda i psikhotekhnika*, vyp. 1 (1928), p. 67.

48. Schultz and McFarland, "Industrial Psychology," pp. 284–95; I. N. Shpilrein, "O trudovom metode v professiografii," *Gigiena truda* 10 (1927): 68–71; and extracts from Shpilrein, "Chto takoe 'Trudovoi metod'?" in *Informatsionnyi biulleten'*, pp. 63–72.

49. Glezerov, "Professional'nyi travmatizm glaz," p. 47.

50. "Obzor russkoi literatury po voprosam travmatizma i gigieny glaza," *GBPT* 6 (1930): 115; *GBPT* 10–11 (1931): 161.

51. "Obzor russkoi literatury po professional'nym zabolevaniiam ukha, nosa i gorla," *GBPT* 2 (1929): 128–129.

52. A. V. Petrovskii, *Istoriia sovetskoi psikhologii, formirovanie osnov psikhologicheskoi nauki* (Moscow: Prosveshchenie, 1967), p. 269.

53. B. L. Markus, "Piatiletnyi plan ozdorovleniia uslovii truda v RSFSR," *Gigiena truda* 11 (1928): 97.

54. *GBPT* 1 (1930): 104; *GBPT* 2 (1930): 119.

55. *XVII Konferentsiia VKP(b), stenograficheskii otchet* (Moscow: Partizd., 1932), p. 113.

56. G. I. Lifshits, "Statistika proftravmatizma na sovremennom etape (v poriadke samokritiki)," *GBPT* 12 (1931): 22.

57. This metaphor is borrowed from Carr's "Preface" to Carr and Davies, *Foundations*, p. vi.

58. I. A. Kraval', ed., "Tsentral'noe upravlenie narodnogo khoziaistvennogo ucheta," *Zdorov'e i zdravookhranenie trudiashchikhsia SSSR, statisticheskii sbornik* (Moscow: TsuNKhU, 1936), p. 25.

59. *Profsoiuzy SSSR*, 7 (1938): 59; V. I. Prokhorov, "Profsoiuzy i voprosy truda," in G. A. Prudenskii, ed., *Voprosy truda v SSSR* (Moscow: Gospollit., 1958), p. 151.

60. Sheila Fitzpatrick, "Cultural Revolution as Class War," in S. Fitz-

patrick, ed., _Cultural Revolution in Russia, 1928–1931_ (Bloomington: Indiana University Press, 1978), p. 28.

61. David Joravsky, "The Stalinist Mentality and the Higher Learning," _Slavic Review_ 42 (1983): 586.

62. The reader is reminded that, just as industrial hygiene was a subspecialty within the field of social hygiene, so industrial psychology was merely one of many applications of psychology.

63. N. F. Kurmanov, "Idealizm v psikhotekhnike rekonstruktsionnogo perioda i otsutstvie rekonstruktsii v psikhotekhnike," _Psikhologiia_ 3 (1930): 385–408. Shpilrein indeed had been an early champion of Stern's personalist approach.

64. I. N. Shpilrein, "Mekhanicheskaia bor'ba za rekonstruktsiiu psikhotekhniki," _Psikhologiia_ 3 (1930): 409–19.

65. I. N. Shpilrein, "Chto takoe utomlenie?" _Psikhotekhnika i psikhofiziologiia truda_ 1 (1931): 67–75. This journal is referred to hereafter as _PPT_.

66. Ibid., pp. 70.

67. "Diskusiia," ibid., 75–76.

68. See L. H. Siegelbaum, "Soviet Norm Determination in Theory and Practice, 1917–1941," _Soviet Studies_, 36 (1984): 54.

69. S. R. Dikhter, "Ob organizatsii nauchno-issledovatel'skoi raboty v oblasty organizatsii i ozdorovleniia truda v period sotsialisticheskoi rekonstruksii," _GBPT_ 11 (1930): 48–50.

70. V. Stroganov, "K voprosam organizatsii nauchnoi raboty v oblasti gigieny i patologii truda," _GBPT_ 11 (1930): 52.

71. Both were attacked (along with Kaplun) in "Za partiinost' v nauke po gigiene i fiziologii truda," _Pravda_, 16 June 1931. For Kaplun's review, see _GBPT_ 4–5 (1931): 147–53.

72. _Pravda_, 20 June 1931; S. I. Kaplun, "Za razoblachenie sobstvennykh oshibok v poriadke samokritiki," _GBPT_ 8–9 (1931): 3–22; and his "Reorganizatsiia IOT kak realizatsiia itogov diskusii na fronte gigieny i fiziologii truda," _GBPT_ 12 (1931): 3–18.

73. On the struggle between the Bolshevizers, led by Mitin, and the Deborinite dialecticians, see David Joravsky, _Soviet Marxism and Natural Science, 1917–1932_ (New York: Columbia University Press, 1961), pp. 250–71.

74. Ibid., p. 261. For the resolutions, see _PPT_ 4–6 (1931): 374–80.

75. Petrovskii, _Istoriia sovetskoi psikhologii_, p. 273. See also T. L. Kogan, "K VII mezhdunarodnoi psikhotekhnicheskoi konferentsii," _Psikhologiia_ 5 (1931): 161–69.

76. See the comment by Iu. O. Shpigel' that "in connection with the political tasks which stood before us at the conference, we sought to criticize bourgeois authorities rather than engaging in self-criticism." _Sovetskaia psikhotekhnika_ 5–6 (1932): 47.

77. K. Pauker, "Obezopasit' put' avto i peshekhoda," _Pravda_, 13 Dec. 1931.

78. _Sovetskaia psikhotekhnika_ 5–6 (1932): 420–28.

79. Joravsky, "The Stalinist Mentality," pp. 591–92.

80. Fitzpatrick, "Cultural Revolution as Class War," pp. 31–32.

81. See for example, Morris S. Schulzinger, *The Accident Syndrome* (Springfield, Ill.: Charles C. Thomas, 1956); W. Ryan, *Blaming the Victim* (New York: Vintage, 1971); and D. Berman, "Why Work Kills," in Vincent Navarro and Daniel Berman, eds., *Health and Work under Capitalism: An International Perspective,* (Farmingdale, N.Y.: Baywood, 1983), pp. 168–92.

82. *Rabochie o nepreryvnom potoke: Vtoraia moskovskaia konferentsiia rabochikh s predpriiatii vvedshikh nepreryvnyi potok* (Moscow: Tekhnika upravleniia, 1931), pp. 34–35, 49–51.

83. D. I. Reitynbarg, *Sotsialisticheskoe sorenovanie na snizhenie neschastnykh sluchaev v proizvodstve* (Moscow: Gostrudizd., 1930).

84. D. I. Reitynbarg, *Plakat po bezopasnosti truda v SSSR i za granitsei* (Moscow: OGIZ, 1931).

85. E. A. Rakhmel', "K itogam I Vsesoiuznogo s'ezda psikhotekhniki i psikhofiziologii truda," *Psikhologiia* 5 (1931): 175; D. I. Reitynbarg, "Plakat po bezopasnosti truda na novom etape," *Sovetskaia psikhotekhnika* 4 (1932): 269–78.

86. M. D. Karnaukhov, "K voprosu ob izuchenii effektivnosti plakata," *Sovetskaia psikhotekhnika* 4 (1932): 289–300; V. V. Reutov, "Ob ustrashaiushchikh plakatakh i novykh kadrakh-rabochikh," *Sovetskaia psikhotekhnika* 5–6 (1932): 397–98.

87. See *Labour in the Land of Socialism: Stakhanovites in Conference* (Moscow: Co-op, Pub. Soc. of Foreign Workers, 1936), pp. 147, 222–23; and B. L. Markus, "The Stakhanov Movement and the Increased Productivity of Labour in the USSR," *International Labour Review* 34 (1936): 23–25. For a recent interpretation of Stakhanovism, see Lewis H. Siegelbaum, *Stakhanovism and the Politics of Productivity, 1935–1941* (Cambridge: Cambridge University Press, 1988).

88. S. I. Kaplun, "Zdorovyi i zhizneradostnyi trud," *Pravda,* 19 Dec. 1935; S. S. Val'iazhnikov and A. A. Alekseev, "Sistema propagandy bezopasnosti (opyt raboty na I GPZ im. L.M. Kaganovicha)," and V. M. Davidovich, K. M. Karaul'nik, Kh. O. Rivlina, and Iu. O. Shpigel', "Psikhotekhnika v dele perenosa stakhanovskogo opyta," in VTsSPS, Vsesoiuznyi nauchnoissledovatel'skii institut okhrana truda, *Tezisy dokladov nauchnoi sessii, 14–19 aprelia 1936 g.* (Moscow: Profizd., 1936), pp. 34, 108–113.

89. Viktor Kravchenko, *I Chose Freedom* (New York: Scribners', 1946), pp. 187–91, 193–94; John Scott, *Behind the Urals* (Bloomington: Indiana University Press, 1973, reprint of 1942 ed.), pp. 163–68.

90. S. I. Kaplun, *Obshchaia gigiena truda* (Moscow-Leningrad: Narkomzdrav, 1940), p. 75. See also p. 45.

91. O. A. Ermanskii, *Stakhanovskoe dvizhenie i stakhanovskie metody* (Moscow: Sotsekgiz, 1940). See especially the note from the publisher and the introduction.

The Stalinist Mentality and
The Treatment of Schizophrenia

David Joravsky

I

PSYCHIATRY IS a hybrid discipline or a chimera: a physician's face on a body of psychological tissues, with the muscled limbs and claws of political dominion. In plain terms, psychiatrists claim the technical know-how of medicine, while working mainly with psychological doctrines, and modern governments have licensed them to treat the mentally ill, a precedure that runs together the functions of physician, moral counsellor, and jailer.

In this field, as in so many others, the political leaders and the scientific professionals of the USSR have followed modern trends, with peculiarly Soviet twists and turns. Fascination with the divergences should not distract us from the opportunity to see in the mirror of Soviet history reflections of our own responses to madness. Authoritarian pragmatism seems an unavoidable response to the insane in any modern society.

Of course, the contrasts are what first catch the eye. In countries with strong constitutional traditions psychiatrists have been notoriously self-assertive and fractious, and significant legal restrictions have recently been placed upon their power to treat patients without consent.[1] In the Soviet Union—before the Gorbachev reforms—the profession still enjoyed almost unrestricted autonomy in its power to treat patients, yet Soviet psychiatrists displayed very little self-assertiveness or fractious spirit. For more than thirty years they quietly accepted subjugation to a school of "clinical dogmatists" headed by Dr. A. V. Snezhnevskii (1904–87).[2] The contrast is not only with the quarrelsome psychiatrists in the West, but also with the stiff-necked natural scientists in the Soviet Union. Geneticists showed far more resistance to Lysenko's rule, at the height of mass terror in the thirties and forties, than Soviet psychiatrists have shown to Snezhnevskii's despotism through the post-Stalin decades of comparatively liberal politics.

This pitiable surrender to the Stalinist mentality is the subject of the following pages. I will argue that the surrender did not spring directly from political interference in the profession. From the 1920s to the late 1940s political power did repeatedly intrude in Soviet psychiatry, sometimes violently, but the profession kept a fundamentally liberal attitude toward conflicting doctrines—until the 1950s, when liberalism was suppressed from within. Of course, repeated capitulations to political interventions in the preceding decades disarmed the profession's commitment to liberalism. But the disarmament was slow and insidious rather than overt. It was fostered not only by the political culture of Stalinism but also by the intractable nature of insanity and the consequent dilemmas of the profession.

II

In the immediate aftermath of the 1917 Revolution, the new regime extended naive trust to a psychiatric profession that conceived itself as a liberal community of medical specialists with a mission to protect the mentally ill from the larger society, which mistreated them. In the prerevolutionary period such psychiatrists had demanded a great increase in the number of insane asylums, for they perceived incarceration as an act of protective healing, not a show of fearful power. They were therefore intensely indignant when police asked them to judge the sanity of shackled criminals. The shackles must be removed, a congress of psychiatrists heatedly and unanimously demanded in 1909.[3] With such a gross symbol of state power removed, the reality could be ignored; momentarily out of shackles, the criminal would be a patient long enough for the psychiatrists to decide whether to recommend the jail or the madhouse.

The eagerness to distance the psychiatrist's role from the policeman's, if only by symbolic rituals, precipitated the first intervention of the Communist regime in the psychiatric profession. At the newly founded Serbskii Institute for Forensic Medicine in the early twenties, specialists routinely judged criminals to be *nevmeniaemye* (not chargeable)—in need of treatment rather than punishment. On a theoretical level such findings were consciously linked with the naturalistic belief that criminal responsibility is a dubious concept, since human behavior is determined by our particular heredities and environmental histories. On a political level such findings were linked with liberal disapproval of the Soviet regime that would try and punish "chargeable" criminals.

Very soon the political authorities grew angry. In their view, liberal psychiatrists were coddling criminals under the pretense of treating sick people. In the midtwenties and early thirties, virtually the entire staff of the Servskii Institute was dismissed. The new staff was politically sympathetic to the Soviet regime and therefore willing to put very sharp limits on findings of *nevmeniaemost'*, unchargeability. Only the most extreme cases of insanity were to be given such exculpation; the rest were to be turned over to the judicial system for punishment. By the early thirties Cecilia Feinberg (1885–1973), the new director of the Serbskii Institute, was boasting that the percentage of psychopaths found to be unchargeable had dropped from 46.5 percent in 1922 to 6.4 percent in 1930.[4] This percentage has remained low ever since, for the authorities' vindictive view of criminals and their indignation at psychiatric exculpation have persisted.[5]

That first political intervention in psychiatry was a fairly minor infraction of professional autonomy. Then as now few psychiatrists were forensic specialists, and few mental patients were involved in criminal charges. The overwhelming majority of psychiatrists and of patients related to each other with very little external regulation by courts or bureaucracy. There was very little feeling among psychiatrists of any need to worry about the lack of regulation.

In the midtwenties, shortly after the forensic psychiatrists bowed to the judicial authorities' vindictive view of criminal behavior, the rest of the profession made a more drastic concession. It surrendered Freud, on the insistence of the ideological bureaucracy.[6] The surrender was eased by a distinction between Freud's teaching as a general ideology, which was utterly condemned, and his teaching as a therapeutic doctrine, which was tolerated until the late forties.[7] Of course, the distinction between ideology and therapy was hard to maintain, and Freudians of any kind were increasingly subdued in the thirties and early forties. But that throttling of psychoanalysis seemed to be of little consequence to the profession as a whole, since Freud had relatively few disciples among Russian psychiatrists. In that respect, as in many others, they resembled the German center of the profession, which was cool to psychoanalysis, rather than the new center developing in America with a heavy Freudian influence.[8]

A far more serious assault on professional autonomy was mounted between 1929 and 1932, during Stalin's "revolution from above." Now the very principle of professional autonomy was rejected in favor of *partiinost'*, the party principle. For psychiatrists, as for all other specialists, there were violent changes in the leading cadres, as professional organizations and publications were subjected to loudly proclaimed control by the Party's Central Committee. But only a few substantive issues were explicitly involved in those upheavals. For example, some of the old leaders were denounced for their occasional talk of mass exhaustion and neuroses among the overstrained builders of socialism. "Psychohygiene" in general, the Soviet version of the mental health movement, was virtually suppressed.[9] The hastily promoted builders of socialism (*vydvizhentsy*) wanted no experts fussing over their mental health. For them,—as for many hand-driving positive thinkers in America,—minds are healthy if we work hard and don't worry about them.

Once again, as in the ban on Freudianism, only marginal concerns of Soviet psychiatrists were at stake. Their overriding concern had all along been psychoses and neuropathology, not neuroses and psychotherapy, as one would reasonably expect of a very small profession in a very large and backward country. (In 1916 there were 350 psychiatrists in the Russian Empire; in 1932 the Soviet Commissar of Health reported 538, plus 743 neuropathologists.)[10] In spite of all the Communist denunciation of "bourgeois" psychiatrists in 1929–32, their competence to deal with severe derangement and neuropathology was never challenged. The intellectual autonomy of the profession was largely preserved in fact, though vehemently denied in principle, during Stalin's revolution from above.

The first political intervention in substantive issues of major concern came in the midthirties, with a campaign to narrow the concept of schizophrenia. *Partiinost'*, the party principle, had been conceded, so no one could openly resist the campaign. Yet the immediate result was a heightening, not a lowering, of the profession's effort to be rigorously scientific. To understand that paradox, a purely technical comparison of narrow and broad concepts of schizophrenia is not enough. One needs to see the intertwined problems that schizophrenia presented to psychiatrists, to public health officials, and to the supreme political bosses, who were intent on building heavy industry rather than mental hospitals, not to speak of mental health clinics (or psychohygiene dispensaries, in the Soviet lingo of the time).

Schizophrenia is the most common of the most extreme mental disorders.[11] It is *not* a split personality on the model of Jekyll and Hyde, as many people imagine. Schizophrenia is a label for severe disruptions of mental functions, with such alarming symptoms as fearful delusions, hallucinations, and senseless speech, and a consequent inability to be a normally functioning member of society. Such disorders may begin insidiously, in the absence of unusual external stress. From within, a person may feel a mounting sense of worthlessness, an irresistible urge toward increasing isolation, and may begin to offer delusions by way of explanation, such as an unbearable stench driving others away from oneself, or terrible voices that others cannot hear. The experienced clinician may sense, without being able to prove, that a cumulative disintegration of mental functions is beginning. Thus the psychiatrist may feel impelled to intervene with some vigorous, not to say violent, empiric remedy, such as sulfur injections or insulin coma in the thirties, prolonged drugged sleep or electric shock in the forties and fifties, or heavy doses of major tranquilizers since the sixties.

Such forceful interventions are justified by the clinicians' interlocking circle of intuitions, actions, inferences, and convictions. If an empiric remedy fails to halt the disintegration of the mind, the diagnosis is confirmed: schizophrenia is an irreversible endogenous disease of unknown etiology. Some other empiric remedy needs to be tried in the place of the one that failed. If the disintegration of the mind is halted, the diagnosis of an irreversible process still stands: the empiric remedy has merely put the disease in remission. In short, severe mental disorder puts the psychiatrist under pressure not only to act with insufficient knowledge but also to repress awareness of such ignorance, to become a "clinical dogmatist." In this respect the clinical psychiatrist resembles other practical authorities who feel duty bound, like the ideal psychiatrist in Snezhnevskii's textbook, to "reconstruct the patient's entire way of life, his entire system of values. . . . The goal is the arrangement of his destiny [*ustroistvo ego sud'by*]."[12] Like policemen and military officers, or teachers and parents, psychiatrists are constantly drawn toward the intuitive self-assurance that is essential to action, and thus toward repression of the question whether they can reasonably justify what they feel compelled to do. The Stalinist mentality is an extreme example of the type, a species of violent insistence that *praktiki,* men of practice, must be right if they are to act on other people, and conversely, that such action proves them to be right.

The natural affinity between Soviet political *praktiki* and "clinical dogmatists" in psychiatry was only fleetingly glimpsed in the thirties. Young Dr. Snezhnevskii, in a 1933 report of chaos overcome in a terribly overcrowded provincial mental hospital, used the characteristic political language of the time. The work had been stormy, the struggle intense. On orders from local party organs, the old staff had been driven out, replaced by Snezhnevskii's team, which had raised bed turnover from one to three per year and depressed the death rate from 10 percent to 2 percent. The characteristic bluster of the time was in those percentages, unsupported by tables of absolute numbers. But—or maybe therefore; Stalinist bluster may have been essential to Stalinist achievement—Dr. Snezhnevskii probably did improve the hospital, if only by moving some patients out to the empty houses of transported *kulaks* and by imposing orderly procedures of hygiene and organized activities.[13]

Concerning psychiatric theories Snezhnevskii had little to say in 1933, but that little was revealing. His practical success proved that "psychiatry was transformed into a science, capable of curing, and of curing far from poorly." He stressed organized "work therapy and cultural therapy," rather than the physiological remedies that would later become an obsession with him, but the obsessive frame of mind was already apparent. Indeed, young Snezhnevskii rediscovered a basic conviction that Pinel and Tuke, the founding fathers of modern psychiatry, had bequeathed to the profession. Science and morality are fused in the personal authority of the psychiatrist: "Work therapy and cultural therapy do not in the slightest exclude, but on the contrary they presuppose the personal individual influence of the doctor's personality on the patient and on his manifestations of illness. The authority of the personality [*avtoritet lichnosti*] of the doctor giving the treatment, and his educative influence both in work therapy and in culture therapy, are decisive."[14]

Foucault and Szasz would no doubt seize upon that declaration as an admission of the authoritarianism that they angrily charge against modern psychiatry.[15] In their polemical passion they ignore the self-corrective liberalism of the profession as a whole, its collective self-questioning, embodied in the toleration of competing schools and doctrines, or teachings (*ucheniia*). In the thirties the Soviet profession was still committed to that liberalism in spite of such portents as the suppression of Freudianism and the acceptance of *partiinost'*. The affinity that a retrospective observer can perceive between the authoritarian pragmatism of the political bosses and the authoritarian pragmatism of clinical psychiatrists was obscured at the time by the bosses' hostility to "bourgeois specialists," who were still the bulk of the profession. Moreover, a crisis of over-crowding in mental hospitals was generating a campaign to make psychiatrists be less free with diagnoses of schizophrenia, the disease—or the disease label—that generates more long-term patients than any other. Thus the political intervention of the midthirties went against clinical dogmatists, in favor of those psychiatrists who demand rigorous self-questioning in diagnosis and incarceration.

Previously, in the twenties, there had been a drive for dispensarization—or deinstitutionalization, as an analagous campaign would be called in the West—without much impact on theories of schizophrenia. At that time the profession could still dream of a great increase in dispensaries—or outpatient clinics, as we would say. Thus self-assurance in pinning the schizophrenic label on patients was not perceived as a threat to overburden the hospital system. Dr. L. M. Rozenshtein (1884–1934), the chief advocate of dispensarization, argued that the population was full of incipient, or mild, schizophrenics, who needed outpatient care, not incarceration. His concept of the disease was broad—perhaps sloppy is the better term—reaching out for millions of new patients.[16] But his scheme of outpatient treatment seemed socially manageable, while political leaders and economists were still indulging in dreams of socialist planning generating a great leap forward on all fronts at once, in the health and welfare of the present generation no less than the industrial base for the future. Rozenshtein's opponents criticized "mild schizophrenia" as a contradiction in terms, but the controversy was relatively sedate, for it was apolitical or purely scientific—until the midthirties, when Rozenshtein's concept of schizophrenia was retrospectively, and unfairly, blamed for the acute crisis that had overwhelmed psychiatric care during Stalin's revolution from above.[17]

In June 1932 Soviet psychiatrists were not yet ready for such a mixture of science and politics. They held a major conference on schizophrenia, the last one, as things turned out, that indulged in a free contest of "teachings" on the subject. No official line had been

established in advance. Rozenshtein presented a paper defending
his broad concept of the disease. O. V. Kerbikov (1907–65) argued
for a different but equally broad concept. Other participants coun-
tered with arguments for narrower concepts, and more rigorous
methods of diagnosis. The participants criticized each other keenly
but politely, ignoring the social crisis that had put their courteous
debate in jeopardy.[18] Forced collectivization and rapid urbanization, with every possible ruble being squeezed into heavy industry,
were blasting the dream of dispensarization, while creating havoc
in the old-fashioned practice of incarcerating schizophrenics for
long periods. Mental hospitals were being flooded with new patients, and psychiatrists were responding in the usual style of
learned specialists: they were holding a conference, politely debat-
ing their divergent concepts of diagnosis and treatment.

Experts argue whether hereditary vulnerability to schizophrenia pulls individuals down into the urban lower classes or whether
the shattering experiences of the urban lower classes precipitate
schizophrenia. Both causal factors may be at work. In any case, the
correlation is beyond dispute. "Schizophrenia is common in all
races and cultures . . . and is commonest in the lower socioeconomic groups in dilapidated areas of large cities."[19] Stalin's
revolution from above caused a huge increase in such groups
down below, while the number of psychiatrists and hospital beds
for mental cases probably declined. Reliable statistics are lacking,
but official comments make it certain that, even if beds and personnel increased slightly, they were grossly inadequate to a huge increase in need.[20]

The characteristic response of Stalinist officials was to rebuff
pleas for increased funding of psychiatric facilities and staff.[21] Instead they stressed the need for administrators like Dr. Snezhnevskii, who imposed order on overcrowded hospitals without requiring large amounts of extra funds. At the same time public health
officials scolded psychiatrists who intensified overcrowding by
facile diagnoses of schizophrenia. Such official scolding had the
eager support of those psychiatrists who had all along deplored
broad, sloppy concepts of schizophrenia. Indeed, one such psychiatrist may have precipitated the midthirties campaign for narrowing the concept; he blamed broad concepts for the political misuse
of psychiatry. Dr. V. P. Osipov (1871–1947), dean of the Leningrad school of psychiatry, in 1935 published a shocking account of
bold young army officers who had been certified as schizophrenic
for criticizing their superiors.[22]

At a major psychiatric conference in 1936 the Stalinist mode of discourse was clearly in evidence. No speaker questioned the demand for narrowing the concept of schizophrenia or challenged Osipov's keynote speech in any way. In place of collective self-criticism, as we may call the liberal habit of open debate among conflicting views, the conference witnessed scapegoat self-criticism, the lurid Stalinist ritual of public confession by errant individuals, including ex post facto sinners, who had strayed from the official line before it was laid down. Most notably, O. V. Kerbikov contritely apologized in 1936 for a paper he had presented to the 1932 conference. He had argued that psychiatrists must be intuitively bold in thought and action, that they must learn to recognize "schizophrenia without schizophrenic symptoms," if they want to stop the disintegration of the mind before the insidious process becomes irreversible. At the 1936 conference he repudiated the argument, and promised to support a narrow view.[23] By such humiliating rituals the Stalinist system pushed psychiatrists toward greater scientific rigor, toward more scrupulous self-doubt when placing the dread label of schizophrenia on disordered minds. Or so it seemed in the midthirties.

III

Seemed—that must be stressed, for dissembling is the natural result of enforced belief. Kerbikov did not really change his mind. Like many other participants in Soviet rituals of the Stalinist type, he put on a mask. In the fifties, when another political intervention reversed the field of force in psychiatry, Kerbikov took off his mask and demanded self-criticism from skeptical critics of broad concepts. In short, he resumed his argument of 1932: timid hesitation to diagnose schizophrenia until mental disintegration is far advanced misses the critical period of insidious onset, when vigorous intervention with shock therapy or drugged sleep might still arrest the disease process.[24]

That sudden reversal in the field of political force, like so many others in Soviet intellectual history, was absurdly irrelevant in origin. The political intervention that permitted Kerbikov to drop the pretense of submission had no connection with the scientific issues of the dispute over schizophrenia, nor even with such relevant social circumstances as overcrowding in mental hospitals. At first patriotism was the only issue. Drs. Snezhnevskii and Kerbikov won power over the psychiatric profession as a part of the anticosmopolitan drive in the late forties. Russian chauvinism raised them to power, which they then proceeded to use autonomously, on behalf of their clinical dogmatism.

As victory over the Germans was turning into conflict with the United States and its allies, A. A. Zhdanov, Stalin's chief lieutenant on the cultural front, launched Russian chauvinist campaigns on all sectors. In psychiatry the climactic media event was a "Pavlov session" in 1951, which was managed by a team of previously obscure men headed by Snezhnevskii, with Kerbikov as the chief theorist. At the time they seemed distinguishable only by their anticosmopolitan abuse of the leaders they were replacing, with emphasis on the Jewish names among them: "As a result of the activity of some psychiatrists with cosmopolitan moods (Professors Shmar'ian, Gurevich, Sereiskii, Edel'shtein), the materialist ideas, the independent originality of our fatherland's psychiatry, have been willfully suppressed."[25] Limitless devotion to Russia's native traditions, Snezhnevskii insisted, must be proved by disdain for Western authorities and by oaths of allegiance to Pavlov's teaching.

We may give Snezhnevskii credit for hypocrisy in mouthing such rhetoric. Before 1948 he had shown no signs of Russian chauvinism. In two modest articles, which were his complete scholarly oeuvre before his rise to power, he had shown the usual reverence for German authorities and had paid special tribute to some of the Jewish teachers and supervisors whom he began to denounce after 1948.[26] We can date the precise year in which he changed from subordinate respect to the self-righteous anger of the "pushed-up person," for 1948 was when the ideological bureaucracy attached him to a commission of distinguished psychiatrists who were preparing a new classification of mental illnesses—or diagnostic manual, as the comparable bible of the profession is called in the United States. Snezhnevskii was sent in with the specific mission of combating cosmopolitanism.[27] He gave only a little lip service to Lysenko, the most exalted god of nativist science at the moment. Belief in diathesis, a hereditary predisposition to mental illness, was and remained basic to Snezhnevskii's clinical outlook.[28] He preferred to join the crusade for Pavlov's teaching, which he had previously ignored, as had the overwhelming majority of Soviet psychiatrists.

This is how Snezhnevskii emerged into the limelight in 1951, as the man in charge of the psychiatrists' "Pavlov Session," calling the profession back to their native teacher, away from the habit of "grovelling" before Western authorities.[29] He compounded the absurdity of the "Pavlov Session" by denouncing one of the very few psychiatrists who had previously shown a serious interest in Pavlov's views on schizophrenia. A. S. Chistovich was that nearly unique person; he had presented patients during Pavlov's visits to a mental hospital and had analyzed Pavlov's speculations in a 1949 article.[30] Snezhnevskii attacked the article for "nosological agnosticism," foreshadowing the campaign he would mount after 1951, as he pressed his clinical dogmatism on the profession—in the guise of "Pavlov's teaching."[31] Chistovich put on a little self-criticism at the 1951 session, but afterward became one of the few hardy souls who offered open resistance to Snezhnevskii.[32]

We may credit Snezhnevskii with hypocrisy in the nativist campaign not only because he joined it late but because he quit it early. Within a few years after 1951, as the post-Stalin political leadership reopened Russia's respectful window to the West, Snezhnevskii's school hastened to stop embarrassing displays of chauvinism. They even dropped Pavlov, except for ceremonial occasions. Pavlov's celebrated teaching had served as a ladder, quickly climbed, soon pushed away. The teacher they most imitated in actual clinical thought—and soon restored to reverence on ceremonial occasions—was Emil Kraepelin (1856–1926), the German founder of the nosological school.[33] To understand the Stalinist version of the school, which Snezhnevskii articulated after he won power over the Soviet profession, one must appreciate the tensions within psychiatric nosology, which do constantly threaten agnosticism, anarchy, and nihilism, as Snezhnevskii repeatedly warned.

Nosology is the classification of diseases. Kraepelin's school, whether in Germany or Russia or the United States—it is indeed cosmopolitan—centers its faith on the power of clinicians to impose taxonomic order on the enormously variable symptoms that mental patients present, to perceive patterns of development or disease processes, which may be classified as disease entities. Dementia praecox was Kraepelin's orginal name for schizophrenia, and a more revealing one too. It is the endogenous dementia that appears precociously, that is, the mental disorder that emerges within young people who have no apparent lesions in their nervous systems, as opposed to senile dementia, which emerges within aging nervous systems.

Kraepelin admitted that the concept of dementia praecox or schizophrenia is a taxonomic *Riesentopf* or giant pot; *wastebasket* is the harsher metaphor of a recent American psychiatrist.[34] Into this concept the nosologist throws diverse symptoms that perhaps should be classified separately and perhaps should not be linked to one particular disease entity any more than fever or fainting or nausea. In other words, the concept of schizophrenia bundles together phenomenal symptoms that should perhaps be considered separately, and ties the bundle to a noumenal reality that is still unproved and may be unprovable. Those viciously circular weaknesses—lumping varied symptoms of mental disorder on the unproved assumption that they jointly evince an underlying process of one particular disease entity—have been the focus of skeptical attack for nearly a century.

In a normally functioning community of psychiatrists the tension between skeptics and believers defines the community. (Of course, many particular versions of this tension are constantly in evidence; I am here offering a schematic outline.) Skeptics note the incongruities that result from a crazy quilt of success and failure in the reduction of mental disorders to physical causes. A patient's delusions and hallucinations may be ascribed to infections, such as malaria or syphilis; or to poisoning, as in alchoholism; or to vitamin deficiency, as in pellagra. But when physical causes are unknown, delusions and hallucinations are ascribed to a mysterious disease process called schizophrenia. Symptoms are hypostatized, transformed from evidence into the thing evinced, the substance or essence of a disease entity. Thus the skeptics. Believers oppose such subversion by appeal to analogies of another kind: somatic processes such as cancer or essential hypertension, which are recognized as disease entities though the etiologies are unknown. Note especially that quaint use of "essential," which equates the evidence with the thing evinced. The symptom, high blood pressure, is declared the essence of the disease—until it may be reduced to some other physical phenomenon. Mental causes are generally assumed to be of secondary importance.

The implicit metaphysics of the profession—medical materialism, in William James's plain speech—is rarely confronted as an issue that requires discussion. The explicit faith of nosological believers is in clinical experience, as epitomized in case histories. They are the physician's equivalent of the exemplary stories that politicians, novelists, and historians draw from *their* experience. Such examples are intended to embody universal truths that may be disgraced if separated from concrete evidence and presented as abstract formulas. Kerbikov crossed the line when he talked of recognizing "schizophrenia without schizophrenic symptoms."[35] So too do psychiatrists who support a diagnosis with the remark:

"This case has the smell of schizophrenia."[36] Clinicians are expected to use such intuitive flair (from the French for smell: compare Russian *chut'e* and German *Spürsinn*), but they may not simply point to the nose in proof. They must tell stories that evoke the persuasive odor in the collective olfactory apparatus of their experienced audience.

In the twenties the German psychiatrist Kurt Schneider (1887–1967) started a movement toward systematic restraint of subjectivity and imprecision in the diagnosis of schizophrenia.[37] This rigorously self-questioning movement significantly limited the incidence of schizophrenic diagnoses in Europe, as contrasted with the United States, where the heavy influence of "psychodynamic" thought expanded the role of subjectivity in psychiatric practice. The Soviet branch of the profession moved through a great zig-zag. In the thirties, as the reader has seen, political pressure reinforced the self-questioning influence of the Germans. In 1935 the official *Soviet Medical Encyclopedia* declared schizophrenia "a problem, one of the most difficult in psychiatry. . . . Every new work in schizophrenia raises more problems than it solves. The situation is best characterized by the [German] authors of the large monograph [recently translated into Russian] . . . who declare: Concerning the essence of schizophrenia 'we do not know anything.' "[38] Thus the Soviet profession moved toward cautious self-restraint, until Snezhnevskii took command in the fifties. He moved his colleagues to bold self-confidence. By 1973, when the World Health Organization published a comparative study, Soviet psychiatrists had overtaken and surpassed the Americans in diagnoses of schizophrenia.[39]

Snezhnevskii did not challenge the diagnostic self-restraint preached by the leaders of his profession until he felt the mantle of authoritative leadership on his shoulders. He opened his campaign against "nosological agnosticism" in 1951, when he was promoted to the editorship of the country's single journal of psychiatry and neuropathology.[40] From that commanding height, which he held until his death in 1987, along with directorships of key institutes, he issued continual pronouncements on the nature of schizophrenia and nosology in general, with occasional conferences organized to demonstrate virtually unanimous support for his views.

The transformation of Snezhnevskii from an unpretentious clinician to an unanswerable boss fits a widespread Soviet pattern. He was dutifully quiet until the higher powers chose him to mount the appropriate tribune and "lay down" or "formulate"—*oformit'*, a favorite term of the Soviet bureaucracy—the theoretical implications of his promotion, which was proof of his practical success. Stalin's career once exemplified that pattern, and hundreds of others, including Khrushchev's and Brezhnev's, have since been held up as ideal types in the Soviet press. The circular logic of the faith that informs those tales of success is one of the crucial meanings of the Stalinist rule that, while theory guides practice, practice has primacy over theory. One might consider analogies with our own cult of success, the pragmatic ideology of those who "make it" in Western countries. Winners take it for granted that they know something that losers do not, and losers often agree. Thus hierarchy is sanctified. But pursuit of such analogies would take us too far from Soviet history.

For a few years in the early fifties Snezhnevskii organized a "discussion" of schizophrenia in his journal. It was a classic Stalinist caricature of a genuine discussion. With disapproving editorial footnotes, he published a few brief defenses of views labeled incorrect from the start and many long expositions of the correct view. At a conference in 1954 he announced the end of the "discussion." (To be precise, he said he was not ending discussion; he was suspending it until decisive data might be collected.) He brushed aside the charge that he was denying freedom of research and publication to psychiatrists with legitimate differences of opinion. He was merely resisting agnostics and nihilists, who would subvert the whole progress of science: "Science can develop only on condition of historical continuity (*preemstvennost'*), and denying the achievements of preceding generations of psychiatrists, denying efforts to define this disease [schizophrenia]—that signifies interruption of the continuity of science, that means opposing scientific development, opposing the progress of science."[41]

In pitiful fact, the critics of Snezhnevskii's clinical dogmatism were very far from such audacious opposition. They were few in number and subdued in tone. Suffice to note that clinical dogmatism, the accurate name for Snezhnevskii's outlook, was offered almost apologetically by a distinguished forensic psychiatrist, who took instant pains to cushion the blow by declaration of his respect for Snezhnevskii's school.[42] By 1963, when he assembled the next conference to endorse his views, Snezhnevskii could note with satisfaction that even fewer critics spoke out. His triumph was supreme: "The rivulets flowing in a single direction have fused in a mighty torent. . . . [Our data] will permit us to specify the precise boundaries of schizophrenia, to erect, so to speak, the boundary marks whose absence has tormented some psychiatrists."[43]

Western psychiatrists have focused on the claim of boundary marks, Snezhnevskii's nosological scheme of schizophrenia, as the distinguishing feature of his school.[44] However important, that focus misses a deeper and more constant theme, which persisted even through the seventies, when Snezhnevskii felt obliged to shift the boundary marks of schizophrenia, though still insisting on his larger nosology. His fundamental, abiding theme was revulsion against nosological agnosticism, nihilism, or anarchism, as he variously called the threat to his most basic value: *preemstvennost'*, continuity, or more precisely, the principle of proper succession, from the Russian root for successor to a throne or office. He found that essential continuity in the ongoing tradition of the clinic, another favorite term of his, which resonated as powerfully in Snezhnevskii's mind as in Foucault's (with opposite feeling, to be sure). He blamed researchers for the "nihilism" that threatens the continuity of clinical wisdom. In his universe, "the laboratory" was granted a place, explicitly subordinate to "the clinic." The practicing psychiatrist cannot allow his self-confidence to be shaken by the academic researcher, who may be of great technical assistance—for example, in the development of new drugs—but must not be allowed to subvert the lessons of the clinic.[45]

In typically Stalinist fashion Snezhnevskii erected a crude, scholastic theory to dignify his vital faith in practice. It may be dealt with summarily here. His scheme of schizophrenia has been well reported and critically analyzed in the West, especially by Dr. Walter Reich. The crushing response of virtually all psychiatrists outside the Soviet Union—including those of East Germany—has been cold indifference, relieved occasionally by little courteous flatteries.[46] Imitation, the sincerest form of flattery, has, as usual, been paid by the backward East to the West, first in the adoption of psychotropic drugs, finally in the attendant theoretical upheavals. In the midseventies Snezhnevskii felt obliged to acknowledge "a crisis in the development of clinical psychiatry," and began to publish extensive reports of Western research in his journal.[47]

He has kept his school intact by restating his nosological scheme, emphasizing the inanity that protects scholastic theories from refutation by any possible evidence. Schizophrenia can be recognized early and confidently as a hereditary disease process that must follow one of three courses: continuous, intermittent, or transitory. (I have used less obscure terms than Snezhnevskii, in order to bring out more clearly the irrefutable nature of his scheme.) The clinician may apply the schizophrenic label with complete confidence, for the patient's symptoms will get worse (continuous course), or they will come and go (intermittent course), or they will disappear (transitory course). In the last case the diagnosis still stands, for the patient without schizophrenic symptoms is still a schizophrenic. "Even as a result of complete recovery the organism does not return entirely to the condition that preceded the disease."[48]

The absence of boundary marks does not torment the Snezhnevskian psychiatrist, whose clinical nose can still discern them. All mental illnesses are still enclosed within the schemes that Snezhnevskii's intuition drew from clinical experience. He literally *drew* the schemes of classification as nested circles, oddly resembling medieval drawings of the earth nested in concentric cosmic spheres. Snezhnevskii thought he had charted the taxonomic relationship of every mental disturbance with every other one, from neuroses to manic depression and schizophrenia, including even epilepsy and feeblemindedness.[49]

Even when he began to concede some significance to contemporary disturbances in nosology, Snezhnevskii clung to faith in historical continuity or succession, in part by recalling that Wilhelm Griesinger (1817–67), one of the founding fathers of modern psychiatry, conceived the diversity of symptoms as manifestations of disorder in the brain, and therefore in some sense a single disease.[50] Snezhnevskii reconciled that stratospheric vision with the grubbing nosology of the Kraepelin tradition by one breathtaking stroke: "*Any* form of mental disorder may emerge in the course of development of many, or of *all* mental diseases."[51] If a patient treated the logic of classification in that wild manner, a Snezhnevskian psychiatrist might well write "cognitive slippage" in his notebook, and leap to a diagnosis of incipient schizophrenia. Imagine someone saying that any form of animal may emerge in the course of development of all animals, that a crab, let us say, may emerge in a woman's womb or in the belly of a man.

Dr. Walter Reich takes exception to my argument here, and very likely many other psychiatrists would too. We agree that Dr. Snezhnevskii deserves to be mocked for disgracing present standards of rigor in psychiatric nosology. My language may suggest mockery of the whole nosological tradition. I do not intend that, but I am a complete layman. I have no license to draw a *precise* line between sensible and ridiculous nosological reasoning in psychiatry. Neither can I reverentially point to a precise line drawn by licensed authorities, for they are notoriously discordant. I can only confess my intuitions, which laugh at Snezhnevskii's mode of reasoning, and respect Kurt Schneider's.

Snezhnevskii's late retreat to almost explicit inanity was forced by foreign, not Soviet, research and debate. In the fifties and sixties, just when he was imperiously suppressing "the anarchy in this whole problem" of schizophrenia, psychiatrists in other countries were letting loose a new wave of anarchy, by the use of psychotropic drugs and by intense efforts to achieve objectivity in research. Used as empiric palliatives, major tranquillizers brought sufficient abatement of symptoms to permit a great increase in the release of patients from hospitals, but efforts at scientific explanation have been persistently frustrated. Probabilistic correlation of particular drugs with abatement of particular symptoms has exacerbated rather than relieved the problems of nosology, that is, of clustering symptoms and processes in disease entities. Neurochemical research on the cellular level has painstakingly pursued an obvious hypothesis—that subtle disorders in neurotransmitters give rise to mental disorders—but without much success. Masses of data have been accumulated, holding out tantalizing possibilities of comprehension but leaving schizophrenia still an essentially unsolved problem.[52]

IV

For more than twenty years, from the fifties to the seventies, Snezhnevskii's clinical dogmatism kept the Soviet profession from significant participation in those new trends of research, including the rising insistence on rigorous skepticism in diagnostics. During the same period the sloppy diagnostic habits that he fostered helped to fill mental hospitals as fast as new ones could be built and staffed. The critically significant fact is that abundant funds were at last flowing to such building and staffing. The political triumph of Snezhnevskii's clinical dogmatists in 1951 was crowned by a decree of the Minister of Health explicitly ordering a great increase in the medicalization of madness and eccentricity. At long last the Soviet Union was to get a truly modern number of psychiatrists, mental hospitals, and patients to occupy them, and Snezhnevskii's school was to be in charge of the process.[53]

The dramatic results can be seen in table 1. In twenty years the number of hospital beds for the mentally ill almost tripled (from 106,500 in 1955 to 312,600 in 1975), while the number of psychiatrists almost quadrupled (from almost 4800 to 18,700). And then,

TABLE 1
DOCTORS AND BEDS FOR THE MENTALLY ILL, 1890–1980

Year	Hospital Beds (thousands)						Physicians (thousands)					
	Total	Mentally Ill	Neurally Ill	Forensic Psychiatric Cases	Mentally Ill Beds/Total Hospital Beds	Hospital Beds/10,000 Pop.	Total	Psychiatrists	Forensic Psychiatrists	Neuropathologists	Psychiatrists/Total Physicians	Physicians/10,000 pop.
1890							14.0	0.18			1:80	
1895							16.0	0.26			1:60	
1902							20.0	0.41			1:50	
1909		35.0					25.0ᵃ					
1912	208	42.2ᵇ (48)				13.0	23.0					1.5
1916								0.35				
1922		12.9ᵇ										
1924		14.0										
1925		16.6ᵇ										
1928	250	26.4ᶜ					65.0					
1932		31.3ᶜ						0.538ᶜ (1.39)		0.743ᶜ		
1935		48.0										

Year										
1940	790	82.0	10.0	1:9.5	40.0	142.0	1.55 (2.36) (2.4)	2.66 (3.21)	1:60	7.0
1950		71.8	15.1			265.0	3.10	5.10	1:90	
1951							2.82	4.21		
1955	1288.9	106.5	18.9	1:12	65.0	310.0	4.78	7.57	1:65	16.0
1958	1532.5	138.2	23.8	1:11	73.0	362.0	5.76	9.24	1:65	17.0
1959	1618.0	149.6	26.1	1:11	76.0	380.0	6.15	9.85	1:65	18.0
1960	1739.2	162.2	29.9 (30.5)	1:11	80.0	431.7 (402)	6.39	10.50	1:65	19.0
1963			1.65				.67			
1970	2663.3	267.9	71.5	1:10	109.2	668.4	14.3 (14.5)	18.1 (17.9)	1:45	27.4
1974	2933.0	300.6	89.4	1:9.5		799.0	17.7	20.5	1:45	
1975	3009.0	312.6	94.0	1:9.5	117.2	835.2	18.7	21.4	1:45	32.7
1980	3324.0	d	d	d	124.9	995.6	d	d	d	37.4

SOURCES: Various publications. For earlier years, see the psychiatric journals, monographs, and proceedings of congresses cited in the notes. For the years since World War II, see especially the statistical series, *Narodnoe khoziaistvo SSSR v 1960 godu* (Moscow, 1961), and for subsequent years.

NOTE: Figures in the public record are sometimes inconsistent. Variations are given in parentheses.

a. Estimate for 1910 by Nancy Frieden, *Russian Physicians in an Era of Reform and Revolution, 1856–1905* (Princeton, N.J.: Princeton University Press, 1981), p. 323. Cf. Gordon Hyde, *The Soviet Health Service: A Historical and Comparative Study* (London, 1974); and Michael Kaser, *Health Care in the Soviet Union and Eastern Europe* (Boulder, Colo., 1976).

b. Patients, not beds.

c. RSFSR only: in 1932 add 11,000 beds outside of hospitals (in sanitoria, "colonies," homes). Cf. note 20.

d. No further data in the public record until 1986: 335.2 beds for mentally ill; 142.3 for neurally ill; and 125.5 for "narcological cases."

after 1975, those indicators of nerve-racking modernity became a state secret—until the Gorbachev era, when it was revealed that beds for the mentally ill totaled 335,200 in 1986, plus 125,500 for . "narcological" cases. No doubt one of the reasons for the new secrecy was the embarrassing contrast with Western trends. The fifties to seventies were the years of "deinstitutionalization." In the United States, for example, the number of mental patients in government hospitals declined from a peak of 558,900 in 1955 to 307,900 in 1971.[54]

It is impossible to get precise figures on the role of schizophrenia diagnoses in the Soviet Union's rising tide of hospitalization. Even in the earlier years, while Soviet health officials had boasted of their low rate of mental illness compared with the decadent West, they had never offered comprehensive data on the incidence of particular illnesses. They may have lacked good data even in their private discussions; in 1948 an assistant minister of health made such a complaint to a conference of psychiatrists.[55] Solid epidemiological studies of mental disorders have begun to appear in Soviet publications only very recently, and they are still very limited. But they suggest that the incidence of schizophrenia has been going up more swiftly than the total increase in all types of mental illnesses.[56] Snezhnevskii's school can claim only some of the credit for that disproportion. They are notoriously quick to pin the label of schizophrenia on disturbed people, but continuing urbanization has been piling up the "lower socioeconomic group in dilapidated areas of large cities," and such groups have the highest rates of schizophrenia even with the most rigorous diagnostic standards.

Snezhnevskii's belated retreat from extreme self-confidence, his reference to a "crisis in clinical psychology,"[57] may have been prompted by dissatisfied health officials, envious of the dramatic deinstitutionalization of mental patients in the West during the sixties and seventies. We may imagine the minister of health chiding Snezhnevskii on the need to reduce incarcerations—but only in private. After they overthrew Khrushchev, Soviet political leaders were extremely fearful of "disorganizing the cadres." There has been nothing like the public campaign of the thirties for "narrowing" the concept of schizophrenia. Nor has there been anything like a return to the open, autonomous debate of the twenties. (Within the openness of 1987/88, some criticisms of arbitrary incarceration began to appear, but that is another story.) Snezhnevskii shared in his superiors' immunity to public criticism, whether of the politically organized type, as in the thirties, or of the autonomous academic type, as in the twenties. Like so many other little Stalins commanding a host of Soviet fiefdoms, he maintained his unquestioned authority while changing his line, offering an insultingly vague explanation and no trace of apology. He and his lieutenants simply began to publish reports of foreign trends in schizophrenia research, eliminating or toning down the most glaring subversions of the original Snezhnevskii scheme, and raising the scheme to a splendid level of irrefutable inanity.

Those belated tactics of Snezhnevskii's school resembled Lysenko's in the fifties and early sixties, when Lysenko conceded the legitimacy of DNA research and offered sophistries to justify his continuing rejection of genetics.[58] But there is a striking difference between the passivity of the psychiatrists and the assertiveness of the geneticists, who attacked Lysenkoism as it retreated, until they finally achieved the withdrawal of political support from the pseudoscience. By contrast, non-Snezhnevskian psychiatrists have continued to show the restraint that they learned so quickly in the fifties. The so-called Leningrad school, to take the most notable center of silent disagreement, was not totally deprived of print by Snezhnevskii's control of the country's one psychiatric journal. Leningrad research institutions publish occasional volumes, in which they systematically avoid offense to Snezhnevskii. They publish very little on schizophrenia; they never make explicit criticism of Snezhnevskii's views; they insert little tokens of explicit obeisance to him, if only in vague terms.[59] One can only assume that these timid psychiatrists are censoring themselves to avoid reprimand by officials in the medical and ideological bureaucracies, who would presumably object to conflicts that might "disorganize the cadres."

Let us seek appropriate standards of criticism, both of the cosmopolitan profession and of the national milieux within which particular branches are submerged. The intellectual fragmentation of the psychiatric profession can approach chaos, as we in the scandalmongering West are reminded every time an especially shocking mass murder brings a carnival of discordant psychiatrists into the courts and the newspapers. In the West we still feel free to indulge our taste for such scandal, as an exciting flirtation with social chaos. Soviet authorities are still obsessively fearful of such flirtation, and most of their subjects give dutiful signs of sharing the fear. There may be some genuine feeling, along with cynical pretense, in those submissive signs of shared fearfulness. The living memory of rulers and subjects retains the terrible experience of murderous chaos on such a massive scale, with such a wild intensity, as we in the West retain only in the ghostly memory of historians.

We must keep in mind not only major differences in social contexts but also differences in the internal standards of knowledge, the implicit epistemologies, of the various learned professions. Soviet geneticists were pushed into militant defense of their profession not simply by the political pressure of Lysenkoism but also by the highly formal character of their discipline. They simply could not do their work without the concepts and methods that Lysenko denounced. In other branches of biology specialists could avoid that clash, and they tended to do so. Plant physiologists, for example, resembled the Leningrad school of psychiatrists in avoiding controversial topics, such as plant hormones and stages of growth, which were areas of conflict with Lysenko's pseudoscientific beliefs. Plant physiology is such a sprawling discipline that its devotees could find tasks to keep them busy without challenging Lysenko's beliefs.[60] They did so, and so have the non-Snezhnevskian psychiatrists, whose discipline is even further than plant physiology from the formal character, the monistic epistemology, of genetics. Epistemological pluralism permits the Soviet devotees of many disciplines to be conscientious professionals while evading conflict with their little Stalins. They can have the sweet cake of a successful career without spending the penny of professional self-respect. Geneticists were an exception to that rule.

V

The practical art of treating disturbed people reveals a striking difference between "backward" and "advanced"—or "underdeveloped" and "developed"—countries. Incidence of hospital confinement for mental illness is low in backward or underdeveloped countries, high in advanced or developed ones. Let us call that Esquirol's law, to honor the first discussion of the pattern in 1824, by one of the founding fathers of modern psychiatry.[61] He noted that the number of psychiatric patients rises to meet or exceed the supply of hospital beds and mental doctors provided for them. He attributed the trend to progress in diagnostic science and in social benevolence, and beat back the gloomier possibility, that the stress of advancing civilization causes more and more minds to break down. He did not even consider the possibility that confinement for mental illness is an artifact of those who would dominate modern society by scientific reason, a way of maintaining confidence in the healthiness of the rational system, by shutting away the sick people who do not spontaneously fit themselves into it.

When we say that the sloppy diagnostic habits of Snezhnevskii's school helped to fill Soviet mental hospitals as fast as they could be built and staffed, we are noting a special instance of Esquirol's law, and we are doing so in hostile fashion. We are showing our eagerness to blame those who dominate the Soviet version of modern development. We are judging them too eager to confine, excessively anxious in their forceful claims of a rational and humane system. In 1980 a Soviet author had a natural inclination to read the increase in psychiatric patients and confining doctors as Esquirol did, as evidence of progress in social benevolence and "improvement in diagnostics," and she was glad to note that "this viewpoint remains dominant among psychiatrists to the present time."[62] She did not ponder the recent decrease in hospitalized patients in Western countries, or wonder whether her own country should start trying to catch up with *this* trend. (In the "reconstruction" of the present days such a move is under way.)[63] It may indicate a decline in arrogant self-confidence among doctors of the mind and political authorities, or a new departure in social benevolence, perhaps toward greater respect for the autonomy of disturbed people, perhaps toward greater stinginess in caring for them, a growing indifference that comes disguised as self-restraint among people at the top and freedom for wretches at the bottom.

Scientific explanation of people is still alienated from human understanding of them, but no one knows what to do about that. Foucault caught some attention with his denunciation of the scientific belief that the insane cannot be understood as persons, that they must be explained as malfunctioning objects in need of repair. But Foucault had no practicable alternative, just inane enthusiasm for Freudian efforts to commune with "the madman."[64] He ignored the record of Freudian or psychodynamic theories of schizophrenia, which were as sloppy as Snezhnevskii's in putting terrible labels on disturbed people, and sometimes crueler in speculative constructs that were supposed to join human understanding with scientific explanation. The "schizophrenogenic mother" was a special shocker of the psychodynamic school. She induced schizophrenia by putting her children in a "double bind," getting them to believe that nothing is more important than pleasing mother and that nothing they might do could possibly please her. Offering such explanation-cum-understanding to disturbed people and their parents seems to me as savagely pseudoscientific as the physical treatments that the dominant medical materialists have used upon severely disturbed people: surgical excision of the organs supposed to be infected, shock to the errant brain by insulin or electricity or induced fever, protracted drugged sleep, and maddest of all the lobotomy: an icepick through the eye socket into the forebrain. In the West a Nobel Prize was given to the inventor of the lobotomy, which was discouraged and then banned in Soviet Russia, in part because Pavlov recommended drugged sleep.[65]

Szasz has denounced his fellow psychiatrists as quasi-Stalinist authoritarians, who lord it over disturbed people by pretending to have scientific explanations of their disturbances and thus the know-how of treatment. But Szasz is as far as Foucault from a practicable alternative, perhaps farther, for he mocks the whole notion of schizophrenia while accepting the medical materialism that engenders it. He promises to accept the reality of schizophrenia if and when it is rigorously defined and demonstrably reduced to specific neural disorders. Until such time he is free to feel holier than the average practitioner confronting severely disturbed persons, knowing the inadequacy of his knowledge yet compelled to do something, especially when suicide is a strong possibility. Snezhnevskii turned that situation to self-pitying justification of authority, mouthing a cliché about "the tragic position of psychiatry," which is obliged to act with insufficient knowledge.[66] Kurt Schneider turned such self-awareness toward self-restraint, by exposing the paradox within the concept of *Wahn* (delusion, mania, madness): "Where there is genuine *Wahn*, there understanding of psychic character ceases; and where understanding is possible, there is no *Wahn*."[67]

That is a psychiatrist's confession—that his profession cannot understand the seriously disturbed person as a person. We—the profession of mental doctors and the society that sustains it—cannot help treating the insane mind as the symptom of some physical disorder, even when we know that we lack knowledge of the disorder. The insane are persons whom we must reduce to physical objects and "treat," whether or not we have the necessary knowledge, sometimes winning their submission to the culturally imposed project, sometimes forcing it. We are not as different as we suppose from Snezhnevskii's school and the Stalinist society that engendered it. Indeed, the medieval French doctor who drove evil spirits from a woman by incising a cross on her scalp and rubbing salt in it seems uncomfortably similar to the mental doctors of our century.[68] The main difference is in the figurative symbols that the doctor's confident mind-brain-hand projects upon the patient's disjointed mind and body.

NOTES

This essay parallels material in my *Russian Psychology: A Critical History* (Oxford: Basil Blackwell, 1989).

1. See Alexander D. Brooks, *Law, Psychiatry, and the Mental Health System* (Boston: Little, Brown, 1974), which has a wealth of references.
2. The term "clinical dogmatists," was offered by the eminent forensic psychiatrist A. N. Buneev (1894–1955), speaking at the 1954 Korsakov conference. See Vsesoiuznaia nauchno-prakticheskaia konferentsiia posviashchennaia stoletiiu so dnia rozhdeniia S. S. Korsakova i aktual'nym voprosam psikhiatrii, *Trudy* (Moscow, 1955), p. 210. Snezhnevskii preferred "traditional clinical psychiatry" as the term for his school. See his *Obshchaia psikhopatologiia; Kurs lektsii* (Valdai: 1970), p. 163. See p. 187 for his effort to rebut the charge of "nosological dogmatism." A Snezhnevskian recently characterized his master's school as "clinical-syndromal." See *Zhurnal nevropatologii i psikhiatrii*, 1980, no. 4, p. 628. That marks a retreat toward the "phenomenological" outlook, which Snezhnevskii derided in 1970, before his recognition of a "crisis in clinical psychiatry."
3. *Trudy tret'iago s'ezda otechestvennykh psikhiatrov* (St. Petersburg: 1911), pp. 532–49; cf. Julie Brown, "The Professionalization of Russian Psychiatry: 1857–1911," Ph.D. diss., University of Pennsylvania, 1981.
4. Ts. M. Feinberg, *Subedno-psikhiatricheskaia ekspertiza i opyt raboty Instituta im. Serbskogo* (Moscow, 1935), p. 15; cf. the figures she gave at I-oe Vsesoiuznoe soveshchanie po subednoi psikhiatrii, *Trudy* (Moscow, 1937), p. 12.
5. G. V. Morozov, D. R. Lunts, and N. I. Felinskaia, *Osnovnye etapy razvitiia otechestvennoi sudebnoi psikhiatrii* (Moscow, 1976), p. 169 passim. I want to thank Walter Reich for giving me this book.
6. The insistence of the bureaucracy is evident in the anti-Freudian articles published in *Pod znamenem marksizma,* and in the gradual suppression of Freudian publications, including translations of Freud's writings. The last Soviet translation of anything by Freud appeared in 1930. The disappearance of Freudian articles from psychiatric publications is evidence of the surrender of the psychiatric profession. The history of Russian Freudianism is still to be written, but see Iu. V. Kannabikh, *Istoriia psikhiatrii* (Leningrad, 1928), ch. 30, 34, 35. Kannabikh (1876–1939) was himself of the Freudian minority, but told nothing about it in this book. Cf. James L. Rice, "Russian Stereotypes in the Freud-Jung Correspon-

dence," *Slavic Review* 41 (1982): 32–34, for many references; and Martin A. Miller, "Freudian Theory under Bolshevik Rule: The Theoretical Controversy During the 1920s," *Slavic Review,* Winter (1985): 625–46.

7. See A. R. Luriia, "Psikhoanaliz," in *Bol'shaia sovetskaia entsiklopediia* 1st ed. (Moscow, 1940), p. xlvii. At a conference in May 1948, A. S. Chistovich made a little plea for a renewal of interest in Freud and the unconscious. See *Trudy III-ego vsesoiuznogo s'ezda nevropatologov i psikhiatrov* (Moscow, 1950), p. 80. The general reaction was so scandalized that he felt obliged to apologize.

8. For the cool reaction of the German profession, see Hanna Decker, *Freud in Germany: Revolution and Reaction in Science, 1893–1907* (New York, 1977).

9. See Joravsky, "The Construction of the Stalinist Psyche," in Sheila Fitzpatrick, ed., *Cultural Revolution in Russia, 1928–1931* (Bloomington: Indiana University Press, 1978).

10. See table 1 below.

11. There is an enormous literature on schizophrenia. The clearest, most sensible introduction that I have seen is Patrick O'Brien, *The Disordered Mind: What We Know about Schizophrenia* (Englewood Cliffs: Prentice-Hall, 1978). On a more advanced level, see John C. Shershow, ed., *Schizophrenia: Science and Practice* (Cambridge, Mass., 1978), which is honestly historical and pluralist in its assortment of views on an unresolved problem. Note especially the contribution by G. L. Klerman, "The Evolution of a Scientific Nosology." For the current official view of the American Psychiatric Association, see its *Diagnostic and Statistical Manual of Mental Disorders,* 3rd ed. (Washington, D.C.: APA, 1980).

12. Snezhnevskii, *Obshchaia psikhopatologiia,* p. 189, as paraphrased by S. Ia. Rubinshtein, *Zhurnal nevropatologii i psikhiatrii,* 1980, no. 4, p. 619. As editor of the journal, Snezhnevskii must have approved the paraphrase.

13. A. V. Snezhnevskii, "Oblastnaia psikhiatricheskaia bol'nitsa v g. Kostrome," *Sovetskaia nevropatologiia, psikhiatriia i psikhogigiena,* 1933, no. 10, pp. 149–54.

14. Ibid., p. 153.

15. See esp. Michel Foucault, *Madness and Civilization: A History of Insanity in the Age of Reason* (New York: Vintage, 1973); and Thomas Szasz, *Schizophrenia: The Sacred Symbol of Psychiatry* (New York: Basic Books, 1976). Foucault charged such authoritarianism against modern medicine in general—see his *The Birth of the Clinic: An Archaeology of Medical Perception* (New York: Vintage, 1973)—while Szasz does not.

16. See the memorial issue of *Sovetskaia nevropatologiia, psikhiatriia i psikhogigiena,* 1934, no. 5, which is devoted to "Rozenshtein and the clinical-prophylactic-psychohygienic trend in psychiatry."

17. See the fine review article by Iu. V. Kannabikh, "K istorii voprosa o miagkikh formakh shizofrenni," ibid., pp. 6–13.

18. The papers were published as *Sovremennye problemy shizofrenii* (Moscow, 1933).

19. *Encyclopedia of Psychology,* vol. 3 (New York: Seabury Press, 1972), p. 177, with references on p. 179. The problem of hereditary vulnerability is most carefully studied by I. L. Gottesman and J. Shields, *Schizophrenia and Genetics* (New York: Academic Press, 1972). Comparative studies of sociocultural factors are summarized in B. D. Petrakov, *Psikhicheskaia zabolevaemost' v nekotorykh stranakh v XX veke* (Moscow, 1972). The extreme paucity of Soviet data is scandalously evident in Petrakov's review of the epidemiological literature. Cf. the brief discussion of schizophrenia and social class in Gordon Hyde, *The Soviet Health Service: A Historical and Comparative Study* (London: Lawrence and Wishart, 1974), pp. 262–64.

20. In 1930 there was plain talk of a crisis of overcrowding in mental hospitals. See *Zhurnal nevropatologii i psikhiatrii,* 1930, no. 3, pp. 109–10; and no. 4, pp. 127–28. For the virtual disappearance of reliable global statistics during the First Five-Year Plan, see the report in *Sovetskaia nevropatologiia i psikhiatriia i psikhogigiena,* 1934, no. 5, pp. 133–38. The statistical compilations that began to appear in the post-Stalin era invariably leap over the twenties and thirties in their data on hospital beds and specialists for the mentally ill.

21. See the repeated complaints by psychiatrists, with occasional agreement of officials; e.g. Ibid., 1933, no. 1, p. 124; and 1936, no. 6, pp. 1078—79. At a major conference in December 1936, A. L. Shnirman complained that psychiatry was the stepchild of health care, and Commissar of Health G. N. Kaminskii (soon to be snatched by the administrators of terror) exclaimed "Pravil'no!" (True!). Vtoroi vsesoiuznyi s'ezd psikhiatrov i nevropatologov, 25–29 dek. 1936 g., *Trudy* (Moscow, 1937), vol. 1, p. 78.

22. See V. P. Osipov, "O raspoznavanii shizofrenii," ibid., vol. 2, pp. 461–66; and "Granitsy shizofrenii i ikh legkomyslennoe raspoznavanie," *Nevropatologiia, psikhiatriia, psikhogigiena,* 1935, no. 7, pp. 1–30. Osipov was the director of the Bekhterev Institute of the Brain, and chief of psychiatry at the Military Medical Academy, both in Leningrad.

23. O. V. Kerbikov, "O gruppe shizofrenii tekushchikh bez izmeneniia kharaktera," in *Sovremennye problemy shizofrenii.* His self-criticism is in Vtoroi vsesoiuznyi s'ezd psikhiatrov i nevropatologov, 25–29 dek. 1936 g., *Trudy* (Moscow, 1937) vol. 2, pp. 516–18.

24. See Kerbikov's speeches at the 1951 Pavlov session: *Fiziologicheskoe uchenie Akademika I. P. Pavlova v psikhiatrii i nevropatologii* (Moscow: 1951), pp. 10–41, 85–92. See especially his articles in *Zhurnal nevropatologii i psikhiatrii,* 1952, no. 5, pp. 8–25; and no. 11, pp. 8–13; et. seq.

25. *Nevropatologiia i psikhiatriia,* 1951, no. 4, p. 34. All four of the names cited were recognizably Jewish.

26. A. V. Snezhnevskii, "O pozdnikh simptomaticheskikh psikho-

zakh," *Trudy nauchno-issledovatel'skogo instituta psikhiatrii im. Gannushkina* (Moscow, 1940), vol. 5. See p. 269 for Snezhnevskii's "profound thanks, for the direction of the present work," primarily to M. A. Sereiskii, whom he would denounce in 1951 as a cosmopolitan. For his other modest article before the late forties, see the bibliography after "Snezhnevskii, A. V.," in *Bol'shaia meditsinskaia entsiklopediia,* 2nd ed. (Moscow, 1963), vol. 30, pp. 756–57. Note the omission of the 1933 article cited in n. 13.

27. *Nevropatologiia i psikhiatriia,* 1950, no. 1, pp. 63–65. Cf. ibid., 1947, no. 2, p. 15, for the original commission.

28. See especially O. V. Kerbikov's amusing use of Lysenko to support an argument *for* diathesis. *Zhurnal nevropatologii i psikhiatrii,* 1952, no. 5, 21–25. Cf. ibid., no. 11, pp. 63–65.

29. See the proceedings of the session cited in n. 24.

30. A. S. Chistovich, "O vzgliadakh Pavlova na shizofreniiu," *Nevropatologiia i psikhiatriia,* 1949, no. 5, pp. 52–55. For Chistovich presenting mental patients to Pavlov, see *Pavlovskie klinicheskie sredy* 3 (1957): 373–74, 430 et seq.

31. For Snezhnevskii's initial attack on Chistovich, see the 1951 Pavlov session cited in n. 24, p. 33.

32. For Chistovich's self-criticism at the 1951 Pavlov session, see ibid., pp. 266–67. For his subsequent leadership of the resistance to the Snezhnevskii school, see his speech at the 1954 conference: Vsesoiuznaia nauchno-prakticheskaia konferentsiia posviashchennaia 100-letiiu . . . Korsakova, *Trudy,* pp. 204–05; in *Zhurnal nevropatologii i psikhiatrii,* 1953, no. 4; 1955, no. 11; a letter of protest, 1960, no. 9, p. 1241; and his remarks at the 1963 IV-yi Vsesoiuznyi s'ezd nevropatologov i psikhiatrov, *Trudy* (Moscow, 1965), vol. 3, pp. 132–36.

33. See O. V. Kerbikov, "Emil' Kraepelin i problemy nozologii v psikhiatrii," *Zhurnal nevropatologii i psikhiatrii,* 1956, no. 12, pp. 925–36. For the virtual dismissal of Pavlov except as a totem, see Kerbikov, "O nekotorykh spornykh voprosakh psikhiatrii," ibid., 152, no. 5.

34. Kraepelin is quoted in *Allegemeine Zeitschrift für Psychiatrie und psychish-gerichtliche Medizin* 65 (1908): 472–73. The wastebasket metaphor can be found in Patrick O'Brien, *The Disordered Mind* (Englewood Cliffs: Prentice-Hall, 1978), pp. 27, 40. It has been used by critics of other diagnostic labels than schizophrenia. See Jan Goldstein, "The Hysteria Diagnosis and the Politics of Anticlericalism in Late 19th-century France," *Journal of Modern History,* June (1982): 211.

35. Kerbikov's 1932 paper is cited in n. 23. The shocking phrase occurs on pp. 99–100.

36. Ibid., p. 154.

37. Kurt Schneider, "Wesen und Erfassung des Schizophrenen," *Zeitschrift für die gesammte Neurologie und Psychiatre* 90 (1925): 542–47.

38. V. A. Giliarovskii, "Shizofreniia," *Bol'shaia meditsinskaia entsiklo-*

pediia, 1st ed. (Moscow, 1935), vol. 32, p. 129. He was quoting from Oswald Bumke, ed., *Handbuch der Geisteskrankheiten,* vol. 9. That volume, entirely devoted to schizophrenia, was translated into Russian in 1933.

39. World Health Organization, *Report of the International Pilot Study of Schizophrenia* (Geneva: WHO, 1973); and WHO, *Schizophrenia: A Multi-National Study* (Geneva: WHO, 1975), esp. pp. 142–43. For a pointed summary, see Walter Reich, "The Spectrum Concept of Schizophrenia: Problems for Diagnostic Practice," *Archives of General Psychiatry* 32 (1975): 493ff.

40. To be precise: *Nevropatologiia i psikhiatriia,* 1951, no. 1, announced the appearance of Snezhnevskii as deputy editor, replacing the "cosmopolitan" A. S. Shmar'ian. O. V. Kerbikov was added to the board of editors in the next issue, and other transformations led to the first issue of 1952, which announced Snezhnevskii's formal designation as editor (replacing the physiologist N. I. Grashchenkov, also known as Propper) and the restoration of the journal's patriotic title, which had been dropped in the radical thirties: *Zhurnal nevropatologii i psikhiatrii im. S.S. Korsakova (The Korsakov Journal of Neuropathology and Psychiatry).*

41. Vsesoiuznaia nauchno-prakticheskaia konferentsiia, posviashchennaia 100-letiiu . . . Korsakova, *Trudy* (Moscow, 1955), pp. 205 passim. For the accusation of repression, and other criticisms of Snezhnevskii's school, see the speeches of P. E. Vishnevskii, A. L. Epshtein, A. S. Chistovich, and A. I. Zelenchuk. The overwhelming majority of speakers were either pro-Snezhnevskii or evasive.

42. See n. 2.

43. IV-yi vsesoiuznyi s'ezd nevropatologov i psikhiatrov, *Trudy* (1965), vol. 4, p. 521.

44. See esp. Walter Reich, "The Spectrum Concept," with its many bibliographic notes. See also Reich, "Kazanetz, Schizophrenia, and Soviet Psychiatry," *Archives of General Psychiatry* 36 (1979): 1029–30; and Reich, "The World of Soviet Psychiatry," *N.Y. Times Magazine,* 30 Jan. 1983.

45. For characteristic statements of these themes, see A. V. Snezhnevskii. editorial note in *Zhurnal nevropatologii i psikhiatrii,* 1953, no. 11, p. 909; Snezhnevskii "O nozologicheskoi spetsifichnosti psikhopatologicheskikh sindromov," *Zhurnal,* 1960, no. 1, pp. 102 *passim;* "Ob osobennostiakh tekhneiia shizofrenii," *Zhurnal,* 1960, no. 9; "Mesto kliniki v issledovanii prirody shizofrenii," *Zhurnal,* 1975, no. 9, pp. 1341 passim. And see esp. his *Obshchaia psikhopatologiia.*

46. Note the persistent Snezhnevskian complaints concerning the indifference of foreigners, especially in the reports of foreign psychiatric literature by E. Ia. Shternberg, e.g., in *Zhurnal nevropatologii i psikhiatrii,* 1980, no. 4, pp. 624–30.

47. For Snezhnevskii's acknowledgment of a crisis, see his article "O

nozologii psikhicheskikh rasstroistv," *Zhurnal nevropatologii i psikhiatrii,* 1975, no. 1, p. 138, with a footnote reference to the "discussion" that he began in his journal in 1973, no. 9.

48. Snezhnevskii, "Mesto kliniki v isseldovanii prirody shizofrenii," *Zhurnal nevropatologii i psikhiatrii,* 1975, no. 9, p. 1344.

49. See ibid. for two charts, pp. 1342, 1343; and ibid., 1960, no. 1, p. 98 for an earlier chart. See also the rectilinear scheme that Snezhnevskii published in his *Obshchaia psikhopatologiia,* p. 176.

50. See Snezhnevskii's articles cited above. For another of his appeals to the authority of Griesinger, see "Prognoz issledovaniia shizofrenii," *Vestnik Akademii Meditsinskikh Nauk,* 1970, no. 6, pp. 84–85.

51. *Zhurnal nevropatologii i psikhiatrii,* 1975, no. 1, p. 140. Italics added.

52. See Judith P. Swazey, *Chlorpromazine in Psychiatry: A Study of Therapeutic Innovation* (Cambridge: MIT Press, 1974). For the impact on diagnosis—intensified descent from confident nosology to skeptical empiricism—contrast the first, second, and third editions of American Psychiatric Association, *Diagnostic and Statistical Manual of Mental Disorders* (Washington, D.C.: APA, 1952, 1968, and 1980). For the origins of that statistical effort to overcome diagnostic confusion, see R. J. Plunkett and J. E. Gordon, *Epidemiology and Mental Illness* (New York: 1960), pp. 21–24. See also M. D. Altschule, "Whichophrenia, or the Confused Past, Ambiguous Present, and Dubious Future of the Schizophrenia Concept," *Journal of Schizophrenia,* 1967, no. 1, pp. 8–17; and Altschule, ed., *The Development of Traditional Psychopathology* (New York: Hemisphere, 1976). The best history I have come across is by G. L. Klerman, "The Evolution of a Scientific Nosology," in J. C. Shershow, ed., *Schizophrenia: Science and Practice* (Cambridge, Mass.: Harvard University Press, 1978).

53. See *Zhurnal nevropatologii i psikhiatrii,* 1952, no. 2, pp. 3–8.

54. See the chart in Swazey, *Chlorpromazine in Psychiatry,* p. 241.

55. III-yi Vsesoiuznyi s'ezd nevropatologov i psikhiatrov, *Trudy* (Moscow, 1950), p. 439.

56. The most detailed and revealing study, in Tomsk, for the period from 1948 to 1971, is reported by E. D. Krasik and I. R. Semin, "Epidemiologicheskie aspekty pervichnoi gospitalizatsii bol'nykh shizofreniei," *Zhurnal nevropatologii i psikhiatrii,* 1980, no. 9, pp. 1354–59. Cf. also the 1970 article by Snezhnevskii cited in n. 50 for a few global figures, including the remark that "up to 70%" of chronic mental patients are schizophrenics.

57. See "Mesto kliniki v issledovanii prirody shizofrenii," *Zurnal neuropatologii i psikhiatrii,* 1975, no. 9, p. 1340.

58. See Joravsky, *The Lysenko Affair* (Cambridge, Mass.: Harvard University Press, 1970), pp. 212–16.

59. See esp. publications of the Bekhterev Institute: Nauchno-issledov-

atel'skii psikhonevrologicheskii institut im. V. M. Bekhtereva, *Trudy*. Note, e.g., G. V. Zenevich, "O primenenii kliniko-nozologicheskogo printsipa v psikhiatrii," *Trudy* (Leningrad, 1966), vol. 34, pp. 93–105. See also M. S. Lebedinskii and V. N. Miasishchev, *Vvedenie v meditsinskuiu psikhologiu* (Leningrad, 1966), with special attention to the evasive discussions of schizophrenia. Cf. V. M. Smirnov, "Zasedanie . . . Leningradskogo . . . obshchestva," *Zhurnal nevropatologii i psikhiatrii*, 1975, no. 8, pp. 1256–60, for a report of a very subdued discussion in Leningrad.

    60. Joravsky, *Lysenko Affair*, pp. 187–201.

    61. E. Esquirol, *Des maladies mentales considerées sous les rapports médical, hygiénique et médico-légal* (Brussells, 1838), vol. 2, ch. 19.

    62. L. M. Shmaonova, in *Zhurnal nevrapatologii i psikhiatrii*, 1980, no. 5, p. 784.

    63. See the interview with the chief psychiatrist of the USSR Ministry of Public Health in *Izvestia*, 27 Apr. 1988. Thanks to Roberta Manning and Lewis Siegelbaum for calling my attention to these recent developments. And thanks to Peter Reddaway for his "Soviet Psychiatry: An End to Political Abuse?" *Survey* 30 (1988): 25–38.

    64. See n. 15.

    65. See Eliot Valenstein, *Great and Desperate Cures: The Rise and Decline of Psychosurgery and Other Radical Treatments for Mental Illness* (New York: Basic Books, 1986).

    66. Snezhnevskii, "Mesto kliniki," p. 1340.

    67. Quoted in G. Huber and G. Gross, *Wahn: eine deskriptiv-phänomenologische Untersuchung schizophrenen Wahns* (Stuttgart, 1977), p. 32.

    68. See C. H. Haskins, *The Renaissance of the Twelfth Century* (Cambridge, Mass.: Harvard University Press, 1928), pp. 326–27.

Images of the Disabled, Especially the War Wounded, in Soviet Literature

Vera S. Dunham

I

FROM THE very moment the Great Patriotic War erupted in 1941, it created a vast audience for tales of war valor, for recollections of the suffering of the Soviet people. Soviet literature responded immediately. It has been responding ever since. And disabled veterans came to the fore.

> I remember my childhood. An invalid
> Attracted us like a magnet.
> He would gather us, kids, and
> Would commence his story slowly.
> He told us about snipers, foxholes,
> Tank attacks. He wore a medal.
> Suddenly he would stare at me
> Like through a haze. He sank
> Into himself for quite a while.
> Then, embarrassed, he would move.
> His old crutch creaked.
> The doleful sound refracted
> Inside me with tremor. It scorched.
> The heart would overflow with pity.
> We understood each other without words.[1]

So let us use this war-bred literature to find out about the disabled and to explore how they were viewed and how they may still be viewed. May we best understand the thrust and splintering of this literature with a synchronic or with a diachronic selection of examples? Let us use both, for the examples available are not that many; and we will need images of disability from long before the war and long after it to follow the evolution of its doleful theme and to identify its patterns.

Let us start with a specimen from 1944. It is from a poem, "I
Shall Come to See You" by Mikhail Lukonin, a well-known war
poet.

> . . . You think
> I'll bring to you
> My tired body.
> No,
> Don't think that.
> That's not the way
> I'll come back . . .
> We shall return to work,
> To puff tobacco,
> To fill the room with smoke.
> I'm not seeking gratitude.
> I offer it to you myself,
> That's what I want.
> What I had to say to the enemy,
> I have said it.
> Now I want to work.
> I'll cross your threshold
> Not to be consoled
> But to console.
> That which I have done
> On my way to you,
> Is not a favor
> But duty.
> I want to work in the smithy
> And sleep in bed.
> I want to write poems about love.
> In the windy conflagration of war
> There was hardly a choice.
> But it is better to return
> With an empty sleeve
> Than with an empty soul.[2]

This poem tells us that of course there were the war wounded, and
of course they were celebrated, and of course there was a mold or
pattern in popular poetry for dealing with their return. It shows
the world of the war wounded the way one would have wanted it
to be, whether one were wounded oneself or a citizen on the home
front. Obviously this poem is a wish; it is heroic literature.

Among the war heroes canonized in fiction, the best known,
perhaps, were the near-autobiographic Colonel Voropaev in Piotr

Pavlenko's (1899–1951) *Happiness;* published in 1947; and the iconic portrait of the famous combat pilot A. P. Meresiev in Boris Polevoi's *The Tale of a Real Man,* published in 1946.[3] Both heroes are amputees.

In creating Colonel Voropaev, Pavlenko—a perfect Stalinist—performed something of a miracle. The colonel, in Stalinist-populist "uniform," turned out to be a rather credible and fetching hero.[4] He had initiated emulation, something like a movement of Voropaevism—a sui generis post–Patriotic War wounded veterans' Stakhanovism. Demobilized after having lost a leg at the front, he moves to the Crimea. He could have retired. Instead, he works as if he were possessed. He hobbles along on a crutch and a creaky and uncomfortable artificial limb. His superman efforts in local party work are thereby underscored. His leglessness is both a tribute to and attribute of his Stalinist courage. *Mirabile dictu,* Stalin makes in this novel a rare appearance and approves of the colonel, precisely because he sees in him a model neopopulist.

As to the combat pilot Meresiev, with both legs shattered in an air-fight crash, this real man, as he is called, manages to crawl out of the enemy zone. After long hospitalization, he returns to active duty. It was not easy. He had to engage in a dreadful fight with the bureaucracy.[5]

One does not anymore see the lingering maimed World War II veterans on city streets in the Soviet Union. Nor is there such a thing as the image of the handicapped in state publishing house (*gosizdat*) fiction, popular or otherwise. There are a few cripples one can find in the literature. But especially diachronically, like the two discussed here, they do not make "a soup," a pattern, an image, much less a reflection of reality.

On the other hand, the splintered, centripetal bundle of themes enveloping compassion for suffering, responsibility for it, and guilt—all of it frequently blending with the apocalyptic memory of war—keeps evolving and reshaping itself with curious tenacity. Therein, the soft, melancholy theme of amazement, the astonishment at anyone having escaped war unharmed, is remarkable. Let us look, for example, at Alexandr Korenev's poem "Buying Bread."

> I have lined up for bread.
> Middle-aged, with a non-sensical briefcase,
> Me, the most unremarkable citizen,
> I move with the others toward the door.

I move. Was I ever shot at?
Did I crawl through forests?
On the run, was I hit by a bullet?
This very same me, standing in line?

It's crazy. How to believe my own eyes
That through the sky's white whirlwind,
Dropped from a Douglass, I landed
As saboteur somewhere at night.

On a crowded street, in a certain year,
This queue quietly moves toward the door.
It's hard to believe I was not killed.
Dropped from the sky, I move on.[6]

Read out of context, this poem seems at times constrained, pinched, strangled and at the same time sentimental. The poem conveys potential pain, as it were. But let us circumvent the trap. Let us not use the label sentimental as an excuse for disregarding the material. Is there not compassion, cosuffering—*sostradanie*—there, as it always has been in Russia for the impaired and the handicapped and the outcast? What seems to be sentimental in one culture need not be in another. In Soviet literature, compassion is especially clear when the theme of suffering involves children: it mandates emotional responsibility, as in Valentin Popov's much more recent "Boarding School for the Blind."

It used to be
when I saw a little tike
wear glasses, my heart
contracted. But here—
children, they are drawing
in total darkness.
It used to be
I would complain
about a billfold thinner
than my bankbook.
And here, these children they
have never seen themselves
nor have they seen
their mother.
It used to be
a pile of rubbish next to
a house just built
would make me sad.
I also grieved that

understanding came late to me—
like newspapers
to a hideaway in winter.
And here—
children play blind man's bluff
with eyes wide open.
It used to be
I howled
because my heart was
broken into with a wrench.
And here—
a small blind girl
listens to TV.
So, I move unseen,
with my enormous seeing eyes,
as if I had stuffed myself
with food
during the Leningrad famine and siege,
survived at the front
when everybody perished,
as if a ship crowded with children
is sinking right now
and no one but me
knows how to swim.[7]

Such personalized guilt for survival blends with responsibility for
the blind, who symbolize, in turn, the vulnerability of all other
unseen handicapped.

Vassily Fedorov's "The Blind Man," published a decade after
the war, offers another insight into this kind of sympathy for the
wounded.

Not seeing anyone in front of him,
Unseduced by a shop in the square,
The blind man goes along the street
Sounding out the ground with his cane.

He will be pushed
As people overtake him.
Quick to interfere,
A seeing man appeals
To others to be careful.

I hear the blind man's voice,
Muted in the din of the crowd:
"Go ahead, push! Nichevo.
It reassures me

> That there are people
> Next to me."[8]

As in our earlier example, so here, there is not objective sympathy with the handicapped. The message here is implied: how easily one might find oneself abandoned. There is active, very gripping reader involvement of a sort one does not find in other literature. It was in such fashion, in particular, that Soviet literature of the postwar period reflected the war wounded.

II

For the sake of a broader perspective, let us look next at a short literary "document" of the early post-Stalinist years. A vignette, involving once more a blind child, turns into a parable or sermon.

> At midnight, I walked along an almost empty street in Moscow. Somewhere, near the Pushkin Theatre, I came upon a girl, who was about ten. At first, I didn't even realize that in front of me walked a blind girl. She walked unevenly along the edge of the sidewalk. She went around a pillar, then paused for an instant, held before it. I overtook and passed her, then glanced back; listening to my footsteps she followed. At Pushkin Square, I turned the corner. But I wanted to see, once more what the blind girl would do. At the corner, the girl stopped, tensely listening, head uplifted. Perhaps she was waiting to hear from what area footsteps would again sound. No one was walking. Nearby cars rushed past. I turned back.
> "Where are you off to?"
> The blind one said, as if not surprised, "If you please, to the Armenian store."
> "And now?"
> "Now, it's close for me. Thanks."
> For an instant she stood, then went on, listening to the steps of a casual passerby. So this meeting ended. Except afterward, I thought, truly you see how often we forget that the echoes of our footsteps remain behind us. And therefore, always, it is necessary to walk straight, correctly, so that we do not deceive others, those, who trust in our steps and follow. And that is all.[9]

This vignette makes clear that the problem of the place of the handicapped in a society, closed or open, is inseparably linked with the question of the bondage of the individual to the social order. This is a tired and melancholy truism, but true nonetheless.

Backtracking to the vagaries and savagery of high Stalinism, one finds fragments in two very different works by two powerful

writers—both victims of the Stalinist terror—each eidetically illu-
minating, per se as well as in relationship to each other. In these
fragments, both writers speak of self-mutilation.

In Vladimir Kirshon's heretical play *Bread,* one of the central
figures—Raevsky—is a party official ordered to requisition grain
from recalcitrant peasants at all costs. And this is no euphemism.
He dreads the assignment. When the woman he loves suggests that
there is an alternative, that he can, indeed, try to disobey the
party's orders, this is what he replies, in one of the most revelatory
passages in all of Stalinist literature:

> RAEVSKY: I've thought of that. Yes, the thong often cuts into my
> flesh, but I can't live without it. . . . Imagine a crowd. A crowd
> composed of identical people, a crowd composed of standardized
> people. They are all wearing ties of the same color. They are all
> walking in the same direction. They all speak the same measured
> words. I don't want to be one of this crowd. There are times when
> I am horrified at the thought that each day I put on the same kind
> of tie everyone else is wearing. But I know a feeling which is even
> more terrifying. Imagine, Olga, this crowd going by without you.
> And that you are left alone, all alone with your thoughts, with your
> doubts while the columns keep passing by. They pass by forever
> without you. They repeat their words. They sing their songs. Not a
> single one of them turns his eyes in your direction. Their measured
> steps are merciless. And precisely because I myself am filled with
> thoughts which are not attuned to those of the others, with emo-
> tions which do not correspond to those of my companions, I cannot
> step out of the ranks. I dare not leave. I must feel another shoulder
> next to mine. I need someone to give me orders, someone to disci-
> pline me. I can't get along without those iron fetters which weld
> together the diverse sides of my "I."[10]

Kolyma concentration camp prisoners, a small group of them,
sit at Christmastime around a stove "in a sleepy lyrical mood," as
one of the greatest writers of the twentieth century—Varlam
Shalamov—says. They meditate aloud:

> "You know, fellows, it would be a good thing to go home. After
> all, miracles do happen. . . . " It was Glebov, the horse driver, speak-
> ing. He used to be a professor of philosophy and was famous in our
> barracks for having forgotten his wife's name a month earlier. "I
> guess I should knock on wood, but I really mean to go home."
> "Home?"
> "Sure."
> "I'll tell you the truth," I answered, "I'd rather go back to

prison. I'm not joking. I wouldn't want to go back to my family now. They wouldn't understand me, they couldn't. The things that seem important to them I know to be trivial. And the things that are important to me—the little that is left to me—would be incomprehensible to them. I would bring them a new fear, add one more fear to the thousands of fears that already fill their lives. No man should see or know the things that I have seen and known.

"Prison is another matter altogether. Prison is freedom. It's the only place I have ever known where people spoke their minds without being afraid. Their souls were at rest there. And their bodies rested too, because they didn't have to work. There, every hour of our being had meaning."

"What a lot of rot," the former professor of philosophy said. "That's only because they didn't beat you during the investigation. Anyone who experienced that method would be of an entirely different opinion.

"How about you, Peter Ivanovich, what do you say to that?" Peter Ivanovich Timofeev, the former director of Ural Trust, smiled and winked at Glebov.

"I'd go home to my wife. I'd buy some rye bread—a whole loaf! I'd cook up a bucketful of kasha. And some soup with dumplings— a bucket of that too! And I'd eat it all. And I'd be full for the first time in my life. And whatever was left over I'd make my wife eat."

"How about you?" Glebov asked Zvonkov, the pickman of our workgang, who had been a peasant from either Yaroslavl or Kostroma in his earlier life.

"I'd go home," Zvonkov answered seriously, without the slightest trace of a smile. "I think if I could go home, I'd never be more than a step away from my wife. Whereever she'd go, I'd be right on her heels. The only thing is that they've taught me how to hate work here. I've lost my love of the land. But I'd find something. . . ."

"And how about you?" Glebov touched the knees of our orderly.

"First thing I'd go to Party Headquarters. I'll never forget all the cigarette butts they had on the floor there."

"Stop joking."

"I'm dead serious."

Suddenly I realized that there was only one person left who had not yet answered. And that person was Volodya Dobrovoltsev. He raised his head, not waiting for the question. From the open stove door the light of the glowing coals gleamed in his lively, deep-set eyes.

"As for me," he said in a calm, unhurried voice, "I'd like to have my arms and legs cut off and become a human stump—no arms or legs. Then I'd be strong enough to spit in their faces for everything they're doing to us. . . ."[11]

In both cases, self-mutilation leads to a dead end. Of course. But it leads to catharsis as well. In Shalamov's ultimate record, self-mutilation turns into strength—a strange and grandiose metaphor going back into the human past with its hubris.

But enough of metaphorical projection. There are two Soviet stories about cripples, one old, one new, which can enlarge our understanding of what seems to be a very Russian theme of deformation and hubris. The cripples are, one might say, binary contrasts. One is a hideous Quasimodo, the other an Apollo. Both are legless amputees. The first is the body and soul of Stalinism; the second is a World War II victim. Both are clairvoyants. They reflect upon their society. They are, somehow, saintly fools both. And one turns out to be more patient than the other with the social order in which they suffer. The Stalinist monster crawls away never to return. The veteran amputee of the Great Patriotic War sits thirty years and then some on the shore of a remote northern lake and waits.

First, Zhachev—the monster—whose first name we never learn. He lives and crawls about a great, dark, frightening, sad book in which not socialist realism but surrealism rises to unprecedented power. Andrei Platonov (1889–1951) must have finished his novel *The Foundation Pit* in the pivotal year of 1930. It is a black testimonial to the Plan, to both Stalinist industrialization and collectivization.

Told in a strangely estranged and at the same time incantational way—in the language of Stalinist malignant bureaucratese—two superhappenings hold the narrative: the excavation of a foundation pit for a high-rise building to house the plebs in the impending Stalinist millennium and the literal sending of kulaks down the river on a raft to drown in the sea.

The *basso ostenato* of the tale is entrusted to a weird relationship between a tiny little orphan girl, Nastya—for whom ostensibly all the ado, since it is she who will blossom in the glorious communist future—and the unsavory legless cripple Zhachev. He keeps Nastya close to his torso in his low cart, which he uses to move and to sleep in. He lost his legs because of what he calls capitalism. Bitter, angry, dirty, denouncing and blackmailing everybody, he loves Nastya. He is passionately committed to kibitzing, to participation in the Plan, and thereby he turns into a holy fool, into a deformed promethean figure, maimed by Stalinism. The sad, hungry, emaciated little Nastya dies from exposure, and since her crippled mentor had failed to save her, he loses faith.

Zhachev alone took no part in anything and watched the digging labor with sad eyes.

"Why are you sitting there like an official?" Chiklin asked him, returning to the barrack. "You might at least be sharpening the spades!"

"I can't, Nikit, I don't believe in nothing now," Zhachev answered on that morning of the second day.

"Why, vermin?"

"Don't you see I am a cripple of imperialism? And communism is the children's business, that's why I loved Nastya. . . . I'll go now and kill Comrade Pashkin, as my parting deed."

And Zhachev crawled away into the city, never again returning to the foundation pit.[12]

So much for our first literary cripple. He is a relic of Russia's past, promethean but ruined. He makes the present seem, by contrast, fair. A literary device, he represents well-lost potential.

Our second cripple is very different. He is the hero of Yurii Nagibin's novella, *Patience*. There were no prosthetic limbs visible in the fiction of the Stalinist period. This post-Stalinist war veteran who has lost both legs also walks on his hands with the help of contraptions much like old fashioned flat irons. The plot involves a weird ménage à trois or, rather, trouble à trois. Before the war, the heroine, Anna, fell in love with handsome and brilliant Pasha. Aleksei, Pasha's best friend, in turn, was in love with Anna. The two men went to war together and served together. Aleksei came back. Wonderful Pasha did not and was assumed lost in action after Anna searched for him all over the country when the war was over. The survivor, then, was lucky enough to marry Anna, to have two children with her, and to proceed rapidly on the scientific elite escalator. So far, so good. But there is a dark secret that Aleksei anxiously hides. During a mutual assignment at the front, Aleksei had acted as a dishonest coward, had betrayed Pasha, and had been responsible for his death. This terrible business surfaces in hazy flashbacks without precise detail.

Now, almost forty years later, the plot deals with a luxurious weekend Anna and her husband—in the company of their nasty, cynical, perverse children—spend on a snow-white luxury tourist vessel that takes them from Leningrad to Bogoyar, a picturesque small island on Lake Ladoga, the site of an ancient monastery. The morning after their arrival, while the husband needs to relax and the dreadful children are nursing a hangover, Anna goes ashore to explore the island.

Passengers approached the boulder. Anna followed them automatically and saw cripples who were selling small, knotty, dirty roots gathered in the forest. And it is here only that she remembered the sad fate of Bogoyar. It served as a terminal shelter for those who were maimed by war and who either had not wanted to return to their homes or who were refused acceptance there.[13]

And . . . this is exactly where she finds Pasha. Swinging his legless torso, he walks on his hands, covering seven kilometers—each step of which he has counted—from the monastery to the harbor, and back. He too comes to sell medicinal roots to tourists, while with each anchored steamer, he waits for Anna.

When she recognizes this stump of a man, she hysterically attacks him with her fists. She screams and demands that he return her life to her, which he had taken away by disappearing. They spend the night together. On the damp ground, in the forest, they have sex for the first time ever. The doleful resumé of the cripple's postwar career and his evaluation of the world he had left behind is told in direct speech.

"This is really the end of the world. Not geographically, of course. I had tried to live among normal people. After the hospital. After they finally finished cutting me down. To Leningrad I didn't return. Anyhow, neither my parents nor my sister were alive anymore. . . . Of course, I thought about you," he said with difficulty. "Why lie? But there is no point in rechewing it all again. Everything is clear as is. I decided to start from scratch, to prove my right to be among the bipeds. But it didn't work out. . . . Do you remember how it was after the war? On every street corner cripples were selling single cigarettes. Commerce maintained by the beggars. I didn't engage in it. I tried to learn the trade of a diamond cutter. But each time I would linger on the street, they would throw at me either change or one-ruble bills. Nobody wanted to insult me. On the contrary. They took the pittance away from their own mouths. Women especially. I was good looking, remember? But it did me in. It seemed to me that they were showing me my real place. Stupid?"[14]

With masochistic fury, he continues the tale of his degradation—how he sold rotten cigarettes, how he spent his measly earnings with drunkards, whores, and thieves who employed cripples in their enterprises; how he took part in brawls, how he learned to use a knife mercilessly—never touching another cripple—and how in a bizarre way he hoped to be murdered by these criminals. But it came to an end without blood. With shame instead. He got into a fight with a young woman who had furnished him with stolen cigarettes. She had cheated him. It wasn't a question of money; it was her flagrant arrogance that made him take after her in his small four-wheeled cart (*telezhka*), which he was using at the time. She mocked him. He tried to hit her and fell out of his cart. Helpless, he rolled down the steps between two steep streets. And that's when he decided to get himself to Bogoyar.

Anna is vehemently, passionately determined to take him away from Bogoyar, no matter what. It is clear that she will be able to handle all the risks. He understands. And he thwarts her with a story of another veteran, a basket case. A Siberian peasant youth, drafted right out of school and sent to the front, had lost all his limbs in battle. Of his own free will, he came to Bogoyar to hide. He did not want his mother to discover him as the stump he had become. His mother refused to believe that he was dead and took off to look for her son "in all of Russia" (*po vsei Rossii*). No one knew how she lived, how she ate. It took her three years to find him. When she did, she stayed with him in Bogoyar. In Pasha's words:

> "Every Sunday she tied her son to her back and brought him to the harbor. She put him on a bench, inserted a burning cigarette be-tween his teeth. He puffed, looked at the people and smiled. (He was over fifty.) His mother's closeness helped him remain a kid with the smile of a child, and with the purity of a child and with a child's lack of anger. When his mother died, I started to drag him out to the harbor. He is now fading away without illness, without a pal-pable reason. I cannot abandon him."[15]

Pasha also adds that he has a woman here, a piece of information that does not make too much of an impresson on Anna as she accuses him of being afraid to leave this hospice. He slashes back. What he hurls at Anna is not exactly what we used to call socialist realism. It is, one might say, anticipatory *glasnost'*, which Yurii Nagibin, for one, had practiced for a long time.

> "The devil I am afraid! . . . I don't want your life. You have gotten used to it. You work at it. And I don't. Out there in the harbor, you think I haven't heard anything, haven't seen anything? . . . Overfed gluttons and philistines, you whine all the time—that's who you are! It's not clear where your mugs are or where your asses are located. And you cry all the time that the situation with food is bad. And that you can't get spare parts. And that garages and repair shops are too far away from your houses. . . . You make me sick. No, I don't want your 'big' life. It will choke me. . . . I bet your

social circle is full of those who crave spare parts, slate roofing, foreign products, and the rest of the rotten junk. Go to hell, all of you! We don't bother you. Leave us alone." The dam had broken and, dismissing all good intentions, he screamed, "We don't want you! Devil take you! What did you drag yourself here for? Who asked you?"[16]

This contemporary novella generated a loud and protracted debate among critics, which is not over yet.[17] To say the least, the author had anticipated *glasnost'* and the lifting of formidable taboos such as suicide; even if accidental. Accidental, perhaps. Nagibin speaks of patience, divisiveness, and bitter-sweet tenacious memories across some thirty-five years. But the significance of the novella in our context lies in its contrast with Platonov's *Foundation Pit* and in Pasha's contrast with Zhachev. For the literary device is in many ways identical. A cripple represents the lost potential of the past. But then one looked forward. Now in today's Soviet society, one looks back. What the Revolution gave, the war took away.

III

At the end of Nagibin's icy and tragic tale, Anna drowns, having jumped from the luxury steamer trying to reach Pasha and the shore. Hereupon, the author speaks through Pasha, who does not know what has happened, of the brotherhood among the handicapped. Pasha's crippled comrades had seen him crawl into the woods with the elegant lady visitor. And he knows that they eagerly await the account of his macho exploit:

> They did not know here what envy was. Success of one of them turned into success for all, affirming their shared capacity to live. But when he entered the dormitory and they threw themselves at him with eager and mocking questions, he reprimanded them in a serious tone of voice:
> "Let it be, fellows. It was my sister."
> They became quiet at once. Not because they believed him, but because Pasha was their commanding officer, their chief, their very own leader, and his word was law.[18]

NOTES

1. Viacheslav Sablukov, "Recollection," in *Almanak 'Istoki'* (Moscow, 1986), p. 346, trans. Vera S. Dunham.

2. Mikhail Lukonin, "I Shall Come to See You," in *Lyrics and Poems*, vol. 1 (Moscow, 1973), pp. 55–56, trans. Vera S. Dunham.

3. Piotr Pavlenko, *Happiness*, (Moscow: Progress Publishers, 1947). Boris Polevoi, *The Tale of a Real Man*. This wounded combat pilot was awarded the medal of Hero of the Soviet Union. Sergei Prokofiev wrote an opera by the same name in 1948.

4. Stalinist-populist is not at all a contradiction in terms, due to the diversified needs of total national mobilization.

5. He thereby became an early brother-in-arms of Vladimir Dudintsev's hero in *Not by Bread Alone*.

6. Alexandr Korenev, "Buying Bread," in *Vzmor'e* (Moscow, 1983), p. 46, trans. Vera S. Dunham.

7. Valentin Popov, "Boarding School for the Blind," in *Den poezii* (Leningrad, 1984), p. 108, trans. Vera S. Dunham.

8. Vassily Federov, "The Blind Man," in *Den Poezii: Izbrannoe, 1956–1981* (Moscow, 1982), p. 238, trans. Vera S. Dunham.

9. Anatolii Pristavkin, "Steps Left Behind," *Trudnoe detstvo, Yunost* 6 (1959), trans. Vera S. Dunham.

10. Vladimir Kirshon, *Bread*, in *Six Soviet Plays* (Boston: Houghton Mifflin, 1934), pp. 242–43, trans. Eugene Lyons.

11. Varlam Shalamov, "An Epitaph," in *Graphite* (New York: Norton, 1981), pp. 281–82, trans. John Glad.

12. Andrei Platonov, in *The Foundation Pit* (New York: Dutton, 1975), p. 141, trans. M. Ginsburg.

13. Yurii Nagibin, *Patience, Novyi mir* 2 (1982): 38, trans. Vera S. Dunham.

14. Ibid., p. 44.

15. Ibid., p. 48.

16. Ibid.

17. See, for instance, a major essay by the well-known critic V. Kardin, "Are these Debates Pertinent?" [Po sushchestvu li eti spory?], *Voprosy literatury* 2 (1983), and a nasty piece by A. Latynina, "The Metamorphosis of Penelope, or a Trap for the Reader" [Metamorfoza Penelopy ili lovushka dlia chitatelia], in *Literaturnaya gazeta*, 27 Apr. 1983.

18. Nagibin, *Patience*, p. 53.

Part TWO

The Contemporary Scene

Programs for the Disabled in the USSR

Bernice Madison

I

THE DISABLED and their survivors constitute a diversified contingent of many million persons in the Soviet Union. There exists a very complex system of material support, assistance in kind, and social services for them. It derives its administrative structure from both all-union and republic statutes; its legal sanctions from labor, *kolkhoz,* and administrative law; and its financing from central, regional, and local sources. Its work involves the trade unions, the employing establishments, *kolkhoz* councils, the educational and medical systems, and the financial and military authorities. The following is a survey of this system.

II

There is no all-union ministry for social security in the Soviet Union.[1] The system's directing organs are fifteen republic ministries of social security. These govern the medical-labor expert commissions (Vrachebno-Trudovye Ekspertnye Komissii—VTEKs), which are the principal executive instruments for determining disabilities. The ministries also supervise the national societies for the blind (Vserossiiskoe Obshchestvo Slepykh—VOS) and the deaf (Vserossiiskoe Obshchestvo Glukhikh—VOG).

The ministries are assisted by the All-Union Central Council of Trade Unions (VTsSPS) and by the All-Union Collective Farm Council. The Council of Ministers has a Union-Republic State Committee on Social Questions, which controls both the social security ministries in the various republics and the Trade Union Council. This committee performs a key interpretive function de-

167

signed to realize "a single state policy" in social security throughout the nation. Its directives are binding on both the trade unions
and the social security ministries, which accordingly find themselves accountable both to the central government and to the Republic Council of Ministers. The ministries all have departments
below the republic level in regions, districts, and municipalities,
which are likewise subject to double subordination. Vertically,
they attach to the higher organs in their own hierarchy, horizontally to the executive committees of appropriate soviets. In addition, there is a special hierarchy of *kolkhoz* councils at the republic,
regional, and area levels, as well as on each collective farm. All but
the last are obliged to include representatives of the social security
and finance ministries.

The 1930s saw the creation of special research institutes for
disability evaluation and assessment of capacity for work, for the
purpose of providing a scientific approach to questions involved in
job placement. These activities have gained in scope, diversity, and
importance since then. Central among the institutes that contribute to this effort is the Central Scientific Institute of Expertise on
Ability to Work and Organization of Work for the Disabled
(TSIETIN). By 1980, there were eight scientific research institutes
in the RSFSR, the Ukraine, Belorussia, and Uzbekistan. They
address not only theoretical matters, but practical concerns as well.

The foundation of any social security system is its financing. In
the Soviet Union many of the costs are absorbed by the all-union
national budget. This budget, for example, carries the entire
weight of institutional care for the aged and the disabled and pays
for the pensions of former military personnel and their survivors,
absorbing all administrative costs. In addition, there is a system of
employer contributions as a percentage of payrolls: a certain percentage of the wages, but not from the wages, is added by the
enterprise; collective farm contributions are made from a tax on
their gross incomes.

Contribution rates for all urban enterprises were set by the
1956 State Pension Act for Workers and Employees and were
raised in 1979. They ranged from 4.4 to 14 percent of payroll,
depending on the degree of hazard which employment in them
entails compared to the original 4.4–9 percent.[2] The intent was
and still is to tie pensions squarely to output. When output rises, it
is reasoned, so does the payroll, and so do contributions into the
state social security fund. Subsidies from the national budget
would be minimal. This assumption has not materialized: subsi-

dies to cover deficits increased steadily and by 1980 amounted to more than half of the total spent.

Financing arrangements for *kolkhoz* pensions date back to 1965 and 1970. Their cost is met on the whole by the Central All-Union Social Security Fund for Collective Farmers and subsidies from the national budget. In addition, there is a 5 percent tax on the gross income of all self-contained *kolkhozy* (since 1978 6 percent on those that show more than a 15 percent return on investment). In 1965, subsidies covered 38 percent of *kolkhoz* pensions; in 1970, 60 percent.[3] Pensions for workers and employees who work in *kolkhozy* are paid from the state social security fund.

Since 1960, pensions have been the most expensive item in the social security–social insurance budget, using up more than 70 percent of it. Increases in expenditures have been reflected in the social consumption budget and in GNP: 26 percent of the former in 1960, 30.2 percent in 1984; and 4.8 percent of the latter in 1976, 5.3 percent in 1983.

Though we cannot know exactly how all these very complex institutions work compared to social security systems in other countries, it seems clear that persistent unresolved administrative problems are endemic to the system. Some of them derive from administrative overlaps. Theoretically, vertical relationships bring about procedural unity in implementing legislation, and horizontal relationships should make possible expedient responses to local conditions. But in many instances, this evidently does not happen, and difficulties arise.

A second set of intractable problems results from the ever-burgeoning multiplicity of laws that governs social security. In 1984, a Soviet authority wrote that "layers of acts . . . [and] constant additions and changes . . . have led to a situation when even specialists find it difficult at times to implement the social security legislation in practice."[4]

A third nagging problem concerns complaints. This has been brought to the fore by Article 58 of the 1977 Constitution, still unimplemented, because it provides access to courts for persons who believe that officials have infringed their rights. In the meantime, the only fair hearings available are via administrative reviews, often by the same officials against whom complaints were lodged in the first place. In many localities, complaints have been increasing.

Another pressing problem regards personnel. The system now requires law and economics degrees for administrators, training in finance for bookkeepers, and specialized medical training for VTEK doctors. An increasing proportion of new workers come with these qualifications, and the level of education in general has been rising, but as yet the situation is not satisfactory.[5] Pay and prestige are low and staff turnover is quite high. Continuing reports refer to social security's failure to do away with causes of complaints brought on by lack of attention, sensitivity, cordiality, warmth, and goodwill—to say nothing of the presence of outright irresponsibility—on the part of some personnel.[6]

A last problem, increasingly urgent, given the huge and complicated social security work load, is the need to create a fully automated system.[7] First steps in this direction were taken more than a decade ago, but as yet automated calculating and payment centers are by no means universal. While it is generally recognized that automation is a progressive step, it is also clear that in many areas automated operations still suffer from deficiencies that cause interruptions and delays.

III

Let us turn now to the quesion of how disability is determined. Responsibility in this matter is, as noted above, assigned to the VTEKs, which are charged with the following duties: (1) determining the degree of loss-of-work ability and the reasons for it, fixing the disability group, defining the conditions and the types of work possible for disabled individuals, and helping them reestablish work ability; (2) fixing the time at which disability began; (3) ascertaining the nature of the reasons for a breadwinner's death; (4) deciding which services will help disabled persons regain work ability; (5) studying working conditions to make sure that the work the disabled are doing is not harmful to their health and is properly organized; and (6) acquainting doctors in the general health care system with the principles and methods of medical-labor expertise. VTEKs handle a huge load: in RSFSR alone, they annually examine 2.4–2.5 million persons.[8]

VTEKs are citywide, interdistrict, and district in scope. They normally include three physician experts—an internist, a surgeon, and a neuropathologist, one of whom serves as a chairman—one representative from social security, and one from a trade union, the latter to furnish guidance on work-related issues and the former on social issues. Specialized VTEKs are organized for persons suffering from tuberculosis, psychiatric disorders, blindness and eye defects, and oncological conditions. In case of need, other special-ized VTEKs may be organized. In all VTEKs there is a medical registrar, and in those that work five or more days a week, a senior nurse. These local VTEKs are responsible to Moscow, Leningrad, regional, and autonomous republic VTEKs, which are composed of four physicians each, and which are responsible for checking lower VTEK decisions, reexamining disabled persons dissatisfied with them, providing consultation, and settling disagreements be-tween VTEK members. The higher VTEKs are also expected to study the reasons for disability and their dynamics, and to make proposals for lowering the occurrence of disabling conditions. In cases where disabled persons do not agree with a VTEK decision, they can, within a month, present a written appeal to the district social security organ, requesting a reexamination. They are then sent to a different VTEK or to a republic, regional, central, or city VTEK—the directors' decisions being final. Nevertheless, if direc-tors have doubts (either on medical or legal grounds) about this final decision, they may send back the documents on the basis of which the judgment was made, requesting that the decision be reviewed.

Most VTEKs examine patients in medical facilities, and a growing number, directly at the workplace. In cases that require a period of observation, they have access to hospitals. They exam-ine only patients sent to them by medical consultative commis-sions (Vrachebnye Konsul'tativnye Komissii—VKK), usually from polyclinics or hospitals in the area where the patient resides. Referrals are made when signs of long-lasting loss-of-work abil-ity have been extablished—not later than four months after the onset of temporary disability, or not later than a combined five-month period during the last twelve months in cases of repeated periods of the same illness. Those suffering from TB are referred to VTEK in the same manner, the only difference being that, instead of four or five months, the period is ten months. Patients who are not working, in addition to medical referral must pres-ent a referral from social security.

The disabled are divided into three groups: Group I includes those who have lost all capacity for work and require constant nursing care; Group II have lost the capacity to work efficiently in their former or any other occupation but may be able to work in specially created conditions, differing from Group I mainly in that they do not need constant nursing care; Group III is the partially disabled, whose loss-of-work ability may be as high as two-thirds and who are unable to work in their former occupations under the conditions obtaining there but can engage in casual, part-time, or less skilled work in another occupation, the last alternative being the one most often used in job placement. Borderline cases are frequent, especially in Group III, which probably takes in 70–80 percent of all disabled.

Regulations call for reexaminations of Group I once in two years and of Group II and III, once every year. Not subject to a specified time are the disabled who have reached retirement age; the war disabled from World War II for whom the disability group remains fixed for a total of fifteen or more years; the disabled of that war who have reached retirement age and for whom the same group of disability has continued without interruption for five years; and some Group I blind.

VTEK decisions must be concrete, designed to describe a correct job placement and, as juridical facts, resolve the questions of objective relevance, admissibility, authenticity; and sufficiency. Often, this is not easy to achieve. Work-connected disabilities include not only injuries, accidents, and diseases sustained on or resulting from the job or from business trips, but also (1) those that occurred while doing something "in the interests of the employing establishment, even if this activity was not requested by management"; (2) incapacities incurred while going to and from work, at the workplace, near the workplace, or "in some other workplace" during working hours and work breaks, "if being at this place does not conflict with rules governing the internal disposition of the workforce"; (3) impairments contracted while putting in order machinery, tools, and work clothes before and after work, as well as accidents that take place during overtime and work on free days; (4) accidents and injuries sustained while carrying out government or social responsibilities, as well as special duties assigned by soviet, party, professional, or social organizations, regardless of whether they are connected with the person's regular employment—as well as those that occur in the process of saving human life, protecting socialist property, maintaining socialist order, donating blood (as well as skin, other tissues, and organs). In short, work-connected disabilities sometimes are not in fact connected with work. For *kolkhozniki,* the concept is interpreted less broadly. For them, (2) above is restricted to incapacities incurred while going to and from work; and (3) is eliminated altogether. Furthermore, Group III *kolkhozniki* are covered only for work-connected disability.[9]

The VTEKs have other problems. Trade union and social security representatives attend VTEK sessions only sporadically, a practice that has become an accepted pattern in many places. (Since such nonattendance is against the law, in a strict sense, decisions made by medical members alone do not have legal force. Apparently, nobody worries about this particular law.) While the outcomes of needed contacts between VTEK and VKK are universally praised, some are nullified by the substitution of VTEK decisions for VKK decisons, when the latter request unnecessary consultations from VTEK. Some censure this practice; others ask, what is to be done with patients who insist that they are disabled, yet who lack certification that their injury was work incurred or that they were wounded at the front? The VKK have neither the legal nor the moral right to turn them down. But can they be refused referral to VTEK? (Actually, the disabled themselves often beg to be permitted to stay with VKK, because sickness benefits are higher than disability pensions. It is when they can no longer receive sickness benefits that they want to be declared disabled.)

Defining the conditions and type of work suitable for individual disabled persons is the most frequently criticized aspect of VTEK work. What is called for is VTEK involvement in socio-labor rehabilitation. In 1980, an important administrator wrote that the level of VTEK expertise does not answer current demands and that it needs basic improvement. Many VTEKs limit their work to examining patients and do not participate actively in prevention and in socio-labor rehabilitation. The number of disabled returned to fully productive work has shown a tendency to decline and was only 4.8 percent in 1978.[10]

Another flaw has to do with the TSIETIN. In some autonomous republics and regions, TSIETIN recommendations are hardly studied and are not applied. Even in Moscow and the Moscow region, in which utilization is quite good, in twenty-four local VTEKs of the twenty-eight studied in 1980, methodological materials issued by TSIETIN could not be found.[11]

Nevertheless, there has been progress. Occurrence of disability diminished by 40 percent during the 1970s. The proportion of physician experts whose principal work is in VTEKs went up to 66 percent in 1980, and increasing numbers of vacancies have been filled by experienced physicians. VTEKs in daily session have also increased; many work in well-organized facilities, during hours convenient for the population. The number of unnecessary referrals to VTEKs has decreased. The number of changed decisions, both those appealed and those controlled, has been diminishing.

VTEKs are carrying out a deep analysis of reasons for initial disability and reporting their findings to soviet and trade union organs. Errors in disability determinations have decreased because of increased participation of physicians from higher VTEKs and of specialists in sessions with lower VTEKs. There is some evidence that VTEK work is assuming a sociological direction, that is, they more often take part in treatment and preventive activities of enterprises directed toward restoring the work ability of the disabled.[12]

IV

There are two main forms of material support for the disabled in the USSR. On the one hand, for one-time members of the work force there are disability and survivor pensions; there are pension supplements for dependents of unable-to-work family members. On the other hand, for persons not eligible for pensions, there are various kinds of grants (*posobiia*).[13]

For disability pensions, eligibility is twofold: loss-of-work ability sufficient for inclusion into one of three disability groups; and, for non-work-connected disability, fulfillment of the requisite work record, not required for work-connected disability. (Students in general secondary schools are eligible only if their disability is work connected, that is, if it resulted from work required by in-service training.) Pensions are either ordinary or privileged. The latter cover workers and employees who work underground, in harmful conditions, or in hot shops (List 1), and those who work under less onerous conditions (List 2).

For Group I blind men and women, the work record is reduced by ten years; for dwarfs, both men and women, by five years. Workers and employees in *kolkhozy* must prove that they worked in the *kolkhoz* after the passage of the 1964 Collective Farm Member Pensions and Allowances Act, and were members prior to this act.

Those eligible for supplements are unable-to-work dependents of nonworking groups I and II pensioners who are workers and employees (such dependents of *kolkhozniki* are not eligible). Included are (1) children—whether natural, adopted, illegitimate, or stepchildren—siblings, and grandchildren under sixteen years of age, eighteen if in school, and older if they become permanently and totally disabled prior to these ages; stepchildren if they receive no support from their own parents; and siblings and grandchildren if they do not have able-to-work parents; (2) parents and grandparents of the disabled if they have reached pensionable age or are groups I, II, or III disabled, and for grandparents, in addition, if there is no other person legally responsible for their support: (3) a spouse, if legally married and he or she has met the same requirements as parents; (4) stepparents, if they have depended on the disabled pensioner for not less than ten years. If the family includes two or more nonworking disabled pensioners, supplements can be paid only on the basis of one pension, the one of the dependent's choice.

Survivor pensions are awarded to unable-to-work dependents of breadwinners who, if they died from nonwork-connected causes, had the requisite work record. Pensions are granted regardless of time of death of the breadwinner. But if he or she was a pensioner, the award is made if death occurred during receipt of pension or during five years following discontinuance of pension. As to family members who are eligible, they are quite similar to family members eligible for supplements.

Grandparents are treated as unable-to-work regardless of age; disability of a spouse must have taken place prior to the death of the breadwinner or during the five years following his or her death, but if the spouse does not have any able-to-work adult children, those restrictions are dropped. Pensions may be paid to children and to parents who were not the breadwinner's dependents if they lose their source of subsistence after his or her death. Also, one of the parents of the remaining spouse is eligible, regardless of age or ability to work, if he or she is raising any of the children—in (1) above—of the deceased. For collective farmers, the circle of family members is narrow. Excluded are parents or spouse who are raising children of the deceased, and only in exceptional circumstances are pensions awarded to children and parents who had not been dependents. For all survivors, the pension is paid to the "collective pensioner," that is, to the family as a single unit. If a member requests a separate share, the pension is divided by the number of family members to arrive at one share.

The social security system adheres to the principle of compensating for loss of wages rather than for the physical or mental harm sustained. For workers and employees, size depends on disability group, reasons for the disability, and former earnings. (Former earnings are average monthly earnings, derived either from the last twelve months of work or from five consecutive years out of the ten preceding application, whichever is the more advantageous. But *kolkhozniki* are not allowed to use the last twelve months: consequently, their historical average earnings may be lower than their more recent ones.) Long uninterrupted work record, family situation, and connection with agriculture are taken into account for worker and employee pensions but not *kolkhoznik* pensions.

The 1974 liberalization introduced two new methods for calculating disability pensions. Method 1 uses a percentage of old age pension, which in turn is calculated as a percentage of earnings. Method 2 uses a percentage of the disabled person's own earnings, a higher percentage being applied to the first part of earnings and a lower percentage to the rest—a double-scale method, which is less advantageous than method 1. Method 1 is the usual one for groups I and II: for Group I disabled by nonwork-connected causes, 100 percent of old age pension; by work-connected causes, 110 percent; for Group II, 90 percent and 100 percent, respectively. Method 2 is used for groups I and II "very rarely," only when it results in a higher pension. For Group III, only the double-scale method is used. This results in relatively low pensions: a Group III disabled who earned 154 rubles 27 kopeks would get a pension of 29 rubles 43 kopeks. Group III are expected to work: pensions only compensate for the part of earnings lost because the disabled person is performing work that is "easier or less in volume."

Available since 1956 for those who do not have the requisite work record for a full pension are partial pensions, awarded to groups I and II who become disabled during work, the only requirement. First, the amount of what the full pension would have been is determined by method 1; then the partial amount is calculated in line with the actual work record, but it cannot be less than a fourth of a full pension. Partial pensions are not payable to *kolkhozniki.*

For Group I workers, employees and *kolkhozniki,* regardless of cause of disability, there is a 15-ruble-a-month nursing care supplement. If, however, the former two are receiving minimum pensions, this supplement "is not awarded because [their] minimum pensions [75.5 rubles a month] are 25 rubles higher than the minimum for Group II disabled [50 rubles a month]." (Apparently, the minimum for Group I is seen as including the sum necessary for nursing care; hence, this part of the pension is not granted as a supplement. It is not stated whether the same rule applies to *kolkhozniki.*) Whether one is working or not, an uninterrupted work record of ten to fifteen years entitles one to a 10 percent supplement; of longer than fifteen years, to 15 percent. For nonworking groups I and II, supplements for unable-to-work dependents amount to a flat 10 rubles a month for one such dependent of

Group I, to 20 rubles for two, and to 30 rubles for three or more. For dependents of Group II, the amounts are 10 rubles for one and 20 rubles for two or more. Group III and partial pensioners do not receive supplements.

Using method 1, for three or more survivors, the pension equals the pension of Group I; for two survivors, that of Group II. Method 2 is used always when there is only one survivor. Method 2 applied to specified intervals of earnings is also used when there are two, three, or more survivors, if the death of the breadwinner was caused by work. For families of workers and employees that include full orphans or children who lost their unmarried mothers, pensions are at the work-connected disability rate; and if among three or more survivors there are such children, a 15 percent increase of basic pension is granted. Partial pensions must not be less than a fourth of a full pension. Since November 1981, full and partial pensions for children under sixteen years of age (eighteen if in school) cannot be less than twenty rubles a month. All pensions must fall within set minimums and maximums, the latter referring to pensions plus supplements. Table 1 presents minimums and maximums from 1956 through 1981 for urban workers and from 1965 through 1980 for farmers.

Grants (*posobiia*) are payable to congenitally disabled children. Since 1980, those older than sixteen receive thirty rubles and twenty-five rubles a month for groups I and II, respectively. (Between 1968, when grants were introduced, and 1980 they got sixteen rubles; children under sixteen remained ineligible until 1980, but since then, both groups have been receiving twenty rubles a month.) Group III individuals are ineligible whether they are under or over sixteen.

Grants for adults in group I and II are awarded only if certain conditions are met: namely, if in addition to ineligibility for pensions they show absence of any means for subsistence; absence of relatives legally responsible for support or able to support; absence of connection with agriculture (in seven republics); inability to find suitable work or a place in an institution. (No grants are awarded Group III adults save in Uzbekistan. Then they are awarded only if it is impossible to arrange job placement and only for six months in a year.) Financed by local budgets, up to 1985, the amounts granted are described by Soviet scholars as "insignificant": in urban communities, ten republics provided 10 rubles a month, the rest 12–16 rubles; for rural residents, eleven republics granted 8.5 rubles a month, the rest 10–16 rubles. These grants

TABLE 1
Monthly Minimum and Maximum Pensions (in Rubles)

Type of Pension and Degree of Disability	Minimum						Maximum			
	1956	1965	1971	1974	1980	1981	1956	1965	1974	1980
Workers and Employees										
Old Age	30		45			50	120	120	120	120
Disability–Gr. I-A[a]	36	50		70		75	120	120	120	
Disability–Gr. I-B[a]	30	50		70		75	90	90	120	
Disability–Gr. II-A	28.5	35		45		50	90	90	120	
Disability–Gr. II-B	23	30		45		50	60	60	120	
Disability–Gr. III-A	21	21		25		30	45	45	60	
Disability–Gr. III-B	16	16		21		26	40	40	60	
One Survivor A	16	21		23		28	45	45	60	
One Survivor B	16	21		23		28	40	40	60	
Two Survivors A	23	30		45		50	90	90	120	
Two Survivors B	23	30		45		50	60	60	120	
3 or More Survivors A	30	50		70		75	120	120	120	
3 or More Survivors B	30	50		70		75	90	90	120	

Collective Farmers

Old Age	12	20	28	102	120 (102)[b]	120 (102)
Disability–Gr. I-A	18	35	45	102	120 (102)	120 (102)
Disability–Gr. I-B	15	30	45	76.5	90 (76.5)	120 (102)
Disability–Gr. II-A	14.4	25	28	76.5	90 (76.5)	120 (102)
Disability–Gr. II-B	12	20	28	51	60 (51)	120 (102)
Disability–Gr. III-A	12	16	16	38.25	45 (38.25)	60 (51)
Disability–Gr. III-B						
One Survivor A	10.8	16	20	38.25	45 (38.25)	60 (51)
One Survivor B	9	16	20	34	40 (34)	60 (51)
Two Survivors A	14.4	20	28	76.5	90 (76.5)	120 (102)
Two Survivors B	12	20	28	51	60 (51)	120 (102)
3 or More Survivors A	18	30	45	102	120 (102)	120 (102)
3 or More Survivors B	15	30	45	76.5	90 (76.5)	120 (102)

SOURCES: Some of the many I examined are: M. L. Zakharov, "Razvitie edinoi sistemy pensionnogo obespecheniia v SSSR," *Sovetskoe Gosudarstvo i Pravo* 11 (1975): 29; Lev P. Yakushev, "Old People's Rights in the USSR and the European Socialist Countries," *International Labour Review* 2 (1976): 246; *Sotsial'noe Strakhovanie v SSSR*, Sbornik Ofitsial'nykh materialov (Moscow: Profizdat, 1983), p. 25ff Pavel Stiller, "Sozialpolitik in der USSR 1950–80," tables on pp. 139, 160.

a. "A" is for work-connected, "B" is for non-work-connected disability.

b. Amounts in parentheses are after deduction for agricultural connection (15%) if the farmer has private plot that is larger than permitted by *kolkhoz* regulations.

were supposed to substitute for pensions, but their amounts were obviously much lower than even the lowest minimum pensions. Given the enumerated conditions, probably only the most helpless and poverty stricken qualified, and given the miserly amounts, most barely survived. In 1985 their grants were raised to 30 rubles a month, a substantial improvement, but still below a harsh poverty line.

V

The congenitally disabled may also obtain material assistance: on the one hand, institutional care and daily life services (for example, prosthetic and orthotic appliances and specialized vehicles); on the other hand, special training. Institutions and "homes" are available in impressive numbers. In 1979, the Soviet Union had 1,500 such homes, accommodating 360,000 persons. Because the institutional population is not given separately for the aged and the disabled, we do not know how many of the residents were disabled. If the findings of a 1982 study–of twenty-two institutions in Moscow, Sverdlovsk, Ivanov, and L'vov regions—are suggestive for the country as a whole, their number would be 14 percent or perhaps 50,000.[14] That the number of places in the homes now in operation is seriously insufficient to meet the need is attested, however, not only by scholars and administrators but also by party resolutions. The failure to open up new homes, a painful problem, is not due to lack of funds but rather to nonfulfillment of construction plans.[15]

Waiting lists of persons who seek entrance are getting longer, not because they prefer to live in homes but because the number of the solitary and those unable to care for themselves is increasing.[16] A 1976/77 experiment that provided services to the old and the disabled in their own homes did not decrease the number of seriously ill who sought to enter institutions.[17] Nothing seems to have come of the idea that some apartment houses should be built to meet the special needs of the aged and the disabled; in 1983 this remained an "unsolved problem."[18] Although it appears that all republics have homes, scattered statistics indicate that in 1978, three republics—RSFSR, Ukraine, and Belorussia (with more than 71 percent of the country's population in 1979)—had 80 percent of the country's homes. Seven of the eleven remaining republics had 249 homes in 1980, thus leaving 51 homes for the other four republics.[19] According to the 1982 study mentioned above, 67 percent of the residents in homes were solitary persons, all of whom received small pensions, averaging forty rubles a month. Another 24 percent received no pensions. It would appear, therefore, that only 9 percent lived in less deprived circumstances, both from social and economic points of view.

Only pensioners, eighteen or older or survivors of pensioners are admitted to the homes. As residents, they keep 10 percent of their pensions, but not less than five rubles a month; one unable-to-work dependent gets a quarter of the pension, two get a third, and three or more, half. Long-service pensioners and their dependents are treated in the same way. *Kolkhozniki* also get 10 percent, not less than five rubles, but the rest of their pensions reverts to the *kolkhoz* for financing their upkeep in the homes. The rules for scientists, personal pensioners, and the military are somewhat different. All three retain the differences between pensions and upkeep but not less than 25 percent of their pensions. The rest, 75 percent, is paid to unable-to-work dependents, if they have them; 25 percent to one dependent, 50 percent to two or more. These arrangements were legislated prior to 1964 and have not been changed.[20]

Inefficient medical and daily life services in the homes evidently give cause for concern. Some have no resident doctors. In many others, doctors stay only the three required years or less, discouraged by poor housing and living conditions. Many dislike the work and feel isolated from modern medicine and colleagues. Shortages of qualified nurses and orderlies add to poor service. Medical councils attached to social security organs are passive, exerting little influence to improve matters.[21] As to daily life services, by 1982, 62 percent of the home population in RSFSR lived in homes that had modern conveniences,[22] but the other 38 percent existed in dismal conditions.[23] In many homes, work therapy was not offered; in others, participation was low. Young residents complained about monotonous and undiversified work, monotonous diets, and negligible amounts of vegetables, fruit, and milk.[24]

A few social security departments have a lot of experience and provide exemplary care in homes.[25] But many have persisted with their inferior performances for years, resisting efforts to bring them up to a higher common level. Another problem is the homes' spotty development of subsidiary farms, despite the knowledge that when serious attention is paid to farming, improved nutrition at low production cost becomes available for the inmates—to say nothing of increasing the availablity of foodstuffs for the entire country. In many regions, serious attention has been absent; in many others, activity has been sporadic and injudicious. As late as 1983, reports from RSFSR showed that in many homes increases in production were either not projected at all or were very small.[26]

Disabled persons who need prosthetic and orthotic appliances can get them under the law of 31 October 1918. In 1930, the responsibility for providing such appilances was transferred from the health system to the social security system; because the provision of appliances was seen as closely related to placing the disabled in jobs, the major objective of the whole undertaking. In 1939, 10,000 appliances were manufactured in RSFSR; in 1981, more than 100 enterprises produced appliances for 800,000 persons.[27] Almost all republics manufacture prostheses on a small scale. (In Kazakhstan, three factories produced 77,000 appliances in 1981, 48.8 percent of them of the "progressive" types; in Kirgiziia in the same year, one factory and its affiliate provided 3,200 prosthetic appliances and 4,000 pairs of orthopedic shoes; in Georgia, 10,000 persons were served; in RSFSR, persons living in outlying areas are served by mobile prosthetic workshops. In 1980, they helped 110,000 disabled.)

The financing of appliances is complicated. Certain prostheses are furnished free of charge to workers, employees, and pensioners; to their dependents; to the aged; to Group I and Group II disabled receiving grants; to the congenitally disabled; to students in secondary and higher schools; to children up to age sixteen; and to the aged, the disabled, and children living in social security institutions and training schools. Costs are absorbed by the social security budget. All other persons pay for prostheses at current prices. "Complicated" orthopedic shoes are furnished free of charge to Group I individuals; to residents of homes (including those for children); to children up to age sixteen; and to personal pensioners and their dependents. Group II individuals get a 50 percent reduction; the rest pay the full price. Travel expenses to and from a prostheses center and for staying in a dormitory while waiting, as well as for a person who accompanies the disabled individual, are paid either by social security or by the center for those who get their "complicated" shoes free of charge and for Group II disabled.[28]

The disabled in the USSR can get motorized or pedal-operated wheelchairs if they are certified by VTEK. Such chairs can be obtained free of charge by disabled personal pensioners and dependent members of their families, by other adult disabled, and by congenitally disabled children up to age sixteen. These chairs remain the property of the government, and when the users no longer need them, they have to be returned. Motorized wheelchairs are renewable every four years; pedal-operated chairs, every seven years. Capital repairs of motorized chairs are free once every five years. As to public transportation (rail, boat, bus, but not taxi), the nonworking disabled, the congenitally disabled, residents of institutions, and one person who accompanies a Group I disabled on a train are entitled to ride free of charge. Once a year, between 1 October and 15 May, all these persons can take an intercity trip at 50 percent of cost.

The major forms of social services available to the disabled in the USSR are training, retraining, and job placement. The drive to return the disabled to work is acquiring ever greater urgency. The authorities explain their interest in work in three ways: social—work improves the material situation of the disabled; moral—work does away with the feelings of uselessness and alienation; economic—work helps to reduce the labor deficit.[29] In 1980, 40 percent of all of the country's disabled were working, including 77.7 percent of Group III.[30]

Training and retraining are almost entirely for the younger disabled. In RSFSR in 1982, there were thirteen technical and thirty-nine professional-technical boarding schools, in which students trained for forty-seven specializations. Every year they graduate 5,000 specialists. The Ukraine's annual graduates number almost 1,000, trained in five boarding schools. In Latvia, there is a sixty-bed hospital (attached to a prosthetic center), which, in a special department, trains for shoe making and prosthesis fitting. Uzbekistan has five schools for 900 students, who train to repair radios and television sets, sew, make shoes, knit, and work as bookkeepers. Some of the disabled train directly in enterprises, in brigades, or via individual instruction by experienced workers.[31]

Three studies by TSIETIN and its Rostov affiliate provide insight into work placement. A 1978 study of ten administrative regions of RSFSR focused on the major reasons that many of the disabled do not work. They include (1) the unwillingness of some managers to hire them, because this inevitably entails "looking after them"; (2) the lack of part-time and home work; (3) the lack of attention to rational placement of the disabled from rural areas; and (4) an insufficient number of specialized work settings (this is linked to absence of data needed by social security for rational planning on a regional and district scale).[32] Some of the disabled consider themselves unable to work, despite VTEK recommendations to the contrary. The investigators concluded that it would be possible to place all of Group III and a considerable part of groups I and II, but this would require a number of changes: (1) VTEK recommendations should correspond exactly to the disabled person's illness and must be strictly observed by management. (2) Together with physicians and trade unions workers, managers should define which professions and occupations are suitable for the disabled. (3) To the extent possible, the disabled should remain on the same jobs but with reduced loads and changed time schedules; in many cases, this may require retraining or transfer to easier work which, however, pays equally well. (4) Prostheses and other devices should be perfected and working conditions improved. (5) Since productivity of the disabled is lower, enterprises that employ them should be granted economic privileges. (6) Labor laws should include legal norms governing job placement, working conditions, safety measures, and so on. (7) Laws on job placement should be systematized and codified; Article 43 of the 1977 Constitution should be implemented by preparing a "regulation of job placement for the disabled." (8) At present, the law does not call for concrete accountability of those who violate the right of disabled persons to be placed on a job; forms of punishment for violating VTEK recommendations should be spelled out. Likewise, there should be a demarcation of social security's competence from that of authorities on labor resources. (9) The rights and responsibilities of regional and city social security organs should be defined precisely in regard to job placement, provision of services, privileges and help, and the development of access to the appeals process. (10) Ministries and departments need to take the initiative to construct homes for their own disabled. For social security, this means that when it constructs new homes, workshops should be included not only for residents but for the disabled of the districts in which the homes are located.[33]

The second TSIETIN study centered on 3,500 disabled who worked in 654 specialized enterprises in Moscow in 1978. It was found that in these settings—characterized by rational organization, a favorable regimen of work and rest, retraining, transfer to easier work arranged individually, work done at each person's own speed, and systematic medical follow-up—productivity was high. But there were problems. Workers were still placed in inappropriate jobs and were forced to quit; Group II disabled, who despite VTEK recommendations remained on their old jobs, harmed their health further. In many enterprises, machinery was outdated, adaptations to compensate for physical defects were absent, and sometimes hygienic norms were violated—this being true of the regimen of work and rest as well. As a result, the disabled complained: 30 percent about working conditions, others about the inattentive attitude of management, about being too far from home, about becoming fatigued. Some quit: in one factory, almost 30 percent, in another, nineteen percent. But this was true of a minority of specialized settings. The majority of the disabled work in regular enterprises, where they are indistinguishable from healthy workers. The investigators concluded that what is needed, for both specialized and regular settings, is more active control by social security. This also holds for VTEKs and VKKs: only through a joint, coordinated effort of all involved will it be possible to create conditions in which the disabled will be able to work successfully.[34]

The Rostov study investigated the situation of 600 Group III disabled in machine-building enterprises, in work that almost 90 percent of them found themselves. Here, the work of 70 percent was in line with the state of their health, but only sixty percent were using their professional skills. About 25 percent remained in their old enterprises; the rest left, but almost all resumed work later in different work settings, a change that for most resulted in worse working conditions.[35]

Complaints continue about lagging development of home work and parttime work. In 1978, there were 250,000 home workers (regulated by a 1928 decree, which remained unchanged until 1981), of whom almost 30 percent were disabled. In the same year, of the 140,000 who worked part time, most were home workers.[36] Another persistent problem is inadequate safety in employing establishments. At present, industrial accidents and professional illnesses still add up to a "heavy specific weight in the general structure of disability."[37]

VI

Foremost among the special groups among the disabled in the USSR are the war veterans, their dependents, and survivors.[38] They get substantially higher pensions than do any other disabled. The act of 1956 raised their pensions to 173 percent of the average 1955 pension, and pensions of their survivors to 206 percent.

Veterans also get many other privileges. If a war-disabled veteran wishes to change his disability pension to an old age pension, for example, he is eligible (since 1968) to receive it five years earlier than other workers. Their minimum pensions are higher (ninety, seventy, and forty rubles for war-connected disabilities); veterans in Groups I and II receive a higher percentage of old age pensions according to method 1 than others in these groups (120 percent and 110 percent, respectively); their old age pensions are raised by fifteen rubles but do not exceed the maximum, which is the same as for other disabled. For those who did not work prior to conscription, pensions are awarded in flat monthly amounts: ninety, seventy, and forty rubles for those in Groups I, II, and III, respectively; for nonwar-connected disabilities, pensions equal seventy-five, fifty, and twenty-six rubles, respectively.

Among unique war veteran supplements is the nursing care allowance for those in Group I (twenty rubles a month); a 10 percent increase in basic pension for nonworking Group II veterans if they are war disabled and their pension is calculated by method 2; a 10 percent supplement for corporals and senior sailors, who receive flat amounts; a 10 percent increase for all war-disabled in Groups I and II, including those who receive flat amounts—within the maximum limits. The circle of eligible survivors is wider than for other disabled.

War veterans in working groups I and II receive full pensions, regardless of size of earnings and other income; the pensions for a veteran in Group III can be paid in full if, together with earnings, it does not exceed 300 rubles a month. *Kolkhozniki* war veterans receive full pensions regardless of income from work in the collectivized sector. For those who change from disability to old age pensions and are working, a full pension is paid regardless of place of work, provided the sum of pension plus earnings does not exceed 300 rubles a month. Other work-related privileges include the proviso that the war disabled are not subject to a probation period. If they work part time, their annual leave (to which they may add two weeks without pay) and work record will not be shortened. When the work force is being decreased, they have first choice to remain. In specialized settings, those in Groups I and II may extend their paid leave by two months of unpaid leave. Management, with the consent of trade unions, can reduce production norms by 10 percent for those in Group III (including home workers), by 20 percent for those in Groups I and II, and can pay home workers in Groups I and II the same rates they receive in the enterprise. Training and retraining is arranged in the same way as for other disabled. While in boarding schools, their full support including the round-trip to the school is at social security expense. If they are pensioners, their pensions are subject to the rules for residents in homes.

On the basis of VTEK recommendations, in addition to motorized or pedal-operated wheelchairs, the war disabled can receive free of charge a Zaporozhets automobile, which is replaced every seven years. When the disabled person dies, his car remains in the family's possession. Driving lessons are free; the car is serviced at special centers; reimbursements for operating costs amount to 120 rubles a year for cars and 48 rubles for wheelchairs. They are exempt from paying for garages and from the tax levied on other car owners. They are entitled to ride free on practically all means of transportation except taxis. For long trips, they pay half the standard fare between 1 October and 15 May, no matter how many trips they make; between 16 May and 30 September they can take one such trip. The same reduction applies to the companion of a Group I disabled veteran. The working war disabled are the first to receive passes to health resorts from trade unions—the nonworking, from social security. Needy veterans in Groups I and II get free round-trips for themselves and one companion. Doctors can sometimes arrange this for those in Group III who have been hospitalized and for those in Groups I and II who are under treatment for the aftereffects of traumas and illnesses. All types of prosthetic and orthotic appliances are free; nor do they pay for trusses, hearing aids, voice development devices, and dentures. Fixing all these is also free.

The war disabled are the first on waiting lists to be assigned housing. They pay half the rent for housing that is not larger than the norm. They also get a 50 percent reduction on the costs for heat, water (hot and cold), gas, electricity, and sewerage. All this applies if they themselves are the owners and to homes owned by collective farms. If there is no central heating, they get a 50 percent reduction in the cost of fuel that does not exceed the norm. All can receive loans for building their own homes: 1,500 rubles without interest, to be paid off in ten years. They may also receive interest-free loans for capital repairs. They are the first to be served in social security offices and in all community facilities. This holds for installation of telephones and for entry into homes for themselves and their disabled children. They also enjoy the right (if certified by social security and military authorities) to have groceries delivered to their homes; to order groceries in advance for holidays; and to be the first to purchase items in short supply—if on credit, at 1 percent interest no matter what the price, with twenty-four months for repayment (twelve months for other disabled), and they can have them delivered without making the first payment.

The war disabled in Groups I and II who have plots in rural communities pay no tax; those in Group III are freed from taxes when they reach retirement age if they themselves are the cultivators. Those in Groups I and II pay no income taxes, regardless of size of income; nor are they subject to taxes levied on bachelors, single persons, and those with small families. They are also freed from the health resort levy and from government duty on passports.

A 1976 TSIETIN study investigated services for the war disabled in two districts of the Moscow region.[39] In regard to housing, it was found that the "level of obtaining good housing" was high: 96.8 percent of those in Group I, 90.6 percent of those in Group II, and 89.4 percent of those in Group III were living in separate apartments or their own homes. As to daily life services, the greatest need among city dwellers was for repair and cleaning of apartments and home delivery of groceries; those in rural areas needed help with fuel, building materials, and cultivation of plots.

Only 24.3 percent received passes to health resorts—61.7 percent paid nothing, 34 percent paid a reduced fee, and 4.3 percent paid the full cost. The major reason for this low figure was the absence of suitable treatment resorts. The disabled veterans did better regarding medical services—88.4 percent were under systematic observation. Almost a third of them (for the most part, those in Groups II and III) used prosthetic and orthopedic appliances; 84.7 percent got them free of charge (all of those in Group I, 84.6 percent of those in Group II, and 80.8 percent of those in Group III. The other two-thirds paid either part or all of the cost.

VII

The other major special groups among the Soviet disabled are the all-Russian unions of the blind (VOS) and the deaf (VOG). These existed in prototype before the Revolution, but they fell apart in 1917. The present VOS and VOG began in 1921, born out of the near desperate situation of the great mass of these handicapped. In 1923 and 1926, respectively, they were recognized by statute and included in the system of invalids' cooperatives; in 1924, they came under the aegis of social security. In 1927, they were accorded the same privileges as producers' cooperatives were.

The first VOS convention, attended by 109 delegates, met in 1925. The objectives it enunciated, later adopted by VOG, have hardly changed since then. In 1983 rehabilitation was still defined as accustoming blind persons to socially useful work; helping them complete secondary and higher education and find suitable employment; and drawing them into the ranks of active builders of Communist society. The histories of the two societies are replete with difficulties and setbacks. They persisted, convinced that only by staying united could they hope for help in meeting their special needs. Much of this is quite vividly described in their two journals: *Zhizn' Slepykh*, later renamed to *Nasha Zhizn'*, published by VOS; and *Zhizn' Glukhikh*, renamed *V Edinom Stroiiu*, published by VOG.[40]

For both societies, the administrative hierarchy starts with local branches in districts, cities, workshops, and state and social organizations, rises to intermediate organs, and ends in a central board. Functionaries for the latter two rungs are elected by the membership. All of the work in both societies is financed by their own resources: membership dues; profits from their training and industrial enterprises (Uchebno-Proizvodstvennye Predpriiatiia—UPPs); and receipts from other activities. Persons who wish to join may do so at age fourteen in VOS and fifteen in VOG. A fixed number of sighted and hearing persons, those who participate actively in the societies' work, may join. Group III blind are treated as sighted members.[41]

Soviet work with the blind and the deaf is based on a theoretically presumed, dialectic interaction between social factors and personality, the former playing the leading role. In teaching, the personality is seen as the subject of cognition and an active agent of changing reality, and is the subject and object of social relations. The defect is not considered to exert a global influence on the formation of personality. Hence, rehabilitation becomes a coordinated system of state, socioeconomic, medical, educational, and psychological measures, which include professional training and job placement. It should be noted that the level of sociolabor rehabilitation that this concept presupposes has not been reached as yet.

The effort to do away with illiteracy among the blind began in 1926, with a cultural revolution of sorts. Clubs, houses of culture, red corners, and libraries multiplied. Night schools were developed; records became available. The first successful experiments with guide dogs were carried out in 1945–48. The construction of industrial structures, apartment houses, and buildings for cultural activities has been included in national plans. Resources have been allocated to improve safety at the workplace and to build eye infirmaries and polyclinics.

In "real life," the process of accustoming the blind to useful work has been "long and complicated."[42] It took two directions: the creation of VOS's own productive base, the UPPs (where special production methods and specially designed tools and accessories are used), and job placement in state enterprises. By 1951, more than 14,000 of the blind were working in UPPs, and in that year VOS began to explore the possibility of cooperative undertakings with state industry. It was claimed in 1963 that for RSFSR the problem of job placement was "completely solved." VOS could then concentrate on a "rational, high quality job placement program based on a scientific organization of work"—a program that called for "creative" cooperation between VOS engineers and technicians, VTEK physician experts, and TSIETIN. There has been substantial progress. In 1967, of 174,800 blind, (55.7 percent of whom were in Group 1—0.04 of sight; 44.3 percent in Group II—0.04–0.08 of sight), those under age sixteen accounted for 2.9 percent of the total; those sixteen to sixty, for 64 percent; and those over sixty, for 33.1 percent. VOS members accounted for 160,00, or 91.8 percent. In addition, there were 3,400 sighted members. On this date, 75,900 of the blind were working; 53,000 in UPPs and other VOS organizations, 13,800 in state industries, and 9,100 on collective and state farms. In 1980, 220 UPPs employed 58,000. In 1983, VOS profits amounted to 198,753,000 rubles, its expenditures to 151,080,000 rubles.

VTEK recommendations are carefully observed in UPPs. Training and work at home is primarily for those in Group I who suffer from additional defects that make movement difficult, or from illness that precludes being in a workshop; who travel long distances or who have no transport; or who care for a child or an unable-to-work family member. Time spent in training is counted toward the work record. "New professions" for the blind have appeared: mathematician programmers, attorneys, scientific collaborators, masseurs, music teachers, and heads of cultural organizations.

In general, VOG has experienced a similar development. At its Twelfth Convention in 1980, there were 300 delegates representing 156,000 members and 5,255 local primary branches. Of its membership, 106,000 or 58 percent were working; 15,000 in seventy UPPs, 68,000 in state enterprises, and almost 23,000 on farms. Every third VOG member was an honored (e.g., shock) worker. During the first four years of the Tenth Five-Year Plan (1975–80), output was worth 855 million rubles, 36 million rubles above target. Profit amounted to 181 million rubles and made it possible for VOG to finance all of its sociocultural undertakings.[43] It also has been noted that VOG members' general educational and professional levels had risen. A 1973 study reported that the deaf were already working in seventy-five professions, had mastered more than thirty new specializations, including some that were considered inaccessible for them in state enterprises, and were actively participating in socialist competition.[44]

In a 1974 article, a writer compared the plight of other handicapped with that of members of VOS and VOG and found that the latter are much better off than the former when it comes to finding suitable work, training, housing, encouragement to study through a system of stipends, paid readers, tape recorders, and so on. She concluded that "it is clear that the corporally handicapped need associations like those for the blind and the deaf. Welfare agencies alone are not capable of solving the problems in this field."[45]

Nevertheless, the two societies are beset by problems. Many originate with poorly trained personnel and result in administrative inefficiencies. Thus, complaints go unanswered, local branches fail to provide material and other services, student dormitories are often in disrepair, personnel do not know how to approach people on an individual basis and do not always make sure that those in Group I arrive at health resorts sober, with attendants and passes. Personnel at higher levels do not always visit local branches or they may check on local activities only superficially. In 1982, a high official from the RSFSR Ministry of Social Security described serious deficiencies in the economic activity of both VOS and VOG UPPs. There were important omissions in planning the cost of production; production and profit goals had been lowered; norm outlays on raw and other materials had not been regulated; and violations of labor laws and remuneration for work were permitted.[46] Quality of production was still poor in some UPPs. The experience of leading UPPs was not followed by others. Losses of work time—due to intrashift stoppages of machinery, illnesses, truancies, and labor turnover—are still great. In some places, because home work is not profitable, people who cannot work elsewhere are without work.

Relatively very little has been done for the blind and the deaf in rural communities. The level of sociocultural services for them is very low, as is membership in VOS and VOG. And professional orientation and rational job placement, which still need improvement for all, are almost absent for those in the villages.

Many believe that education is problem number one of the deaf and the blind. While all who want to work can get jobs, this is not enough: technical progress demands skills that can be acquired only if the deaf or the blind person has completed general education. The movement of the adult deaf and blind into engineering, technical, administrative, and managerial positions is stimulating the young to raise their education and professional sights. But a 1983 study of a number of graduates from schools for the blind found a "rupture" between intellectual development and moral "formation" of personality and inadequate readiness to realize their potential, to adapt to new conditions of life, to be independent in daily living, and to get along in mixed groups.[47] There is a need to improve the upbringing of young deaf and blind workers in the direction of self-reliance, self-care, and self-growth. Social development—judged to be at a rudimentary stage in 1973[48]— apparently still requires careful study and planning and sufficient resources to help the blind and deaf achieve their full potential in modern society.

VIII

With the aid of the figures in table 1 one may gain some inkling of the economic situation of the disabled in the USSR. It has been estimated that in 1970–75 the Soviet poverty line was 66.4 rubles per month. The minimum monthly pensions for disabled workers and employees in groups I–III ranged over the decades between 1956 and 1981 from 16 to 75 rubles. Among *kolkhozniki,* the corresponding figures ranged between 12 and 45 rubles. We do not know exactly how many disabled pensioners received the minimums; but among all urban worker pensioners in 1981, 36 percent received the minimum. Among old age *kolkhoznik* pensioners in the same year, 40—50 percent received the minimum.[49] It seems most unlikely that the proportions among the Group III disabled were any better.

These figures are the more disturbing when one regards them comparatively. During the years between 1956 and 1978, minimum wages for workers and employees were raised on four separate occasions, increasing by 160 percent, to seventy rubles a month. Between 1956 and 1981, minimum old age pensions for those workers and employees went up twice, increasing 67 percent. *Kolkhozniki* did even better statistically, because their wages and pensions started at an extremely low level. The pensions for the disabled showed no such impressive increases. Since, as Soviet authorities tell us, pensions are often the sole source of material support for their recipients, this means that in relative terms the disabled were doing less well, were falling backward, in recent years.

It does not help their situation that all those in Group III are almost constantly exposed to unremitting pressure to continue to work, not only by the need to supplement their meager pensions, but also by VTEK decisions. The fact that degree of disability is not a static concept, especially for Group III, often creates situations of conflict between their interests and those of the state: in some cases the health of the Group III disabled may deteriorate because of an incorrect job placement—to the point where he or she thinks it necessary to be reclassified into Group II.

There is growing official recognition that disability rehabilitation should involve a socio-labor approach joined with medical services to bring about a clear-cut system. It is also being urged that such an approach begin in the school and follow the disabled when they enter the general health system or deal with VTEK, social security, and the employing establishment, as well as the network of communal services. Clearly, the situation is due to improve. Still, it is in the "socio" area that scarcity of meaningful and technically reliable research is especially pronounced. Available studies center almost entirely on work in its various contexts. Although Soviet scholars are aware of the gaps and are calling for a deep analysis—sociological, economic, and demographic—we have yet to read a study that investigates how the disabled actually live, not only as productive or unproductive entities, but as full-fledged human beings with all their spiritual, emotional, social, and physical needs.

It is to be hoped that the overemphasis on the need to engage in socially useful work will give way in the near future to a more balanced approach, which, together with more adequate material support and more effective social services (made possible by an anticipated new pension law), will make room for greater participation in cultural, educational, and social activities that are so essential for enriching the quality of life for all human beings, including the disabled.

NOTES

1. See the following: B. Q. Madison, *Social Welfare in the Soviet Union* (Stanford: Stanford University Press, 1968); "Social Services for Families and Children in the Soviet Union since 1967," *Slavic Review* 31 (1972): 831–52; and "Trade Unions and Social Welfare," in Arcadius Kahan and Blair A. Ruble, eds., *Industrial Labor in the USSR* (New York: Pergamon Press, 1979).

2. For a detailed breakdown of contribution rates from 1956 to 1979, see V. Krulikovovskaia, P. Kiseleva, and A. Gorbunov, *Planirovanie biudzheta sotsial'nogo strakhovaniia* (Moscow: Profizdat, 1959), p. 17; and M. S. Lantsev, *Sotsial'noe obespechenie v SSSR. Ekonomicheskii aspekt* (Moscow: Ekonomika, 1976), p. 42. For 1979 rates, see Decree of the Soviet of Ministers, 18 (1979); 118.

3. M. S. Lantsev, "Progress in Social Security for Agricultural Workers in the USSR," *International Labour Review* 107 (1973): 250.

4. A. E. Kozlov, "Sovershenstvovanie material'nogo obespecheniia netrudosposobnykh, sotsial'nye faktory," *Sovetskoe gosudarstvo i pravo* (1984): 58.

5. In 1979, in the district social security organs in RSFSR more than two-thirds of lower and senior inspectors (line workers and supervisors) had neither higher nor secondary special education: E. G. Azarova, "O zashchite pensionnykh prav grazhdan," *Sovetskoe gosudarstvo i pravo* 2 (1979): 46–47. In 1980, the RSFSR system employed 147,000 personnel; in this year, Turkmenistan had 1,200.

6. D. Komarova, minister of social security for RSFSR, "Na blago sovetskikh liudei," *Sotsial'noe obespechenie* 2 (1981): 8 (henceforth *Sots. obes.*); and "Vazhnyi kanal sviazi s massami," *Sots. obes.* 4 (1983): 4, 5, 8.

7. In RSFSR, the nation's leader in social security, more than two million pensions and grants are awarded annually and about the same number of recomputations are made. In 1980, this republic had fifty-four automated centers, which served 60 percent of its clients; D. Komarova, "Na blago sovetskikh liudei," p. 4. Administration is complicated by the fact that ministries do not maintain earnings records of eligible individuals nor are such records maintained in any centralized facility: they must be developed at the time claims are made at individual enterprises and farms: *Sots. obes.* 11 (1983): 8.

8. The VTEKs, established in 1920, are regulated by special acts and by a multitude of "unmatched" legal norms that deal with different kinds of benefits. But certain aspects of their work, despite their direct effect on the rights of citizens to material support, have not received needed normative ratification: I. I. Rybakova, "Pravovoe polozhenie vrachebnotrudovykh ekspertnykh komissii," *Voprosy sotsial'nogo obespecheniia, sbornik nauchnykh trudov* 10 (1978): 82; and I. A. Fogel', "Sotsial'noe obespechenie naseleniia i zakon," in Ministerstvo Vysshego i Srednego Spetsial'nogo

Obrazovaniia SSSR, Nauchnotekhnicheskii Sovet. Sektsiia narodnose-
leniia, *Naselenie i sotsial'noe obespechenie* (Moscow: Finansy i Statistika,
1984), p. 53.

9. Some Soviet scholars believe that the more restricted treatment of
the *kolkhoz* disabled is unfair because of the peculiarities of employment
relations on collective farms: see Rybakova, "Pravovoe polozhenie," pp.
86–88.

10. E. Zhumatova, "Po individual'nym programmam," *Sots. obes.* 8
(1980): 34–36; and M. Kravchenko, "Nasushchie problemy profilaktiki
invalidnosti," *Sots. obes.* 2 (1980): 3–7.

11. V. Sokolov, doctor of medical science, professor, acting director
of science of TSIETIN, "Nauka-Praktike," *Sots. obes.* 1 (1980): 33, 34;
E. Udintsov, director of TSIETIN, professor, "Uchenye-Prakticheskim
Rabotnikam," *Sots. obes.* 8 (1982): 36.

12. M. Kravchenko, "Nasuschie problemy," pp. 3–7; V. Kotel'nikov,
"Kazhdyi chelovek dorog," *Sots. obes.* 7 (1980): 5; M. Emel'ianova,
"Povyshat' otvetstvennost' i organizovannost'," *Sots. obes.* 8 (1980): 4;
S. Pastukhov, chief physician-expert of Kemerov oblast', "Deistvennost'
analiza," *Sots. obes.* 1 (1980): 35.

13. Much of the following is based on the laws and regulations compiled in M. L. Zakharov, *Pensii rabochim i sluzhashchim* (Moscow: Profiz-
dat, 1983), pp. 31–71.

14. V. Kogan, "Sotsial'noe obsluzhivanie pozhilykh liudei," in Ministerstvo Vysshego Obrazovaniia, *Naselenie*, pp. 30–32.

15. D. P. Komarova, minister of social security of RSFSR, wrote that
in 1976, only 68 percent of a plan to open homes with 1,600 places was
completed; in 1979, there was failure to open homes for 665 persons in
Kemerov region; in 1981, Komarova expressed alarm over the fact that in
six regions, including the Moscow region, the five-year construction
plan had been fulfilled by less than half; in 1982, a special correspondent
reported that some construction plans remained paper creations. He
found that in Kalinin region (RSFSR), a home started in 1972 is still
unfinished; for another, started in 1974, "completion is still out of sight."
Some, battered by snow and rain, have become dilapidated and will have
to be rebuilt. In 1983, Komarova wrote that the problem of home care
for the solitary and disabled remained "urgent"; Komarova, "Effektivnost' i kachestvo v osnovu nashei raboty," *Sots. obes.* 2 (1977): 7; "Na
blago sovetskikh liudei," p. 6; "Vazhnyi kanal sviazi s massami," p. 7.
The situation in the Kemerov region was reported by the Board of the
RSFSR Ministry in "Vnimanie k zhiteliam domov-internatov," *Sots obes.*
9 (1980): 25. The correspondent was A. Lysenkov, "Emblema obiazy-
vaet," *Sots. obes.* 9 (1982): 28.

16. V. Kotsur, "O nikh maksimum zaboty," *Sots. obes.* 6 (1972): 26.

17. N. Semenova, "Eksperiment daet resul'taty," *Sots. obes.* 4 (1977):
36–38.

18. M. Kravchenko, "Zadachi gosudarstvennykh organov sotsial'-

nogo obespecheniia v svete novoi konstitutsii SSSR," *Sots. obes.* 4 (1979): 42; V. Strashnov and A. Kazakov, "Doma s kvartirami dlia invalidov," *Sots. obes.* 4 (1983): 29. In 1971, the Moscow City Social Security Division opened a home for paying residents. It accommodated 537 persons, with five of its twelve floors reserved for those who were ambulatory. The top floor was occupied by an extensive library and dining hall. Each room had its own bathtub and toilet. The cost of a single room was ninety-five rubles per month, while double was seventy-nine rubles for each occupant: Vladimir Rabichev, *Literaturnaia Gazeta,* 13 Sept. 1972, p. 12. Nothing in the literature indicated that the paying idea has spread. I was not shown this facility on my trips to the USSR, and I do not know whether it still exists.

19. M. Zakharov and R. Tsivilyev, *Social Security in the USSR* (Moscow: Progress Publishers, 1978), p. 55; in reports of all but two republics (Moldavia and Belorussia) in *Sots. obes.* 2 (1981) and 5–11 (1982) I have not found any clear-cut data on how many homes for handicapped children there are or how many children reside in them. In 1976, there were 168 such homes in RSFSR; in 1980, there were 11,000 children in such homes in the Ukraine. In 1977, 2,400 special schools provided full board and room for 400,000 congenitally handicapped children. The full cost of their training and upkeep (over 1,000 rubles per pupil per annum, compared with about 150 rubles in an ordinary school) is borne by the state; Vladimir Lomeiko, "Security and Safeguards for the Elderly in the USSR," *Soviet Life,* Oct. 1977, p. 21.

20. Iu. Ivakin, "Pravovye voprosy, sviazannye s prozhivaniem v domakh-internatakh," *Sots. obes.* 8 (1982): 53–55.

21. A. Samarina, director of homes in RSFSR, "Vrach doma-internata," *Sots. obes.* 4 (1982): 25–27; A. Nuzhnov and N. Iudin, "Problema staraia, podkhod novyi," *Sots. obes.* 2 (1982): 38–40.

22. Samarina, "Vrach doma-internata," pp. 25–27.

23. A correspondent reporting on a home for 200 residents in Kostroma region in 1983 found it in total decay, its linoleum full of holes, and floorboards that "walk around" with every step. Overcrowding was such that in many rooms there was no place for anything but beds, which were pushed against each other. Despite the local soviet's appeal to social security to reduce the number of residents by 100, the latter kept sending new residents—87 in 1982 and 52 in the first nine months of 1983. The kitchen was in almost total disarray, and there was no hot water and no sewage disposal. There was nothing to do in the home—there was one sewing machine in the workshop—so, those who were still able went into town to get small jobs, or simply got drunk. See G. Alekseev, "Dom internat vzyvaet o pomoshchi," *Sots. obes.* 12 (1983): 29. In 1980, s. Martynova inspected a two-story home in Kazininsk region for 70 residents that had one working toilet and one washbasin: "Nesostoiatel'nye opravdaniia," *Sots. obes.* 12 (1980): 56–57.

24. Komarova, "Vazhnyi kanal," pp. 7–8.

25. See, for example, the description of two good psychoneurological homes, one in the Moscow region the other in the Altai region: N. Udal'tsova, "Uvlechennost'," *Sots. obes.* 12 (1981): 23–25; and V. Boltenko, "Dva uchrezhdeniia—dva stilia raboty," *Sots. obes.* 12 (1983): 28.

26. Boltenko, "Dva uchrezhdeniia," p. 7.

27. B. P. Popov and N. A. Shenk, "Protezno-ortopedicheskaia pomoshch naseleniia," in D. P. Komarova, ed., *50 Let sovetskogo sotsial'nogo obespecheniia* (Moscow: RSFSR Ministry of Social Security and TSIETIN, 1968), pp. 131–34; D. P. Komarova, "Garantirovano konstitutsiei," *Sots. obes.* 11 (1982): 7; N. Kondrashin, "Nauchno-tekhnicheskii progress v protezirovanii i protezostroenii," *Sots obes.* 1 (1980): 16.

28. M. D. Grishina, ed., *Sbornik normativnykh aktov o l'gotakh invalidam* (Moscow: Iuridicheskaia Literatura, 1977), pp. 52–53, 60.

29. P. Povarov, "Trudovoe ustroistvo invalidov i prestarelykh—vazhnaia sostavnaia chast' politiki KPSS v oblasti sotsial'nogo obespecheniia," *Sots obes.* 1 (1980): 47; Povarov, "Trudovoe ustroistvo invalidov i prestarelykh", *Sots. obes.* 12 (1980): 10–11; Kotel'nikov, "Kazhdyi chelovek dorog," pp. 5–6.

30. In RSFSR, 84.6 percent of Group III were working; in Turkestan, 31 percent of all groups. Povarov, "Trudovoe ustroistvo," p. 49.

31. Grishina, *Sbornik normativnykh aktov,* pp. 66–71.

32. In 1980, there were about 1,500 such settings, with 400,000 places—not enough. For the mentally disabled, the situation is especially acute: there were seventy-eight specialized workshops, with 3,000 places, mainly in five republics—RSFSR, Ukraine, Latvia, Lithuania, and Estonia. "Obviously this does not meet the need which exists in almost every city"; Kravchenko, "Nasushchie problemy," p. 7.

33. E. Udintsev and N. Gorbunova, "Zadacha gosudarstvennoi vazhnosti," *Sols. obes.* 3 (1980): 31–34.

34. D. Komarova, "Dostoino zavershim desiatuiu piatiletku," *Sots obes.* 1 (1980): 5; Komarova, "Novoe proiavlenie zaboty o blage sovetskikh liudei," *Sots. obes.* 1 (1974): 6–7; and N. Gorbunova and V. Petrova, "Trudoustroistvo invalidov: pliusy i minusy," *Sots. obes.* 8 (1980): 7–9.

35. Iu. Ellanskaia, "Rabota dlia invalida," *Sots. obes.* 8 (1983): 33–34.

36. A. G. Novitskii and G. V. Mil, *Zaniatost' pensionerov. Sotsial'no-demographicheskii aspekt* (Moscow: Finansy i Statistika, 1981), pp. 157–58; see also pp. 133, 173–76.

37. I. Zenin, "The Law Is Binding upon Everyone. What Some People Will do for a Bonus!" *Trud,* 19 Dec. 1973, p. 4. Translated in *CDSP,* 26 (1976): 30; K. Voinov, "Vinovat postradavshii!" *Trud,* 13 Sept. 1974, p. 2; N. Zemlianushin, "Poka grom ne grianet," *Trud,* 25 Oct. 1974, p. 2; Kravchenko, "Nasushchie problemy," p. 4.

38. See Zakharov, "Razvitie edinoi sistemy," p. 33; L. A. Mirosh-kina, "L'goty invalidam voiny," *Sovetskoe gosudarstvo i pravo* 2 (1980): 122–27; L. Vul'f, "Pensionnoe obespechenie zhen voennosluzhashchikh, pogibshikh na fronte," *Sots. obes.* 11 (1980): 50–51; Vul'f, "Pensii byvshim voennosluzhashchim," *Sots. Obes.* 9 (1982): 54–56; and ibid., *Sots. obes.* 10 (1982): 56–58.

39. La. M. Fogel' and Z. D. Vinogradova, "Sotsial'noe obsluzhivanie invalidov Velikoi Otechestvennoi Voiny," in *Voprosy sotsial'nogo obespecheniia,* vypusk 9 (Moscow: Ministerstvo Sotsial'nogo Obespecheniia, RSFSR, TSIETIN, 1976), pp. 80–92.

40. M. Ksenofondov, "Zadachi i perspektivy sotsial'nogo obespecheniia," Voprosy sotsial'nogo obespecheniia 1 (1926): 1; editors, *Voprosy sotsial'nogo obespechniia* 7 (1926): 16; 1 (1928): 6; 13 (1928): 6; and 2 (1929): 1; editors, *Nasha zhizn'* 4 (1975): 2; E. Ageev, "50 Let *VOS,- v edinom stroiu* 10 (1975): 14; B. Zimin, "Sotsial'naia reabilitatsiia," *Nasha zhizn'* 2 (1933): 2.

41. M. I. Fliaster, *Trudovye prava invalidov—voprosy sotsial'nogo obespecheniia i usloviia truda* (Moscow: Iuridicheskaia Literatura, 1968), p. 80.

42. For the following, see B. Zimin, chairman of the central adminis-tration of VOS, "*VOS*—50 Let. Sogretye zabotoi partii," *Sots. obes.* 11 (1975): 8.

43. Editors of *V edinom stroiiu,* "Novaia piatiletka—novye zadachi," *Sots. obes.* 9 (1980): 31–33.

44. It should be added that by 1972, the theater of mimicry and gesture in Belorussia was producing such plays as Moliere's "Plutni Skapana" at a professional level. And in 1981, at the Fourteenth Interna-tional Games for the Deaf (in Cologne), in which forty-two countries participated, the Soviet delegation—107 sportsmen and -women—was awarded twenty-one gold, twenty silver, and fourteen bronze medals. L. Godin, "Vsemirnye igry glukhikh," *Sots. obes.* 11 (1981): 62–63.

45. Yelena Rzhevskaya, in *Literaturnaia gazeta,* 14 Aug. 1974, p. 12. Abstract in *CDSP* 27 (year): 17–18.

46. V. Babkin, "Za vysokuiu effektivnost' kontrolia," *Sots. obes.* 2 (1982): 5–6.

47. M. L. Zakharov, *Pensii rabochim i sluzhashchim* (Moscow: Profiz-dat, 1983).

48. P. Sutiagin, "Sotsiologiia na sluzhbe," *V edinom stroiiu* 10 (1973): 12–13; and 11 (1973): 16–17.

49. P. Lopata, "Desiataia piatiletka—vazhnyi rubezh v razvitii sistemy pensionnogo obespecheniia," *Sots. obes.* 11 (1981): 7.

Everyday Life of the Disabled in the USSR

Stephen P. Dunn and
Ethel Dunn

I

THIS CHAPTER attempts to estimate the quality of life for disabled people in the Soviet Union on the basis of both legally published and underground materials and the testimony of Soviet émigrés with special experience in this field. We focus on the long-term orthopedically disabled and, within that group, primarily those who are disabled from birth or early childhood. Other contingents—particularly those who, as mature people, have been knocked out of the labor force by, for example, cardiovascular or pulmonary illness or by accidents—are dealt with tangentially, in terms of how their treatment differs from the treatment of those who were never in the labor force. Omitted from consideration are those who suffer from sensory impairments and, for the most part, the mentally retarded and the psychiatrically disabled.

Ours is a topic of the utmost philosophical importance. It has been said with a great deal of justice—and the point is quoted by Soviet writers—that the spiritual quality of a society can be judged by the lifestyle it gives to its disabled members.[1] With this in mind, let the reader be warned that, while we make every effort to reflect the sources accurately, we cannot claim to maintain the usual scholarly distance from our subject. In the first place, since we are outsiders to the Soviet world, our assessment will of necessity be comparative, both with the situation in our own country and in the capitalist world generally and with the claims and statements of intention made by Soviet spokesmen about policy toward the disabled. For this reason alone, our work is inevitably, perhaps regrettably, subjective. In addition, when we discuss the position of the long-term orthopedically disabled, whether in the Soviet Union, in the United States, or anywhere else, we are talking about something that involves us personally. It would be difficult if not impossible for disabled people like ourselves not to feel involved in such a subject and, in addition, not to be critical.

II

How can we estimate the number of the long-term orthopedically disabled in the Soviet Union as a whole, or relative to the total population, or relative to other contingents of the disabled? The sources we have found offer no estimate on a USSR-wide basis. All are regional and hard to work with. A study conducted in Krasnodar and reported in 1971, for example, gives a figure of 1,833 persons disabled from childhood registered with the social security organs of the city.[2] This evidently represented 10 percent of all disabled persons in the town and 61.4 percent of all disabled persons under nineteen years of age receiving pensions. A more recent study of Krasnodar, with a broader data base, placed the number of persons disabled from childhood per 10,000 total population at 38.4.[3] The most frequent causes of such disability are (in rank order) deafness and dumbness, poliomyelitis, psychiatric disorders, and tuberculosis, followed by other categories of disease. Cerebral palsy shows a rate of 1.71–2.5 per 1,000 children. The last issue of *Ogonek* for 1988 gives a figure of 4 per 1,000 children with cerebral palsy, and 24 per 1,000 with pathologies of the motor apparatus. The total number of those with some sort of psychoneurological disorder, including cerebral palsy, is said to be 48 per 1,000 or 1,185,000 children. So far, the Ministry of Public Health has entangled in red tape the creation of a USSR-wide Pediatric Center and Research Institute for Psychoneurology of Children and Adolescents.[4]

In matters of this kind, the general trend is sometimes more important than either absolute figures or percentages. Many Soviet sources point out that the number of people with impaired motor function in the population is increasing at a steady pace. This is particularly true if one includes among them people who have had strokes and who, while not orthopedically disabled in the strict medical sense, resemble this category in terms of the kind of care and facilities they need. The reason for the rapid increase in the numbers of the disabled is, in part, the aging of the population and, in part also—just as elsewhere in the world—the survival of many disabled children who in earlier times would have died.

What does the Soviet government do for the disabled? In approaching this question, one should know that Soviet policy draws a sharp distinction between the disabled worker—the person who has a certain job senority and standing in a work collective—and the person who cannot claim this status. The official Soviet view (which we share) is that human dignity is preserved and maintained by the ability to be useful. As is spelled out by Bernice Madison in this volume, there is a fairly elaborate medico-juridical network that oversees the treatment and rehabilitation of disabled workers and their working conditions when they return to the job. The central component of this network is the Medical-Labor Expert Commission (VTEK). Almost all our information about treatment comes from VTEK sources, but this in no way implies a blackout on the treatment of the born disabled.

One group of experts describes a comprehensive program for the rehabilitation of stroke patients operating at an inter*raion* city hospital in Kiev. The program has at its disposal a full medical and paramedical staff—neuropathologist, cardiologist, internist, orthopedist-traumatologist, physiotherapist, psychotherapist, acupuncturist, specialist in physical medicine, and speech therapist. The guiding principle by which these specialists function is characterized as follows: "The maximum task of rehabilitation is the attainment of the complete level of social, labor, and household activity; the minimal task is to increase the ability of the patient to care for his own needs, to the point where outside help is not required."[5] The specific forms of treatment mentioned in connection with this program include some which seem to us peculiar to Soviet practice, such as occupational therapy performed in hot water at a specially equipped table. When patients are not able to come to the center, home rehabilitation is set up with the limited goal of increasing the patient's mobility to the point where treatment outside the home is possible. Another expert, A. F. Kaptelin, describes a program for bringing patients to rehabilitation centers by car, a system which probably does not exist in every treatment center in the Soviet Union, but neither is it universal in the United States.[6] The system described by Kaptelin implies that the rehabilitation center has its own fleet of cars with its own staff of drivers.

Equally comprehensive programs are described in the literature for Leningrad[7] and for Vinnitsa in the Ukraine.[8] It is worth noting that, according to the Leningrad study, the percentage of patients referred to the program through VTEK is extremely low. Most, apparently, are referred by the district physician or through the health department at their place of work. The sources unfortunately do not give any indication of the total capacity of rehabilitative programs for stroke victims and similarly disabled patients in terms of those treated over a specific time period. However, we can safely assume that this capacity is small relative to the need. We know from experience in the United States that rehabilitative treatment of stroke and orthopedic patients is extremely labor intensive.

The Leningrad Institute of Prosthetic Research has developed standard plans for apartments for the disabled—particularly those with disturbances of function in the lower extremities and with arms missing. The standard apartment included an entryway, a room, a kitchen, and a bathroom area; the width of the apartment was determined on the basis of a wheelchair 70 cm wide and 105 cm long. (This is a very small wheelchair.)[9]

The standard apartment was well received by those disabled people who were asked to comment on it, because its arrangement permitted the occupant complete autonomy in daily life and potentially allowed him or her to work at home. The requirements set forth by the researchers in terms of the dimensions of the apartment and its various parts are significant, because standards for the amount of living space to which each person is entitled are laid down rigorously and in great detail in Soviet housing law. Housing for the disabled—at least those who use wheelchairs—would require a detailed set of exceptions to the existing housing law. A current legal source states that there is an increased quota of housing space for persons suffering from certain disabling conditions but does not specifically mention motor disabilities or discuss accommodations for those using wheelchairs. We do not know whether any apartments like the one described above actually have been built, and if so, where, but the researchers do not anticipate unusual technical problems or major obstacles in their construction. Bureaucratic problems and obstacles may be another matter.

A recent Soviet discussion of housing law cites a case indicating that the courts will make available special housing for the handicapped, in the face of resistance by the housing authorities. The Executive Committee of the Lenin *raion* Soviet of People's Deputies in the city of Petrozavodsk brought suit in court to evict the family of D. from an apartment, making another one available. The plaintiff pointed out that pursuant to the decision, the house in which the D. family lived was to be converted from a residential to an administrative building, but the defendant refused to move into the apartment allotted to him, and, objecting to the suit, explained that his refusal of the transfer was caused by the fact that the apartment was assigned without taking into account the state of health of his minor daughter. The Supreme Court of the Karelian ASSR, considering the case as the court of first instance, found for the plaintiff, finding the objections of the defendant unfounded. The Civil Panel of the Supreme Court of the RSFSR reversed this decision, emphasizing that in accordance with Article 37 of the Fundamentals of Housing Law and Article 41 of the Housing Code of the RSFSR, in the event of a decision of a legally competent organ converting a residential building into a nonresidential one, citizens are to be provided with other well-equipped housing, taking into account the state of health of citizens, and other circumstances which are deserving of attention. The court did not take into account the fact that the defendant's minor daughter suffered from a severe progressive disorder of the cardiovascular system and the kidneys, and that her going to school in the second shift, as would be the case at their new place of residence, would be contraindicated, according to the conclusion of the medical authorities.[10]

On the rehabilitation of the orthopedically disabled, Krasnov and Naumov describe a program at the Orthopedic Hospital in Kuibyshev for adolescents with congenital dislocations of the hip.[11] This program includes surgical correction of the condition, postoperative therapy and rehabilitation, and schooling, both general and specialized, which for the older patient is under the supervision of a local secondary school. During the nine years that the program had been in operation when the article was written, 511 pupils passed through the course of schooling, and none ever failed to be promoted from one grade to the next. The score in the basic subjects remained stable, and every fourth student scored higher than he or she did on entering the program. The authors compared this situation with the results for a group of control pupils who were studied and treated in the same way between 1963 and 1969, when no coordinated program of combined treatment and schooling existed. At that time, the rate of success among all students was much lower, and every fourth student had to repeat a grade, in some cases twice. Seventy-nine graduates of the program were covered by a follow-up study. Of these, eleven had seven to nine grades of schooling, twenty-four had general secondary education, twenty-three had specialized secondary education, thirteen did not complete postsecondary education, and six had graduated from postsecondary institutions. This is a rather favorable picture for people with severe motor disabilities.

According to those authors, certain trades, such as those of machinist and lathe operator, are not recommended for people with dislocated hips, even when the condition has been surgically corrected—presumably because these trades require prolonged standing. The same is true for such predominantly female occupations as physician's assistant, nurse, and kindergarten supervisor. "We recommend that persons having the above-named specialties work in the departments in charge of special procedures, in physical-therapy departments, as dispatchers at first-aid stations, and in the admitting offices of large hospitals."[12] The authors describe the material status of the families of these patients as on the whole quite satisfactory. The average income per family member among the twenty-two people studied was over 150 rubles per month. Twenty-four women were married and were coping with the obligations of wife and mother. More than two-thirds of them had children; ten with one child each, and six with two. Two women who were housewives bore and were raising four children each. Twenty-one males were studied. All of them had, in the past, been subjected to operations for congenital dislocation of the hip. Four were married, of whom two were helping to raise one child each, and one was raising two. Not one of the men had received higher or specialized secondary education. The majority of them carried out heavy labor such as that of machinists, welders, and painters.

This report is significant because it is the only substantial body of data that we have found on the rehabilitation of people in the Soviet Union who have been orthopedically disabled from birth or shortly thereafter. It indicates at least that there are Soviet physicians and educators who are aware of what is necessary to provide a near-normal life for persons with this type of disability and who realize that the effort of rehabilitating them will pay for itself.

For comparative purposes, we can cite a roughly similar U.S. study (although it lacks the diachronic character of the Soviet one, and the sample is rather smaller) reported by Janet Rosenberg. She studied a group of seventy-nine graduates of a public high school for orthopedically handicapped students. The respondents suffered from a wide range of conditions of varying degrees of severity, deriving from congenital disorders, childhood illnesses, and injuries. Rosenberg's conclusion is forthright:

> Of the small group (14) of seriously handicapped, 10 were in the job market. Though all but one had had postsecondary educational experience, only 3 had full-time jobs and none were earning more than 50% of the amount needed to meet their minimum financial needs.

> Our data suggest that a strong motivation to achieve and intense efforts to acquire skills, though very important factors in overcoming the serious impediments to the employment of handicapped adults, do not fully guarantee economic security. The alumnus with the best chance for full economic functioning is the moderately handicapped graduate with vocational training or a college education leading to a position in areas of the occupational structure where opportunities are protected by law.[13]

On a different but related problem, Dement'eva and Modestov reported on the training of mentally retarded adolescents in special boarding schools under the Ministry of Social Security. The adolescents, classified as imbeciles, are trained in therapeutic workshops and in a subsidiary farming operation. A special study was made of the inmates of a boarding school in the Krasnoiarsk Television Factory, which included a box workshop and a sewing workshop, with thirty places each, and a machine tool workshop, with twenty places. On reaching the age of eighteen, the inmates of the boarding school were transferred to a psychoneurological boarding facility, where forms of labor were used that, in many cases, did not correspond to the skills that they had been taught earlier, and where the conditions were monotonous. As a result, some inmates lost interest in their work and lost the skills that they had learned. In order to remedy this situation, a special program with its own staff of supervisors and physicians was set up. The skills taught were those of press operator, welder, and thread cutter. In order to ensure safety, all the presses were converted to hand operation, and the trainee's labor was made independent of the assembly line. The other workers were also briefed over the plant radio on what to expect from their new colleagues, and what attitude to take toward them.

> The study showed that not only work skills, but also specialties that are not too complex, are within the grasp of adolescents suffering from pronounced mental retardation. The social experience required in the course of work training can be the basis of their integration

into society. At the same time, it turned out that such adolescents needed an intermediate stage in which, with the help of supervisors and preceptors, they could acquire social experience. There are as yet no institutions [in the USSR] which carry out such work. Within the social security system, these functions can to some extent be fulfilled by specialized boarding facilities for young retarded people.[14]

The existence of model and pilot programs such as those just described does not mean that the facilities available for rehabilitation are necessarily adequate, even in the view of Soviet physicians and public health officials. For instance, Kaptelin made a restrained but forthright critique of Soviet rehabilitation clinics—one which raises significant policy questions. The problems to which Kaptelin drew attention relate both to medical practice per se and to public health—that is to say, the availability and distribution of facilities. On the first point, Kaptelin observed: "The low effectiveness of restorative treatment, directed toward the removal of a physical defect, is also determined by the incompleteness of the set of means applied, which is often based, by the old tradition, on the use of various physical factors, and not of physical exercises, and which in motor disorders is a pathogenetic method or therapy."[15] We take this to mean that the patient, instead of receiving general exercise, or exercise for the part of the body in need of treatment, is too often put in traction, which makes the condition worse. The major problem is that, after the patient is checked out of the hospital, the restorative treatment in most cases either stops completely or else continues on a catch-as-catch-can basis.

Kaptelin—and in this he is echoed by many Soviet authors writing in public health journals—emphasized that many important forms of rehabilitative therapy are available only at widely scattered institutions and, in some cases, only at one or two places. The training of paramedical personnel to provide rehabilitative services (occupational therapy, hydrotherapy, medical gymnastics, and the like) suffers from the same spottiness and general quantitative inadequacy. Unfortunately, we do not know how decisions are made as to the siting of a facility that either is unique in the Soviet Union or is one of only two or three of its type. Nor do we know, specifically and in detail, how its patients are selected. *Samizdat* literature and the testimony of an émigré family, which is discussed in more detail below, have indicated that admission is by special pass or referral. *Samizdat* literature implied—and in some cases has stated explicitly—that admission procedures are open to corruption and political manipulation.

The production of special orthopedic equipment and apparatuses is another often-cited sore point. Models of such equipment have been developed by the Central Institute of Traumatology and Orthopedics (TsITO). But the number actually produced falls far short of the need. Kaptelin, by implication, placed the responsibility for this at the door of the Ministry of the Medical Industry. But, once again, we do not know the details of the decision making process with regard to funding and allocation of materials. Kaptelin's overall conclusion was as follows:

> Thus, we may conclude that there exist a large number of trauma patients and disabled persons requiring medical, and later social rehabilitation, and that the basic principles of scientific methodology for the application of restorative treatment, and positive experience in doing this kind of work, are at hand. An acute need is felt for better coordination of the work of the existing institutions of rehabilitative type. It may well make sense to organize, under the Main Administration of Medical and Prophylactic Aid of the Ministry of Public Health of the USSR, a group concerning itself with the questions of the coordination of work in the medical rehabilitation of patients. In order to carry out adequate restorative treatment, we need to create specialized institutions for the rehabilitation of disabled persons, to train specialized personnel, and to produce a broad spectrum of specialized equipment.[16]

Kaptelin defined medical rehabilitation to include not only surgical correction and other medical treatment in the narrow sense but also the adaptation of the disabled person to the conditions of daily life and work by means of various kinds of compensatory apparatuses, and the adaptation of the disabled person's environment to his or her own individual characteristics. This is a rather broader concept of medical rehabilitation than the one generally used in this country. By contrast, he defined social rehabilitation as consisting mostly of vocational retraining. His rather acerbic conclusions are emphatically backed up by Nesterov and Poddubnyi, who described the results of failure to treat orthopedic injuries adequately and in a timely fashion. "In many cases, the onset of disability is due to incorrect types of treatment and the absence of rehabilitation in the given group of injured persons. The absence of regular observation of injured persons under polyclinic conditions makes it impossible to restore working capacity, and in a

number of cases leads to the deterioration of the state of health and
consequently to an exacerbation of the degree of loss of working
capacity."[17] Disability due to injury affects young people to a
greater degree than most other forms of disability, and therefore is
particularly damaging to the society as a whole in an economic
sense.

To cap this discussion of how the disabled are officially treated
in the USSR, let us introduce some comparative material. We
recently became acquainted in San Francisco with a Soviet émigré
couple originally from Baku. Their twenty-five-year-old son is
very severely disabled with cerebral palsy, and perhaps also mental
retardation—although, since he is unable to speak so as to be understood by anyone outside his family, this is difficult to determine.
The parents stated explicitly that they emigrated for their son's
sake. While we have not conducted full-scale life-history interviews with them, the picture we get of their experience of trying
to get help for their son is as follows: they took him to a number of
different treatment centers in various parts of the Soviet Union,
including the Turner Children's Orthopedic Hospital in Leningrad
and a similar institution in Kaluga, where he was treated for relatively short periods of time and with varying degrees of success. In
one instance, he was placed in a full-body cast, and when the
treatment period was over and the cast was removed, he had lost
whatever mobility he had originally had. This is significant in
view of Kaptelin's criticism of the traditional method of treating
orthopedic conditions, quoted above. This story sounded familiar
to us: we both, in our childhood and early adolescence forty years
ago, experienced the same thing, and furthermore, the surgery
which made our immobilization necessary is now generally recognized as having been mistaken.

We do not mean to reflect, by this anecdote, on the quality of
Soviet medicine or on Soviet policy toward the disabled. The
young man's mother emphasized to us that she had known first-
rate doctors and concerned therapists and had witnessed at least
one recovery that seemed miraculous. However, we do wish to
call attention to a structural problem. Anyone desiring treatment
at one of the well-known Soviet centers must get an admission
permit, good for a specified length of stay—usually several
months—which, in the case of a condition like cerebral palsy (not
to mention mental retardation), is quite inadequate to produce any
marked or lasting improvement. Patients who are workers in good
standing can renew such permits without difficulty through the

VTEK, but persons disabled from childhood have trouble. In the case in question, when the young man reached the age of sixteen, there were no further admission permits, and further treatment was not available unless he were to be permanently institutionalized, which the parents would not consider. They were urged to seek help nearer home, but in fact, there was no appropriate institution for young disabled adults in or near Baku. A Soviet émigré specialist on Siberia now living in France told Ethel Dunn in 1988 that his son's disability (cerebral palsy) was the reason for his decision to emigrate: "there was nothing for him [the son] there." Once again, this was a basically familiar story. Our personal experience as young adults and increasingly as we age is that by far the greatest rehabilitative efforts are made for children. As a policy, this cannot be faulted in terms of medical cost effectiveness, but it is no less tragic on a personal level for all that.

The émigré family's experience in this country shows some interesting points of contrast. Although the father is unable to practice his profession of civil engineering, and although the family income fluctuates because ot the unskilled and seasonal nature of his work in construction (and also because the mother is only occasionally employed outside the home), the family seems to enjoy a fairly good standard of living, inasmuch as it has a two-bedroom apartment not far from the ocean. The apartment is not adequate, since the son and a thirteen-year-old daughter must share a room, and the bathroom facilities make it extremely difficult to give the son proper care. But considering the family's presumed income and the shortage of low-rent housing suitable for the disabled in San Francisco, conditions are still favorable. The son is enrolled in several training and recreation programs and spends two weekends a month away from home as part of a respite program; the mother receives an allowance for caring for him, and he also receives a disability allowance. The parents consider this subvention superior to what was available to them in the Soviet Union, and add that, whereas in the Soviet Union they were more concerned about the son, here they are more concerned about their daughter, who initially lacked the educational and particularly the artistic opportunities that she had in Baku. She was preparing to enroll in a private Jewish school, where she could get education of a higher quality than was available in the public schools, including access to a full music and dance program of a kind that has been eliminated in recent years by most California public-school districts, because of fiscal constraints.

An American Communist journalist and party official, Mike Davidow, told a contrasting story about his experiences in trying to get help for his mentally retarded epileptic son, both in the United States and the Soviet Union.[18] As one might expect, the contrast came out strongly in favor of the latter. Davidow stated that the Kashchenko Psychiatric Hospital, where his son was placed and eventually died, had a patient/staff ratio in the early 1970s of nearly one to one, in contrast to a figure of twenty to thirty to one at a hospital in upstate New York. We cite this here not to indicate, necessarily, what is available to the ordinary Soviet citizen (the Soviet public health literature is full of complaints about the overconcentration of doctors in the large cities), but rather as an example of what the Soviet system can accomplish when appropriate decisions are made on the highest level.

The American journalist and translator William Mandel, who has traveled extensively in the Soviet Union and has published several books on his experiences there, reported the following:

> I have often been asked about the status of people handicapped by birth. On my last visit to Tashkent, capital of Uzbekistan, Soviet Central Asia, I taped the following in a conversation with G. A. Khidoiatov, a historian whom I had first met when he visited San Francisco. . . . Mr. Khidoiatov says: "the Admission Committee [of the college] decided to accept this lad without arms. He studied the full five years. Inasmuch as he was unable to get along without assistance, we put his mother on the payroll. She was uneducated, but we took her on in the category of a cleaning-woman. And we assigned them a room of their own in the dorms, in which the two of them lived. The president [presumably of the college] allocated them a living grant of 100 rubles per quarter. He completed the course of instruction and then was found work with the assistance of our college. He is now employed at a publishing house here in Tashkent."[19]

This is not necessarily a typical experience. When we asked the parents of the disabled young man in San Francisco what schooling he had received in the USSR, they merely shrugged and replied that the schools were not accessible—a problem very familiar to us. Andrew Sutton, who visited special schools in the Armenian SSR in October 1986 noted that no children with mobility or incontinence problems, or who were unable to use their hands, were admitted. He was, on the whole, very favorably impressed with the theoretical level and the pedagogical skills of the teachers he observed.[20]

Mandel's case history shows again what can be done within the

Soviet system. It is, we suppose, conceivable that the president of an American private college could do something equivalent, but at a public institution, it would be extremely difficult. It is also true that certain American universities and colleges have residential programs for severely handicapped students, but this is quite recent.

III

The official Soviet public health literature says little about the quality of daily life of the disabled in the USSR. We found one official report on such a subject, a brief and rather ambiguous survey of 336 disabled persons in Novosibirsk for the years 1970–73.[21] The report is very dry: of these people, 41.3 percent worked in subsidiary departments of large industrial enterprises; 21.7 percent had been disabled for less than a year, 19.6 percent, four to five years, and 26.5 percent, from one to three years; 7.1 percent were classified as Group I disabled. About 48 percent of the sample were under thirty years of age. Only 4.7 percent of the sample were single, and 37.4 percent of families consisted of four persons. Thirty-three persons lived in private houses where water and heating required physical effort. The authors express satisfaction at the fact that 41.3 percent had nine square meters of living space per family member; 20.5 percent had less than seven square meters. Only 21.7 percent had one-room apartments, and 16.3 percent were situated on the fourth floor. However, 96.4 percent of the families had individual apartments. In the sample, 33 percent received a pension of seventy rubles; 25.8 percent got thirty to forty rubles, and 14.8 percent got less than thirty rubles. When figured on a per-family-member basis, 37.4 percent had more than seventy rubles of income, and only 0.9 percent had less than thirty rubles. Only 3.5 percent of the sample visited the doctor more than nine times a year. However, 44.6 percent said they felt worse than they had; 1.8 percent were addicted to alcohol. Only 2.3 percent complained about the size of the pension, apparently about as many (2.4 percent) as complained about the medical service. Over the period in question, nineteen were considered partially rehabilitated. None of the sample had been retrained, but 95 percent were working as recommended by VTEK.

In order to get a better feel for the daily problems behind such statistics, we will in this section consult a variety of unofficial and nontechnical sources. The popular journal *Nauka i religiia,* more than any other source we know of,[22] has published material on the daily lives of disabled Soviet people. In addition, its material consists in part of letters from disabled readers and interviews with the letter writers by the journal's staff writers. The reader thus has a rare opportunity to hear the actual voices of the Soviet disabled—those who are neither dissidents nor émigrés. What struck us in reading this material was how close the inner experience of the Soviet disabled was to that of disabled adults—particularly older ones—in the United States. A reader of *Nauka i religiia,* who asked that she be referred to only as Tanya, wrote:

> I am over 30 and have a secondary education. I work, but I have a Group III disability rating [the least severely affected group of disabled persons, who can work in the general labor force but cannot be put to work without their consent, as able-bodied persons can]. In childhood I was often sick and suffered severely from loneliness— I had no friends. Even today, there are many people around me, but I seem to be alone. Each one is occupied with his own concerns, and they have no time for disabled people. As long as I can remember, I have suffered not only physical but also psychological pain from my shortcomings.
>
> Do healthy and able-bodied people understand how hard it is for people like me—how hard it is in our position to remain a human being? It's not at all easy not to become rude and mean, not to bear a grudge against the whole wide world. Do people understand that the most terrible thing for a disabled person is loneliness? Neither books nor music nor TV—nothing can replace the goodness of the human heart. Whether a person is healthy or sick, everyone needs support in a difficult moment.
>
> I'm getting older and feel more and more attraction to people. To live without friends is unendurable. Print my letter, and perhaps through the magazine I will find a good friend, male or female. I ask only that you not write my address in the magazine, since I fear the ridicule of my fellow villagers. But if someone wants to correspond with me, please give him or her my address.
>
> This letter has probably turned out badly: I have never written to a magazine before. You can correct this, but please retain the meaning: I seek friends.[23]

In 1985, *Nauka i religiia* informed Tanya and its readers that it had received an unexpected number of responses to Tanya's letter— more than three hundred. Some of what Tanya received in reply to her *cri de coeur* is described by the staff writer, Inga Ballod, as "sententious letters—fortunately few in number—which are full or unarguable, but fleshless truths, and words which everyone knows." Those who wrote this kind did not ask for Tanya's address; the staff writer opined that their feeling for pain in others remains undeveloped. "You and I are flying forward, oh, how high the destiny is! The wind blows strongly in our faces, in our throats, and the sand whistles in our lungs." Ballod commented: "A dangerous type of person! Not so much because he is full of pretense, and 'high demands' on the society surrounding him, and is absolutely incapable of self-accusation. He is dangerous because he lives easily in two worlds at once: in the world of his own thought, the wordy and exhibitionist world, where poems, self-admiration, and the soul 'which no one understands,' float over the earth, and in the other world, the real world where he has robbed, killed, and stolen from crippled people." What is interesting here is Ballod's assumption that everyone has to one degree or another "robbed, killed, and stolen from crippled people." Another letter also not forwarded to Tanya asked her to think of the writer for the time being as Mr. X and asserted that he wanted only to love and be loved in the way that he has read about in books.[24]

Most of the letter writers expressed sympathy for Tanya, saying that they knew how she felt and were ready to be her friends. The most detailed response was from a construction foreman, who wrote that he was over fifty-six years of age and also had a Group III disability rating, since he lost his hand when he was in the fifth grade. However, he always had friends and always did the things that boys his age did. He learned to write with his left hand. Since he lived in the German-occupied Ukraine, he was not able to go to school during the war, and had to go to work as an agricultural laborer immediately after it. He also worked as a stone cutter, a painter, and a carpenter, and graduated from the evening ten-year school. He married, had children, and took his whole family into the Virgin Lands (Kazakhstan). Then his wife left him, having fallen in love with someone else, taking the children with her, and he began to drink. But then he found a new set of friends and stopped drinking, entered the Omsk Polytechnic Institute, and received the diploma of engineer. His wife looked him up and said that she wanted to begin over again, but he couldn't forgive her. He paid alimony faithfully and helped the children. The children grew up and made the choice to live with him, and he saw them married. His second wife became ill and died, but with the help of friends, he raised their daughters and gave them away in marriage. His third wife has three children and they now live in peace and harmony, inviting all the grandchildren to visit.

Not all the letters from the disabled were so cheerful. A

woman with a Group III disability rating wrote that she too feared
the ridicule of her fellow villagers, even though she worked and
had a specialized secondary education. "I am well over 30; my life
has gone by and I've experienced nothing bright in it. What kind
of friends can there be if people, especially men, are embarrassed
to be seen with people with a limp? I was surprised that you
published a letter about this. I am accustomed to the fact that no
one pays us any special attention."[25]

A limp didn't seem much of a handicap to another staff writer
of *Nauka i religiia,* who commented on the letter of a lady he called
Ol'ga Andreevna. She wrote to explain how she became a believer
after having served as an atheist propagandist. She was born during the war, her father had died before her birth, and her mother
raised three children alone. In the sixth grade, Ol'ga came down
with a spinal disease and for four years walked ten kilometers to
school in hellish pain. After graduation she spent six months in the
hospital and had two serious operations, one of which injured her
nerves; she came out "a cripple." Nevertheless, a young man
wanted to marry her. His parents were against it. "He even cried,
but he went away without saying goodbye to me." She spent three
years in a school for clubhouse workers, "the only bright spot in
my life." Afterwards, she was asssigned to a run-down village
clubhouse, which kept her working from early morning till late
night. After six months, things got a little better. She lived in a
private apartment and there were lots of livestock around—sheep,
cows, goats, and turkeys. A young man proposed marriage, and
they were married, but there were no children and her mother-in-
law spread rumors that she was bewitched. After some years, she
divorced and moved away. It seemed to her that three years was
about as long as she could spend in any one place. The story
doesn't end there. One winter, all the wood in her shed was stolen;
another time, someone had the key to her house and took away
everything valuable. At this point she decided to return to her
home village. She enrolled by correspondence in a journalism
school and was accepted on the *raion* newspaper. But then she
began to drink. "Men are forgiven for this, but for women it is
considered impermissible." Ol'ga Andreevna thought that what
men could do women should be allowed to do as well. She fell in
with a man who also drank; he beat her unmercifully, either from
jealousy or in a drunken rage. This made her drink even more, and
she was dismissed from her job and from the university.

For two months, she couldn't find any work: "For good jobs

they wouldn't take me, and I couldn't work with a shovel because of my poor health." Someone from the *raion* executive committee (where she had gone for assistance) said of her situation, "What is she supposed to do now—steal?" She remembered this as she took a rabbit-fur hat, brought it home, and placed it in her closet. Of course the police and the investigators arrived, and that night she swallowed some pills that she had in the house. "But instead of death, I had a significant dream. God called me to him and promised me salvation."

The staff writer was not impressed by this tale, saying that Ol'ga Andreevna tended to see things in black and white, as being either from God or from the Devil, which was an excuse to avoid facing the fact that she herself was responsible for her problems. She called herself a cripple, but in fact she had only a barely noticeable limp.[26]

The story of Ol'ga Andreevna and the staff writer's reaction to it show the highly subjective nature of disability in its social aspect, where it operates (and is perceived) more like a disfigurement than like an actual, practical handicap. It is clear that the staff writer refused to accept Ol'ga Andreevna's self-evaluation, and it is also clear that Ol'ga Andreevna herself was a rather disturbed individual, quite apart from her physical problems.

Another case described in detail in *Nauka i religiia* was that of Leonid Krasov, a thirty-four-year-old neurosurgeon and sports enthusiast, who on 4 March, 1963 fell off a trampoline and suffered a fracture and dislocation of the first lumbar vertebra and compound fractures of the second and third. At that time, the conventional wisdom was that a patient with such an injury would never walk again. Immediately on being brought to the hospital, Krasov sent for a notebook and began writing down his impressions. Although in constant pain, he refused the morphine that was offered him, saying, "All I have is my hands and my head, and you want to turn off my head."

Contrary to the usual behavior of spinal patients, Krasov took charge of his own case, arguing with the doctors who advised postponing physical therapy and (according to the standard practice of the time) applying elaborate braces, which were to run from the waist down to the heels. Krasov taught the nurses and his friends massage methods and, with their help, improvised the needed equipment for exercise and training, which was lacking at the institute. After he left the institute, a bedroom in his apartment in Moscow was fitted out as a small gymnasium, and he exercised at all hours of the day and night. Someone lived permanently in the apartment with him, helping him keep house, maintain the equipment, and live through the inevitable depressions and illnesses. Relatively soon after the accident, he achieved some movement of his legs, which indicated that part of the spinal cord was intact. His recovery was to be virtually complete: an illustration to the article shows him paddling a raftlike vessel in the water.[27]

This account is in many ways a typical inspirational piece, such as one might find in many American mass magazines or on primetime TV. In fact, the editors of *Nauka i religiia* received many letters asking whether Krasov were not an isolated case and whether it was really a good idea to publicize his methods and experiences. Krasov himself admitted that few could do what he had. To be what he has become takes a tough attitude, a love of life, an awareness of where one fits in, and an ability to rise above pain by becoming absorbed in intellectual pursuits. Krasov spent some part of his childhood in an orphanage, and he says he learned early that he was not the navel of the universe.

Another case reported by Inga Ballod contrasts in certain respects with Krasov's. It shows us a person who has not yet begun to find out what Krasov apparently knew even before he became disabled. Sasha Chizhkov was twenty (and had already served as a parachutist in the army) when he dove into a river and broke his neck. People were kind to him, but his reaction was to "drop out of life." Compared to Krasov, he had no goals, much less education, and many fewer friends. In the beginning, he had indicated that he wanted to complete the ninth grade of school by correspondence, but the inspector in the local department of education, who had promised to help with textbooks, failed to follow through, and though Sasha would have liked to visit the village library, he did not want to go through the village in a wheelchair (perhaps there were no paved roads or sidewalks; perhaps he was simply ashamed). Sasha was cared for by his mother, and was lonely. Now, in his village of fifty households, he waited for people to bring him small appliances to repair, and he took pictures of the people around him. Correspondence with Ballod, lasting a year, was his way out of loneliness. In the beginning, he confessed that he could not call himself a believer. Faced with death, however, he did start to think and to question. Later he told Ballod: "Precisely because there is death, I would like to live. If we were immortal, we would not want to act. Life and death do not contradict but rather complement each other."

Ballod replied that Sasha could find friends and satisfaction from life if he would make the first move. She recalled a young man in a wheelchair, who, though disabled from birth, took part in the social and intellectual life of his village. Then she told Sasha to do likewise. As one of the steps toward becoming more mobile and more involved in social life, Sasha thereupon acquired a Zaporozhets (a small Soviet-made passenger car), and this brought a whole range of new concerns—assistants, spare parts, a garage. He became so active that a local psychotherapeutic center made plans to appoint him external associate, a kind of peer counselor for others in his situation.[28]

The social aspect of recovery from the effects of disability is emphasized in an account of Natasha Smeikal, who when a student in the tenth grade in Cheliabinsk fell four storeys and broke her neck. Operations did not help, but her devoted parents heard about Leonid Krasov, and Natasha began to follow his instructions. While still on crutches, she entered a school for paramedics and graduated as a teacher of massage, and then began to work in the medical facilities of the Cheliabinsk Tractor Factory. Since she liked to help people, she began to travel around, apparently without crutches, visiting the spinal disabled, bringing small presents, hope, and a fresh look at life. She was asked how she bore pain, and she answered that at first she was sorry for her parents, and then she gained a sense of her connectedness with life that never left her. She went to visit a man who was disabled as the result of a partisan action in his village during World War II (he had been a very young civilian), and the next day went to the village soviet to chew out the members of the local Komsomol unit for forgetting him. She told them that the attitude toward the sick, the disabled, and the elderly is a measure of public morality and an index of social health.

Natasha Smeikal had a fierce faith in the power of personal friendships. She traveled around the Soviet Union, supporting herself mostly as a tour guide. In Dushanbe, Christian believers were so taken with her that they tried to recruit her into their congregation, and even helped her to find a job as a paramedic. Her idea of friendship was very exacting: "If I find that a person is not what I thought, I break off relations with him without resentment. I need trustworthiness as I need food." Apparently, she found this in her relations with the elderly and the disabled she met on her travels. In September, 1984, having rejected the profession of patient, Natasha Smeikal died.[29]

These documents from *Nauka i religiia* show that, at least in this Soviet source, the handicapped are treated as human individuals, without any kind of generalization or stereotyping on the basis of their disability—even though in some cases (such as Ballod's comments on the replies to Tanya's letter) extremely far-reaching conclusions are drawn on the basis of very slender evidence. At the same time, the documents also show that the disabled themselves frequently feel that they are stereotyped and arbitrarily assigned to certain roles by the able-bodied. There is, of course, no basis here for statistical conclusions, but it seems clear that physical defect and its psychological sequelae are extremely widespread in the Soviet population, and that a great many of those suffering from some degree of disability are not reached by corrective and supportive measures other than the purely medical ones. A Soviet journalist summed up a situation that changed little until 1988:

The most acutely painful question for all of us, the handicapped people write, is the lack of opportunity to engage in socially useful activity.

Here are lines from various letters received: We are in the position of parasites. We bear this as a brand, as a mark of shame. Work is my convalescence, my happiness. I experience enormous happiness when I am of use to my beloved country. How many handicapped people from the ages of 18 to 45 ask themselves: where is my place in life? Inactivity is a great sorrow. You only get one life and there won't be a second. Something has to be done so that there will be a place for us in the middle of things and not in carriages for the wounded. . . .

In spite of the universal need for laborers, homebound labor is at present little used; it is extremely difficult to find jobs for the handicapped. But paradoxically if you lack a hand or even both hands and are in addition blind, you can be sure that you will be suitably cared for and that work will be found for you. The All-Russian Society for the Blind (*VOS*) and the Society for the Deaf (*VOG*) see as their main task allowing a person to work.

It is quite evident that handicapped people need an organization similar to *VOS* and *VOG*. Social security agencies alone are not competent to solve this problem. In the life of a handicapped person there is nothing of secondary importance. Several steps leading from the home in which he lives can cut him off from the external world. And the lack of suitably modified items in everyday use or specially made clothing . . . and the levered wheel chair which only a normal person can use. . . .

Scientists think that 80% or the handicapped can be returned to active life. Special centers should be created for this, where in the process of rehabilitative treatment and prosthetic outfitting, the inclination and gifts of the patients would manifest themselves and the possibility of making them able to work would be explored. There must be in these centers shops which have many specialties. And the handicapped should study not, as is done at present, shoe repair or primitive bookkeeping, but electronics, precision mechanics, artistic crafts. For the physically disabled person completely preserves his intellect and can master a complicated advanced profession which demands a smaller expenditure of physical labor. And in addition, finding him a job is made easier.

One of the first stages on the road to implementing the complex task of rehabilitation, it seems to me, should be the creation of homes and boarding schools for young people outfitted with a variety of shops and a network of producing living facilities paid for by working handicapped people.[30]

This striking statement, we must stress, was written four years before the appearance of a disabled rights movement in the USSR and essentially supports all the demands the movement's leaders later made.

IV

The use of dissident and *samizdat* sources constitutes one of the most difficult and potentially explosive problems for anyone attempting to write accurately and fairly about any aspect of life in the Soviet Union. One is faced with the alternatives of, on the one hand, ignoring these sources completely and seeming to assume the role of an apologist for the regime, and on the other, using the sources without specific caveats and qualifications (for which, as a rule, adequate corroborating information is not available), and seeming to assume the role of a prosecutor—or, still worse, of an apologist for the other side. We are profoundly unwilling to assume either role, but the emotional reaction of the more severely disabled of us to the horror stories contained in this literature is so strong that something had to be said about them.

Some of these stories are not overtly political at all. For example, a paralyzed woman in the Crimea lives in what used to be a bathroom. Twice a day, she is visited, fed, and attended to by her son, who works some distance away: for everything else, she must depend on passersby, whom she summons by shouting, and who invariably ask her on entering, "How do you live?" She is listed with the city committee as being eligible for improved housing, but there are about 100 applications ahead of her.

Other *samizdat* stories are very evidently political, however. For example, Iurii Kiselev, the disabled rights activist who is discussed in a later chapter of this volume, had his specially built house burned down by persons unknown. When he tried to get redress, he was prosecuted because the house did not follow the standard plans. Again, the disabled activist and inventor Gennady Gus'kov was personally vilified by the minister of social security, hauled out of his bed, and sent 700 miles away to be placed in an old folks' home (he was in his thirties at the time). He traveled there in a railway car sitting up under guard of two policemen, although he was supposed to be moved only on a stretcher.

How should such material be interpreted? Are these just meaningless atrocities? A complex subtext of the Gus'kov story gives us some hints. Gus'kov once had some legitimacy within the system. His activities and achievements were features in the national press during the late 1960s and early 1970s. At Boarding Home No. 1 in Voronezh, where he lived, Gus'kov, a victim of polio in childhood, set up a cottage industry producing parts for motors and other specialized equipment. The response to Gus'kov's initiative was widespread and on the whole favorable, although some people were disturbed at meeting Gus'kov, who traveled around on a primitive cart. His shop began to receive large orders. A gifted engineer, he developed many models for devices to assist the disabled, including a stair-climbing wheelchair and a small automobile, which he drives himself. His eviction from the boarding home seems to have been the result of a conflict with certain politically powerful elderly people, many of them war veterans, whose quarters in the boarding home were taken over for the expansion of the sheltered workshop.[31] Gus'kov's workshop was due to be removed from the jurisdiction of the social security organs and placed under the authority of local industry: it is reported that Gus'kov's eviction from the boarding home was the result of a campaign of slander mounted by local social security officials in a battle over bureaucratic turf, and by the elderly inmates just mentioned, in defense of their living quarters.[32] It appears from this story that Gus'kov was caught in the middle of two power struggles, one bureaucratic and the other political. We should also note in connection with Gus'kov's story that a distinguished colleague of ours, who personally knows the minister of social security involved, expressed strong doubts that she took a direct part in the events described or that her actions were accurately reported in the *samizdat* sources. These considerations do not make the Gus'kov report less disturbing, but they do show how carefully *samizdat* material must be treated.

Other caveats emerge from an appeal by Iurii Kiselev published in *Novoe Russkoe Slovo* at the end of December 1984. He entitled it: "The Most Terrible Thing Is Our Separateness" and addressed it to all societies of war veterans and camp prisoners, to societies of disabled in Western countries, and to pacifist groups. He began by saying that the Initiative Group to Defend the Rights of the Disabled in the USSR consists of four persons. Two were forced to emigrate, and a third, categorized as belonging to the most disabled Group I, was silenced out of fear for his relatives. Kiselev pictured the life of the disabled as being taken up with mundane problems: wheelchair repair, transportation, and household purchases, since they do not have enough money to buy furniture and sufficient food.

> We [in the USSR] always hid the disabled, and we continue to hide them from curious eyes. No one needs them. They are a burden to the state, and sometimes they do not hesitate to say so openly. The mass media play down the dark side of the "heroics" of war and labor and do not show disabled with obvious injuries (in the USSR there are no accidents). Soviet citizens make every effort not to think of the cause-and-effect connection of these injuries. The nation is being taught cruelty toward the weak, the sick and the disabled, who are of no use anywhere. Therefore the regime ignores the most vital needs of the disabled and forbids their organizations and societies. Such societies, organized by the disabled themselves in the USSR, have been broken up several times as "antistate" and contrary to the interests and goals of the leaders of the Communist Party.[33]

Since pensions for the disabled range from thirty to seventy-five rubles, Kiselev doubted that the Soviet disabled could travel to the West, and he invited interested Westerners to visit them, starting with himself, in order to open the eyes of the Soviet disabled and bring them into the peace movement, so that "together we may succeed in holding a peace march in the streets of Moscow." There seems little doubt that Kiselev's main concern was to alter the isolation leaders experience as a result of having their letters stolen and their phones cut off, and of being incarcerated in special psychiatric hospitals and treated with neuroleptic drugs.

A number of other points should be made also in order to put the contents of Kiselev's appeal in perspective. First, his statement that Soviet disabled people are considered useless because they do not work is flatly contradicted in much of the public health literature, where we read that even many in Group I (who cannot be put to work without their own consent) do in fact hold jobs, and that less severely disabled persons are in many cases better workers than their able-bodied fellow citizens. Iakobashvili and Dashkovskaia, reporting on a study in 1968 of social hygiene in Krasnodar, state that

> 31.4% of disabled persons in Group I are working, 29.3% of persons in Group II, and 72.5% of persons in Group III. The participation of disabled persons of Groups I and II in labor has to be considered a positive phenomenon. At the same time, the large percentage of disabled persons of Group III who are not working indicates that the public health organs and the social security system are paying insufficient attention to recruiting them for labor and giving them rational job placement. We should note that among men the percent of those disabled from childhood who are working is greater than among women (76.1 as against 68.3).[34]

The relative unemployment of disabled women in the USSR seems to represent a pattern, but by way of comparison, we should cite data from the United States for the same period showing that between 65 and 76 percent of all disabled women are unemployed and that "while 94 percent of disabled men who are rehabilitated receive training in wage-earning occupations, only 68 percent of the women are so trained."[35]

Second, the charges that Soviet people are being taught callousness and cruelty toward the disabled, and particularly that they practice these things habitually, should rest, if they are to be taken seriously, on something more than the subjective impression of an interested party. The Initiative Group appears to claim that the privileges granted to disabled war vetarans discriminate against other categories of the disabled.[36] There are indications that these privileges for veterans are resented by some Soviet citizens—particularly younger ones—just as any privilege for anyone tends to be resented. However, it seems doubtful that the Initiative Group's view is widely shared.

To put the *samizdat* material in focus, it seems useful to insert here some comparative data from the United States. In 1979 and 1980, a number of letters, editorials, and op-ed articles were published in the *New York Times* and the *Washington Post* stating that government policy on the federal and local levels had gone too far in mandating conveniences for the handicapped. Some of this material is discussed by Spiegel and Podair.[37] One of the cases cited by these authors deserves to be considered in more detail. In May 1980, the Museum of Modern Art in New York City mounted a large and prestigious exhibit of the work of Pablo Picasso. The arrangements for accommodating the handicapped at this exhibit provoked a vehement protest from Michael E. Levin, professor of Philosophy at City College, CUNY, expressed in a letter to the *New York Times,* dated 20 May, 1980. After describing the inconveniences caused by the effort to accommodate the disabled, Levin wrote:

> This discomfiture imposed on the vast majority for the dubious benefit (or "mainstreaming") of a tiny minority is being duplicated all over the country. It is one of the most astonishing phenomena, and greatest scandals, of the current American scene that this absurdity is receiving virtually no press coverage. . . .
>
> It would be nice if no one were crippled or blind, and one should make every provision for the convenience of those less fortunate. But it is insane to gear everything to those in wheelchairs. People so confined simply cannot lead the life of someone not handicapped, and it is stupid to pretend they can.
>
> It is equally stupid to impose innumerable inconveniences, and the cost of imposing them, on the majority for the sake of a very small minority.

Several cogent and equally vehement rebuttals to Levin's letter were published, but he also received support from an unexpected corner. Lee Baxandall, while distancing himself from some of Levin's more extreme positions, ventured the opinion that the drive for equal access for the handicapped to public facilities was due largely to the efforts of the construction lobby.[38]

These and similar statements raise the basic question: To what extent do the disabled have an inherent right to make nuisances of themselves—to demand special treatment and facilities, and thereby potentially or conceivably burden or inconvenience the able-bodied? In a recent study of disability policy in Western Europe and the United States, Deborah Stone argued that disability is

> an administrative category in the welfare state, a category that entitles its members to particular privileges in the form of social aid and exemptions from certain obligations of citizenship. . . . Disabil-

ity accounts for a substantial portion of income redistribution and,
in much smaller measure, for the distribution of some fundamental
privileges and duties of citizenship—the obligation to serve in national defense, to obey the laws of the state, and to honor financial
agreements. The reverse side of the "privilege" of being disabled is
the harshness of social treatment of those who are not categorized as
disabled but are nonetheless unable to achieve a decent standard of
living. The very act of defining a disability category *determines what
is expected of the nondisabled—what injuries, diseases, incapacities, and
problems they will be expected to tolerate in their normal working lives.*[39]
[emphasis ours.]

To our knowledge, no disabled activist in the United States has
yet been committed to a psychiatric hospital or received the kind
of treatment meted out to Gennadii Gus'kov. But in general, the
life of the Soviet disabled, as Kiselev has depicted it, is reminiscent of that experienced in the United States by unemployed,
uneducated, and poor disabled people. The range of appliances
available to the disabled in the West is certainly greater, but by no
means necessarily better suited to the individual, precisely because the appliances are mass produced and there is no "standard"
disability. Furthermore, it is by no means a foregone conclusion
that a particular needed appliance—which may be anything up to
and including a specially outfitted automobile—will be available
to a particular disabled person if he or she lives in a state where
there is no program for supplying those in need with such articles. The United States has its own horror stories of this type,
some of which one may see on television's evening news or
"Sixty Minutes."

Further, even if we accept the idea that the *samizdat* horror
stories derive from policy decisions at the highest level, which
seems dubious, at least when stated as a general proposition, we
should not lose sight of the fact that under the right (or wrong)
political conditions, similar policy decisions are in fact made at the
highest levels of our own government: witness the attempted social security purge by the Reagan administration, described by
Piven and Cloward in one of their latest books.[40] A large part of
that welfare purge was disallowed by the courts, but this does not
bear on our argument here. The fact is that the American judiciary
is more independent than the Soviet one and that the appellate
procedure is more highly developed says little about the position
of the disabled under either regime or about the nature of government policy in either country at any given moment.

V

The mid-to-late 1980s saw some changes in the situation of the disabled in the USSR, including increasingly frank admissions that the disabled were being poorly integrated into Soviet society. A recent study on work adaptation by Dobrovol'skaia and Shabalina[41] shows a relatively high level of professional skills among the disabled, but also a large number (almost a third) with low levels of social adaptation. The disabled workers in question had little contact with management and considered themselves superfluous on the job. The same attitude was found in a smaller percentage of able-bodied workers in a control group. Not surprisingly, the lowest level of on-the-job adaptation was found among those in the first year of disability; with the passage of time, this level fell sharply, and was reduced to 9.7% after ten years. The highest level of job adaptation was among workers with war-related disabilities. The authors state that those with war-related disabilities "are skilled career workers, who received their disability ratings shortly after the war. They learned their trades and became adapted to the changed working conditions long ago. Many of them are of pension age, and therefore those whose occupational adaptation is low have simply stopped working." We know from other sources that disabled World War II veterans enjoy respect and a degree of material and moral support apparently not extended to other disabled persons, whether working or not. Among the group of persons disabled from birth, those with low levels of on-the-job adaptation amounted to 16.3 percent, as compared with 17.9 percent among those the cause of whose disability was a general disease (non-war-related). The poorest on-the-job adaptation was among those with occupational diseases, who were also poorly educated, and hence unable to pass over to other skilled and highly paid work. Women, generally speaking, were at a disadvantage in terms of job adaptation: a low level was found in 35.3 percent, as opposed to 23.1 percent among men, and a high level among only 34.5 percent as against 53.5 percent of men. The sample involved is small—only 220 individuals—and limited to a number of enterprises in Moscow. The authors call for a more flexible system of job placement for the disabled and also for what is currently referred to in the United States as "mainstreaming," as opposed to the placement in special disabled cooperatives which is commonly practiced in Czechoslovakia, Poland, and certain other countries.

Dobrovol'skaia, Demidov, and Shabalina did a study early in

1987 to find out whether the establishment of a Society of the Disabled was advisable.[42] They noted that the question of creation of such an organization had been dragging on for years. The results showed that social-security workers at the upper and middle level did not consider the present system adequate. Of the 260 persons questioned in Moscow, Riazan', and Kishinev, 80.4 percent called the aid only partially satisfactory and 19.6 percent called it poor. Specialists at the secondary level—inspectors at the *raion* departments of social security, who work directly with the disabled— were more optimistic, but among them only 9.7 percent considered the existing aid to the disabled satisfactory. Only 22.6 percent of specialists at the upper level considered that the consequences of disability were fully compensated for by the existing measures and privileges.

The question was put to 590 disabled persons: "Do you have adequate opportunities for finding a job?" From 50 to 76.5 percent of the disabled, depending on the area, answered negatively. From 50 to 70 percent of the experts whose job it was to help the disabled to find jobs said that it was very difficult to do so. Two percent of the jobs at enterprises are supposed to be held open for the disabled. By way of comparison, the authors say the Federal Republic of Germany has a quota of 6 percent, and if this is not honored, the enterprise pays a monthly fine into the funds set aside for rehabilitation. (Speakers at the Founding Conference of the Russia-wide Society of Disabled People repeatedly spoke of the 2 percent rule as being more often violated than honored.[43])

Those with motor and spinal disabilities have the greatest difficulty, and these are usually young people. They have often graduated from secondary schools, professional-technical schools, specialized secondary schools, and sometimes even university. This in itself takes a great deal of courage, but even the most talented look for work for years, and when they find it, a bookkeeper, for instance, will be working as a typist, and an economist as a registrar in a polyclinic. (Bookkeepers and economists are in short supply in rural areas.) One of the problems seems to be that the professions that the disabled can acquire in professional and technical schools and specialized secondary schools are very limited in number, lacking in prestige, and not in demand; 35.7 percent of the experts cited this as a difficulty. From 15.1 percent of those at the upper level and 38 percent of the experts at the middle level considered material difficulties significant, while 48.7 percent of the disabled themselves considered that a problem.

More than a third of the disabled said that they lacked the opportunity to take part in public life; 25 percent expressed psychological discomfort surrounding the problem of making contact. Those with visible disabilities (primarily of the motor apparatus) said that the able-bodied related to them with some hostility; 18 percent noted indifference or hostility, and 16 percent connected their troubles with the indifference of people who were supposed to be helping them. Only 13 percent of the disabled surveyed turned to the trade union for help, and only 3 percent to Party and Konsomol organizations, and the authors take this as a sign of the work that needs to be done in integrating the disabled into society.

Dobrovol'skaia and her colleagues say that it is important to address the psychological problems as well as the material ones, "because a truly humanistic society cannot accept the indifference or hostility by the able-bodied toward the disabled." Forty-five percent of the middle level specialists said that they were completely unequipped to deal with this question. In the opinion of 85 percent of the experts, this society could help with employment; 68 percent thought that it could organize leisure and social interaction; 68 percent thought it could be a legal defender; 62 percent that it could help with everyday living; 58 percent that it could create workers' cooperatives; 56 percent supplementary medical aid; and 55 percent thought the society could broaden the system of professional training.

A Founding Conference of the Russia-wide Society of Disabled People was held in August–September 1988, at the clubhouse of the enterprise "Kozhkombinat." This enterprise has established a special workshop for fifty disabled persons, with hopes for expansion if things go well. One of the most sharply expressed opinions at the conference in September was that VTEK should be entitled to say that a disabled person was capable of working, but not what job he or she should hold. There seemed to be consensus that no organization defended the right of the disabled to work, a right considered basic in the Soviet Union. A partial description of the proceedings of this conference contained an edited version of the report given by the minister of social security of the RSFSR, V. Kaznacheev, whose remarks were preceded by an editorial comment that the presence of the ministry at this conference is in sharp contrast to the actions of the minister in 1973 in the case of Gennady Gus'kov, described above. The minister assured his audience that "a truly humanistic approach to the disabled is not a slogan, and not a campaign, but one of the links of state policy in the social sphere."[44] He pointed out that in 1987 more than 450,000 with diminished work capacity were employed, which is almost 100,000 more than before April 1985. However, in 1987 only 30 percent of the total number of disabled were employed, which was actually 4 percent less than in 1985. Among those employed, Group III disabled were doing the best (79 percent); only 10 percent of Group II disabled and 9 percent of Group I were employed. A sociological study revealed that about 40 percent of the disabled were dissatisfied with the character and content of the work, and 39 percent were not satisfied with working conditions.[45]

One of the first tasks of the society in Kuibyshev (urban) *raion* of Moscow was to discover how many disabled people lived in the *raion* (9,000 persons were eventually contacted). The society inquired at the *raion* social security department and at seven adult and six children's polyclinics for addresses and sent out questionnaires, but the responses were in many cases anonymous. The information number of Moscow telephone was of limited help: two requests for telephone numbers are free; each additional number costs fifteen kopeks. Even when the society had the number, if the subscriber lived in a communal apartment, whether the society got through to him or her depended on the good will of the operator on duty. Now the society is temporarily housed on the first floor of a residential building and has its own telephone number. Later it will move into a remodeled three-storey building. The relative speed with which the society was given facilities is said to reflect the Communist Party's interest in the successful functioning of the new organization.[46]

A small but significant step toward breaking the psychological barrier between the disabled and the able-bodied was the broadcast on Soviet television's First Program in January 1988 of a segment called "Nashi Dolgi" (Our Debts)—one of the rare instances in which persons on crutches or in wheelchairs have been shown on Soviet television.[47] Perhaps the ongoing discussion of the costs of the Soviet Union's involvement in Afghanistan—costs including maimed and alienated Soviet soldiers—accounts for this change. In September and October 1988, Marilyn Golden, an American "disability rights citizen diplomat," visited members of the Moscow Society of Disabled as part of a delegation which included American Vietnam veterans, "prosthetists, an orthopedic surgeon, readjustment psychologists, computer system designers, and transportation (wheelchair) specialists." The trip, organized by Earthstewards Network in the state of Washington and the Soviet Foundation for

Social Inventions, is considered so successful that other exchanges are planned.[48]

VI

In a paper prepared for a conference in Uppsala in 1978, three Polish scholars set up a model for the attitude toward the handicapped and their position in three kinds of societies.[49] In societies at the first stage of development (such as the Third World countries now), the handicapped are not segregated from the rest of society, and no particular attention is paid to their problems, because there are so many other problems. In this type of society, the handicapped are invisible because no one notices them. Such a society is characterized by the "spontaneous participation" of the disabled.

The second type of society, which is at the next stage of development, is marked by the "separation" of the handicapped. At this stage, the problems of the disabled begin to be seen as serious problems for the society as a whole, and particular methods and programs begin to be set up to try and deal with them. These programs involve the segregation of the handicapped, either in closed institutions or in their own apartments, simply because there are not enough devices of the right kind to allow the handicapped to be integrated into society with the same rights and capabilities as normal people. The handicapped are still invisible, because they are locked away and do not appear physically in public.

The third type of society is marked by "integration." This is where the handicapped appear on the social scene, equipped with the necessary appliances to make them as equal as possible to normal people. The authors say that this situation exists, or should exist, in Western Europe, but they pointedly, and for good reason, do not mention the United States. From our point of view, the stage-three society plays the same role in this model as full communism in the Marxist theory of history, or the Second Coming in Christian theology.

The authors describe Polish society as being at the beginning of stage two. They do not mention the Soviet Union in this connection, but our feeling is that it is at the same stage, with the United States somewhat ahead in terms of the presence of technology—but, as we have pointed out, not necessarily in terms of the *availability* of technology to those who need it. The importance of technology varies from one form of handicap to another. In compensating for sensory impairments (blindness, deafness, and the like), it is absolutely crucial. In motor handicaps, except for the most severe, it is somewhat less so, since what is chiefly needed in teaching people to move is unlimited, skilled manpower and specialized knowledge.

The result of the model strikes us as something like a dead heat between the United States and the USSR on the issue of provision for the disabled. This is hardly a brilliant record for the richest country in the world, compared with one which many observers rank as part of the Third World. Our overall conclusion is that Soviet policy makers, in allocating funds and efforts in the field of public health as well as elsewhere, tend to concentrate on those projects and activities they consider cost effective, and that this largely leaves out of account the long-term orthopedically disabled, particularly those who have never been part of the labor force. The emphasis on cost effectiveness is certainly not uniquely Soviet, but the interpretation of this concept largely in terms of returning disabled workers to the job as soon as possible is more distinctive to Soviet conditions than the emphasis on cost effectiveness as such. By the same token, the extreme centralization of the Soviet system means that there is only one interpretation of cost effectiveness, rather than (as in the United States) a potential multiplicity of them—one for the federal government in any given administration, one for each state, and an unspecified number for various powerful private institutions and organizations.

One final point remains: it is clear from the Soviet public health literature, including even celebratory articles like that of Kaziew,[50] that the Soviet system for rehabilitating the disabled and providing services to them is still under construction. There is no reason to assume that after ten or fifteen years it will look the way it does now.

If *perestroika* for the disabled proceeds along the lines which have been indicated in other parts of Soviet society, we can expect that a wide range of problems will be addressed, using both foreign and domestic sources, with results which cannot even be forecast at this point.

NOTES

1. Antoine de St. Exupéry, as quoted in N. Uvarova, "Neudachi menia ne ostanavlivali," *Nauka i religiia* 12(1985): 8–11.

2. V. A. Iakobashvili and Zh. Ts. Dashkovskaia, "Mesto invalidnosti s detstva sredi prichiny invalidnosti," *Zdravookhranenie Rossiiskoi Federatsii* 1(1971): 16.

3. M. N. Nikitina, "Mediko-sotsial'naia reabilitatsiia invalidov s detstva," *Pediatriia* 2(1981): 3–5.

4. *Ogonek* 52(1988): 16–20. For more details, see *The Station Relay* 4, nos. 1–2 (1988).

5. G. L. Apanasenko, V. G. Karepov, and L. G. Rusakovskaia, "Vosstanovitel'noe lechenie bol'nykh, perenesshikh insul't, v usloviiakh mezhraionnogo tsentra reabilitatsii," *Sovetskoe zdravookhranenie* 10(1983): 23.

6. A. F. Kaptelin, "Voprosy organizatsii meditsinskoi reabilitatsii bol'nykh i invalidov posle povrezhdenii oporno-dvigatel'nogo apparata," *Ortopediia, travmotologiia i protezirovanie* 2(1976): 3.

7. N. A. Shestakova and E. A. Bogdanov, "Reabilitatsiia invalidov v usloviiakh polikliniki," *Sovetskoe zdravookhranenie* 4(1983): 41–43.

8. V. S. Kilivnik, "Effektivnost' reabilitatsii bol'nykh v tsentral'noi raionnoi bol'nitse," *Sovetskoe zdravookhranenie* 10(1983): 18–22.

9. A detailed description of the dimensions and fittings of the model apartment follows:

Considering the need to maneuver in a wheelchair, the room was planned for a width of not less than 3.3 meters. For a disabled person moving around in a wheelchair, it is important that the central part of the room be free [of obstructions], and therefore the furniture was placed around the edge of the room and was attached to the walls in console style. . . . Considering the fact that the zone which a disabled person can reach while moving around in a wheelchair is limited both horizontally and vertically, shelves in cabinets, boxes, switches for electrical appliances, and a folding desk for reading and writing must be at a level lower than the usual one (between 0.3 and 1.6 meters). . . .

One of the basic tasks of domestic rehabilitation of disabled persons is to give them the opportunity to carry out sanitary and hygienic procedures without outside help. This requires special planning of the toilet area. The toilet area in the experimental apartment must have all the facilities combined in one place and must be larger than usual. The commode and the bathtub must be approachable from any side. Handles and grab bars are provided to assist in making transfers. The height of the commode is identical with that of the chair. The sink is located side by side with the commode, and the commode is provided with an appliance for hygienic procedures [a bidet?]. The bathtub and shower are provided with a seat on a level with the seat of a wheelchair. A handle is mounted beside the tub to facilitate transfers. The floor covering in the bathroom must not be slippery. The door to the bathroom is on hinges and must be

provided with a latch which permits the door to be opened from
outside. . . .

[A]n optimal plan was developed for apartments for disabled
people with disturbance of function in the lower extremities. At the
present time, a technical plan has been worked out in several versions for such apartments in standard housing, in accordance with
which large prefabricated sections contain, in the first stories, apartments for disabled people. In addition to this, there are in the same
place special rooms for storing the wheelchairs of the disabled (both
for street and indoor use). A special ramp permits the disabled person in a wheelchair to travel from the street to the first floor without any particular effort. The entrance vestibule and the door open-
ings have been expanded to accommodate wheelchairs.

N. I. Filatov, N. G. Agarcheva, and V. V. Kleimenov, "Organizatsiia
zhilykh pomeshchenii dlia invalidov s defektami nizhnykh konechno-
stei," *Ortopediia, travmotologiia i protezirovanie* 6(1981): 1–5.

10. M. Ia. Shiminova, "The Legal Powers of the Parties in Concluding a Contract: Prescribed Terms and Contracts of Association," unpublished manuscript translated from the Russian by Stephen P. Dunn for
International Research and Exchanges Board; the original source for the
opinion in the Petrozavodsk case was *Biulleten' Verkhovnogo Suda RSFSR*
3(1984): 13–14.

11. A. F. Krasnov and A. S. Naumov, "Sotsial'naia adaptatsiia
bol'nykh zabolevaniiami oporno-dvigatel'nogo apparata," *Ortopediia,
travmotologiia i protezirovanie* 6(1981): 59.

12. Ibid., p. 9.

13. Janet Rosenberg, "The Relationship of Types of Post-High School
Education to Occupation and Economic Independence of Physically
Handicapped Adults," in Allen D. Spiegel and Simon Podair, eds., *Reha-
bilitating People with Disabilities into the Mainstream of Society* (Park Ridge,
N.J.: Noyes Medical Publications, 1981), p. 247.

14. N. F. Dement'eva and A. A. Modestov, "Organizatsiia trudov-
ogo obucheniia umstvenno otstalykh podrostkov v usloviiakh promysh-
lennogo proizvodstva," *Zdravookhranenie Rossiiskoi Federatsii* 9(1984): 25.

15. Kaptelin, "Voprosy organizatsii," p. 2.

16. Ibid., pp. 3–5.

17. V. A. Nesterov and N. P. Poddubnyi, "Izuchenie invalidnosti pri
travmakh soprovdaiushchikhsia narusheniem funktsii oporno-dvigatel'-
nogo apparata," *Zdravookhranenie Rossiiskoi Federatsii* 9(1984): 23.

18. Mike Davidow, *Cities Without Crisis* (New York: International
Publishers, 1976), pp. 80–89.

19. Radio broadcast, 18 Mar. 1985; transcript provided by W. Mandel.

20. Andrew Sutton, "Special Education for Handicapped Pupils," in
Soviet Education: The Gifted and the Handicapped, ed. Jim Riordan (London: Routledge, 1988), pp. 70–94.

21. V. P. Agarkov, A. D. Federov, and A. V. Onishchenko, "Iz opyta kontrol'ia za usloviiami truda i byta invalidov," *Zdravookhranenie Rossiiskoi Federatsii* 4(1975): 41–42.

22. Some of the material in this section can be found in Stephen P. Dunn and Ethel Dunn, "Distant Voices," *Kaleidoscope* 15(1987).

23. "Ponimaiut li eto zdorovye liudi?" *Nauka i religiia* 11(1984): 25.

24. I. Ballod, "Daite ee adress," *Nauka i religiia* 5(1985): 25–28.

25. Ibid.

26. V. Khazarov, "Ol'ga Andreevna ishchet Boga," *Nauka i religiia* 10(1984): 51–53.

27. L. Krasov, "Znanie, volia, vera," *Nauka i religiia* 12(1984): 13–17. This material and the following appeared in slightly different form in *The Station Relay* 1, no. 5(1986): 11–12, 15.

28. I. Ballod, "Shag cherez katastrofu," *Nauka i religiia* 10(1979): 8–11.

29. Uvarova, "Neudachi menia ne ostanavlivali."

30. E. Rzhevskaia, in *Literaturnaia gazeta* 14 (1974): 12. The article is translated as "The Disabled in the Soviet Union," *The Station Relay* 1, no. 4 (1986): 21–22.

31. Ibid. pp. 18–21.

32. Steven Marc Glick, "Disability in the USSR—A Dissident View: A Case Study of the Action Group to Defend the Rights of the Disabled in the USSR," Master's thesis, London School of Economics, 1980, p. 7.

33. Iurii Kiselev, "The Most Terrible Thing Is Our Separateness." An undated clipping of this article from *Novoe Russkoe Slovo* is in our possession.

34. Iakobashvili and Dashkovskaia, "Mesto invalidnosti," p. 18.

35. Michelle Fine and Adrienne Asch, "Disabled Women: Sexism Without the Pedestal," in Mary Jo Deegan and Nancy A. Brooks, eds., *Women and Disability, The Double Handicap* (New Brunswick, N.J.: Transaction Books, 1985), p. 7.

36. Glick, *Disability in the USSR,* p. 56.

37. Allen D. Spiegel and Simon Podair, "Introduction," in Allen D. Spiegel and Simon Podair, eds., *Rehabilitating People with Disabilities into the Mainstream of Society* (Park Ridge, N.J.: Noyes Medical Publications, 1981), p. 1.

38. Lee Baxandall, Letters to the Editor, *New York Times,* 12 June 1980.

39. Deborah A. Stone, *The Disabled State* (Philadelphia: Temple University Press, 1984).

40. Frances Fox Piven and Richard A. Cloward, *The New Class War: Reagan's Attack on the Welfare State and Its Consequences* (New York: Pantheon Books, 1982).

41. T. A. Dobrovol'skaia and N. B. Shabalina, "Osobennosti proizvodstvennoi adaptatsii invalidov," *Sotsiologicheskie issledovaniia* 3(1985): 121–25; for more details, see *The Station Relay* 4, nos. 1–2 (1988).

42. T. A. Dobrovol'skaia, N. A. Demidov, and N. B. Shabalina,

"Sotsial'nye problemy invalidov," *Sotsiologicheskie issledovaniia* 4(1988): 79–83.

43. *Sotsial'noe obespechenie* 11(1988).

44. Ibid., p. 6.

45. Ibid., p. 7.

46. E. Potapova, "Kogda est'opora," *Sotsial'noe obespechenie* 12(1988): 40–42.

47. R. L. L'vovskaia, "Nabolevshie problemy," ibid., pp. 42–43.

48. Marilyn Golden, "Mission: Moscow," *Challenge,* January–February 1989, pp. 18–25; Drew A. Hittenberger, "A Unique Soviet-American Exchange," *Almanac,* January 1989, pp. 43–46.

49. Magdalena Sokolowska, Antonina Ostrowska, and Anna Titkow, "Creation and Removal of Disability as a Social Category: The Case of Poland," in Gary L. Albrecht, ed., *Cross-National Rehabilitation Policies: A Sociological Perspective* (Beverly Hills: Sage Publications, 1981), pp. 223–34.

50. M. J. Kaziew, "Entwicklung des umfassenden Rehabilitationssystems für die Behinderten in der UdSSR," *Zeitschrift für die gesammte Hygiene und Ihre Grenzgebiete* 27(1981): 104–06.

Disability as Dissidence:
The Action Group to Defend the
Rights of the Disabled in the USSR

Paul D. Raymond

I

A CONSIDERABLE literature describes the political dissent that has manifested itself in recent decades in the USSR.[1] We know about the human rights, cultural, religious, and national activist movements through a veritable flood of documents, memoirs, and secondary studies published both in the West and underground in the Soviet Union. Little attention has focused, however, on a group which calls itself the Action Group to Defend the Rights of the Disabled in the USSR, although in many respects it has an extraordinarily clear mandate to exist. A dissertation has been written about it in the West, but this remains unpublished.[2] The Action Group is rarely mentioned in the dissidence literature.[3] This chapter outlines its history since May 1978, when it emerged, and analyzes the factors that led both to its persecution by the Soviet authorities and to its persistence—which continued well into the 1980s, before a variety of circumstances led to its de facto disbandment. Perhaps the most poignant irony is the fact that it was precisely at this low ebb that the Gorbachev regime began to show signs of embracing some of the issues and demands the group advocated. Only time will reveal the extent to which the Soviet disabled will be able to benefit from the twin themes of *glasnost'* and *perestroika*.

II

Iurii Kiselev was sixteen years old in 1948 when an industrial accident led to the amputation of both his legs. Valerii Fefelov was an apprentice electrician of seventeen in 1966 when a thirty-foot

235

fall broke his back, permanently confining him to a wheelchair. Kiselev went on to achieve a measure of success as a free-lance artistic designer after his accident. Fefelov had to subsist on a state pension and his wife's earnings. But each became acutely aware through experience and observation of the difficulties the disabled faced in the Soviet Union. It was their efforts to ameliorate what they came to consider the low status of the handicapped that led them finally, in May 1978, to found the Action Group.

The catalyst for their action was unmistakably the Helsinki Conference on Security and Cooperation in Europe (the Helsinki accord) of 1975. Prior to that date, Kiselev had intermittently associated himself with the larger dissident movement, primarily through the signing of various petitions against regime human rights violations.[4] Fefelov, nearly twenty years his junior, had confined himself to petitioning the authorities in his native western Russia for an improvement in his particular situation.[5] In the aftermath of Helsinki, however, they—like many others—sensed an opportunity to join forces. Now, together with Faizulla Khusainov, a Crimean Tatar paraplegic from Chistopol, Kiselev and Fefelov steeled themselves to request that the Soviet government approve the formation of an all-union society for the disabled, similar to those that already existed for the blind and the deaf, and which had indeed once existed for the disabled until its dissolution in 1956.

There is clear evidence that before they acted, the Action Group founders were in close touch with the Moscow Helsinki Watch Committee. Three months before the group's manifesto, Helsinki Watch addressed an appeal to the Supreme Soviet as well as to the United Nations' Human Rights Commission, UNESCO, and Norman Acton, the chairman of the World Federation of Disabled Persons, proposing the formation of a Soviet Invalid's Association, demanding improvements in the social services to the disabled in the Soviet Union, and accusing the Soviet government of massive insensitivity to the constitutionally mandated rights of the disabled. In May 1978, coincident with the first Action Group manifesto, the Moscow Helsinki Watch Committee issued a strong endorsement, calling upon the Soviet disabled "not to reconcile themselves to their humiliating conditions," and pledging help.[6]

At the start, however, the leaders of the Action Group clearly viewed themselves above all not as yet another dissident group but as the nucleus of a wider and legally sanctioned official association. According to the initial programmatic document of May 1978, the group's basic objectives were (1) to collect and disseminate information on the situation of the disabled in the USSR; (2) to petition before competent Soviet organs for the improvement of social security for the disabled; (3) to garner help from world opinion in the event that their appeals were turned down; and (4) to establish contact with international organizations for the disabled.[7] As Fefelov put it in an editorial preface to the first issue of the group's *Information Bulletin:* "Having a sufficiently loyal attitude towards the authorities, we make no pretense towards any sort of 'opposition' or 'independent activities,' as might appear at first glance."[8]

Six months after its foundation, the group again informed the Soviet state and the public that "it is engaged only in the question of the rights of the disabled and their immediate needs within the framework of the Soviet legal system, and that it has no underlying political motivation."[9] The founding declaration did state quite openly that "since we consider that in present circumstances only the disabled themselves can defend their rights, we cannot delegate this [defense] to an indifferent protector such as the Ministry of Social Security."[10] This independent stance applied not just to the Soviet authorities. The Moscow Helsinki Watch Committee was induced early on, for example, to explain that, while it sympathized with the Action Group's aims, it was "not really a 'sister' organization. We neither take part in, nor direct [the Action Group's] activities."[11]

Such declarations of political loyalty combined with firm expressions of autonomy sound rather naive in the Soviet context, and as we will see, were shortly proved to be so. Yet judging from the group's early documents, they were serious. Again and again at the start, pragmatic, legitimate demands predominated. First and foremost, of course, was the creation of an all-union organization. Second came the question of pensions. As seen in the preceding chapter of this volume, disability pensions in the Soviet Union are calibrated according to three degrees of ability to work. But they range from only seventy rubles for the totally disabled—less than half the average working person's monthly salary—to as little as fifteen rubles for those who can still do limited work. Not surprisingly, therefore, one finds numerous references in Action Group publications to the "pauperization" of the disabled resulting from this support scale.

The Action Group also campaigned for the improvement of living conditions, not just for improved availability and quality of goods, the elimination of long lines, and the reduction of shortages. They specifically demanded improved ease of movement and of access. The group issued as one of its first publications a monograph by Kiselev entitled "Transport."[12] This pamphlet explained dramatically why there was need for more automobiles and public vehicles with modifications for the handicapped, for reliable wheelchairs, for easier access to public buildings, for pedestrian underpasses, for street crossings with handicap provisions, and for preferential allocation of functional, handicapped-designed ground-level apartments. There was likewise complaint about the poor quality of special programs and services for the disabled. Rehabilitation facilities, physical therapy, reeducation and job training programs, prostheses and orthopedics, medical personnel, on-going research support—all were perceived as currently inadequate and inferior.

To repeat, the spirit behind all this petitioning was not suggestive of opposition to the Soviet government itself. The group's second *Samizdat* document detailed the issues that concerned the founders but then expressed the hope that the USSR would eventually catch up to the levels of care in other societies.[13] As late as December 1980, the group editorialized: "We love our homeland, and we would like to see it in the front ranks of peoples who are realizing humane actions. And it would be shameful to realize that our government has not responded to this UN initiative [to participate in the "Year of the Disabled" in 1981]."[14] Supporters from the dissident community at large seemed to recognize the largely emotional, nonoppositional character of the Action Group. In an essay about the disabled evocatively entitled "Erased from the Facade," Viktor Nekipelov, a writer who later emigrated to the West, wrote: "One can only welcome the formation of such a group, for these people, more than any others, need to be united if they are to impress on the state their right to get onto the street and join the stream of life."[15]

What was present even in the early period, however, was anger, an anger such as the disabled everywhere must feel toward the society that surrounds them, once they start emerging from their isolation and compare themselves to others. As Fefelov and his wife would put it much later: "Among the overall population of the USSR, the most cruel and refined economic and moral exploitation falls on the shoulders of the invalids. . . . Separated from the entire world and each other, they lead a beggarly existence. From a sociological survey that we have conducted among the disabled, we have been able to determine that they exist on the verge of extreme poverty."[16] Fefelov once again captured the everyday despair of the handicapped when he wrote in 1982 that "after fifteen years of life as an invalid I have reached the conclusion that being disabled in the USSR is a double, if not a greater misfortune. It is not only a physical oppression, but a constant battle for survival against inertia, rudeness, effrontery, poverty."[17]

In general, the Action Group's *Samizdat* material produces an impression of overwhelming dismay at the way the state reacts— or rather fails to react—to the presence of the disabled, perceiving them as a physical blemish and embarrassment of the ideal society. In a very real sense, they believed that "invalids are a ballast which impedes the pace of the heroic construction of the new society. Therefore the regime has no interest in investing money in the more important measures for an improvement in their lives, despite the obviously beneficial economic and prestige gains it would bring."[18] The disabled are segregated in rural areas, small towns, and convalescent homes that appear to be little more than dumping grounds. Kiselev, Fefelov, Khusainov, and Zaitseva (Fefelov's wife) best expressed the spirit of their movement in a letter sent abroad in 1982: "Both the young and the old, the disinformed optimists and pessimists who no longer believe that anything good will come their way or that any changes for a brighter future are possible in their life-time, are eager to hear about themselves and their counterparts abroad and, given the opportunity, to share their bitter experiences. This will give them new strength in their fight against bureaucratic stagnation and ineptitude, for their human dignity and their own union. This would also be quite useful for those people who have no connection to the disabled."[19]

III

Within weeks of the Action Group's establishment, however, signs appeared that the authorities regarded it as subversive and, despite all the denials, as an opposition group. Harassment, illegal searches, interference with correspondence, and threats from various sources began to plague the group's members and sympathizers.[20] Fefelov soon became the subject of particular attention. The authorities in his hometown of Iuriev-Pol'skii first sought to curtail his movements by suspending his driver's license. When he persisted, they arrived unannounced at his residence in October 1978 and, without producing any authorization, conducted a search.[21] Shortly thereafter, they decided to make "street repairs by digging an open pit in front of his garage. That December he

was visited by four local officials: the chairman of the Iuriev-
Pol'skii Soviet Executive Committee, the district director of the
Department of Social Services, and two officers from the KGB.
During the two-hour "discussion" that followed, the group was
labeled an "illegal organization," its *Bulletin* an "underground publication," and Fefelov himself was threatened with prosecution.[22]
He denied all of the above accusations and in turn responded with
a letter of his own to KGB chief Iurii Andropov, defending his
actions, reiterating the apolitical purposes of the group, and accusing the state of acting illegally.[23]

The harassments and threats continued nonetheless. Local
state security officials pressed his relatives to use their influence on
him to cease his "anti-Soviet" activities. More charges and denials
were exchanged. In June 1980, he was accused of drunk driving on
his suspended license. When the authorities forcibly removed his
license plates, Fefelov threatened a hunger strike and in fact spent
a night in front of the city police station in protest. The plates
were subsequently returned, but he was still fined thirty rubles
and had his suspension extended for another five years.[24] That
December saw yet another search and the confiscation of more
"illegal materials."[25]

On 28 January 1980, a KGB delegation delivered an "official
warning" to the Fefelovs to cease their activities or face prosecution. Zaitseva's workplace was visited (she was employed as a
school nurse), and allegations against her were collected. The authorities further threatened her with the loss of parental rights
over her children from a previous marriage.[26] That April came the
next highest threat: a Warning According to the Decree.[27] In mid-
May, Iuriev-Pol'skii's local newspaper, *Za Kommunizm,* weighed
in with an article entitled: "What Do You Want, Fefelov?" which
in turn sparked several anti-Fefelov resolutions in local factories.
The article itself reproduced the by now standard litany of accusations: anti-Soviet activities, receipt of illegal funds from the West,
listening to foreign radio broadcasts, and, in general, of being a
"fanatic."[28]

Fefelov dispatched a reply, which was, of course, never published in *Za Kommunizm.* The version that ultimately appeared in
Samizdat contained a recitation of his "wants": (1) that the disabled
be given permission to have their own association and press; (2)
that the disabled should not be in such a low position that they are
ashamed of their clothes and their hideous pedal and motorized
wheelchairs, and that public transport and the streets be adapted

for them; (3) that the disabled have the opportunity to obtain an education and work corresponding to their infirmity or ailment; (4) that the disabled have access to all public places (i.e., theaters, cinemas, libraries, etc.); (5) that the disabled have the opportunity to purchase an automobile as an item of primary necessity; and (6) that the disabled be able to obtain medical assistance and access to holiday resorts. In sum, Fefelov demanded a right for disabled people in the USSR to lead a full life.[29] Thereupon, his wife was threatened with firing; and then, alternately, promised a better apartment if she would divorce him. The remainder of the year saw more searches and warnings.[30]

IV

Under such circumstances of regime unresponsiveness and intimidation, it is not all that surprising that the Action Group would soon make two fundamental changes. First, it essentially abandoned the view that change in the Soviet Union could ever be brought about through the existing system. In an April 1980 open letter to the émigré newspapers *Russkaia mysl'* and *Novoe Russkoe Slovo,* Fefelov and Zaitseva declared that the socialist system "has brought oppression to man in innumerable ways. A scrutiny of our life reveals the deception of the pledges that were inscribed on the banners of the communist revolution. Having promised every blessing in words, socialism . . . in practice cannot even guarantee its citizens a normal standard of living." Nor was the link between domestic and foreign policy ignored: "The struggle of the CPSU for hegemony in the world communist movement, the policy directed toward the achievement of world supremacy, the extensive spy network and the all-powerful punitive security organs, the maintenance of an army of bureaucrats of all ranks, the ostentatious space race, management inefficiency (inevitable in socialist conditions) and so forth, bring irreplaceable losses to the national economy. The country cannot even provide its own citizens with bread: Russia, which was once a granary, has now become a beggar."[31] Although the group would still periodically address petitions to the authorities, they were half-hearted and nearly always prefaced with an updated catalogue of ongoing illegalities.

A second change flowed logically from the first. Increasingly, the group saw its activities as part and parcel of the broader human rights movement. Searches of group members' and dissidents' apartments now turned up growing numbers of materials on each other's activities. Nekipelov, for instance, had several issues of the group's *Information Bulletin* in his possession at the time of his arrest. KGB searches of Fefelov's house, in turn, landed numerous nongroup items. Fefelov himself was later moved to write openly in defense of Nekipelov and others: "Man's greatest natural gift is one he values more than any other blessing that may fall his way: that gift is freedom. By virtue of his freedom, man has the right to use his own judgment in deciding his own actions. And all countries which are just in the civilized and moral sense recognize this freedom as being a natural and unalienable right of man. Except the USSR."[32] By the early 1980s, then, the circle had seemingly been completed: the Soviet government perceived the group as a form of dissidence, other dissidents embraced them as kindred spirits, and the leaders of the group themselves accepted this designation.

That the authorities chose to respond in the way they did can be explained partly by mind-set and partly by the simple exigencies of politics. Repeated and persistent actions in the face of obvious regime displeasure could be interpreted as nothing less than rejection of the ground rules of the Soviet system. Shortly before the Fefelovs emigrated to the West, the KGB conducted another search of their dwelling. In preparing his subsequent report, the chief investigating officer made the revealing and typical observation that "Fefelov is one of the founders and leaders of the so-called 'Action Group to Defend the Rights of the Disabled,' which prepares and distributes in the USSR and abroad the illegal typewritten collection called 'Bulletin' and other materials discrediting the Soviet state and social system. The material prepared by the Action Group are used by foreign centers of anti-Soviet propaganda to perpetuate acts of ideological sabotage against the USSR."[33]

In a more pragmatic sense, the regime sought to counter the group in two complementary ways. First, the official viewpoint was that the level of attention devoted to the disabled was adequate to meet their needs. Discussions of social welfare programs generally treated the disabled as among the recipients of state programs, not as a separate category deserving preferential treatment.[34] Therefore, second, the disabled needed no additional benefits, no organization of their own, nor links to organizations abroad. For an economy facing serious budget strains and growth contractions, this policy of denial ostensibly eased the financial burden. After all, the disabled constituted a potentially large slice of the total population. Just how large that is remains difficult to calculate, for the problem is both quantitative and qualitative. The fact that sympathetic estimates have ranged from twenty million to as many as fifty million suggests the perils involved.[35] In each case, the numbers are in part dictated by the breadth of the definition of the word *disabled,* extending as it does beyond those with debilitating physical impairments. Yet even using a narrow designation, the Soviet government admitted in 1988 to the existence of over four million disabled in the Russian Republic alone, with nearly a half-million more being added each year.[36] In the crudest of senses, then, this would suggest the existence of upward of ten million disabled in the country as a whole, a not insubstantial number by anyone's reckoning.

Depressingly indicative of the state's position was the manner in which it chose to note the United Nations' declaration of 1981 as the International Year of the Disabled. The International Year was barely and perfunctorily noted in the official media. As 1981 progressed, each issue of the Action Group's *Information Bulletin* devoted its lead section to the ways in which the regime was ignoring the whole question of the plight of Soviet disabled.[37] As a retrospective outside analysis put it: "The official mass media, evidently working on the theory that in the USSR disabled persons are fully integrated in the Social system, portrayed the situation as if the measures provided for in the program of the International Year were only necessary in a capitalist society."[38]

V

Several references have already been made to the Action Group's *Information Bulletin*. During its short existence, this remarkable collection became the voice of Soviet disabled rights activists. Between the founding of the group in 1978 and the emigration of Fefelov in 1982, some fourteen issues were compiled and clandestinely distributed.[39] A survey of them illustrates the rather wide range of concerns confronted by Fefelov and the other editorial board members: Olga Zaitseva (Fefelov's wife), Iurii Kiselev, and Faizulla Khusainov. It also helps illuminate how those concerns and the group itself evolved over time.

A typical issue usually ran forty to fifty pages in length and had a consistent format. An editorial statement constituted the introduction. This could be a plea or demand, the text of a document, or a reaction to some current event. Examples would be an appeal to an international body, an open letter to the Soviet government or the *Bulletin*'s readership, the results of a special study or survey, or a general information account. This latter form was quite common at the outset, almost deserving a category of its own. The group was not only interested in disseminating pertinent information to Soviet disabled, it also tried to elicit from its readers some sense of their concerns. Questionnaires on housing, transport, living standards, and employment, to name a few, would then be compiled into a statistical report. In this way, the editors hoped to attune their efforts to the concerns of their unseen constituents.

When the regime escalated its response, the *Bulletin* reported repressions and obstructions. A special section was devoted to actions directed against the editorial board. Indeed, the *Bulletin* provided a most detailed account of the various threats, searches, and harassments the authorities undertook. Occasionally, the case of another activist would be highlighted. That of Gennady Gus'-kov was depressingly typical. A Group I paraplegic, Gus'kov had helped set up an engineering cooperative in his Voronezh residential center. It later proved so successful that plans were drawn up to increase production, expand the work force, and bring in disabled from other areas. At the same time, in so doing the cooperative would have shifted from "occupational therapy" to "work," thus transferring control from the social security ministry to local Voronezh authorities. Loathe to accept even this minor loss, the ministry began a slander campaign against Gus'kov, eventually closing down the cooperative and having him transferred to a nursing home.[40] Despite appeals to the ministry and a petition with 600 signatures on Gus'kov's behalf, the decision was not reversed. But the point is that it was only through the *Bulletin* that such cases could be aired and monitored.

Within a few issues, the *Bulletin* also began carrying information on the fate of other Soviet human rights activists. The 1980 relocation of Andrei Sakharov and his wife Yelena Bonner (herself a Group II war disabled) to Gorkii was noted and condemned. Concern was increasingly expressed for prison camp inmates—many of whom were incurring disabilities as a result of their confinement. One particularly graphic account of a former inmate at a camp for the disabled reported that during the mid-1970s many had died, including a blind prisoner supposedly "shot trying to escape."[41] While still small in proportion to the other sections, it did reflect the broadening of the group's scope of concerns.

Toward the end of its existence, a growing amount of *Bulletin* space was taken up by letters and personal appeals from readers. Few at the outset, they ultimately constituted upward of half the space of individual issues. They came from all over the Soviet Union, perhaps testifying to the fact that after nearly five years the Action Group, its message, and its readership were expanding. Although it is impossible to know how much of a ground swell had been created, it may not have been coincidental that precisely now the authorities closed down the *Bulletin* once and for all.

VI

In retrospect, 1982 was a watershed in the group's history. Moscow's overall nonobservance of the International Year of the Disabled moved Fefelov to some of his harshest and most sarcastic commentary. Early that January, he sent an open letter to the Politburo and Supreme Soviet, contrasting their "special hospitals, sanatoria, dachas . . . luxuries, and privileges" to their "70 year hysteria about the most humane and just of societies. . . . In the future," he concluded, "I shall believe not in evil, violence, boorishness, or mockery, but in reason, justice, and morality—in other words, not in you."[42] The state replied in kind. After numerous searches, Fefelov was charged that summer with "resisting a representative of the authorities" and threatened with arrest.[43] With arrest and trial apparently looming, he chose to give in. That October, he, his wife, and their two young children packed their belongings and drove into reluctant emigration in West Germany.[44]

Fefelov's departure was a serious blow to the group. The driving force behind the *Bulletin* was gone. No new issues have appeared since 1982. In Moscow, Iurii Kiselev has been unable to shoulder the burden alone. Unlike the treatment handed out to Fefelov in tiny Iuriev-Pol'skii, the authorities in Moscow have been much less persistent in hounding him. Aside from the vandalism and revocation of his specially designed house in the Crimean city of Koktebel, he has endured only occasional searches and threats from organizations such as the Moscow War Veterans Committee. At other times, his license and vehicle registration have been suspended.[45]

As an activist with a long record of disabled rights agitation, Kiselev has peformed noteworthy functions. Residing in Moscow made him a natural liaison to the wider dissident community. In his capacity as a *Bulletin* editor he contributed many appeals to the state, the party, and foreign audiences. Among the latter were an appeal to Lord Killanin (chairman of the International Olympic Committee) to hold the 1980 Disabled Olympics in Moscow concurrent with the summer games[46] and an appeal to the International Red Cross and Amnesty International to intervene on behalf of prison camp inmates and disabled veterans of the Afghan conflict.[47] Lacking the *Bulletin* as their outlet, these statements generally made their way to the pages of *Samizdat*.

Although *Samizdat* continues to make occasional formal reference to the Action Group, it seems safe to say that since the mid-1980s the organization has essentially existed only on paper. From abroad, Fefelov and Zaitseva continue their efforts, with their names still appearing on some Moscow communiques. They have also sought to utilize the Western media to advance their cause.[48] Obviously, this is no substitute for direct involvement. Once again the tactic of forced emigration appears to have paid dividends for the Soviet authorities.

One can still see some signs of the Action Group, however. Beginning in the spring of 1985, direct ties were established between it and the Group to Establish Trust Between the USSR and the USA, a group formed in January 1982 to encourage a revival of détente and a resumption of the arms control process. From this time on, many Action Group documents included the signatures of Trust Group members, and by December 1985 Kiselev himself was being identified as a Trust Group adherent and signatory.[49] In time, Kiselev would come to be identified solely as a Trust Group member, merging his more particular interests within the broader context of its democratization and international tension-reduction goals, itself given new impetus by the resumption of super power summitry.

Not that Kiselev has totally abandoned disabled rights concerns. In November of 1985, for example, he staged a hunger strike to protest police beatings and mistreatment of the disabled.[50] Letters of support for individuals undergoing repression have continued.[51] In the aftermath of Chernobyl, he penned an extended critique of the regime's disregard for environmental issues, warned of the potential physical disabilities this could produce, and then complained that those displaced by the accident had received better treatment than other equally deserving Soviet citizens.[52] What the Trust Group offers, however, is a cadre of activists who can sustain and persevere in its activities.

VII

On the whole, then, prior to Gorbachev, the Action Group had registered mixed results. In terms of the four basic objectives enumerated in its May 1978 charter, one could argue that each has to some extent been realized. Information was collected and disseminated, numerous appeals to competent authorities were made, world public opinion was tapped, and formal contacts with other disabled rights organizations were established. From a purely practical standpoint, the group probably did all that it could under the circumstances. An identifiable organization was constituted, an agenda and objectives were formulated, a constituency was cultivated, and appropriate agencies were pressured for change. Although the *Bulletin*'s editors resided in different parts of the country and were limited in their physical mobility, they were still able to maintain for a time the semblance of communications and coordination. In the process, they came to be accorded legitimacy by their peers as well as by other representatives of the dissident community.

Yet despite all this, they were unable to achieve their policy objectives. Instead, they came to be perceived and treated as just another group of malcontents who refused to work through existing channels. Regime hostility thus led to Action Group counter-hostility. Its struggle to survive would come to rival the causes it championed. Defined in these terms, the regime had no difficulty rationalizing its suppression. And while the group's overall treatment might have been "milder" when compared to others, its story became tragically familiar.

Unorthodox behavior was only one of its downfalls. The content of its issues and the implications of its size undoubtedly played a part. Unlike other groups who pushed for more nebulous political rights, religious freedom, or nationalistic autonomy, the Action Group's agenda involved potentially staggering budgetary outlays. The sputtering Soviet economy was simply in no position to absorb such costs. Nor was the representation of the disabled in the economy even remotely sufficient to make the threat to withhold their services credible. More consumer than producer, they lacked the leverage to pry even half-measures from the authorities. The disabled, it would seem, make unlikely candidates for revolutionaries. And while it is easy to ascribe heroic attributes to the Fefelovs and the Kiselevs, one can easily conjure up the image of an invalid isolated in an apartment with a disconnected phone and an unserviced elevator, to say nothing of an open pit before his small town garage.

While much of this story is distressingly familiar and pessimistic, there is reason to hope that changes for the better may be forthcoming. The consolidation of the Gorbachev leadership has carried with it a palpable relaxation of Soviet society and the mass media. Topics, personalities, and historical events once considered tabu are now a frequent element of public discourse. The rhetoric and tentative initiatives of change from above are reflected in changing attitudes on the part of even the most "incorrigible" of dissidents. In many ways, Gorbachev has been co-opting and assimilating portions of their critique into his own words and policy platforms.

For now, all we can do is point to harbingers and nascent stirrings that carry significant implications for the Soviet disabled. Shortcomings in goods and services are openly discussed in the press, which also publishes letters about lack of facilities and resources and about general public indifference toward the disabled.[53] Even more significant have been recent decisions to establish (or perhaps we should say reestablish) societies for the disabled in both the Russian Republic and the city of Moscow. After all, the creation of their own society was the founding rationale and hallmark of the Action Group. Perhaps it is not too farfetched to envision a Iuri Kiselev in Moscow or a Valeri Fefelov in exile contemplating the day when they might resume their activities with an officially sanctioned imprimatur.

In closing, then, we might consider the remarks of N. T. Trubilin, vice-chairman of the Russian Republic's Council of Ministers. The decision to establish a society for the disabled is "Primarily because of disabled people's desire to play a more active role in public life, to have broader opportunities for socializing, and to hold the kinds of jobs they are capable of handling and at which they can be most productive. The latter is especially important, as it gives them a sense of independence and the knowledge that they are being useful to society."[54] How eerily reminiscent of Kiselev and Fefelov! Clearly, this is an important starting point. But much remains to be done. Residents of Western societies, after all, are almost daily brought into contact with the reality of the disabled, be they affirmative action programs, building access modifications, or preferential parking places. For the Soviet disabled, conversely, while the reality of these programs remains in the future, the prospects for taking some steps in a more positive direction are as great as they have ever been.

NOTES

1. For general surveys of Soviet dissent, see Peter Reddaway, *Uncensored Russia: The Human Rights Movement in the Soviet Union* (New York:

American Heritage Press, 1972); and "Dissent in the Soviet Union," *Problems of Communism* (Nov.–Dec. 1983): 1–15; George Saunders, ed., *Samizdat: Voices of the Soviet Opposition* (New York: Pathfinder Press, 1974); Rudolph Tokes, ed., *Dissent in the USSR* (Baltimore: Johns Hopkins University Press, 1975); Michael Meerson-Aksenov and Boris Shragin, eds., *The Political, Social, and Religious Thought of Russian "Samizdat": An Anthology* (Belmont, Mass.: Nordland, 1977); Marshall Shatz, *Soviet Dissent in Historical Perspective* (New York: Cambridge University Press, 1980); Mark Hopkins, *Russia's Underground Press: The Chronicle of Current Events* (New York: Praeger, 1983); and Ludmila Alekseeva, *Istoriia Inakomysliia v SSSR: Noveishii Period* (New York: Khronika, 1984), also available in an English translation as *Soviet Dissent: Contemporary Movements for National, Religious, and Human Rights* (Middletown, Conn.: Wesleyan University Press, 1985). Memoirs are too numerous to mention, while much of the primary source material comes from the *Chronicle of Current Events* (Amnesty International) and the *Arkhiv Samizdata* (Radio Liberty, Munich).

2. Steven Marc Glick, "Disability in the USSR—A Dissident View: A Case Study of the Action Group to Defend the Rights of the Disabled in the USSR," Master's thesis, London School of Economics, 1980. The author wishes to thank Mr. Glick for kindly providing a copy of his thesis.

3. In her over 400 pages of text, for instance, Alekseeva, *Istoriia Inakomysliia*, devotes a scant two pages to the group; but see Walter Parchomenko, "The Soviet Union's Hidden Minority," *America* 16 April 1983, pp. 296–98.

4. See S. P. deBoer, E. J. Driessen, and H. L. Verhaar, eds., *Bibliographical Dictionary of Dissidents in the Soviet Union, 1956–1975,* (The Hague: Martinus Nijhoff, 1982), p. 255; *Chronicle of Current Events* 52 (1979): 114–19.

5. See *Chronicle of Current Events* 51 (1978): 167; and "We Arrived in the West with Hope," *Samizdat Bulletin* (San Mateo, Calif.) 118 (1983).

6. *Arkhiv samizdata* (hereafter referred to as *AS*), 3224 (Moscow Helsinki Watch Committee Document 37). Further support was contained in a companion document of the same date (*AS* 3255) listing the disabled among those discriminated against by the political system.

7. *AS* 3482.

8. *AS* 3511.

9. *Chronicle of Current Events* 52 (1979): 118.

10. *AS* 3482.

11. *AS* 3506.

12. *AS* 3465.

13. *AS* 3496.

14. *AS* 4322.

15. Nekipelov's article appeared in the fifth issue of the Action Group's *Information Bulletin*, 24 April 1979. See also *Chronicle of Current Events* 52(1979): 119.

16. Valerii Fefelov and Olga Zaitseva-Fefelova, "A Letter from the USSR to Russians Residing in the West," *Samizdat Bulletin* 118 (1983).

17. *AS* 4614. Also referred to in the *Chronicle of Current Events* 64 (1982): 32–34.

18. *AS* 3766.

19. Kiselev, Zaitseva, Fefelov, and Khusainov, "Open Letter: To the Russian Departments of Radio Stations *Voice of America, BBC, Deutsche Welle,* and others," *Samizdat Bulletin* 105 (1982).

20. For a general review of these initial actions see *Chronicle of Current Events* 52(1979): 114–19; and 53(1979): 156–59.

21. *AS* 3466.

22. *Chronicle of Current Events* 52(1979). One of the group's early documents (#3: "On the Position of the Disabled in the USSR") quoted a deputy minister of social security as having said of Fefelov: "There was someone in Ivanovo who wanted to organize a society for the disabled. If you knew what they did to him, you wouldn't envy him." At the time, the statement was more exaggeration than fact.

23. *AS* 3517.

24. *Chronicle of Current Events* 54(1979): 136–37. In this issue one can also find photographs of the Fefelovs and the celebrated excavation in front of their garage.

25. Ibid. See also *AS* 3938 for an anonymous report on the campaign against him in Iuriev-Pol'skii.

26. *Chronicle of Current Events* 56(1980): 203–04.

27. Ibid. 57(1980): 26–29.

28. *AS* 4127 gives an account of the letter and the campaign.

29. *AS* 4128 and 4129 give Fefelov's account of these events and the text of his reply.

30. *Chronicle of Current Events* 57(1980): 26–29.

31. *AS* 3770.

32. *AS* 4341. In that same article he also declared that: "If we do not want our lives to become meaningless and empty, to become enslaved, we will come to the defense of such remarkable and thinking people as Anatolii Marchenko, Viktor Nekipelov, Tatiana Velikhanova, Feliks Serebrov, Tatiana Osipova and many, many others who are today languishing in the depths of the bottomless Gulag, which continues to devour more and more victims."

33. *Chronicle of Current Events* 64(1982): 33–34.

34. Representative surveys of social welfare programs by Soviet writers would include V. S. Andreev, *Sotsial'noe obespechenie v SSSR* (1971); Andreev, *Pravo sotsial'nogo obespecheniia v SSSR* (1974); and the collection *Naselenie i sotsial'noe obespechenie* (1984). For a sampling of Western studies see Bernice Madison, *Social Welfare in the Soviet Union* (Stanford, Cal: Stanford University Press, 1968), and Vic George and Nick Manning, *Socialism, Social Welfare, and the Soviet Union* (London: Routledge & Kegan Paul, 1980).

35. Respectively: Fefelov, "A Measure of the Humaneness of 'Developed Socialiam,' " *Samizdat Bulletin* 128(1983); and Parchomenko, "The Soviet Union's Hidden Minority." Each made their calculations using such disability categories as industrial accidents, birth defects, alcoholism, drugs, age-related infirmities, pollution, prison conditions, poor diets, World War II, Afghanistan, and even the industrialization/collectivization campaign of the 1930s. Such wide disparities are testimony to the importance of determining precisely who to include or exclude. Inclusion of the war disabled is dubious in that the Soviet government has long had benefits for this, as detailed in Bernice Madison's contribution to this volume.

36. This was revealed by N. T. Trubilin, vice-chairman of the republic's Council of Ministers, in *Izvestiia*, 14 February 1988.

37. *Information Bulletin* 11(1981) contained appeals to the United Nations and the recently convened Twenty-Sixth Communist Party Congress on the need for amnesty and the recognition of invalids' rights, as well as a lead editorial deploring the regime's silence. *Information Bulletin* 12(1981) noted the continuing silence and appealed to the World Council of Churches in Geneva for assistance.

38. Sergei Voronitsyn, "Soviet Observance of the International Year of the Disabled Person," *Radio Liberty Research Bulletin* 24/82, 3156 (20 Jan. 1982): 3.

39. Their respective publication dates are issue 1 (20 May 1978); 2 (22 June 1978); 3 (26 Aug. 1978); 4 (11 Nov. 1978); 5 (27 Jan. 1979); another issue 5 (24 Apr. 1979); 6 (12 July 1979); 8 (20 Feb. 1980); 9 (July 1980); 10 (10 Dec. 1980); 11 (30 Mar. 1981); 12 (30 July 1981); 13 (25 Dec. 1981); and 14 (20 June 1982). Several complete issues are reprinted in the *Arkhiv samizdata* series.

40. The Gus'kov case was prominently featured in *Information Bulletin* 1 (reprinted in *AS* 3511).

41. A. Zelyakov, "You are an Annoying Burden of our Society . . . ," *Samizdat Bulletin* 132 (1984).

42. *AS* 4614.

43. *Chronicle of Current Events* 64(1982): 33–34.

44. See their initial statement: "We Arrived in the West with Hope," *Samizdat Bulletin* 118(1983).

45. For accounts of the treatment of Kiselev, see *Chronicle of Current Events* issues 52; 60; 61; and 63. Also consult *AS* 3519; 3571; and 4448. As for the other member of the editorial board—Faizulla Khusainov—his remoteness from Moscow and travel difficulties ultimately severed his links to the group.

46. *AS* 3767. As it turned out, the Soviet government denied the request.

47. *AS* 4702. The final issue (14) of the *Information Bulletin* contained a feature article on disabled Afghan war veterans and their neglect by the Soviet authorities. Presumably, had the *Bulletin* continued, more such stories would have appeared.

48. Examples are "Disabled Prisoners," *Radio Liberty Research Bulletin* 124/84, 3270 (1984): "Medical Care in the USSR," *Samizdat Bulletin* 143(1985): and "The Fate of a Political Prisoner," *Samizdat Bulletin* 152(1985).

49. *AS* 5455; 5556; 5571; 5573; and 5577. Along with supporting the general goals of the Trust Group, Kiselev also signed several petitions in defense of Vladimir Brodskii, one of its arrested activists.

50. See *Samizdat Bulletin* 156(1986).

51. *AS* 5589 (an appeal to Gorbachev protesting the abuse and ridicule of Soviet disabled); *AS* 5697 (a defense of invalid Viktor Smirnov's support of the Trust Group); and *AS* 5755 (another appeal to Gorbachev, this time asserting that ongoing repression contradicts the "openness" campaign).

52. *AS* 5766.

53. See, for example, the letter to *Izvestiia*, 15 April 1988, from the mother of a deaf child in Gorky, who added that the nearest school for the deaf was over 1,300 miles away. The magazine *Ogonek* (Feb. 1988) likewise sympathetically chronicled the travails at Moscow State University of Iuri Borisov, a paraplegic victim of military parachute training.

54. *Izvestiia*, 14 February 1988.

Dissidence as Disability:
The Medicalization of Dissidence
in Soviet Russia

Mark G. Field

I

IN 1836 the Russian writer, P. Chaadaev, wrote several philosophical essays, in which he called Russia essentially a wasteland. It happened that Tsar Nicholas I read these papers. He pronounced them a "farrago," offensive, and "obviously" the work of a madman; whereupon Chaadaev was declared insane, confined to his home, and placed under the supervision of a physician.

From that famed incident one may not conclude that there is a well-established Russian tradition of using medicine, and notably psychiatry, to dispose of inconvenient citizens whose expressed views affront the majority and particularly the holders of power. A review of the record reveals very few cases of such abuse in tsarist times and, as noted in an earlier chapter of this book, even during the Lenin and Stalin years the use of psychiatry as a means of social or political control was simply not institutionalized, though in the early years after the Revolution there were a few such cases. Indeed, in the Stalin years there were instances when individuals were placed in mental hospitals as a protection from a worse fate at the hands of the regime.[1] But since the early 1960s, individuals who have gone beyond prescribed limits of behavior have, with some frequency, been diagnosed as suffering from some form of mental illness, placed in mental hospitals, and thereby silenced and isolated. The medicalization of dissidence is, in practice, surely rare relative to the vast overall dimension of Soviet medicine, or even of Soviet psychiatry. But it occurs.[2]

This sort of political incapacitation is, of course, very far from the physical disability that forms the subject of this book. Here a fake medical or psychiatric diagnosis is imposed on normal people.

Elsewhere, the volume deals with truly daunting medical conditions, which sometimes are, sometimes are not, given civic recognition. In some ways it seems improper to mix the two. Yet such is the complexity of the situation of the handicapped in the Soviet world that it is important to recognize a murky common ground between the really disabled and those who bear a medical label. The Soviet mind allows, as it were, a part of normal society to be seen as handicapped, crippled, or defective. Soviet attitudes, it may follow, are not so cut and dried about the exclusion of the handicapped from society as attitudes might be elsewhere. Hence the following chapter, which recalls the dimensions of the recent abuse of psychiatry and attempts some explanations of it.

II

At this writing (1988), the use of psychiatry in the Soviet Union to control and repress the public expression of dissidence seems to be about thirty years old. One of the first cases reported in the West was that of Valerii Tarsis, a writer who had, in the post-Stalin era, written a book, *The Bluebottle,* highly critical of Soviet society. Tarsis's book naturally could not be published in the Soviet Union, so he let it appear in the West. Unauthorized publication of Soviet works abroad is a transgression of Soviet law. Shortly after the publication of *The Bluebottle,* Tarsis found himself forcibly taken to a psychiatric hospital. Released later on, he wrote a thinly disguised autobiographical account of his experience in a book (also published in the West), *Ward 7,* a title inspired by Chekhov's *Ward 6,* in which he detailed his experiences as a "patient" at the Kashchenko Psychiatric Hospital near Moscow.[3]

The next important case, and one that caused an international furor, was that of Zhores Medvedev, a biologist, whose activities, like Tarsis's, were not to the liking of Soviet authorities. In particular, he was the author of a book on Lysenko that exposed that charlatan for what he was, a book that was almost published in the USSR but that finally appeared in the United States. Medvedev had also written critical essays on Soviet postal censorship, on the problems encountered by Soviet scientists when invited to give papers abroad, and other sensitive subjects. In 1970, he was invited to report to a psychiatric hospital, ostensibly to discuss his son's school problems. He found himself detained in a locked room. He managed to escape, but was forcibly picked up the next day with the help of the police and was hospitalized "for observation."

Medvedev's wife immediately notified Zhores's twin brother, Roy, a noted dissident historian, who set in motion a national and international campaign on behalf of his brother. After Zhores's release a few weeks later, the brothers wrote a book together, which they published in the West as *A Question of Madness*.[4] Their work laid to rest, once and for all, whatever doubts there might have been about the misuse of Soviet psychiatry for political or ideological control. They showed that such misuse had become institutionalized, in spite of Soviet protests to the contrary.

Let us at this juncture make a semantic distinction between dissent (or the dissenter) and dissidence (or the dissident). The former term comes from the Latin *sentire*, which means to feel, to experience. It is a subjective, an individual phenomenon, locked in the individual's consciousness and usually inaccessible to others. Certainly the comportment of individuals *may* reflect these inner feelings or thoughts, but they may remain hidden from all. The term dissidence, on the other hand, has a quite different origin and meaning. It is again derived from the Latin, but from the verb *sidere* which means to sit. In ecclesiastical disputes in the Middle Ages, those who did not agree with the majority view took a seat apart from the others, thereby publicly signifying their position in the same way as legislators sit on the left or right of the aisle in Congress. Closet dissenters need never show themselves as dissidents. It is our impression that Soviet authorities have not been particularly concerned with silent dissenters. They have been concerned primarily with public expression of dissent, that is, dissidence, fearing that dissident ideas may contaminate orthodox elements in society. The Soviet Union is thus a long way from the state that Orwell described in *1984,* in which the regime obsessively (and in the end successfully) engages in brainwashing to eliminate not only dissidents but also dissenters.

But this distinction does not make the practice under consideration any pleasanter. As Tarsis notes, in the mental hospital in which he was incarcerated there were neither doctors nor patients, only guardians in charge of inconvenient citizens. Not without irony, he remarked that the mental hospital ward was about the only place in the Soviet Union where people enjoyed absolute freedom of speech. The days were filled with endless discussions and debates about many subjects, including those not ordinarily discussed in public. The reason was simply that whatever was said by individuals diagnosed or certified as mentally ill, incompetent, or irresponsible did not matter, could not be taken seriously: what they said were rantings, the products of demented or deranged minds, without significance. And here lies, according to Soviet dissidents, the particular horror of being declared mentally ill: whatever one says or writes tends to be interpreted through the prism of the diagnosis. It is not judged on its manifest contents but as an expression of illness. In the same way, psychiatrists report that mentally ill patients claim they are not crazy—the claim itself being a symptom of their condition. The patient usually cannot win.[5]

For Soviet dissidents, as for the mentally ill, there are two pathways to the mental hospital. The first involves civil commitment. This is a procedure whereby any person can be forcibly hospitalized on suspicion of being mentally ill and of presenting a danger to himself or herself, to society, or to both. In recent years, the procedure has been simplified and streamlined. The initial commitment procedures must be approved or ordered by one psychiatrist, and if one cannot be found, by one physician. Every case must then be reviewed within twenty-four hours, at which time the individual must be examined by three psychiatrists, who must decide on the course to follow: continued hospitalization and observation; release and placement under the supervision of an outpatient psychiatric clinic; or simple release with no need for treatment. There are a very few formalities and legal safeguards for the individual. Physicians cannot be sued for false or wrong diagnoses, although a new set of regulations on psychiatric treatment that came into effect on 1 March 1988 states that "the internment in a psychiatric hospital [section] of a person known to be mentally healthy is a criminal offence."[6] Civil commitment is the preferred way to dispose of dissidents who have not committed criminal offenses but whose behavior is considered offensive or alarming. Zhores Medvedev and Valerii Tarsis were forcibly hospitalized, examined, and treated under this kind of commitment procedure.

The second path is criminal commitment. This is reserved for those who stand accused of a crime, including the crimes of libeling Soviet reality or engaging in anti-Soviet propaganda, as well as the crimes of murder, theft, rape, and so on. During the period of instruction (when the case and the evidence are developed), the prosecution (in this case the procurator) may suggest to the court that the defendant was mentally ill (insane) at the time the offense was committed, or that he or she is now mentally ill or incompetent, and thus should not be made to stand trial.[7] To do this, the prosecution suggests to the court that the defendant be examined by a panel of psychiatrists to determine mental competence, responsibility, or in legal terms, sanity. Should the panel find against the defendant, that he or she is indeed mentally ill, then the criminal charges are dropped by the prosecution and the individual is remanded for treatment and incarceration either in a special hospital for the criminally insane or in a regular psychiatric hospital. It should be noted that, in the case of dissidents charged with such crimes as libel or propaganda, it is invariably the prosecution and not the defendant or the defendant's attorney who request psychiatric examination. Indeed, it is the greatest fear, and thus the object of the greatest resentment on the part of dissidents, to be declared mentally incompetent, or irresponsible.

The significance in all this lies, of course, in the fact that the civil authorities and the KGB possess more than adequate administrative devices for curbing dissidence. For example, dissidents may be informally warned by the secret police to mend their ways. This may take the form of "friendly" chats, in which they are told that their actions are known to the police, that they are being watched, and that, unless they desist, unpleasant consequences are likely to follow. Such warnings may also include more physical measures, like beatings. Further, a dissident may be extruded, that is, gotten rid of, either through exile at home or by being sent abroad.

In addition to such informal procedures, dissident behavior may be formally defined as criminal, as seen earlier, through two well-known articles in the Penal Code of the RSFSR and corresponding articles in the other republics. They are articles 70 and 190, which punish as a crime either the defamation of Soviet reality through the spreading of statements that are patently false, or engaging in anti-Soviet propaganda aimed at undermining the Soviet Union. It should be emphasized that the definition of crime in the Soviet Union is broader than in the West. Thus according to a former Soviet psychiatrist: "From the viewpoint of Soviet law, a person who criticizes government institutions can be committing a crime. A person who has in his personal library a book considered undesirable by the authorities can be committing a crime. A person who expressed dissatisfaction with certain aspects of society can be committing a crime."[8]

Given the array of other means to curb dissidence at the Soviet state's disposal, why does it resort to medicalization? Why, in the late twentieth century, go back to the method Tsar Nicholas used against Chaadaev? All in all, this question remains large. The balance of this chapter is an attempt to suggest why and how, at this juncture of Soviet history, medicine and psychiatry became involved in the political process of curbing political and ideological dissidence.

III

Whatever the internal steps and machinations that led the Soviet authorities to use psychiatry to curb dissidence, the practice is in line with a more generalized phenomenon of contemporary society: the medicalization of deviance. Two social scientists, Peter Conrad and Joseph Schneider, call this a conversion of "badness into sickness." It epitomizes an increased humanization and compassion of present-day society and a more caring and less punitive social order.[9] Its origins can be traced to such physicians as Pinel in France and Tuke in Great Britain, who about two centuries ago asserted that individuals who behaved in a bizarre fashion, who heard voices and had visions, who acted in a violent or self-destructive way, might not be criminals or possessed by the devil or sinners in need of punishment, but sick persons whose brains had been affected. People who nowadays are routinely defined as mental or psychiatric patients were, in prior times, punished, flogged, caged, exhibited like animals for the amusement of the populace, or loaded on barges—ships of fools—to drift downriver and out of sight. Other behaviors that have been partly medicalized include compulsive gambling, obesity, alcoholism and drug addiction, hyperactivity among children, senility, and juvenile delinquency. A few years ago, homosexuality—which had in the past been considered as both a sin and a crime—became medicalized in the United States when the American Psychiatric Association declared it a type of mental illness. More recently, in the only case we know of demedicalization, homosexuality was redefined as a normal alternative sexual lifestyle, on petition by gay activists.

Historically, medicalization has thrust physicians into a new role. They often became, whether they realized it or not, agents of social control.[10] This was because they were considered uniquely qualified, as applied scientists, not only to diagnose and treat illness but also to separate the sick from the healthy, and sometimes from the guilty. The change in the doctor's role has been so great that one might ask whether the process of medicalization can be attributed to some kind of medical imperialism or colonization, in which doctors are only too eager to stake new territories to aggrandize their already considerable power. This may be a gross exaggeration. There is evidence that, in many instances, physicians have been asked by society to perform certain tasks, or that these tasks have been thrust on them by law (for example, the definition of disability in compensation cases). Finally, it should be emphasized that medicalization is but a modality, a technique. It can be used, like any other procedure, either to help or to harm. Undoubtedly, behind a great deal of medicalization lies the humanitarian impulse that is central to the medical tradition and that sees the individual as the victim of forces over which he or she has little or no control. And yet, like a drug, medicalization can cure or cripple or kill, depending on the dosage and the intent of the one who administers it.

Psychiatrists are, in this context, like any other doctors. They are seen as experts, whose function is to determine whether an individual suffers from a medical condition that accounts for his or her behavior and over which that individual has little or no volitional control. It is on the basis of that determination, then, that courts (the world over, and not only in the Soviet Union) decide whether the individual should be forcibly hospitalized—and in criminal cases, whether criminal charges should be dropped. The other, and more important, function of psychiatrists is the therapeutic one: they are expected to help the individual. When treatment is of no avail, then the psychiatrist, should the patient present a danger to him or herself or others, must create and supervise such custodial conditions as will protect both society and the individual.

There is, however, a specific feature of mental illness that distinguishes psychiatry from other medical specialties and that makes it an often controversial branch of medicine.[11] Behavior *is* the symptomatology the psychiatrist is called upon to diagnose and treat. Insofar as behavior is also judged normatively by the community, particularly in terms of conformity and deviance, then the distinction between a clinical and a social judgment becomes a complicating factor and tends to fudge the diagnostic procedure. To this we must add that every psychiatrist is a child of the same culture as the patient. It would indeed be very difficult, practically impossible, for such a clinician to treat patients whose language and culture were alien. An orthopedic surgeon would face no such difficulties; but the psychiatrist may be expected to have the same reactions as the rest of the population to eccentric, bizarre, nonconformist, or sick behavior. In fact, part of the training of the psychiatrist is precisely to learn to parse out social from clinical judgments. The person in the street does not face the same problem. It is common in most societies to make the summary judgment that someone is crazy, sick, out of his or her mind, if he or she does not agree with you!

Now to come to the point: the task of the Soviet psychiatrist in dissident cases is to medically certify that what is in essence social, political, or intellectual behavior is or is not the result of a medical condition—a mental illness. There is little doubt, in addition, that Soviet psychiatrists who deal with dissidents are usually pressured to find against the individual by the organs of state security. To comply with these organs may be seen by the Soviet doctor as simply performing the civic duty of an obedient citizen. In the Soviet context, given the nature of the system of controls; given the educational and propaganda systems; given the fact that physicians and psychiatrists are not an autonomous professional group but are state employees or functionaries; given that most psychiatrists are, just like the rest of the population, often turned off by dissidents if not hostile to them, then it may not be too difficult for the average psychiatrist to detect and diagnose a mental illness. And it is possible that some Soviet psychiatrists think that dissidence is a sign of mental unbalance.

IV

Let us now move to another set of factors that led to the outbreak of medicalization of dissidence in the Soviet Union. Let us recall that in the Stalin years (1928–1953), far more than today, the state used a host of other quite effective means to silence those it did not trust or suspected of subversion, means that are well known and that include the use of terror, arbitrary arrests, and the establishment of a vast Gulag Archipelago. There was little need then for psychiatric hospitals as instruments of repression and control. Those who succeeded Stalin decided, however, to dissociate their policies from those of the late dictator, particularly in the areas of arbitrariness and terror. What they wanted was to establish a system with a degree of internal stability. Indeed, they set in motion a process of limited normalization, if not liberalization. The consequences of this policy were hardly those anticipated: as a result of the elimination of terror and the dismantling of the apparatus of mass repression, there emerged in the Soviet Union a group of individuals which, though very small in size, began to point openly to the discrepancies between reality and the claims of the authorities. They began to state more and more forcefully that indeed the emperor had no clothes, that the so-called Soviet democracy was but a sham. The situation was the more ominous to the authorities because, coincidentally, a new generation of Soviet citizens had grown up who had not known (except by hearsay) the numbing Stalin years, a generation more critical and more outspoken than its elders and, by definition, more susceptible to dissident ideas. The question therefore arose: How should one curb the expression of dissident views without recourse to the discredited means of Stalin?

The medicalization of dissidence was an ideal response. Medicalization means that the dissident's behavior is defined (or redefined, as the case might be) into a medical condition, an illness, for which the individual is not willfully accountable. And therefore the individual, instead of being punished, is transformed into a patient and placed under the jurisdiction of physicians and the medico-psychiatric establishment. This politicizes psychiatry, but it depoliticizes (or trivializes) dissidence by making it the result of madness. Whatever the dissident says or writes is depicted as the result not of a rational mind making a political or intellectual judgment but of a manifestation of a disturbed brain, itself the consequence of an underlying physical condition. As we shall see, Soviet psychiatry sees mental illness as the result of a physiological disturbance. Dissidence becomes naturalized. In addition, medicalization has the advantage of avoiding a court trial, often used by articulate dissidents (as was also the case under tsarism) to make public statements of their beliefs, often embarrassing to the authorities.

In defense of such an explanation one may of course cite numerous statements by high-level authorities. Khrushchev is reported, for example, to have said that one would have to be a lunatic to want to leave the Soviet Union! But attitudes were not the whole of it. The rationale behind medicalization, according to the Medvedevs, was not just that the "successors to Stalin affirmed the principle of strict legality, but soon were up against many difficulties caused by the relatively democratic Constitution and the nondemocratic nature of the government. It was frequently necessary to punish people who, in fact, had not gone beyond what was allowed by the law." They add: "And then someone [presumably it was Dr. Morozov of the Serbskii Institute] had the simple idea that the growing number of political prisoners made a very bad impression, whereas the increase in the number of patients in the hospitals would be a very good indication of social progress. From that time on, psychiatric hospitals began to grow."[12] Dissident medicalization was made easy, because Soviet psychiatric theory then was, and today is, dominated by the so-called Moscow or Snezhnevskii school.[13] As suggested earlier in this book, that school detects pathology in behavior that, in the West, would be dismissed as inconsequential or perhaps merely neurotic. Its underlying belief is that mental illness, particularly psychosis, is of primarily genetic origins; that it tends to be inherited; that it tends to be incurable, and thus is of lifelong duration; that it may manifest itself in a variety of ways; and that it may include long periods of remission, during which the individual acts in an absolutely normal way.[14] Furthermore, the view is that there can be mental illness in the absence of overt symptomatology and that only well-trained specialists are able to detect the presence of that illness. And thus the claims of those who daily interact with the individual (relatives, co-workers)—that there is no detectable pathology—tend to be dismissed by psychiatrists as laymen expressing uninformed judgments. As two Soviet psychiatrists put it:

> Certain patients' outwardly normal behavior is not always an absolute index of their mental health: since it may be combined with delirious ideas of persecution and grandeur, messianism or delusions that they are great reformers or inventors . . . and exert a certain influence on mentally healthy individuals who, not being specialists, cannot make a correct assessment of the . . . person's condition. . . . These patients are suffering primarily from exaggerated or delirious ideas that manifest themselves within the framework of a psychopathic-like paranoia or hallucinatory-paranoic syndrome. It is these patients, once outside the Soviet Union, who are widely used by certain circles in Western countries. . . . The fact that these same patients have been or are being treated in mental hospitals while in the West is hushed up.[15]

The Snezhnevskii school is particularly outspoken about so-called borderline schizophrenia: it claims that this condition is schizophrenic, though it included the ability, not usually found in schizophrenics, to accurately assess reality. Snezhnevskii and his colleagues thus find it possible to diagnose schizophrenia in a patient without having to show that the patient is out of touch with reality.[16]

It is not our impression that Professor Snezhnevskii developed his theories specifically to assist the state in suppressing dissidents through psychiatry. Nor did he come to prominence during the 1950s for such service. These ideas of his were first enunciated some years before psychiatry became involved in a systematic way to control and isolate dissidents.[17] But this approach to psychiatry proved a boon when it came to using psychiatric practice to cover a wide range of actions that in other countries would be considered part of normal political discourse.

V

A few years ago, a group of American psychiatrists gave an exhaustive examination to former Soviet General Peter Grigorenko, who had, on more than one occasion, been diagnosed in the Soviet Union as mentally ill, and who had spent a great many years incarcerated in mental hospitals. The Americans reported that they could not find any trace of mental illness. As one of them wrote in concluding an article on the case: "Where they [Soviet psychiatrists] claimed obsession, we found perseverance; where they cited delusions, we found rationality; where they identified psychotic recklessness, we found committed devotion; and where they diagnosed pathology, we found health."[18] This does not necessarily rule out, by any means, that some of those dissidents who have been declared mentally ill might also be diagnosed as such outside of the Soviet Union. But in most instances, the harshness of the measures taken against the dissidents judged to be mentally ill, the forcible incarceration, and the use of medications in a punitive rather than therapeutic manner do not seem in the least bit justified or defensible as treatment.

At the same time, it is impossible to estimate the scope of psychiatric repression, that is, the number of dissidents who have been handled in the psychiatric mode. There are some indications that the numbers are relatively small[19] but that the threat of mental hospitalization and of being declared mentally incompetent are powerful blackmailing instruments. In addition, any individual who has had any brush with the psychiatric system may be put on the psychiatric register, which will follow him or her for the rest of life and will involve such disabilities as being denied permission to drive or to hunt or to travel abroad. That would mean more than 5 million people in the country as a whole.[20] Recent discussions in the press indicate that, in 1985, 1,923 of every 100,000 Soviet citizens were registered as having psychiatric disorders. Recent discussions suggest that a large proportion of such persons ought to be removed from the register, probably 30 percent, or 1.5 to 2 million people.[21]

Thus, in addition to the elements mentioned earlier, Soviet psychiatrists may make social judgments instead of clinical ones and may make (or be forced to make) such clinical judgments on people who are mentally healthy. We must also entertain the possibility (as in the Grigorenko case) that aspects of Soviet psychiatric theory and practices may lend themselves to the labeling of illness where, faced with precisely the same case, Western psychiatrists would find none. Or at least none that would lead to the forcible hospitalization and (often punitive) drug treatment reported in Soviet psychiatric hospitals. And it is also possible that there may be honest differences of opinions. We are all aware of the common observation that several psychiatrists examining the same patient may come up with several different diagnoses and recommendations. We know of the different schools of psychiatry that co-exist in most countries. It is thus possible, and perhaps plausible, that differences of opinion may arise between Soviet and non–Soviet psychiatrists, and that different interpretations (tied to cultural peculiarities) may be entertained.

Many Western psychiatrists, not to speak of the veterans of the dissident movement, tend to dismiss this possibility. An example is an extraordinary document written by Vladimir Bukovsky, a well-known dissident who had been hospitalized several times in mental hospitals for his activities, and by Semyon Gluzman, a psychiatrist who wrote a counterexpertise on the Grigorenko case, holding that the diagnosis of mental illness was completely unjustified.[22] Their *Manual for Dissidents Undergoing Psychiatric Examination* contains a veritable typology of Soviet psychiatrists, and it instructs dissidents on how to deal with each type. As the typology proceeds, dishonesty manifests itself more and more.

1. Novice psychiatrists, they say, are young and capable of finding pathology where there is none. From the dissidents' viewpoint, they are not particularly dangerous, because, usually, they are not asked to participate in forensic examinations.

2. Academicians are psychiatrists who have kept their passion for the profession and who do not like to participate in the examination of dissidents, arguing that they are physicians, not investigators. The advice to the dissident is to help the academicians by using the correct technique (suggested in the *Manual* for the presentation of the self).

3. Dissertation writers are psychatrists who, unconsciously per-haps, may extend the borders of the illness they describe. Advice: by your behavior, convince them that you are not good material for a thesis.

4. The Voltairians are clever and experienced psychiatrists—intelligent, well read, but somewhat cowardly. Under pressure, they may declare a dissident mentally competent, but they will do so cleverly and convincingly, in order to allay any suspicion of sympathy, so that there cannot be accusation of complicity.

5. The Philistines are psychiatrists of average intelligence with a good sense of adaptation to reality. In a sense, their mentality is closest to that of the *rentier* (described later on). They may sin-cerely see dissidents as abnormal, particularly if they left a good job, gave up an apartment, and became outcasts for their beliefs. The Philistines' feet are solidly anchored in reality; they are suspi-cious, for example, of nonrepresentative or modern art, preferring to use socialist realism as their artistic canon. They are the ones who will ask dissidents whether they really believe that horses fly. From the dissident's viewpoint, these are dangerous psychiatrists, because they can always detect pathology, even without symp-toms. As people with supple backbones, they are the ones who submit to, and quote authority (political and scientific), and who always document their findings in terms of a school of psychiatry or well-known names to justify their action.

6. The hangmen, or professional torturers are the psychiatrists who routinely exculpate mentally healthy dissidents (or other per-sons, for that matter) on the basis of a nonexistent mental condi-tion.[23] Psychiatrists at the Serbskii Institute, who certified many dissidents as mentally ill when they had been found healthy by other Soviet psychiatrists (General Grigorenko, for example), fall into that category. The manual's advice to the dissident: "do not allow him to find a single symptom. Under these circumstances, he might decide from the viewpoint of professional pride not to dirty his hands with an open forgery." From the dissidents' van-tage point, these last two categories of psychiatrists are the most dangerous. It is they, indeed, who have put on the map the con-cept, now widely accepted in the Soviet Union, that dissidence is per se a possible symptom of mental illness. They have become moral entrepreneurs. They have undertaken to define dissidence as a sickness and have made careers out of it. This definition has become their stock in trade in the same way that, during the McCarthy era in the United States, specialists in communism took

upon themselves to define and identify those who were Communists, even those who did not openly act like Communists. And furthermore, these psychiatrists have benefitted from that function and from being of some utility to the state: honors, visibility, perquisites, increased credits, hospital beds, and so on. They are the ones who, of course, speak for Soviet psychiatry at home and abroad.

Bukovsky and Gluzman, in sum, make no apologies for the recent behavior of Soviet psychiatry. They perceive dishonesty in the medicalization of dissidence. Yet, curiously, they start their whole typological discussion with reference to what they call the *rentier* mentality. *Rentier* is a French term that denotes an individual who lives on a pension (or an income) received either from a patron or some bureaucratic authority (like the state). The *rentier* mentality, according to them, is the normal mentality in the Soviet Union. "A *rentier*," they write, "is a person of mediocre intellect and bourgeois tastes, civilized rather than cultured, who does not want to take risks—he is the support of any authority; the light that guides him is his instinct for personal preservation. His life is monotonous but quiet. He regards his life style as the only one that is correct in an existence fraught with danger." The *rentier,* they say, is unlikely to go to Red Square and wave a banner asking for Soviet troops to leave Czechoslovakia, Hungary, or Afghanistan. Bukovsky and Gluzman advise dissidents to present themselves as *rentiers* to psychiatrists who examine them. They say that if dissidents describe themselves as people who have always had normal lives, have always conformed, have gone through the stages of growth, education, job, and family in a normal manner, then the dissidents stand some chance of being declared competent and healthy, and their nonconformist behavior will be interpreted as a random aberration, not symptomatic of a deep-lying mental disturbance.

The need for a manual, Bukovsky and Gluzman suggest, is that the concept of mental health and illness is vague, elastic, capricious, and manipulable. They point to the following situation. When dissidents are brought to court for a trial, it is possible to deal with the charges through their knowledge of the Constitution (fundamental law) and the Penal Code, where the articles are spelled out in black and white. Thus, dissidents may often be able to defend themselves in court, indeed often may run circles around the judges and assessors, because most of their actions are not crimes in the strict definition of the law. But where, the authors ask, are the equivalent of the legal articles in psychiatry? Where are the objective criteria that make it possible to determine whether an individual is mentally sick or healthy, the criteria that will decide whether what he did was simply the expression of individual judgment, of personal opinion, of simple eccentricity? What do Soviet psychiatrists use to differentiate the healthy from the sick?

The ultimate test for Soviet mental health, for normality, Bukovsky and Gluzman assert, is conformity—the *rentier* mentality. In this, their definition joins that of Ambrose Bierce, who in his *Devil's Dictionary* defined the adjective mad as "affected by a high degree of intellectual independence; not conforming to standards of thought, speech and action derived by the conformants from study of themselves; at odds with the majority; in short, unusual." Bukovsky and Gluzman also claim that there is a universal feeling in the Soviet Union that the real possibilities for change and reform (unless implemented by the state itself at its own initiative, as Gorbachev is now trying) are practically nil. It follows that, once a dissident has gone public, his or her personal situation is likely to drastically deteriorate; not only will such a step lead to ostracism by most of his or her erstwhile friends and colleagues, but there is danger of losing one's job or apartment, the last, one of the greatest possessions. The psychiatric diagnosis may follow the dissident forever and may limit as seen earlier choice of a job, ability to drive a car, or to travel abroad. Thus from the viewpoint of the average reasonable person, and also evidently from that of the average psychiatrist, public dissidence does not make sense. In a way, it is a kind of suicidal behavior, which, again from a psychiatrist's viewpoint, may be defined as sick, pathological, schizophrenic, and so on; or as some would put it, as poor adaptation to reality, which it certainly is.

There is a line in one of the fables by LaFontaine ("The Fox and the Lamb") that goes: "The reason of the stronger is always the better." This puts the Bukovsky-Gluzman message another way. It means that the reasoning, the definition of reality, the determination of the truth by the stronger person constitutes the social definition, the reality, the orthodoxy that will have official currency and general support. Those who fail to accept that orthodoxy, who have their own different (i.e., deviant) version of reality, will tend to be labeled as subversive, misguided, deluded, treasonous, criminal, or mentally ill; as suffering from schizoheterodoxy, from reformist mania, from obsessive truthseeking, from delusional thoughts, or from an incorrect or exaggerated view of their own importance. George Orwell referred to the same phenomenon in his novel *1984* by saying that the truth is not some objective, universally defined and accepted decision, but what the party defines as true. Truth here becomes not a universal, positivistic statement but a relative one, tied to circumstances, expediency, and the conjunction of political and ideological orthodoxy. The refusal on the dissidents' part to accept the official definition of reality is, per se, madness.

To this, one may add one further, and truly terrifying, aspect of what happens as a result of the medicalization of dissidence. Conditions in Soviet mental hospitals (as in most public psychiatric hospitals the world over) are hardly likely to be a rest cure, but they are particularly difficult for individuals whose only illness is a disagreement with the state. Tarsis, as we mentioned earlier, reported that in the hospital where he was confined there was freedom of speech and endless intellectual discussion and debate. But this seems to be more the exception than the rule. In the Special Psychiatric Hospitals (for the criminally insane), the regimen is penitentiary and only secondarily medical. The institution is under the KGB rather than the Ministry of Health, and medical personnel are usually uniformed members of the security organs.

It has recently been announced that the Special Psychiatric Hospitals would be transferred to the jurisdiction of the Health Ministry, though it is difficult at this writing to determine whether the transfer has taken place and what real difference it will make.[24] Dissidents are placed in the same wards as those who are genuinely sick, those who have committed murders, rape, arson, and those who hallucinate and scream for no apparent reason. In such hospitals, orderlies tend to be criminals (or exprisoners who are purging their sentences, and who tend to abuse the inmates and extort bribes for every service (such as permission to go to the toilet). In the same vein, medications tend to be given in punitive and harmful doses, and protest against their administration is likely to lead to even greater amounts. Injections of certain substances (sulfazin, for example) make it impossible for the individual to relax and are simply chemical tortures.[25] Complaining may lead to even harsher regimens. Some dissidents have suggested that a mentally healthy person, subject to that kind of treatment for any length of time, is likely to become truly mad.

VI

The medicalization of dissidence through the use of psychiatry in the Soviet Union represents, in my view, the peculiar national manifestation, at a certain juncture in the history and development of Soviet society, of the more generalized phenomenon that has to do with the increased intrusion and importance of medicine in the modern world. It is thus a special case of the misuse or the abuse of an approach that traditionally has been utilized to protect the individual, rather than the state or society. Medicalization may be pictured in the most humane and traditional medical terms. And it is in these terms that Soviet psychiatrists officially, and some sincerely, defend their actions: they claim that the dissidents they have diagnosed as sick or mentally incompetent are *really* sick, should be treated like patients, and should not be punished for their deeds because they do not know what they are doing or are incapable of measuring the consequences of their deeds.

The weight of the evidence in the last quarter century or so does not lend much credence to those claims. Rather, it illustrates that medicalization is like any other modality of treatment: it depends on who wields it, with what motives, how it is applied, and with what purposes. The legitimacy of the medical profession, however, lies in a specific commitment and devotion to the welfare of the individual. This commitment may be diluted, and indeed lost, when physicians cast their lot with the larger society, with the state or the party, and use their skills and knowledge to defend the state's interests, not those of the individual. As Szasz puts it: "When treatment is imposed on a person, inevitably he sees it as serving not his own best interests, but the interests of those who brought him to the psychiatrist (and who often pay him)."[26] In many instances, physicians in both East and West walk a delicate line between those two interests.

In the Soviet case, we are left with a large question mark: are psychiatrists aware of the fact that they may be performing a charade, a game imposed upon them by a powerful polity whose suggestions they are unable to resist? Or are they convinced that they are truly within the tradition of medicine and of benevolence toward the patient, that they are shielding the dissidents from a worse fate, and that these dissidents do not really know or understand the gravity of their acts? Obviously, both views must exist among Soviet psychiatrists. But the situation is extremely complex, and no easy solution or explanation can be accepted.

The existence of these alternatives (psychiatric abuse as a charade imposed upon the physician; or psychiatric abuse denied) has important implications for the future. If the first one prevails then the charade can come to an end overnight: for example, a decision could be made by the Kremlin that dissidents henceforth will not be placed into mental institutions for political reasons. Thus, if it is a game, then the rules can be easily changed. The other alternative is more ominous: if physicians are sincerely and professionally convinced they are accomplishing a clinical (and not a political) task, then the practice may be much more difficult to eliminate.

There is evidence that the top leadership of the Soviet psychiatric establishment is very sensitive to the accusations coming from their foreign colleagues that psychiatry is exploited in the Soviet Union for political repression. They, of course, emphatically and indignantly deny this charge. As members of the World Psychiatric Association, they attended two congresses of the association, one in Mexico in 1971, the second in Honolulu in 1977. In 1971 Soviet psychiatric abuse was still relatively new, poorly documented, and not well known in the West. The Soviet delegation easily brushed aside questions on the subject, dismissing the allegations as part of the cold war and as fabrications of anti-Soviet circles.

In Honolulu the situation was quite different; the perversion of psychiatry by then had been well documented, and the congress passed a resolution that specifically condemned the Soviet Union and requested that it stop such practices. A decision would then be made at the next congress to be held in Vienna in 1983 on whether to suspend or expel the Soviets from the world body. There was every indication, toward the end of 1982, that Soviet psychiatrists would attend the Vienna congress and would use it as a platform to denounce attacks on the Soviet Union and to affirm that psychiatry was not used to repress and silence dissidents. Indeed, they had even paid thousands of dollars in back dues, a sure sign of their intent to remain members in good standing.[27] Then we can only surmise that something happened, for in January 1983 the All Union Scientific Society of Neurology and Psychiatry, the constituent Soviet member of the World Psychiatry Association, informed the association of its withdrawal.[28] Subsequently, the psychiatric associations of Czechoslovakia, Bulgaria, and Cuba followed suit.[29]

The arguments the Soviet body used both in its letter of resignation and in an article informing the medical community, published in March 1983, were that "certain circles" in the West, particularly in the United States and Great Britain, engaged in a deliberate campaign of slander against the Soviet, alleging abuses of psychiatry. Such slander, they claimed, were inspired by governmental

and other forces interested in heating up antagonism toward the
Soviet Union and its allies. The WPA, claimed Moscow, instead of
uniting psychiatrists the world over in a common scientific effort
to alleviate the sufferings of mental patients, "has embarked upon a
path . . . of disuniting them; it has become an obedient instrument
in the hands of forces that are using psychiatry in their own political interests, . . . aimed at fanning conflicts and hostility among
psychiatrists of various countries"[30] In other words, the Soviet
organization turned the argument around, accusing Western psychiatrists of using their discipline for political purposes.

It is plausible to assume that the sudden decision to withdraw
from the World Psychiatric Association came from the Kremlin,
not the psychiatric society. One motivation was to avoid the possible humiliation of an expulsion or a suspension from the WPA. It
is also possible that this was a signal by the Soviet political leadership that it was contemplating a review of the whole political use of
psychiatry because of the embarrassment it caused the Soviet
Union. (On an earlier occasion, the authorities repudiated Lysenko,
who had practically destroyed the science of genetics in the Soviet
Union, by shunting him and his disciples aside.) As David Joravsky
has pointed out earlier in this volume, the major figure in contemporary Soviet psychiatry, Professor Snezhnevskii, occupied until his
death in 1987 a position analogous to that of Lysenko at the height of
his hegemony in Soviet genetics. Maybe Snezhnevskii's fall was
considered imminent.

Unfortunately, Snezhnevskii's viewpoints have been taught to
new generations of psychiatrists. He elbowed aside the so-called
Leningrad School, whose traditions were closer to the West. He
saw his disciples and students move into positions of power and
control. Thus, unless there is a dramatic turnaround, it is most
likely that Snezhnevskii will be succeeded by his students and
collaborators, men like Vartanian, Morozov, Nadzharov, and
Babaian, all of whom are already occupying positions of influence.[31] As long as Snezhnevskii's school remains the dominant and
hardly challenged one, one may expect the use (and abuse) of
psychiatry to continue and to be defended as legitimate.

It should be noted that, with the advent of *glasnost'*, increased
attention has been paid in the Soviet Union to corrupt practices
and the abuse of psychiatry, and particularly to the extreme ease
with which (at least until now) it was possible to forcibly hospital-
ize an individual in a psychiatric hospital. It is indeed easier, as
Sergei Grigoryants wrote early in 1988, to put people in a hospital

than in a prison.[32] From various recent exposés in the Soviet press, a picture emerges of how easily inconvenient citizens—those who complain, who seek truth or justice, who have grievances against their bosses, who are too conscientious and criticize their lazier co-workers, who blow the whistle against dishonest officials on the take, or whose possessions are coveted by others (a room or an apartment, for example)—can be removed to psychiatric hospitals in violation of the law and regulations. In one reported case, a party official was declared mentally incompetent and sent to a mental hospital after a falling-out with his superiors. Some psychiatrists, who unjustifiably have signed certifications of mental illness, have been reprimanded or removed from their positions.[33] In several cases, the doctors involved (Babaian included) are the same ones who engage in repressing dissidents.[34] No instance, as far as we know, has been reported in the Soviet press of the use of psychiatry against dissidents, and the official Soviet line is that such abuses have never taken place.[35] And yet the increasingly available evidence of the ease with which psychiatry can be manipulated suggests that it would present no obstacle whatever to repress political or ideological dissidents.

And now to return to the theme of this volume. What do these conclusions about the medicalization of dissidence imply for the handicapped in the Soviet Union? On a certain level, the answer may paradoxically be that they convey hope. The principle of the medicalization of deviance, the idea that people who are behaving in a bizarre fashion are not bad, not sinners, not criminals, but sick—and thus deserve the humanitarian umbrella of medicine—is a sign of progress and humanitarianism, in line with parallel developments in other countries. The pity is that precisely that redefinition of deviance has been applied in a punitive if not destructive way to individuals who are not sick. It destroys individuals whose only deviance is a political or an ideological one, and not a clinical one. And thus the humanitarianism of medicine has been distorted to accomplish precisely the opposite of what the physician is mandated to do.

It is possible that in the near future, the Gorbachev regime will really clamp down on the abuse of psychiatry, that psychiatrists will concern themselves exclusively with those who are sick, and that Soviet psychiatry will rejoin the international comity and become once more a member in good standing of the World Psychiatric Association.[36] This would bring to an end a bizarre thirty-year episode in the abusive medicalization of dissidence in the Soviet Union.

NOTES

1. This was suggested by the poet Naum Korzhavin, who did spend some time in a psychiatric hospital in 1948. Personal unpublished letter to Peter Reddaway, 28 Sept. 1976.

2. See, for example, Sidney Bloch and Peter Reddaway, *Psychiatric Terror* (New York: Basic Books, 1977), and their *Soviet Psychiatric Abuse: The Shadow over World Psychiatry* (London: Victor Gollancz, 1984).

3. Valerii Tarsis, *Ward 7: An Autobiographical Novel* (New York: Dutton, 1965).

4. Zhores A. Medvedev and Roy A. Medvedev, *A Question of Madness* (New York: Knopf, 1971).

5. D. L. Rosenhan, "On Being Sane in Insane Places," *Science* 179 (1973): 250–58.

6. "New Soviet Regulations on Psychiatric Treatment," International Association on the Political Use of Psychiatry, *Information Bulletin* 18 (1988): 30–34.

7. See Bloch and Reddaway, *Soviet Psychiatric Abuse*.

8. Edgar Goldstein, "Compulsory Treatment in Soviet Psychiatry," *Psychiatric Opinion* 468 (1975): 25.

9. Peter Conrad and Joseph W. Schneider, *Deviance and Medicalization: From Badness to Sickness* (St. Louis: Mosby, 1980).

10. Irving Kenneth Zola, "Medicine as an Instrument of Social Control," *Sociological Review* 20 (1972): 487–504.

11. Thomas Szasz has argued that psychiatry is not really a medical specialty. See his *Law and Psychiatry: An Inquiry into the Social Uses of Mental Health Practices* (New York: Macmillan, 1963); his *Myth of Mental Illness: Foundations of a Theory of Personal Conduct* (New York: Paul B. Hoeber, 1961); and his *Ideology and Insanity: Essays on the Psychiatric Dehumanization of Man* (Garden City: Anchor Books, 1970).

12. Medvedev and Medvedev, *A Question of Madness*, p. 199.

13. Walter Reich, "The World of Soviet Psychiatry," in Eric Stover and Elena O. Nightingale, *The Breaking of Bodies and Minds* (New York: Freeman, 1985), pp. 206–22.

14. Walter Reich, "The Schizophrenia Spectrum: A Genetic Concept," *Journal of Nervous and Mental Diseases* 162 (1976): 3–12; and "The Spectrum Concept of Schizophrenia," *Archives of General Psychiatry* 32 (1975): 489–98; and "Soviet Psychiatry on Trial," *Commentary* 65 (1978): 40–48.

15. G. Morozov and G. Likhachev, "We Condemn This Unseemly Activity," *Meditsinskaia Gazeta*, 25 Mar. 1983. For an English translation, see *Current Digest of the Soviet Press*, 25 Apr. 1983.

16. Statement by Walter Reich in *Abuse of Psychiatry in the Soviet Union*, Hearing before the Subcommittee on Human Rights and International Organizations, Committee on Foreign Affairs, 98 Cong., 1 sess (Washington, D.C.: Government Printing Office, 1984), pp. 31–35.

17. A. V. Snezhnevskii, "The Symptomatology, Clinical Forms, and Nosology of Schizophrenia," in J. G. Howells, ed., *Modern Perspectives in World Psychiatry* (New York: Brunner/Mazel, 1977), pp. 425–47.

18. Walter Reich, "Grigorenko Gets a Second Opinion," *New York Times Magazine,* 13 May 1979.

19. Bloch and Reddaway, *Soviet Psychiatric Abuse.*

20. Felicity Barringer, "Despite Gorbachev Changes, Punitive Psychiatry Lingers," *New York Times,* 21 Oct. 1987.

21. International Association on the Political Use of Psychiatry, "Numbers on Psychiatric Register in USSR To Be Reduced," *Information Bulletin* 18 (1988): 34–36.

22. Vladimir Bukovsky and Semyon Gluzman, "A Manual on Psychiatry for Dissidents," *Survey* (1975): 176–98.

23. Exculpation is what many dissidents resent most: to be excused for their actions on the basis of a nonexisting, fictitious illness.

24. International Association on the Political Use of Psychiatry, "The New Soviet Regulation on Psychiatry—Or, Anatoly Koryagin's View," *Information Bulletin* 18 (1988): 3.

25. See the ample documentation provided by Amnesty International, such as *Political Abuse of Psychiatry in the USSR* (New York: Amnesty International, 1983), as well as periodic *Information Bulletins* of the International Association on the Political Use of Psychiatry.

26. Szasz, *Ideology and Insanity,* p. 81.

27. Wayne Biddle and Margot Slade, "Soviet Symptoms of Withdrawal," *New York Times,* 13 Feb. 1983.

28. Letter to the president of the World Psychiatric Association in *Abuse of Psychiatry in the Soviet Union,* pp. 25–30.

29. Statement by Harold Visotsky, in ibid., p. 17.

30. Morozov and Likhachev, "We Condemn." Basically the same arguments had been presented by the Soviets ten years earlier in "An Open Letter from the Presidium of the All-Union Scientific Society of Neurologists and Psychiatrists," *Literaturnaia Gazeta,* 3 Oct. 1973. For an English version, see *Joint Publications Research Service,* No. 60447, USSR Series, No. 452 (Washington, D.C.: Department of Commerce, 1973).

31. Babaian was removed recently for corrupt practices. "Revelations of Corruption among Soviet Psychiatrists," *Radio Liberty Research,* RL 61/87, 12 Feb. 1987.

32. Sergei Grigoryants, "Soviet Psychiatric Prisoners," *New York Times,* 23 Feb. 1988.

33. E. Maksimova and I. Martkovich, "Defenseless," *Izvestiia,* 11 July 1987, in *Current Digest of the Soviet Press* 39 (1987): 1–4; "Soviet Journals Begin to Publish Accounts of Abuse by Psychiatrists," *Soviet East European Report* 4 (1987); "Case Histories in Soviet Psychiatry: When Justice Is Just Another Form of Insanity," *New York Times,* 24 Jan. 1988.

34. Julia Wishnevsky, "Izvestia Exposes Psychiatric Abuse," *Radio Liberty Research,* RL 277/87, 16 July 1987.

35. A. Novikov, "Let's Examine It: A Sore Point—Or, Who Needs Psychiatric Terror in the USSR," *Komsomolskaya Pravda,* 15 July 1987, in *Current Digest of the Soviet Press* 39 (1987): 4.

36. For a thorough review of such possibilities, written in mid 1988, see Peter Reddaway, "Soviet Psychiatry: An End to Political Abuse?" *Survey* (London) 30, no. 3 (Autumn 1988).

Attitudinal Change in Eastern Europe: The Case of György Konrád

William O. McCagg

I

PUBLIC ATTITUDES are among the most difficult things in the world to measure, because the public is every man, yet all people are different. How can one generalize about public attitudes even toward objects less likely to arouse mixed feelings than handicapped fellow human beings? There is no infallible way.

Nonetheless, conventional modes of approaching such attitudes exist. One of them is certainly to take samplings of literary opinion. Reading literature is in some part a sampling of what the greater public thinks, and in Russia and Eastern Europe this is particularly the case, because very often in the past two centuries writers have been the recognized spokesmen of the peoples there. Hence this chapter, which studies the work of a prominent contemporary Hungarian writer, György Konrád.

It goes with mere mention that literature is not only a mirror of society, but also a weapon designed to influence what people think. Because of this mirror-weapon duality, literary sociology never yields absolute certainty. While studying writers, one is always hovering between the reflector and the influencer. This again is especially the case in Russia and Eastern Europe, where even writers who see clearly often falsify what they see in order to get published—or write to false ends. Nonetheless, there is one constant in this business: when they express attitudes, all writers take a stand far more heroic than that of the ordinary person in society. Writers cannot take back what they write, because their words belong to us as well as to them. When a writer expressed an attitude (as toward the disabled) one may test it out. One may investigate at length how such an attitude came to be expressed and investigate, equally, how the attitude has influenced other people. Indeed, we the critics can thus enter into the writer's society, plunging to its depths. This is what I plan to do in this chapter. I first point to the extraordinary empathy that György Konrád has expressed in many writings toward handicapped persons. I inquire how he came to do so, and then ask whether he has had influence—whether he has induced changes among his friends and in the broader public.

II

Let us deal first with biography and oeuvre. Konrád was born in 1933 in small-town rural Hungary.[1] His parents were prosperous—second- or third-generation propertied middle class. He has memories of childhood in a two-story house, of gardens and orchards, uncles who were big-city gay blades, a grandfather factory builder. His memories also concern peasants living in a misery that contrasted with his comfort. He mentions at one point the indifference with which his family devoured five-course meals, despite the barefoot poverty of the common folk on the street outside—an indifference typical of prewar, still feudal, central Europe with its aristocratic past and its backwardness vis-à-vis the West. Konrád is Jewish, and his parents did not abandon their faith despite their prosperity. He has memories of childhood hours at the synagogue and Jewish school. And he remembers the catastrophe of World War II—the distortion of social relations after 1938 by the military draft and by anti-Jewish measures; the German invasion of Hungary in March 1944; the bombings and deportations that followed; and the horrors of battle and mass murder in the second half of that year. He endured this last experience without his parents, alone in Budapest.

Konrád returned to Budapest during the years of Communist power seizure and Stalinist construction, studying literature at the university. He suffered discrimination because of his class background and thus had political doubts. But for young intellectuals of that time, these were not necessarily depressing years. The horrors of Stalinism were, if not secret, at least not discussed, whereas the revolutionary aspects of the period had positive meaning for all who had suffered under fascism. Even class aliens were often filled with socialist enthusiasm and campaign spirit. Precisely this quality of the Stalinist period made the next stage of Hungary's development—and Konrád's own—so traumatic. With the death of Stalin, the precipitous reforms and the return of the prisoners from the camps, one's blinders fell away with shattering effect. This is why such young people as Konrád joined suddenly, spontaneously, in the summer and fall of 1956 with broad elements of the Hungarian populace to make a new revolution; and when that uprising was beaten down, the disillusionment was the greater because youthful idealism had been so high.

In the 1950s, Konrád worked as an editor and a librarian at first, and was already a writer. Then after the revolution he reached his accommodation with the new Kádárist authorities by working for seven years as superintendent (a case worker) of a slum-district welfare institution in the capital city. This was a determining experience for his whole later career. He witnessed with a clinician's eye the naked universe of the bottom of big city society—the world of the street people, the retarded, the impoverished, the downcast and outcast; a world in constant conflict with the conventional, lying world of authority and the state. This was the material of his major literary work: the novels *The Case Worker,* published in Hungary in 1969, *The City Builder,* published abroad in 1977, and *The Loser,* published abroad in 1980.[2] The underworld experience informed also his major sociological and political statements: *The Intellectuals on the Path to Class Power,* a neo-Marxist historical study written jointly with the sociologist Ivan Szelényi in the early 1970s and published abroad in 1979; *The Temptation of Autonomy,* published (in Hungarian only) abroad in 1980; and *Antipolitics,* published in English in this country in 1984.[3]

In the later 1960s, Konrád earned his living not just by writing but as a sociologist advising the authorities about urban planning.[4] By 1970 he was deep in historical-sociological investigation of where the new classes in Eastern Europe had come from. His tendency was to perceive behind the official Marxist-Leninist explanations a seizure of power by bureaucrats and intellectuals. Such ideas got him into trouble with Kádár. This is ironic, because the Hungarian regime was by then notorious the world over for the mildness of its social and cultural communism, and for its increasing return to capitalism in the sphere of economics. For Konrád and his friends, however, the reforms by no means expunged or excused the state's fundamental autocracy, its foreignness to Hungary, its bourgeois hypocrisy, and its sheer corruption. The more it softened, the more they spoke their minds. In 1974 the police managed to confiscate a manuscript of *The Intellectuals on the*

Path to Class Power. The consequences were that Konrád was barred from publication at home, that he spent a short time in prison, and that he was then pressed to emigrate. Konrád's collaborator, Szelényi, did emigrate, and Konrád himself went abroad in 1977, spending two years in Berlin.

It was during this trip that his political involvement sharpened, though he still speaks of himself as a writer first and a sociologist second. His essay on individual autonomy, written in Paris, is bent on explaining why as a writer he simply would not and could not stay abroad; and why as a citizen of Hungary he would not and could not stay silent about the hypocrisies of Hungarian society and the Hungarian state. In 1979 he returned to Budapest despite the regime's threats to subject him to legal prosecution if he did. The regime backed away; whereupon Konrád came West again for two years (1982–84) with the manuscript of *Antipolitics,* which is nothing more nor less than a manifesto of central European intelligentsia defiance of the entire cold war division of Europe. In this book, Konrád cries out as a Magyar-speaking intellectual against the tyranny of the great powers, East and West alike, which maintain the central European status quo. He screams his indignation over the repression of the Czechs in 1968 and of the Polish Solidarity Movement in 1981. He hails the peace and environmental movements of the West for their rejection of the nuclear atrocity, but calls on them to undertake as well the liberation of Europe from outside rule. And in detail he explains how intellectuals may defy regimes such as Kádár's by day in and day out driving the hated bureaucrats to acknowledge individual and national rights.

One may worry about Konrád's intellectualism a little, about his antirationalism a little, but one must recognize that he consciously and intelligently has taken on his shoulders the historic burden of speaking for his whole country. Quite as much as Solidarity in Poland seeks to be the voice of Poland or the nineteenth-century Russian intelligentsia sought to be the voice of Russia, he seeks to be Hungary's voice.

III

Konrád's absorption with the handicapped is most evident in his first book, *The Case Worker.* This short, pungent novel takes the form of nigh-Joycean musings by a professional social worker, a bureaucrat somewhat older than Konrad himself, who is responsible for a variety of clients from the bottom of society, but especially for abused children. This man, who is by no means insensitive, has personal knowledge of the atrocities committed in the 1950s by the revolutionary state. He was then a public prosecutor—one of those Stalinists who sentenced legions of men and women to long prison terms for imaginary crimes.

Subsequently, just before 1956, he was in charge of physically exhuming the rehabilitated victims of the terror. For a while after the revolution, he worked at a slaughter house, a regular butcher. This is why he is a good case worker: he can accept the daily sleaze, stench, and grimy horror of society's underworld, because he knows that it is cleaner, more honest, and more human than what goes on up above. He is a refugee as it were from the revolutionary bureaucracy. The case worker's protagonist is a victim of the Revolution, a five-year old, just-orphaned child born with the rhomboid frontal missing from his skull. This creature, totally incapable of learning, wild, covered with wooly hair, soiled with his own excrement, is the son of parents from the old ruling class, people of education and one-time dignity whom the new state has not just degraded and cast down, but whom it has also driven to insanity and suicide.

Feri Bandula, the boy, is a symbol of what the revolution destroyed, a residual of the old society. Yet as the case worker can tell, this child is human—he can weep just like any other child, he can feel just like any other. And the questions of the book are: What is the new society going to do about this human being, cast out because he was born that way? Are there limitations to humanity? May the modern state, dedicated to the betterment of humanity, let this bit of humanity die? Doesn't even the employee of the state, the underling without ultimate responsibility, have an obligation to give human attention to such a case?

Konrád's hero wrestles for an answer. On the morrow of the parents' suicide, he has to dispose of the child. No institution has space for it at the moment. He has therefore to find a guardian. By evening he locates someone, and returns to his family and grubby life; but meanwhile he has dreamt to the limit the possibility of leaving his job and assuming responsilibity himself, trying to educate the child, trying to give it the love and attention that might prevent death. In the book's allegory, this dream brings the citizen of the state, even the anonymous employee, to acknowledge his obligation to all humanity, regardless of label. Compassion for humanity emerges as a responsibility altogether lacking limits. In the end, Konrád's hero finds that compassion in such extreme form will lead him to insanity—a prospect that fills him with dread. But he discovers also (to his relief) that in practice the bureaucracy would step in and take the child away from him before his insanity was complete. The case worker thus escapes (cops out?). But the importance of the book, especially in the context of the handicapped world, is its assertion that such problems exist, and that all members of society must face them.

It is not only in this first and finest novel that Konrád deals with the handicapped. In his third novel, *The Loser,* he raises again the question of insanity, from which the hero of *The Case Worker* retreats. In form, the two books are similar; once again we enter the mind of a central character and, though we never really learn his name, we follow his most private musings. Once again the hero has been an actor in the development of the revolutionary state, albeit the loser was far more pivotal than the case worker. He is an erstwhile leading Communist, a Milovan Djilas. But just like the case worker, he is now a refugee wrestling with questions of responsibility. The difference is that the case worker, no intellectual, fled downstairs and wrestled with the problem of society's base. The loser, very much the intellectual—a professional no less—has fled upstairs by accepting the label *deranged.* We meet him in an elegant asylum—Hungary's equivalent of the Hartford Retreat.

Initially, this hero views his life record as one long, ghastly, and inexplicable mistake. He calls himself a loser because all his revolutionary acts have furthered violence and have led to political autocracy. He is staying in the asylum, in some part voluntarily, to free the world, as it were, of his loathsome touch. The drama thereupon begins when, in a spirit of human tolerance, he helps make it possible for a truly demented woman to take her own life. For his humanistic act he is expelled from the asylum, back into normal society; and the action of the book lies in his progressive recognition that exactly such humanism has characterized his whole life. All his revolutionary acts (which we review in gory detail) and all his killings turn out to have been acts of tolerance toward humanity, and it is humanity that turns out to be insane. And why not? This is the question of the book. Why should not humanity be allowed to take its chances and move as it wishes? Why the arbitrary labels: *sane* and *insane?* Is there in nature any difference?

At the end of this book the hero is about to abet another suicide, this time in the outside world; and to accept as punishment his own reincarceration. But this suicide is no longer the consequence of a loser's fatal touch. It is a rational almost sentimental act of natural justice against the internal demon that has driven a normal man to kill. And now the asylum is no longer a garbage bin full of creeps. It is a haven for people of dignity who, better than the rest of us, acknowledge that they cannot handle themselves.

Konrád's compassion for the injured and the impaired, his inclusion of the handicapped into the human fold, affects even his recent political tracts. In *Antipolitics,* for example, over and over again he acknowledges the frailty of the central European society for which he undertakes to speak. It is not altogether adult, he declares.[5] It is characterized by a strange "old youngness," not entirely reliable.[6] Its past political record is "grotesque."[7] In this "ill-starred corner" of the earth, he claims, "folly" frequently has taken over.[8] Hungary since about 1940 has been "possessed, in both senses of the word." She is still "sick from the restraints."[9] The book is strewn with such imagery; and Konrád even seems to perceive himself, Hungary's voice, as a case worker of sorts. He speaks consciously for a fragile and contemptible reality; he has no illusion that he is leading heroes into war. Withal, he demands that his country be set free and given self-determination. He virtually personifies Eastern European society as handicapped; and then he makes clear that in his view the handicapped of humanity, along-side the outwardly sound and healthy, have rights. The impor-tance of György Konrád for the disabled of Eastern Europe lies in all these metaphors.

IV

With Konrád's references to the handicapped in mind, let us now ask the vital questions of literary sociology: Is Konrád a reliable witness? What kind of influence has he had? To the first of these questions we initially seem to have a ready answer. Konrád has been out there. His is the voice of experience. No doubt one may detect occasional exaggeration in his vocabulary—a predilection for words evoking grime and sleaze, blood and gore. But surely this is a writer's privilege, and no excuse for distrusting his word.

Yet a problem exists here, as is easily suggested by my own experience when I invited him in 1984 to participate in a confer-ence on the situation of the handicapped in Eastern Europe. He protested that he knows nothing about them, that he is a writer interested in social work. He declined the invitation for an assort-ment of reasons, but among them was a puzzling plea of non-qualification. Further, when during my research for this chapter I consulted with a number of Konrád's close friends and collaborators, the response was identical. All seemed puzzled by my proposition. One, a sociologist by profession, declared that he simply would not know how to start a study of the handicapped in Hungary; and reminded of the subject matter of Konrád's books, he said, as if seeing that evidence for the first time, that he would have to think it through. How to reconcile these seeming disavowals of Konrád's expertise with the evidence that Konrád is a true witness of the situation of the handicapped? One may find an answer by looking carefully at the literary contexts of his work. It detracts but little from the reliability of his mirror but a lot from the sharpness of his knife.

Let us start at the end, by positing that all of his works, but most of all the recent political essays, respond to a parlous situation. Since the 1930s Eastern Europe has lost its political independence— no matter that in some versions of history, the region never effectively had political independence and that some people doubt whether it is desirable. The great powers dominate the place; and for Hungary the pill is more bitter, because to some extent the loss of the independence the country enjoyed between the wars may be attributed to her own behavior—to the mistakes of her leaders between the wars. What is more, the noose around Eastern Europe has grown tighter and tighter over recent years. In 1956 when the Hungarians pioneered resistance to Soviet domination by rebelling violently, the Russians as violently intervened and repressed all opposition. In 1968 the Czechs, learning from 1956, sought to engineer an escape by subtly restructuring their political system without changing its form. The Russians intervened nonetheless. In 1980, thereupon, the Poles accepted the lessons of experience. They sought their escape through demonstrative eschewal of traditional politics; they expressed in organized fashion what they considered the will of the people, and then left it to the authorities to introduce reforms; withal, they incurred repression.

In the face of this ever-tightening noose, one may observe throughout Eastern Europe expressions of desperation, which take a peculiar form. In Poland for example, there is an ongoing stress on universal solidarity. In the past, Poles would fight for their nation, but invariably the nation turned out in practice to be partial. The nobility did not fight for the peasants, the workers fought neither for the nobility nor for the peasants, the intelligentsia fought against the church, and the peasants in their exasperation sometimes didn't fight. Today, however, the national messianism of the past has given way to social universalism. No one is to be left out. Among Czechs, resistance takes a different form, but the universalism of despair is equally present. The writer Milan Kundera, for example, has taken to composing manifestoes in which he speaks of the old concept of a *Mitteleuropa* composed of smaller national cultures, whose very nature separates them from the East and binds them to the West.[10] His vision is apocalyptic; whereas the Poles have no doubt that Poland will live again, Kundera dreads that his nation's language will once again, as in the seventeenth century, simply become extinct. But like the Poles he speaks of universals. Without weapons, he appeals to humanity to take responsibility for the existential fact that *Mitteleuropa* is being denatured.

Konrád is clearly enough writing in a similar vein—a genre, one might call it. Because of the mildness of the Kádár regime, he enjoys much more leeway for self-expression than do the Poles and Czechs. He is not in forced exile, as Kundera is. Further, he writes in a national idiom. He takes his advocacy of personal autonomy from the greatest of Hungary's midcentury political voices, that of István Bibó, the moralist and essayist whose calls for national and personal autonomy provided an ideology to the revolution of 1956.[11] But in his appeal to Hungarian intellectuals to develop their spiritual autonomy, Konrád is no less a voice of desperation than the underground Solidarity leaders and Kundera. Indeed, in *Antipolitics* he spells out specifically that there is no other way—that all other paths have been tried and blocked.[12]

So now to the point: it is no surprise that he includes the handicapped and the insane in his ideal of society. The desperate genre in which he writes entails reference to the universality of mankind. Nor should it be any surprise that he does not consider himself an expert on the handicapped. He speaks for them not because of their special need but because all society now has similar needs. This sort of argument seems the stronger, because it is not only a political genre that determines Konrád's references to the handicapped and the insane. There are also literary genres. Dostoevsky stands tall in the pantheon of every European writer of note in the past fifty years. In Dostoevsky, the barrier between insane and sane is abolished, atomized, and the human psyche appears as wild. Thomas Mann likewise ranks high among the central European literary gods. Mann described the asylum as a microcosm of the sickness of bourgeois Europe. By implication, if

Zauberberg is normalcy, the outside world is sick. Kafka, likewise, has his heroes struggle with the ineffable forces that compel them to deny the reality of the world in which they live. In Hašek, the peasant idiocy of Schweik turns out to be rational intelligence, as the great world surrenders to the insanity of war. Kundera uses freely the imagery of the asylum and traces with delight the light-footed, evasive mentality of the insane. To say that Konrád draws on this rich heritage for his literary imagery is no deprecation of his compassion for the disabled; but it does point up a limitation to his commitment to their special cause.

All the more is this limitation visible when we approach the literature of the grotesque. The single best known literary representation of the experience of fascism in Eastern Europe, Günther Grass's *The Tin Drum,* lies squarely in this genre. Grass describes the monstrosity of the Nazi era as a great hump growing on a changing child, who has no normal voice but a scream that shatters glass. This Oskar is out of touch with society, yet as symbolic of it as Konrád's Feri Bandula; and Grass has his exiled Danzigers in post-1945 West Germany haunted by a murderous, wicked, black witch who presages the inner demons of *The Loser.*

When we look at the literature of the animal grotesque—the *Metamorphosis, Animal Farm,* and *Painted Bird* literature—the genre character of Konrád's novels seems ever stronger. Ludvik Vačula published his novel *The Guinea Pigs* in 1971, suggesting through the behavior of tortured furry little beasts the behavior of human society under bureaucratic rule. This most egregious example of animal grotesquerie may thus be a consequence, rather than a cause, of *The Case Worker,* which appeared two years earlier not just in Hungarian but in Czech. That both novels stand in a single tradition, however, seems beyond dispute. And in that tradition also stands the masterpiece of postwar Hungarian poetry, Ferenc Juhász's long dramatic poem *The Boy Changed into a Stag Cries Out at the Gate of Secrets.*[13] Written during the post-Stalin thaw by a peasant boy turned poet, by a darling of the new regime, this poem was published on the eve of 1956. No literary work has more captured the imagination of contemporary Hungarians. It describes the new industrial Hungary allegorically, as a boy transformed into a beast with high-tension wire antlers, steel hooves, and fur-covered genitals. This monster yearns for a return to the rural peace of the past, cries out from the crags to his mother that he will come back to die, but meanwhile he acknowledges that he is irretrievably urban, a monster capable only of goring the old world if he comes near it, yet a symbol of the present—alive.

In Konrád's fur-covered Feri Bandula, the roles are reversed, but the community of the living is the same. This is why we can state that Konrád's seeming commitment to the handicapped is a matter of genre above all; and that quite naturally he would be puzzled by suggestions that he was dedicated to their specific cause.

V

What about Konrád's impact? May it be said that his imagery of the disabled has lent to change in the attitudes of the Hungarian public toward handicapped people—to greater sympathy and understanding? Once again, one's initial inclination might be to respond affirmatively; but then a problem appears.

Certainly Konrad's voice has gotten through. *The Case Worker* was published in Hungary and was received favorably enough to make possible its republication in Czechoslovakia, another socialist land. It is imbedded in Hungary's literature and cannot be erased. No doubt it has long been out of print and, because of Konrád's political disfavor, cannot be used as propaganda, for example by organizations for the handicapped. No doubt, also, his other works, banned at home, are far less well known. But to balance this, one may mention that he still lives in Hungary, circulates socially in Budapest, and is in fact a lion of its youthful intelligentsia. In a society dominated historically by its intelligentsia, such prestige is almost more important for the propagation of ideas than publication.[14] Further, most of Konrád's work has been published in Hungarian abroad by the exile community in Paris. Given the increasing ease with which Hungarians can travel, this means that his books are in all probability widely imported and even more widely read.

But does his true depiction of the handicapped get through to his readers, and does it have beneficial results? These are crucial questions. As it happens, we can discuss them on the basis of hard evidence: a film directed by János Xanthus, a young friend and protégé of Konrád's, which centrally features a character who is deaf.[15] From the opening scene onward it is clear that sympathy for the handicapped is getting through, but only limited understanding, and that they are still regarded as grotesque.

The film opens with beautiful photography of an autumn street in the villa section of Budapest, where the intelligentsia lives. It is dawn. A man is lurking in the shadows, watching a house. He is shaggy headed, rather dark in complexion, somber in mien, not unsympathetic. We will learn that he is named János and is stone deaf. Shortly, a second man emerges from the house, lighter in weight and color, more artistically dressed. This we later learn is a successful rock musician. He is played by the same Polish actor who played the aristocratic jacobin, Saint Just, in Andrzej Wajda's film *Danton*. He is naturally arrogant, supercilious. As the two men approach, Laci recognizes János and attempts a grin. János then plunges a knife into his belly.

The rest of the film consists of a flashback explanation of this melodramatic beginning. It turns out that the two men are linked by their involvement with Éva, who is petite, blond, and sexy. She is married to János but has become Laci's lover. She is a good wife, in the sense that she uses sign language to communicate with János, shares his humble apartment in Pest, and expresses love for him, as well as a moral responsibility to his disability. But she is also ambitious as a singer and regularly visits night spots where she can meet the likes of Laci, who has international success and lives part time—and very expensively—in London. She attracts him, he seduces her. He helps her achieve a success abroad as considerable as his own. János manfully stands aside, silently suffering. Mournfully, then, she abandons not only him but also Laci, who for love of her has become a drunk. We catch our final glimpse of her headed for her first American tour. The murder has happened, but she probably doesn't know. She is on a channel ferry gazing soulfully at the rough seas and murmurs the title line: "The Eskimo lady is cold." This recalls a love name Laci gave her. She speaks it in English, and the words are captioned in the Hungarian version, in Magyar, an ultimate snob symbol of the high life she has attained.

Throughout the film, the depiction of János is highly sympathetic. The director shows real understanding of the loneliness of the deaf, of their permanent depression, and of their latent paranoia—which in this case wells up and explodes into murder. It is accordingly the more shocking when, midway, it turns out that our deaf man makes his living at the zoo as a monkey keeper. Xanthus even shows him seeking solace for his tragedy by using sign language with the apes. Those who know something about deaf people, know that there can be no higher insult. Yet the mockery is continued in another scene when Laci and Éva try to include János in their lives by teaching him, stone deaf as he is, to hammer rythmically on the drums while they make music. He shows gratification by protruding his eyeballs, and the audience howls. Further, the bulk of the film simply does not concern him but depicts in grotesque distortion the superstar life available beyond Hungary's frontiers. Laci wines here, there, and everywhere, expensively. In England he has a Jaguar, which he uses casually to take his lady friend into the woods for penetration from the rear, like a goat. There's a motorboat around there somewhere, too, and airplanes galore. Even in Budapest, the penetrations are frequent, graphic, and exotic. The result is certain distraction of the viewer from the theme of the handicapped.

Possibly this film aspires to suggest a tension modern Hungarian young people must experience between the attraction of life at home, chained but spiritual, and the tug of a dreamed about West. Possibly, Xanthus wishes to polarize the alternatives by characterizing life at home as handicapped, just as Konrád does, and then by juxtaposing it with a deliberately parodied high life abroad to create in film language the coldness mentioned at the end. Xanthus has taken over from Konrád the expression of sympathy for the handicapped as a matter of style. He has taken over nothing of Konrád's sense of mission. And as we have seen, even in Konrád's work the helper vocation was limited.

Even more disappointing, Xanthus's audience did not seem to learn from this exposure. I can report two sorts of response. On the one hand, the people I went with to the film were simply unimpressed. They are intellectuals, already conversant with the problems of the handicapped, and sympathetic. They were somewhat put off by all the sex but accepted the depiction of János. I had to explain to them that the film was an insult to the deaf. They did not learn this from the film. On the other hand, the bulk of the audience clearly relished the sex but, in at least some part, had a complaint. They wondered why Xanthus had to rub their noses in something so unseemly, so socially inappropriate, indeed, so shameful as physical deficiency—as a disability.

VI

The work of György Konrád represents a breakthrough for the Eastern European handicapped, albeit particularly for those of Hungary. Embedded in the high literature of the region there are now attitudes favorable to them. It has been written that the whole society is handicapped and should feel bound to the actually handicapped by ties of common fate as well as by human sympathy. These attitudes are new and pregnant with possible benefit to the disabled, if they are absorbed.

Still, one must acknowledge that Konrád's work itself has literary rather more than missionary value. His compassion is not in question, but his specific dedication to the handicapped is. His writing is genre writing and perhaps may not cause an eruption of popular zeal to help the crippled, the deaf, and the blind. Certainly this is the lesson of the cinematographic examples of how his work is being passed on. Empathy for handicapped people comes through, but they are nonetheless perceived as grotesque.

And to conclude, it seems appropriate to cite an incident in the recent past where the intervention of an intellectual on the side of the handicapped backfired. A few years ago sociologist critics of Budapest authorities organized a great conference on the theme of poverty. The regime did not wish to acknowledge the existence of poverty in a socialist country and asked a most prominent and cosmopolitan figure, the late Alexander Szalai, to defuse the enterprise. Szalai did this with a slightly devious trick. He expanded the agenda to include the handicapped and reentitled the conference The Multiply Disadvantaged (Többszörösen hátranyos helyzetben).[16] The result was a bitter row; the handicapped were discussed, but they did not benefit.

This incident suggests the extent to which, given engrained prejudices, the interference of a subversive intellectual such as Konrád on the side of the handicapped might also have a negative impact.

NOTES

1. There is an autobiographical interview with Konrád by Ivan Sanders in *The New Republic,* 5 Jan. 1980, pp. 24–28. I am indebted also for the following account to personal communications from Yvette Biro, Ivan Sanders, and Iván and Kati Szelényi.

2. *The Case Worker,* trans. Paul Aston from *A Látogató;* (New York: H. and K. Wolf, 1974); *The City Builder,* trans. Ivan Sanders from *A városalapító* (New York: H. and K. Wolf, 1977); and *The Loser,* published first in French (Paris: Editions du Seuil, 1980), then in English, trans. Ivan Sanders from *A cinkos* (New York: H. and K. Wolf, 1982).

3. *The Intellectuals on the Path to Class Power,* trans. Andrew Arato and Richard E. Allen from *Az értelmiség útja az osztályhatalomhoz* (New York: H. and K. Wolf, 1979); *Az autonómia kísértése* (Paris: Magyar Füzetek, 1980); and *Antipolitics,* trans. Richard E. Allen (New York: H. and K. Wolf, 1984).

4. This work resulted in Iván Szelényi and György Konrád, *Az új lakótelepek szoziológiai problémai* (Budapest: Akademi K., 1969); and their "Social Conflicts of Under-Urbanization," in A. A. Brown et al., eds., *Urban and Social Economics in Market and Planned Economies* (Boulder: Praeger, 1974).

5. *Antipolitics,* p. 154.

6. Ibid., p. 116.

7. Ibid., p. 124.

8. Ibid., p. 128.

9. Ibid., pp. 241–42. This is the last page but one of the book, so one may assume that the metaphor is not accidental.

10. See, apart from Kundera's well-known manifestoes in *The New York Review of Books,* his interview with Alain Finkielkraut and the follow-up essay by Roman Szporluk in *Cross Currents* (Ann Arbor) 2 (1982): 15–19 and 30–38.

11. On Bibó, see most recently the introduction by Zoltán Szabó to *Bibó István, 1911–1979* (Paris: Magyar Füzetek, 1979), pp. 7–43.

12. Compare T. G. Ash, "Does Central Europe Exist?" in *New York Review of Books,* 9 Oct. 1986, pp. 45–52.

13. See the excellent English translation by Kenneth McRobbie in Miklós Vaida, ed., *Modern Hungarian Poetry* (New York: Columbia University Press, 1977), pp. 206–17.

14. For information about the regime's odd treatment of Konrád in recent years, see Ivan Sanders's review of *The Loser* in *Irodalmi Ujság* (Paris), no. 1 (1983): 17–20.

15. *Eszkimó asszony fázik* (Budapest: Hungarian Films, 1983).

16. The conference materials have been published in *Szociál-politikai Értesítö,* nos. 1–5 (1985). I am indebted to Ivan Sanders for background information.

Conclusion

William O. McCagg and
Lewis Siegelbaum

Already in the earliest stage of the development of the Kievan state, the distinctiveness and unique qualities of Russian life gave birth to a purely national phenomenon—community care for the "crippled children." The law providing for social supplements for the deaf—as stipulated in the "Pilot Books" *(Kormchikh knigakh)* and receiving elaboration in the circumstances of Russian reality—influenced the organization of social welfare and education for deaf children.

—*A. I. D'iachkov*

I

Would the authors of the chapters in this volume unanimously agree with the boastful nationalism of this opening paragraph of a history of Russian deaf education published by a Soviet academic press in 1961? Perhaps not. Judging from their contributions, however, they clearly would agree that our topic in this volume has unique features. The history of the disabled in Russia is much more than just a footnote to their history in Western Europe and the United States; and a survey of the situation of the disabled there today is much more than just a localized version of the situation elsewhere in the world.

Some of these unique features appear in the historical chapters of this volume. In early modern times, for example—just as in Europe, so in Russia—new secular attitudes developed toward the disabled, and modern states undertook to usurp the management of public welfare from the churches and local authorities, which had tended the disabled in the past. In Europe, however, the result was, as it were, competitive interplay between the new state and

293

the older institutions. In Europe, the apparatus of welfare expanded in the new age, because, on the one hand, the churches retained their charitable and benevolent institutions, adapting to the times; and on the other hand, local authorities strove more vigorously in their attention to public welfare. In Russia the expansion was far less rapid, because the state, despotically and heavy handedly, barred the other helpers yet was itself ill equipped to supply the needed support. Characteristically, Peter the Great abolished church care for the insane but then introduced one lonely committee, located in St. Petersburg, to assess all cases of madness throughout the empire. Granted, this legislation affected only the gentry mad, the peasantry—the bulk of the population—being treated as chattel! Still, the enormity of his approach to the disabled set back instead of advanced the humanitarian cause he pretended to favor.

And in the two centuries between Peter's reform and the Revolution, the loggerheads between the state and private welfare institutions persisted. No doubt, officialdom early recognized that it could ill afford to pay for a welfare system. For such reason, in the nineteenth century the financial responsibility for the disabled shifted back into the private sector. Yet at the same time, the state over and again insisted on control, discouraging any genuine autonomous undertaking in the welfare area, rejecting as it were with one hand what it decreed with the other. The story here is not dissimilar to what one finds in other areas of Russian educational and medical history. By the early twentieth century, the net result was very real progress, which was however vastly inadequate and conducive to immense impatience.

All told, this history of the disabled in old Russia is a story very different from the tale of essentially private policing and philanthropy one encounters nearer to the heart of Europe and in America.

Most of the material in the present volume deals with post-1917 Russia, not with prerevolutionary times; and here again one finds an apparently unique pattern of developments in care of the disabled. First, from the very moment of the Revolution there was an explosion of innovation. Out of the universities, out of the old state institutions, out especially of private sector institutions that the state has so hampered in the past, initiatives sprang for the application of the most modern scientific ideas to every field of public care. We have observed this frenzy of innovation particularly in Lewis Siegelbaum's chapter on the investigation and prevention of industrial accidents, but also in William McCagg's chapter on the beginnings of Soviet defectology, in the contributions of David Joravsky, and of Jane Knox and Alex Kozulin on various aspects of Soviet psychology. In extraordinarily short order the new worker state founded by the Bolsheviks "caught up with, and surpassed"—one can readily admit the validity of the typical Communist Party boast in this context—the rest of the world in the articulation of its welfare system. By the middle 1920s, a Western visitor could happily report home "that there was more industrial hygiene in Russia than industry."

Then came the comeuppances, first a budgetary, then a political one. As Siegelbaum details, but as our other authors clearly suggest, the middle 1920s brought not only an overflowing of fascinating theoretical publications about the condition of the disabled but also the beginnings of the great Soviet leap forward into industrialism, and the new state's growing insistence that all costly—and a great deal of noncostly—activity on the part of the citizenry be subordinated to the economistically defined cause of "socialist construction." Within a few years the innovators of the early revolutionary era were beleaguered, deprived not just of their budgets but also of their very consciences, as Five-Year-Plan expediency replaced revolutionary humanitarianism as the law of the land.

What in actual practice happened to the disabled in the Soviet Union during the Stalin era is apparently beyond our knowing, because statistical information simply does not exist. The Soviet census of 1926 did mention the disabled, the first time ever that this had been done in Russia; but the mention was tangential and allows no deep analysis; and the next censuses, those of 1937, 1939, and 1959, simply did not touch on this problem. Apparently, it had become a matter of embarrassment to a state that had putatively eliminated class struggle and achieved socialism that there should be cripples, much less a population of cripples, resulting from the activities of the new regime.

We do know that, despite its destructiveness, the Stalinist state steadily expanded its schooling system, the medical and hospital system, and the health and pension system, at least in the cities. Gradually, in the midst of the terror, the USSR constructed one of today's greatest modern welfare systems. But of the details, in so far as they relate to defectology, we are sadly uninformed. Characteristically, just as in Soviet psychology the name of the "foreigner," Sigmund Freud, simply ceased to be mentioned in the

Stalin era, so in defectology the name of Lev Vygotsky fell into disuse, though he was an authentically Russian genius who worked in the disabled area, the equal of the adulated Pavlov. One is reminded, in listening to this sad story, of the loggerheads between state and private charitable enterprise in tsarist times. Forward looking and powerful as it may have been, the Bolshevik undertaking massively held itself back when it came to actual welfare improvement. In the West it would be hard to find such a history of self-retardation—of akinesia, to use a neurological term.

Yet as our chapters on the present situation of the disabled clearly show, the extraordinarily interesting work undertaken during the great decade of Soviet experimentation in the 1920s produced a worthy heritage. Today, an enormous defectological machine exists in the Soviet Union. It must be stressed that, until Khrushchev's time, village Russia was simply not included in the welfare state, and that even today its inclusion is on a scale distinctly less than urban Russia's. Further, as Bernice Madison shows especially well in her chapter on disability pensions, the system creaks. It is bureaucratic to a degree, also autocratic, and frequently inadequately staffed. Its regulations are often contradictory, overlapping, or just plain unclear. The financial provisions both for paying the welfare bureaucrats and for extending benefits to the disabled population are frequently inadequate. Yet the more the wealth of the nation increases, the more the once solely paper structure of the government extends the benefits of modernity to a mass population. As Stephen and Ethel Dunn, who are themselves the victims of cerebral palsey, remark, this places Russia for all her enduring poverty on a par in some respects with some of the great Western countries, which have enormous wealth, which enjoy the benefits of every variety of modern technology, but which are unwilling to set up a distribution system that will guarantee these benefits to every citizen.

One last peculiarity in the history of the disabled in Russia bears mention here. It originated in the medieval period. As we have learned especially from Julie Brown's chapter on the insane in prerevolutionary Russia, one could find, even in Mongol times in that land far out on Europe's Asian frontier, a whole category of persons, the so-called holy fools, who out of religious altruism made as if they were insane, albeit they were not so, and who thus won a peculiar reverence from the population—a reverence which carried over in part to the truly insane. These "saintly" figures proliferated in the early modern period of Russia's history and could be found in rural areas until the eve of 1917. Their presence did not bring all insane presons, much less all of the disabled, the favor of the population and correspondingly sympathetic treatment. As elsewhere in the world, so in Russia, the early history of the disabled abounds with tales of cruel abuse. But because of the popular respect for the holy fools, there was an ambivalence from way back in popular Russian attitudes toward the disabled, a documentable willingness to empathize with and to offer warm spontaneous help to the disabled, that one does not hear of in the history of other countries.

Is it possible that this difference may survive even to this day? Both Vera Dunham, in her moving review of Soviet literary references to the war wounded of World War II, and Stephen and Ethel Dunn, in their report on the actual life of the disabled today in the USSR, give hints of some sort of specially Russian warmth and understanding that crops up among ordinary people when they encounter the disabled. Whether such humanity can be framed as a direct descendent of the respect for the holy fools we self-evidently cannot know. But something is there that, according to a wide range of witnesses, is unusual, is not nearly as present in other places, and has been manifest since long ago. What that something is and why it has persisted is a major question posed but not answered in this volume.

II

At the core of this volume is a suggestion that may be fundamental to any historical consideration of the disabled. David Joravsky in his study of the politics of Soviet psychiatry finds that it was not just the immense political pressure that Stalinism placed on psychiatrists that led them to become among the politically most craven of Soviet professional groups, but in part also the very etiology of disability. Joravsky suggests that the professionals who treat the insane have a special problem that distinguished them from other medical personnel. There is no answer for the patients here involved; their disease or defect is simply not understood or understandable in the same way that other diseases are by modern science; much less is it curable as other diseases are. The physicians here—that is, the psychiatrists—must, accordingly, invent a pseudo answer if they are to deal on a day-to-day level with the imponderables of their patients' condition. Further, they must then willfully apply their remedy, always exposed to the probability that they are wrong, as if they were bearers of science and truth. They must consciously assume a pose. This leaves them singularly dependent on institutional stability.

From this it might follow that, whereas in Western societies psychiatrists are inherently adventurous because of etiological difficulties, in the USSR they have tended to the other extreme: they have been addicted to rigidity, have been especially susceptible to bureaucratic pressures, in some part have been involuntary collaborators with political power.

Joravsky very carefully limits his suggestion. He makes it specific to psychiatry, where there is manifestly an extraordinary difference between the adventurous behavior traditional among psychiatrists in the Western world and the behavior of their Soviet counterparts. Whether the suggestion will be useful in discussing the treatment of other defects in the Soviet, or even in a worldwide context, we cannot say. In this volume we have not been able to devote full-scale attention to the development of Soviet defectology in the Stalin period. We can note, of course, that though there was no scandal there, such as Snezhnevskii caused among the psychiatrists, Vygotsky was, as mentioned above, forgotten, though he had virtually founded the field. One can also make some important distinctions between those who treat the insane and those who treat other defects. Psychiatrists, who deal with the unfathomed delicacy of the human mind, are inordinately driven to experiment with different theories, and they seem correspondingly delinquent when, for political reasons, they conform to just one approach. Defectologists are different. They deal with physically much more limited problems—how, for example, to get through to the mind of a child who is born deaf and who cannot conceive of speech. And the choice of oral (lipreading) training as opposed to sign language training will neither vitiate the main effort to educate the deaf nor seem scandalous if politically inspired. One might generalize that defectologists do not stick their necks out, because they do not need to do so; and that in the Soviet Union it may even be advantageous for the defectologists in their caring professional work to rely on a strong political dogmatism and not to have to worry about basic technique.

Clearly, however, cold war morality has no place in such comparisons and contrasts. For all the freedom of inquiry that Western psychiatrists possess, for all their admired adventurousness, they also have been susceptible to dogmatically received ideas. Their orthodoxies, indeed, have often lent them a wholly false reputation for competency—witness their indiscriminate enthusiasm for lobotomies during the 1930s and 1940s, just those Stalin years when fear repressed the search for innovation among their colleagues in the Soviet Union.

Clearly also, the whole question of the relationship between etiology and political behavior is a very important one, which must be investigated in future studies of the disabled in both our area and in other political and social contexts. The virtue of this volume has been to raise the issue, though we cannot resolve it.

III

Our volume ends with three chapters dealing with special topics that give hints as to what may lie in the future for the disabled in the Soviet Union and Eastern Europe. The first is Paul Raymond's chapter about the rudimentary disability protest movement that emerged in the USSR during the 1970s—about the Initiative Group to Defend the Rights of the Disabled. Raymond shows above all that, though there exists the population basis for such a movement in the USSR, just as in the United States or Western Europe, the movement shows small promise of winning for the Soviet disabled the enormous psychological gains that the disability movements of the 1960s and 1970s captured for the disabled of the West. The Initiative Group has already encountered the fate of the many other varieties of private pressure groups in Russian history: from the very moment of its establishment in 1978, despite its disclaimers, it was viewed by state authorities as subversive, and repressed as such. One can derive some hope, perhaps, from the peculiar fact that the Initiative Group's organizers kept on protesting even after the repression. They did not retreat; with their problems, perhaps they could not. And the state did not, and perhaps even could not, bring itself to place them in the usual depository of unuseful Soviet citizens—the camps. Are these examples of obdurance and abstention signs for hope? Quite possibly, for even if the fate of the Initiative Group remains precarious at best, thanks to *glasnost'* the plight of the disabled has become better known to the Soviet public.

The second of these chapters is Mark Field's study of the Soviet use of insane asylums to quiet political dissidence in the Brezhnev era. Field's subject matter is in many ways distant from the topic of the volume. He deals with normal people who are treated as defective, rather than with defective people who are trying to find a place in the normal world. But his discussion of the eruption of political misuse of psychiatry serves us twofold in this volume. First, he brings to light the immense power of conformity in the middle class and educated sectors of Soviet society (and Vera Dunham has emphasized this factor too). The pressures are strong enough to induce public acceptance of a *mad* label, with all the pariah consequences that it conveys, for people who simply voiced their opinions differently. What amidst such circumstances can the genuinely disabled expect?

Here too, as in the case of the Initiative Group's efforts, there are hopeful signs. In seeking to break with the administrative command system that was erected under Stalin and that gained a lease on life under Brezhnev, the Gorbachev administration has introduced legislation that makes it more difficult to consign people to mental institutions. But the evidence that Field discussed fortifies whatever impression we may have from other sources about the appalling barriers of intolerance that surround the disabled and "just different" persons in the USSR.

Yet Field also leads us to an interesting corollary finding, namely that there is a place in Russia, both historically and in more recent times, for the disabled. In other countries and other societies, the great distress of the disabled is precisely that they have no place in the memory or the mentality of the normal world. In Russian history, and now in the Soviet present, the normal cannot conceive the fullness of their own record without recognition of the fate of the really insane.

William McCagg's concluding chapter both carries the story of this integration of the disabled into society a step further and probes for its limits. This is our only chapter on Eastern Europe, which is of course in many many respects very different from the inner expanses of the USSR. Yet among the many features that Eastern Europe shares with Russia, one stands out: literature makes an enormous difference, because in history as in the present time, a literate intelligentsia, with writers in its lead, has played an enormously important political role. And certainly György Konrád, the writer with whom McCagg is concerned, is comparable in his use of the imagery of defectiveness to the great Russian writers, from Gogol and Dostoevsky to Voinovich and Solzhenitsyn, who have used the imagery of illness and insanity to discuss essentially political problems. Konrád, like the great Russian writers, equates backwardness with defectiveness, and asks the question, pregnant for the entire world today, whether the humanity of a people is the less because it cannot, for essentially physical reasons, keep up with the West.

McCagg's conclusions, and concurrently those of this book, are on the first level certainly pessimistic. He reports that even in the face of so direct an effort to force public self-identification with the disabled as Konrád made in the later 1960s, the Hungarian public, and even Konrád's own associates, proved rather resistant. This intellectual's intervention for the disabled was not effective; it did not really work. In some respects, it may even have been counterproductive, stirring resentments where sympathy was desired. Yet on the other side, the evidence suggests a curious participation by the disabled in the life of the normal society. Because of Konrád's work—and by implication, because of Gogol's and Solzhenitsyn's—the disabled have a permanent place in the history and literature of the European East, a place from which they can enter the minds of all future generations of the population, and from which, short of the most obscurantist and long-standing censorship, they cannot be deposed. In the USSR and Eastern Europe the disabled are part of the popular culture, not outside it as in the West; and however miserable may be their lot at the moment, once it does change—once at some future date they do surmount the natural obstacles that hold them back—they may stand a better chance of social integration there than in the West.

Notes on Contributors

JULIE V. BROWN is Associate Professor of Sociology at the University of North Carolina at Greensboro. She is the author of a number of articles on the psychiatric profession and societal responses to mental disorders in late Imperial Russia. Her research interests include psychiatrists during the revolutionary era and the social organization of medical work in the USSR.

VERA SANDOMIRSKY DUNHAM is Professor Emerita at Wayne State University and the City University of New York. An associate of the W. Averell Harriman Institute at Columbia University, she is the author of *In Stalin's Time: Middle Class Values in Soviet Fiction*.

ETHEL DUNN has an M.A. in history and a Certificate from the Russian Institute at Columbia University. She is the Executive Secretary at Highgate Road Social Science Research Station. Her major interests include Russian religious dissidence, the Small Peoples of the Soviet North, and the status of Soviet rural women.

STEPHEN P. DUNN received his Ph.D. in anthropology from Columbia University in 1959. He is the editor emeritus of *Soviet Anthropology and Archeology* and *Soviet Sociology*. With Ethel Dunn he coauthored *The Peasants of Central Russia,* and both are contributing editors to *The Station Relay: Facts and Views on Daily Life in the USSR,* published by Highgate Road Social Science Research Station, where he is Director of Research.

MARK G. FIELD received his Ph.D. in Social Relations (Sociology) from Harvard University in 1955. He is Professor Emeritus of Sociology at Boston University, Fellow in the Russian Research Center and Adjunct Professor at the School of Public Health at Harvard University, and Assistant Sociologist, Department of Psychiatry, Massachusetts General Hospital. He is the author, coauthor, or editor of eight books, including *Success and Crisis in National Health Systems: A Comparative Approach* (1989).

DAVID JORAVSKY is Professor of History at Northwestern University. His books include *Soviet Marxism and Natural Science, 1917–1932; The*

Lysenko Affair; and *Russian Psychology: A Critical History.* He is a contributor to the *New York Review of Books.*

JANE E. KNOX is Associate Professor and Chair of the Russian Department at Bowdoin College and a Research Fellow at the Harvard Russian Research Center. She has been a National Academy of Sciences Exchange Scientist at the Institutes of Linguistics, Psychology, and Defectology, Soviet Academy of Sciences and Pedagogical Sciences, Moscow. She is co-translator of volume 2 of L. S. Vygotsky's *Collected Works.*

ALEX KOZULIN is Associate Professor of Psychology at Boston University School of Medicine. He received his degree (Ph.D. equivalent) in psychology from the Moscow Institute of Psychology. He is the author of *Psychology in Utopia: Toward a Social History of Soviet Psychology* and editor of the revised translation of L. S. Vygotsky's *Thought and Language.*

WILLIAM O. McCAGG received his Ph.D. from Columbia University. Since 1964 he has been professor of East European and Russian history at Michigan State University. His publications include *Stalin Embattled, 1943–48; Soviet-Asian Ethnic Frontiers* (with Brian Silver); and *A History of Habsburg Jews.*

BERNICE MADISON holds a Ph.D. in social services from the University of Chicago. She has taught at San Francisco State University and been a visiting scholar at the Woodrow Wilson International Center for Scholars and at the Kennan Institute for Advanced Russian Studies. She has written widely on the social security system in the Soviet Union.

PAUL D. RAYMOND received his graduate degrees in political science and Soviet area studies from Pennsylvania State University. He has taught in the University of California system and at James Madison University. Currently he is an associate acquisitions editor in the College Department of Harcourt Brace Jovanovich, Inc., San Diego.

LEWIS H. SIEGELBAUM, Professor of History at Michigan State University, received his D.Phil. in history from Oxford University and taught at La Trobe University in Melbourne, Australia, for seven years. He is the author of *The Politics of Industrial Mobilization in Russia, 1914–17* and *Stakhanovism and the Politics of Productivity in the USSR, 1935–41* as well as numerous articles on Russian labor history.

Pitt Series in Russian and East European Studies

Jonathan Harris, Editor